Accelerating DevSecOps on AWS

Create secure CI/CD pipelines using Chaos and AIOps

Nikit Swaraj

BIRMINGHAM—MUMBAI

Accelerating DevSecOps on AWS

Group Product Manager: Rahul Nair
Publishing Product Manager: Meeta Rajani
Senior Editor: Sangeeta Purkayastha
Content Development Editor: Yasir Ali Khan
Technical Editor: Shruthi Shetty
Copy Editor: Safis Editing
Project Coordinator: Shagun Saini
Proofreader: Safis Editing
Indexer: Subalakshmi Govindhan
Production Designer: Shyam Sundar Korumilli
Senior Marketing Coordinator: Sanjana Gupta
Marketing Coordinator: Nimisha Dua

First published: April 2022

Production reference: 1060422

Published by Packt Publishing Ltd.
Livery Place
35 Livery Street
Birmingham
B3 2PB, UK.

ISBN 978-1-80324-860-8

www.packt.com

To my father, Nagendra Ram.

I would have been a terrible software engineer if you had not bought me a desktop and taught me cut, copy, and paste in Windows 98.

– Nikit Swaraj

Contributors

About the author

Nikit Swaraj is an experienced solution architect. He is well versed in the melding of development and operations to deliver efficient code. Nikit has expertise in designing, developing, and delivering enterprise-wide solutions that meet business requirements and enhance operational efficiency. As an AWS solution architect, he has plenty of experience in designing end-to-end IT solutions and leading and managing complete projects within time and budgetary constraints. He contributes to open source projects and has experience working with start-ups as well as enterprises including financial service industries and public and government sectors. He holds various professional certifications from AWS, Red Hat, CNCF, and HashiCorp. He loves to share his experience with the latest technologies at AWS meetups.

When he's not in front of his computer, you might find him playing badminton or golf or trying out new restaurants in town. He enjoys traveling to new places around the world and learning about various cultures.

I must begin my acknowledgment by thanking a couple of people who have had a significant effect on my profession. First and foremost, I want to thank my mentor and friend, Rahul Natarajan, who basically taught me AWS and continues to help me with architecture challenges whenever I get stuck. My former manager, Jason Carter, taught me a lot about application architecture and security. I'd also like to thank Stephen Brown and Gergely Varga for advancing my career by exposing me to AI and global reach. Finally I want to thank my girlfriend Lee Lee who has supported me in this journey.

About the reviewer

Julian Andres Forero is a DevOps consultant at Endava, with more than 7 years of experience in different private and public companies related to media, payments, education, and financial services. He holds a degree in systems engineering and other professional certifications as a Professional and Associate Solutions Architect on Amazon Web Services and as a Terraform Associate Engineer. He has broad experience with cloud architectures and enterprise DevOps frameworks and helps companies to embrace DevOps and site reliability engineering principles. He is the author of various academic articles and has spoken at multiple events on the IT scene. Outside of work, he is an amateur footballer and enjoys visiting new places around the world.

To my partner, for always being there for me, and supporting me when I need it the most. I really appreciate all the moments that we have shared together. I love you.

Table of Contents

3

CI/CD Using AWS Proton and an Introduction to AWS CodeGuru

Section 2: Chaos Engineering and EKS Clusters

4

Working with AWS EKS and App Mesh

5

Securing Private EKS Cluster for Production

6

Chaos Engineering with AWS Fault Injection Simulator

Section 3: DevSecOps and AIOps

7

Infrastructure Security Automation Using Security Hub and Systems Manager

8

DevSecOps Using AWS Native Services

9

DevSecOps Pipeline with AWS Services and Tools Popular Industry-Wide

10

AIOps with Amazon DevOps Guru and Systems Manager OpsCenter

Index

Other Books You May Enjoy

Preface

CI/CD has never been simple, but these days the landscape is more bewildering than ever, its terrain riddled with blind alleys and pitfalls that seem almost designed to trap the less-experienced developer. If you're determined enough to keep your balance on the cutting edge and are equipped with a resource like this book, though, the landscape of CI/CD is one that you will navigate with ease.

Accelerating DevSecOps on AWS will help you discover all the most modern ways of building CI/CD pipelines with AWS by placing security checks, chaos experiment, and AIOps stage in pipeline, taking you step by step from the basics right through to the most advanced topics in this varied domain.

This comprehensive guide wastes no time in covering the basics of CI/CD with AWS. Once you're all set with tools such as AWS CodeStar, Proton, CodeGuru, App Mesh, Security Hub, and CloudFormation, you'll dive into chaos engineering, the latest trend in testing the fault tolerance of your system using AWS Fault Injection Simulator. After that, you'll explore the advanced concepts of AIOps using AWS DevOps Guru and DevSecOps, two highly sought-after skill sets for securing and optimizing your CI/CD systems. The full range of AWS CI/CD features will be covered, including the Security Advisory plugin for IDEs, SAST, DAST, and RASP, giving you real, applicable expertise in the things that matter.

By the end of this book, you'll be confidently creating resilient, secure, and performant CI/CD pipelines using the best techniques and technologies that AWS has to offer.

Who this book is for

This book is for DevOps engineers, engineering managers, cloud developers, and cloud architects. All you need to get started is basic experience with the software development life cycle, DevOps, and AWS.

What this book covers

Chapter 1, CI/CD Using AWS CodeStar, introduces the basic concept of CI/CD and branching strategies, then you will create a basic pipeline using AWS CodeStar and enhance it by adding multiple stages, environments, and branching strategies. Doing this will cover all of the AWS developer toolchain, such as CodeCommit, CodeBuild, CloudFormation, and CodePipeline.

Chapter 2, Enforcing Policy as Code on CloudFormation and Terraform, walks through the concept of policy as code and its importance in security and compliance, and the stage of CI/CD at which infrastructure can be checked. You will use CloudFormation Guard to apply policies on an AWS CloudFormation template. After that, you will learn how to use AWS Service Catalog across multiple teams. You will also do hands-on implementation on Terraform Cloud and policy implementation using HashiCorp Sentinel.

Chapter 3, CI/CD Using AWS Proton and an Introduction to AWS CodeGuru, introduces the new AWS Proton service and how AWS Proton helps both developers and DevOps/infrastructure engineers with their work in software delivery. You will learn the basic blocks of the Proton service and create an environment template to spin up multiple infrastructure environments and service templates to deploy the service instance in the environment. This chapter will also walk you through the code review process and how to find a vulnerability or secret leak using AWS CodeGuru.

Chapter 4, Working with AWS EKS and App Mesh, guides you through the architecture and implementation of an AWS EKS cluster. It explains the importance of and need for the AWS App Mesh service mesh and implementing features such as traffic routing, mutual TLS authentication, and using the X-Ray service for tracing.

Chapter 5, Securing Private EKS Cluster for Production, contains an implementation guide to set up a production-grade secure private EKS cluster. It covers almost all the important implementations on EKS, such as *IAM* Role for Service Account (IRSA), Cluster Autoscaler, EBS CSI, App Mesh, hardening using Kubescape, policy and governance using OPA Gatekeeper, and the backup and restore of a stateful application using Velero.

Chapter 6, Chaos Engineering with AWS Fault Injection Simulator, covers the concept of chaos engineering and when it is needed. It walks through the principles of chaos engineering and gives insights in terms of where it fits in CI/CD. You will learn how to perform chaos simulation using AWS FIS on an EC2 instance, Relational Database Service (RDS), and an EKS node.

Chapter 7, Infrastructure Security Automation Using Security Hub and Systems Manager, includes some important solutions to automate infrastructure security using AWS Security Hub and Systems Manager. The solutions include enforcing only running compliant images from ECR on an EKS cluster, config rule evaluation as an insight into Security Hub, and integrating Systems Manager with Security Hub to detect issues, create an incident, and remediate it automatically.

Chapter 8, DevSecOps Using AWS Native Services, walks you step by step through creating a DevSecOps CI/CD pipeline with a branching strategy using AWS native security services such as CodeGuru Reviewer and ECR image scanning. It includes the powerful combination of the developer toolchain, App Mesh, and Fault Injection Simulator. It also covers the canary deployment of microservices and analysis using Prometheus and Grafana.

Chapter 9, DevSecOps Pipeline with AWS Services and Tools Popular Industry-Wide, walks you through the planning to create a pipeline. It shows how to implement security at every stage of software delivery, starting from when you write code. It also shows the usage of the Snyk Security Advisory plugin in an IDE, git-secrets to scan sensitive data such as keys and passwords, SAST using Snyk, DAST using OWASP ZAP, RASP using Falco, chaos simulation using AWS FIS, and AIOps using AWS DevOps Guru. It also includes operational activities such as showing a security posture and vulnerability findings using AWS Security Hub.

Chapter 10, AIOps with Amazon DevOps Guru and Systems Manager OpsCenter, introduces the primer artificial intelligence and machine learning concepts. It covers what AIOps is, why we need it, and how it applies to IT operations. You will learn about the AWS AIOps tool DevOps Guru and implement two use cases about identifying anomalies in CPU, memory, and networking within an EKS cluster, and analyzing failure insights and remediation in a serverless application.

To get the most out of this book

All the tools used are the latest version while writing the book.

Software/hardware covered in the book	Operating system requirements
Cloud: AWS services, Terraform Cloud, HashiCorp Sentinel	Linux
Shell script, Python, Node.js, Terraform	
cfn-guard, Snyk, Anchore, OWASP ZAP, Falco, OPA, Kubescape	

All the tools used in this book are open source or have a trial version that you can subscribe to.

If you are using the digital version of this book, we advise you to type the code yourself or access the code from the book's GitHub repository (a link is available in the next section). Doing so will help you avoid any potential errors related to the copying and pasting of code.

It is important to have cloud, DevOps, or development work experience to understand the content of the book.

Download the example code files

You can download the example code files for this book from GitHub at https://github.com/PacktPublishing/Accelerating-DevSecOps-on-AWS. If there's an update to the code, it will be updated in the GitHub repository.

We also have other code bundles from our rich catalog of books and videos available at https://github.com/PacktPublishing/. Check them out!

Download the color images

We also provide a PDF file that has color images of the screenshots and diagrams used in this book. You can download it here: https://static.packt-cdn.com/downloads/9781803248608_ColorImages.pdf.

Conventions used

There are a number of text conventions used throughout this book.

Code in text: Indicates code words in text, database table names, folder names, filenames, file extensions, pathnames, dummy URLs, user input, and Twitter handles. Here is an example: "To verify the policy, we will issue a command in the EKS cluster to run the node:10 image."

A block of code is set as follows:

```
{
    "detail-type": ["Config Rules Compliance Change"],
    "source": ["aws.config"],
    "detail": {
        "messageType": ["ComplianceChangeNotification"]
    }
}
```

When we wish to draw your attention to a particular part of a code block, the relevant lines or items are set in bold:

```
$ wget https://raw.githubusercontent.com/PacktPublishing/
Modern-CI-CD-on-AWS/main/chapter-07/ecr-compliance.yaml
```

Any command-line input or output is written as follows:

```
$ docker push <yourAWSAccount>.dkr.ecr.us-east-1.amazonaws.com/
node:latest
```

Bold: Indicates a new term, an important word, or words that you see onscreen. For instance, words in menus or dialog boxes appear in **bold**. Here is an example: "Select **System info** from the **Administration** panel."

> **Tips or Important Notes**
> Appear like this.

Get in touch

Feedback from our readers is always welcome.

General feedback: If you have questions about any aspect of this book, email us at customercare@packtpub.com and mention the book title in the subject of your message.

Errata: Although we have taken every care to ensure the accuracy of our content, mistakes do happen. If you have found a mistake in this book, we would be grateful if you would report this to us. Please visit www.packtpub.com/support/errata and fill in the form.

Piracy: If you come across any illegal copies of our works in any form on the internet, we would be grateful if you would provide us with the location address or website name. Please contact us at copyright@packt.com with a link to the material.

If you are interested in becoming an author: If there is a topic that you have expertise in and you are interested in either writing or contributing to a book, please visit authors.packtpub.com.

Share Your Thoughts

Once you've read *Accelerating DevSecOps on AWS*, we'd love to hear your thoughts! Scan the QR code below to go straight to the Amazon review page for this book and share your feedback.

https://packt.link/r/1-803-24860-2

Your review is important to us and the tech community and will help us make sure we're delivering excellent quality content.

Section 1: Basic CI/CD and Policy as Code

This part includes chapters that cover how to create a CI/CD pipeline using AWS CodeStar with a branching strategy and adding multiple stages and environments. It covers how to leverage the AWS Proton service to create a CI/CD pipeline for applications and infrastructure at scale. It also covers how to avoid any secrets and vulnerabilities in code by integrating AWS CodeGuru Reviewer with CodeCommit. After that, it covers how to enforce policy on infrastructure code using CloudFormation Guard and HashiCorp Sentinel.

This section contains the following chapters:

- *Chapter 1, CI/CD Using AWS CodeStar*
- *Chapter 2, Enforcing Policy as Code on CloudFormation and Terraform*
- *Chapter 3, CI/CD Using AWS Proton and an Introduction to AWS CodeGuru*

1
CI/CD Using AWS CodeStar

This chapter will first introduce you to the basic concepts of **Continuous Integration/ Continuous Deployment (or Continuous Delivery) (CI/CD)** and a branching strategy. Then, we will implement basic CI/CD for a sample Node.js application using **Amazon Web Services (AWS) CodeStar**, which will deploy the application in Elastic Beanstalk. We will begin by creating a CodeStar project, then we will enhance it by adding develop and feature branches in a CodeCommit repository. We will also add a manual approval process as well as a production stage in CodePipeline. We will also spin up the production environment (modifying a CloudFormation template) so that the production stage of the pipeline can deploy the application. After that, we will create two lambda functions that will validate the **Pull Request (PR)** raised from the feature branch to develop branch, by getting the status of the CodeBuild project. Doing this entire activity will give you an overall idea of AWS Developer Tools (CodeCommit, CodeBuild, and CodePipeline) and how to implement a cloud-native CI/CD pipeline.

In this chapter, we are going to cover the following main topics:

- Introduction to CI/CD, along with a branching strategy
- Creating a project in AWS CodeStar
- Creating feature and development branches, as well as an environment
- Validating **PRs/Merge Requests** (**MRs**) into the develop branch from the feature branch via CodeBuild and AWS Lambda
- Adding a production stage and environment

Technical requirements

To get started, you will need an AWS account and the source code of this repository, which can be found at `https://github.com/PacktPublishing/Accelerating-DevSecOps-on-AWS/tree/main/chapter-01`.

Introduction to CI/CD, along with a branching strategy

In this section of the chapter, we will dig into what exactly CI/CD is and why is it so important in the software life cycle. Then, we will learn about a branching strategy, and how we use it in the source code repository to make the software delivery more efficient, collaborative, and faster.

CI

Before getting to know about CI, let's have a brief look at what happens in a software development workflow. Suppose you are working independently, and you have been asked to develop a web application that is a chat system. So, the first thing you will be doing is to create a Git repository and write your code in your local machine, build the code, and run some tests. If it works fine in your local environment, you will then push it to a remote Git repository. After that, you will build this code for different environments (where the actual application will run) and put the artifact in the artifact registry. After that, you will deploy that artifact into the application server where your application will be running.

Now, suppose the frontend of your application is not too good, and you want some help from your frontend developer. The frontend developer will clone the code repository, then contribute to the repository either by modifying the existing code or adding new code. After that, they will commit the code and push it into the repository. Then again, the same steps of build and deploy will take place, and your application will be running with the new **User Interface (UI)**. Now, what if you and the frontend developer both want to enhance the application, whereby both of you will be writing the code, and somehow you both used the same file and did your own changes, and tried to push back to the repository? If there are no conflicts, then your Git repository will allow you to update the repository, but in case there are any conflicts then it will highlight this to you. Now, once your code repository is updated, you must again build the code and run some unit tests. If the tests find a bug, then the build process will fail and you or the frontend developer will need to fix the bug, and again run the build and unit test. Once this passes, you will then need to put the build artifact into the artifact registry and then later deploy it into the application server. But this whole manual process of building, testing, and making the artifact ready for deployment will become quite troublesome and slow when your application gets bigger, and collaborators will increase, which in return will slow the deployment of your application. These problems of slow feedback and a manual process will easily put the project off schedule. To solve this, we have a CI process.

CI is a process where all the collaborators/developers contribute their code, several times a day, in a central repository that is further integrated into an automated system that pulls the code from the repository, builds it, runs unit tests, fails the build, gives feedback in case there are bugs, and prepares the artifact so that it is deployment-ready. The process is illustrated in the following diagram:

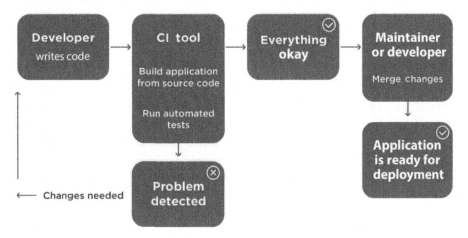

Figure 1.1 – CI process

CI makes sure that software components or services work together. The integration process should take place and complete frequently. This increases the frequency of developer code commits and reduces the chances of non-compatible code and redundant efforts. To implement a CI process, we need—at the very least—the following tools:

- Version Control System (VCS)
- Build tool
- Artifact repository manager

While implementing a CI process, our code base must be under version control. Every change applied to the code base must be stored in a VCS. Once the code is version controlled, it can be accessed by the CI tool. The most widely used VCS is Git, and in this book, we will also be using Git-based tools. The next requirement for CI is a build tool, which basically compiles your code and provides the executable file in an automated way. The build tool depends on the technology stack; for instance, for Java, the build tool will be Maven or Ant, while for Node.js, it will be npm. Once an executable file gets generated by the build tool, it will be stored in the artifact repository manager. There are lots of tools available in the market—for example, Sonatype Nexus Repository Manager (NXRM) or JFrog. We will be using the AWS Artifact service. The whole CI workflow will be covered in detail after the *Branching strategy (Gitflow)* section.

CD

CD is a process where the generated executable files or packages (in the CI process) are installed or deployed on application servers in an automated manner. So, CI is basically the first step toward achieving CD.

There is a difference between continuous deployment and delivery, but most of the time, you will be seeing or implementing continuous delivery, especially when you are in the financial sector or any critical business.

Continuous delivery is a process whereby, after all the steps of CI, building and testing then deploying to the application server happens with human intervention. Human intervention means either clicking a button on **Build Tools** to deploy or allowing a slack bot by approving it. The continuous deployment process differs slightly, whereby the deployment of a successful build to the application server takes place in an automated way and without human intervention.

The processes are illustrated in the following diagram:

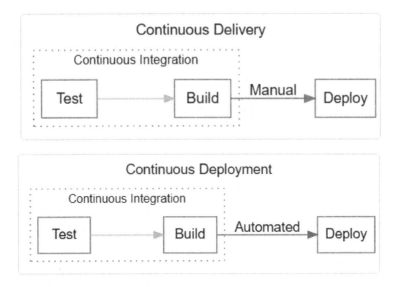

Figure 1.2 – CD processes

On reading up to this point, you must be thinking that the CI process is more complex than the CD process, but the CD process is trickier when deploying an application to the production server, especially when it is serving thousands to millions of end-user customers. Any bad experience with the application that is running on your production server may lose customers, which results in a loss for the business. For instance, **version 1 (v1)** of your application is running live right now and your manager has asked you to deploy version v1.1, but during the deployment, some problem occurred, and somehow v1.1 is not running properly, so you then have to roll back to the previous version, v1. So, all these things now need to be planned and automated in a deployment strategy.

Some CD strategies used in DevOps methodologies are mentioned in the following list:

- Blue-green deployment
- Canary deployment
- Recreate deployment
- A/B testing deployment

Let's have a look at these strategies in brief.

Blue-green deployment

A blue-green deployment is a deployment strategy or pattern where we can reduce downtime by having two production environments. It provides near-zero-downtime rollback capabilities. The basic idea of a blue-green deployment is to shift the traffic from the current environment to another environment. The environments will be identical and run the same application but will have different versions.

You can see an illustration of this strategy in the following diagram:

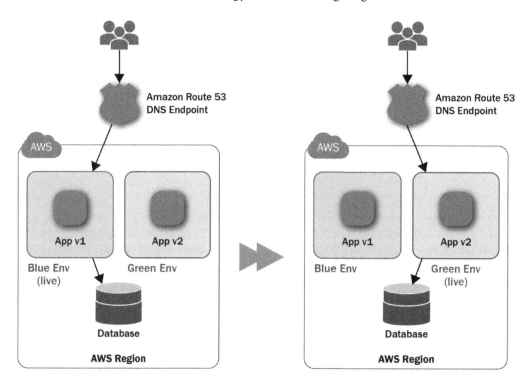

Figure 1.3 – Blue-green demonstration

In the preceding diagram, we can see that initially, the live application was running in the blue environment, which has **App v1**; later, it got switched to green, which is running the latest version of the application, **App v2**.

Canary deployment

In a canary deployment strategy, applications or services get deployed in an incremental manner to a subset of users. Once this subset of users starts using an application or service, then important application metrics are collected and analyzed to decide whether the new version is good to go ahead at full scale to be rolled to all users or needs to roll back for troubleshooting. All infrastructure in production environments is updated in small phases (for example, 10%, 20%, 50%, 75%, 100%).

You can see an illustration of this strategy in the following diagram:

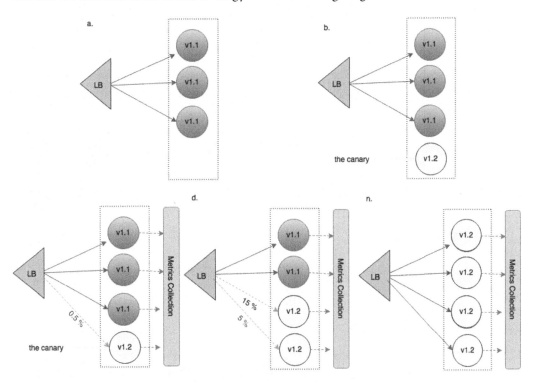

Figure 1.4 – Canary deployment phases

Let's move on to the next strategy.

Recreate deployment

With this deployment strategy, we stop the older version of an application before deploying the newer version. For this deployment, downtime of service is expected, and a full restart cycle is executed.

You can see an illustration of this strategy in the following diagram:

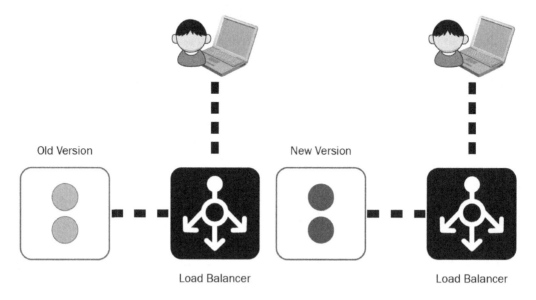

Figure 1.5 – Recreate deployment steps

Let's have a look at the next deployment strategy.

A/B testing deployment

A/B testing is a deployment whereby we run different versions of the same application/ services simultaneously, for experimental purposes, in the same environment for a certain period. This strategy consists of routing the traffic of a subset of users to a new feature or function, then getting their feedback and metrics, and after that comparing this with the older version. After comparing the feedback, the decision-maker will update the entire environment with the chosen version of the application/services.

You can see an illustration of this strategy in the following diagram:

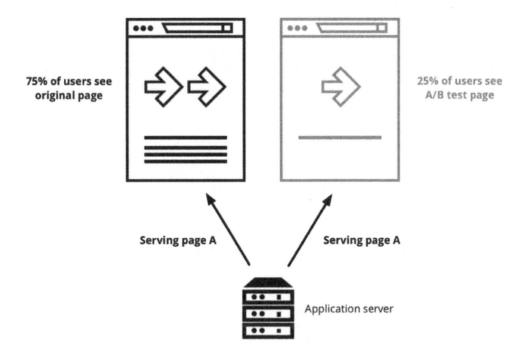

Figure 1.6 – A/B testing demonstration

So far, we got to see the deployment strategies, but we do not deploy the application in the production server just after having the build artifact ready from the CI process. We deploy and test the application in various environments and, post success, we deploy in the production environment. We will now see how application versions relate to branches and environments.

Branching strategy (Gitflow)

In the preceding two sections, we got to know about CI and CD, but it is not possible to have a good CI and CD strategy if you do not have a good branching strategy. However, what does *branching strategy* mean and what exactly are branches?

Whenever a developer writes code in a local machine, after completing the code, they upload/push it to a VCS (Git). The reason for using a VCS is to store the code so that it can be used by other developers and can be tracked and versioned. When a developer pushes the code to Git for the first time, it goes to the master/main branch. A branch in Git is an independent line of development and it serves as an abstraction for the edit/commit/stage process. We will explore the Gitflow branching strategy with a simple example.

Suppose we have a project to implement a calculator. The calculator will have functions of addition, subtraction, multiplication, division, and average. We have three developers (Lily, Brice, and Geraldine) and a manager to complete this project. The manager has asked them to deliver the addition function first. Lily quickly developed the code, built and tested it, pushed it to the Git **main/master** branch, and tagged it with version 0.1, as illustrated in the following screenshot. The code in the main/master Git branch always reflects the production-ready state, meaning the code for addition will be running in the production environment.

Figure 1.7 – Master branch with the latest version of the code

Now, the manager has asked Brice to start the development of subtraction and multiplication functions as the major functionality for a calculator project for the next release and asked Geraldine to develop division and average functions as a functionality for a future release. Thus, the best way to move ahead is to create a **develop** branch that will be an exact replica of the working code placed in the master branch. A representation of this branch can be seen in the following screenshot:

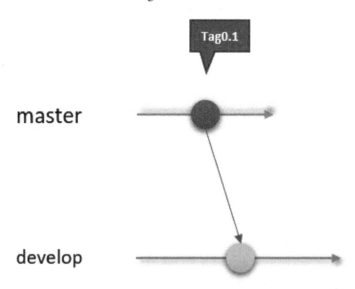

Figure 1.8 – Checking out the develop branch from master

So, once a develop branch gets created out of the master, it will have the latest code of the addition function. Now, since Brice and Geraldine must work on their task, they will create a **feature** branch out of the develop branch. Feature branches are used by developers to develop new features for upcoming releases. It branches off from the develop branch and must merge into the develop branch back once the development of the new functionality completes, as illustrated in the following screenshot:

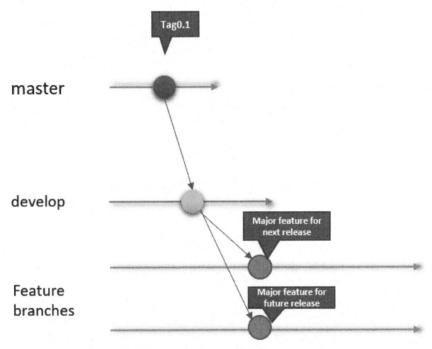

Figure 1.9 – Creating feature branches from the develop branch

While Brice (responsible for subtraction and multiplication) and Geraldine (responsible for division and average) have been working on their functionality and committing their branches, the manager has found a bug in the current live production environment and has asked Lily to fix that bug. It is never a good practice and is not at all recommended to fix any bug in a production environment. So, what Lily will have to do is to create a **hotfix** branch from the master branch, fix the bug in code, then merge it into the master branch as well as the develop branch. Hotfix branches are required to take immediate action on the undesired status of the master branch. It must branch off from the master branch and, after fixing the bug, must merge into the master branch as well as the develop branch so that the current develop branch does not have that bug and can deploy smoothly in the next release cycle. Once the fixed code gets merged into the master branch, it gets a new minor version tag and is deployed to the production environment.

This process is illustrated in the following screenshot:

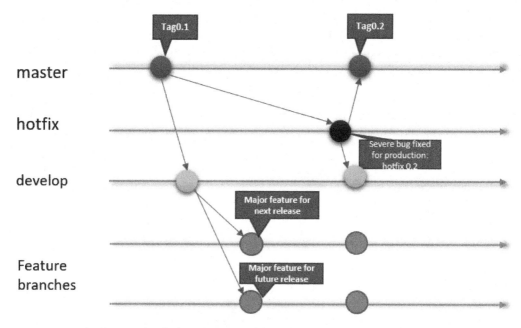

Figure 1.10 – Checking out hotfix from master and later merging into the master and develop branches

Now, once Brice completes his development (subtraction and multiplication), he will then merge his code from the feature branch into the develop branch. But before he merges, he needs to raise a PR/MR. As the name implies, this requests the maintainer of the project to merge the new feature into the develop branch, after reviewing the code. All companies have their own requirements and policies enforced before a merge. Some basic requirements to get a feature merged into the develop branch are that the feature branch should get built successfully without any failures and must have passed a code quality scan.

You can see an example of a PR/MR in the following diagram:

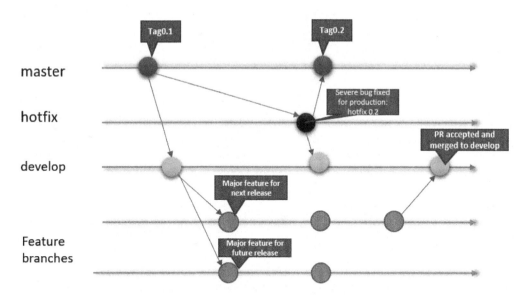

Figure 1.11 – PR raised from the feature branch, post-approval, merged into the develop branch

Once Brice's code (subtraction and multiplication feature) is accepted and merged into the develop branch, then the **release process** will take place. In the release process, the develop branch code gets merged to the **release** branch. The release branch basically supports preparation for a new production release. The code in the release branch gets deployed to an environment that is similar to a production environment. That environment is known as staging (pre-production). A staging environment not only tests the application functionality but also tests the load on the server in case traffic increases. If any bugs are found during the test, then these bugs need to be fixed in the release branch itself and merged back into the develop branch.

The process is illustrated in the following screenshot:

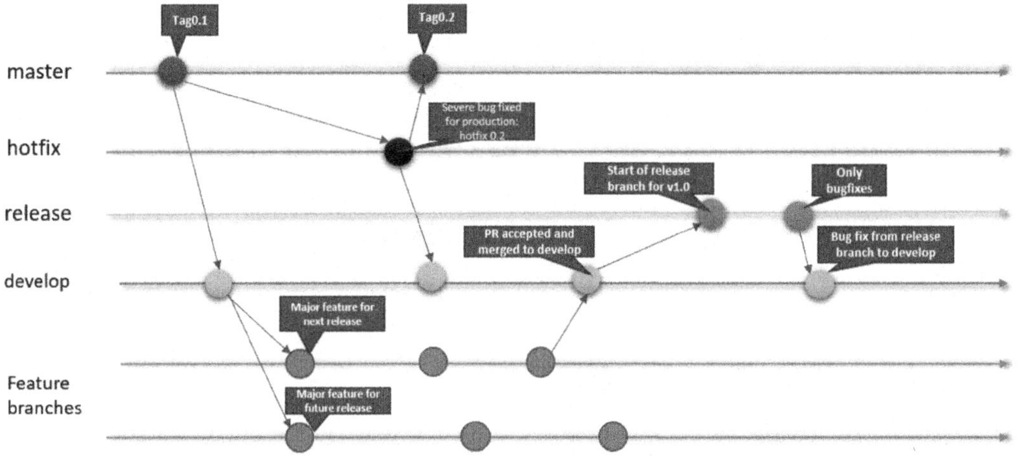

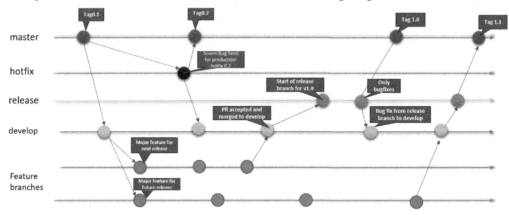

Figure 1.12 – Merging the code into release branch from develop branch, fixing bugs (if any), and then merging back into develop branch

Once all the bugs are fixed and testing is successful, the release branch code will get merged into the master branch, then tagged and deployed to the production environment. So, after that, the application will have three functions: addition, subtraction, and multiplication. A similar process will take place for the new features of division and average developed by Geraldine, and finally, the version will be tagged as 1.1 and deployed in the production environment, as illustrated in the following diagram:

Figure 1.13 – Merging code from the release branch into the master branch

These are the main branches in the whole life cycle of an application:

- Master
- Develop

But during a development cycle, the supporting branches, which do not persist once the merge finishes, are shown here:

- Feature
- Hotfix
- Release

Since we now understand branching and CI/CD, let's club all the pieces together, as follows:

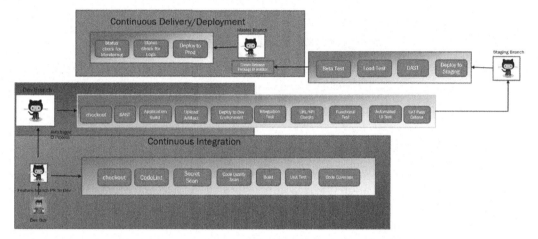

Figure 1.14 – CI/CD stages

So, in the preceding diagram, we can see that when a developer finishes their work in a feature branch, they try to raise a PR to the develop branch and the CI pipeline gets triggered. The CI pipeline is nothing but an automated flow or process in any CI tool such as Jenkins/AWS CodePipeline. This CI pipeline will validate whether the feature branch meets all the criteria to get merged into the develop branch. If the CI pipeline runs and build successfully, then the lead maintainer of the project will merge the feature branch into the develop branch, where another automated CI pipeline will trigger and try to deploy the new feature in the development environment. This whole process is known as CI (colored in blue in the preceding diagram). Post-deployment in the **development** environment, some automated test runs on top of it. If everything goes well and all the metrics look good, then the develop branch gets merged into the staging branch. During this merge process, another automated pipeline gets triggered, which deploys the artifact (uploaded during the develop branch CI process) into the **staging** environment. The staging environment is generally a close replica of the production environment, where some other tests such as **Dynamic Application Security Testing (DAST)** and load stress testing take place. If all the metrics and data from the staging environment look good, then staging of the branch code gets merged into the master branch and tagged as a new version.

If the maintainer deploys the tagged artifact in the **production** environment, then it is considered as continuous delivery. If the deployment happens without any intervention, then it is considered as continuous deployment.

So far, we have learned how application development and deployment take place. The preceding concept of CI/CD and branching strategies were quite important to be familiar with to move ahead and understand the rest of the chapters. In the next section, we will be learning about the AWS-managed CI/CD service CodeStar and will use it to create and deploy a project in development, staging, and production environments.

Creating a project in AWS CodeStar

In this section of the chapter, we will understand the core components of AWS CodeStar and will create a project and replace the existing project code with our own application code.

Introduction to AWS CodeStar

AWS CodeStar is a managed service by AWS that enable developers to quickly develop, build, and deploy an application on AWS. It provides all the necessary templates and interfaces to get you started. This service basically gives you an entire CI/CD toolchain within minutes using a CloudFormation stack. This service is quite good for any start-up companies that want to focus only on business logic and do not want to spend any time on setting up an infrastructure environment. It is so cloud-centric that it is integrated with the Cloud9 editor to edit your application code and CloudShell to perform terminal/shell-related action. AWS CodeStar is a free service, but you will be paying for other resources that get provisioned with it—for example, if you use this service to deploy your application on an **Elastic Compute Cloud (EC2)** instance, then you will not pay to use AWS CodeStar but will pay for the EC2 instance. AWS CodeStar is tightly integrated with other AWS developer tools mentioned next.

AWS CodeCommit

AWS CodeCommit is a VCS that is managed by AWS, where we can privately store and manage code in the cloud and integrate it with AWS. It is a highly scalable and secure VCS that hosts private Git repositories and supports the standard functionality of Git, so it works very well with your existing Git-based tools.

AWS CodeBuild

When it comes to cloud-hosted and fully managed build services that compile our source code, run unit tests, and produce artifacts that are ready to deploy, then **AWS CodeBuild** comes into the picture.

AWS CodeDeploy

AWS CodeDeploy is a deployment service provided by AWS that automates the deployment of an application to an Amazon EC2 instance, Elastic Beanstalk, and on-premises instances. It provides the facility to deploy unlimited variants of application content such as code, configuration, scripts, executable files, multimedia, and much more. CodeDeploy can deploy application files stored in Amazon **Simple Storage Service** (**S3**) buckets, GitHub repositories, or Bitbucket repositories.

AWS CodePipeline

AWS CodePipeline comes into the picture when you want to automate all the software release process. AWS CodePipeline is a CD and release automation service that helps smoothen deployment. You can quickly configure the different stages of a software release process. AWS CodePipeline automates the steps required to release software changes continuously.

Getting ready

Before jumping into creating a project in AWS CodeStar, note the following points:

- The project template that we will be selecting is a Node.js web application.
- We will be using Elastic Beanstalk as application compute infrastructure.
- Create a **Virtual Private Cloud** (**VPC**) with a private subnet and an EC2 key pair that we will be using later.
- If you are using Elastic Beanstalk for the first time in your AWS account, make sure the t2.micro instance type has enough **Central Processing Unit** (**CPU**) credit (see https://docs.aws.amazon.com/AWSEC2/latest/UserGuide/burstable-credits-baseline-concepts.html).

Let's get started by following these next steps:

1. Log in to the AWS Management Console by going to this site: `https://aws.amazon.com/console/`.

2. Go to the search box and search for **AWS CodeStar**, click on the result, and this will redirect you to AWS CodeStar intro/home page.

3. Click on **Create project**, and you will be redirected to **Choose a project template page** where you will see information on how to create a service role. Click on **Create service role**, as illustrated in the following screenshot:

Figure 1.15 – Service role prompt

4. Post that, you will see a green **Success** message, as illustrated in the following screenshot:

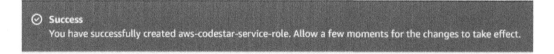

Figure 1.16 – Service role creation success message

5. Click on the dropdown of the **Templates** search box, then click **AWS Elastic Beanstalk** under **AWS service**, **Web application** under **Application type**, and **Node.js** under **Programming language**, as illustrated in the following screenshot:

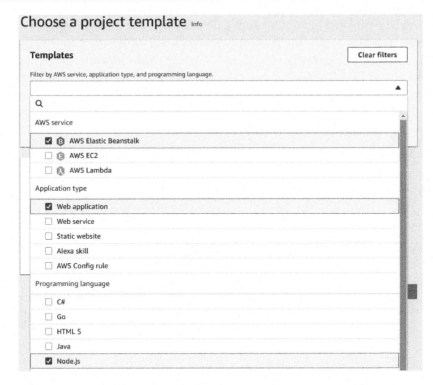

Figure 1.17 – Selecting service, application type, and programing language

6. You will see two search results, **Node.js** and **Express.js**. We will go ahead with **Node.js** by clicking on the radio button and then on **Next**, as illustrated in the following screenshot:

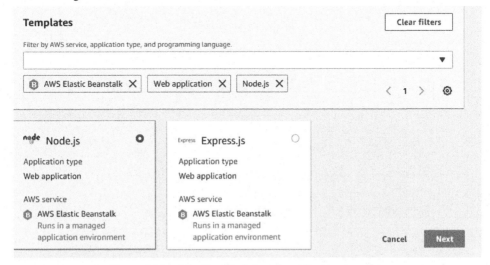

Figure 1.18 – Selecting Node.js web application template

7.   We will be redirected to another page called **Set up your project**, where we will be
     entering northstar in the **Project name** field. This will auto-populate the **Project
     ID** and **Repository name** fields. We will be using **CodeCommit** for the code
     repository. In **EC2 Configuration**, we will be going ahead with t2.micro and
     will select the available VPC and subnet. After that, we will select an existing key
     pair that we should already have access to and then click **Next**, as illustrated in the
     following screenshot:

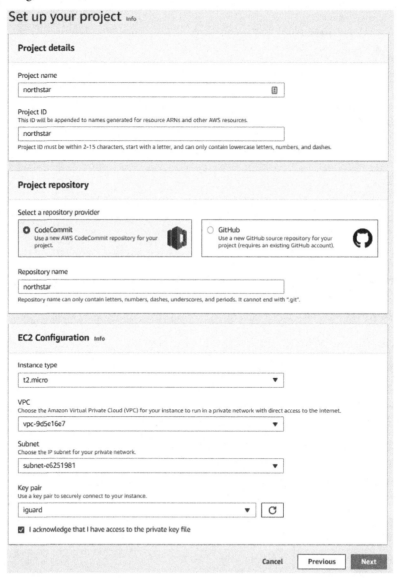

Figure 1.19 – CodeStar project setup details

8. Post that, we will be reviewing all the information related to the project and will proceed to click **Create project**. This process will take almost 10-15 minutes to set up the CI/CD toolchain and Elastic Beanstalk and deploy the sample Node.js application in Elastic Beanstalk. During this process, we can go to CloudFormation, search for the `awscodestar-northstar` stack, and see all the resources that are getting provisioned, as illustrated in the following screenshot:

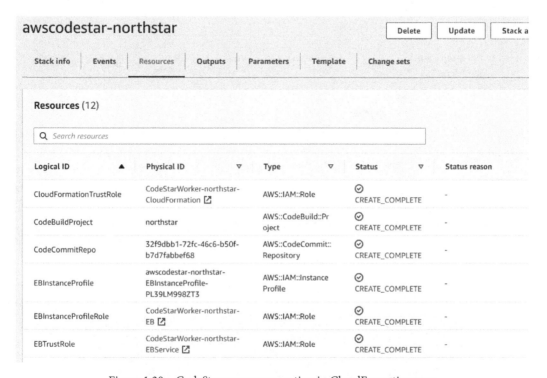

Figure 1.20 – CodeStar resources creation in CloudFormation page

9. We can also have a look at the Elastic Beanstalk resource by going to the **Environments** view of the Elastic Beanstalk console, as illustrated in the following screenshot:

Figure 1.21 – Elastic Beanstalk page showing northstarapp

10. After 10-15 minutes, we will keep monitoring the project main page. Once the **View application** button gets enabled, this means that the creation of a project, including a CI/CD toolchain and an environment infrastructure, and the deployment of an application have been completed. We can access the application by clicking on the **View application** button.

11. This will redirect us to a Node.js sample web application, as illustrated in the following screenshot:

Figure 1.22 – Default Node.js web application page

Now, before replacing the sample application with our own application, let's get to know what exactly happened at the backend, as follows:

- CodeStar triggers an AWS CloudFormation stack to create an entire CI/CD toolchain and workload infrastructure.

- The toolchain includes the following:

  - A CodeCommit repository with the master branch having a sample Node.js application

  - A CodeBuild project with the preconfigured environment to run the build

  - CodePipeline to trigger the build and deploy the application

- The workload infrastructure includes Elastic Beanstalk with one EC2 instance.

- IAM roles with certain permissions that allow CloudFormation to perform actions on other services.

To replace the sample application with our own sample application, perform the following steps:

1. Our sample code provided by AWS CodeStar resides in AWS CodeCommit, but we are not going to edit the application code in CodeCommit directly; instead, we will use the **AWS Cloud9 Integrated Development Environment** (IDE) tool. Switch to the CodeStar console from Elastic Beanstalk. We need to create an IDE environment by going to the **IDE** tab, as illustrated in the following screenshot, and clicking on **Create environment**:

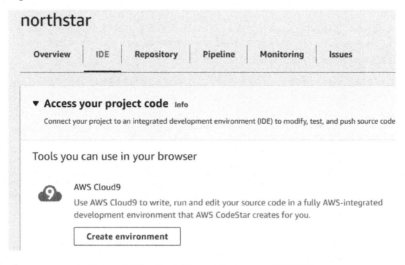

Figure 1.23 – CodeStar project page at IDE tab

2. The second page will ask you for the environment configuration for the Cloud9 IDE. This IDE environment will stop automatically if it is in an ideal state for 30 minutes to save on cost. Once you fill in all the details, click on **Create environment**, as illustrated in the following screenshot:

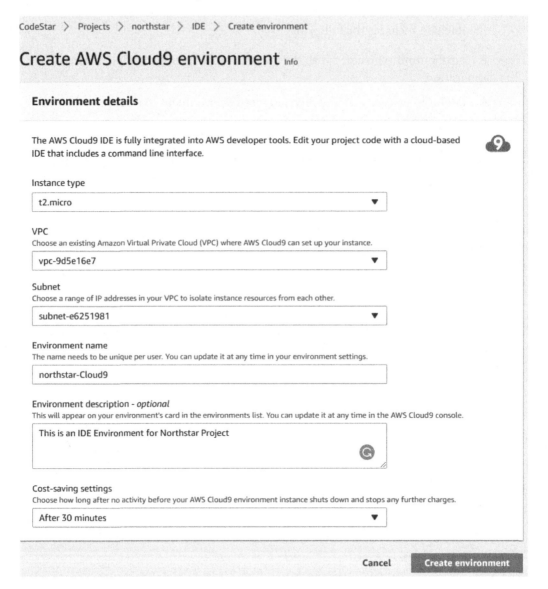

Figure 1.24 – Cloud9 environment configuration

3. After 10-15 minutes, you will be able to see the Cloud9 IDE environment available for you to open it and start using it. Click on **Open IDE** to get to the Cloud9 IDE.

4. The following screenshot shows you the Cloud9 IDE. This IDE will automatically clone the code from CodeCommit and show it in the cloud9 explorer. It also comes with its own shell:

Figure 1.25 – Cloud9 IDE console

5. Go to the shell of the editor and type the following commands. These commands will set the Git profile with your name and then clone our own application code:

```
$ git config –global user.name <your username>
$ git clone https://github.com/PacktPublishing/Modern-CI-
CD-on-AWS.git
```

6. Once you clone the application code, you will be able to see a folder with `Accelerating-DevSecOps-on-AWS` on the left side, as illustrated in the following screenshot. AWS-CodeStar, in your case it will be Accelerating-DevSecOps-on-AWS folder. That folder contains all the application code and some lambda code that we will use in this chapter:

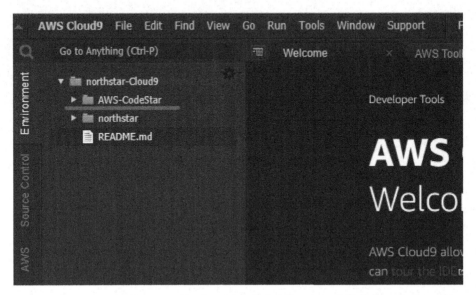

Figure 1.26 – Cloud9 IDE with the cloned Git folder

7. Now, type the following command into the shell to replace the application code:

```
$ cd northstar
$ rm -rf package.json app.js public tests
$ cd ../Modern-CI-CD-on-AWS/chapter-01
$ cp -rpf server.js source static package.json ../../
northstar
```

8. After that, go to the editor and edit the `buildspec.yml` file. Comment *line 16* where it is using the `npm test` command because our application does not include a test case for now.

9. After that, push the code into CodeCommit by typing the following commands:

```
$ cd ../../northstar
$ git add .
$ git commit -m "Replacing application code"
$ git push origin master
```

10. The moment we push the code into CodeCommit, CodePipeline will trigger automatically. This will pull the latest code from CodeCommit and pass it to CodeBuild, where the build will take place using `buildspec.yml`, and then it will deploy to Elastic Beanstalk using the `template.yml` CloudFormation template. The process is illustrated in the following screenshot:

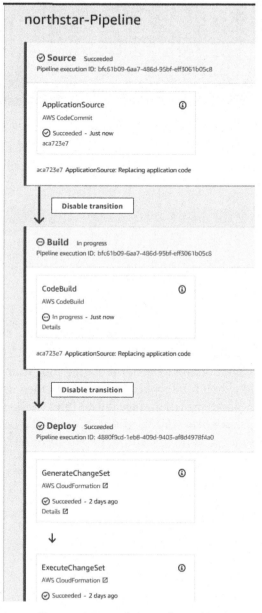

Figure 1.27 – northstar code pipeline

11. Once the pipeline completes successfully, go to the CodeStar Northstar project page, as illustrated in the following screenshot, and click on **View application** button in the top right. Alternatively, you can also access the new application via the Elastic Beanstalk page:

Figure 1.28 – New Node.js application deployed by CodePipeline

So, in this section, we created a CodeStar project, created an IDE environment, and replaced the sample application with our own application. Basically, the current flow looks like this:

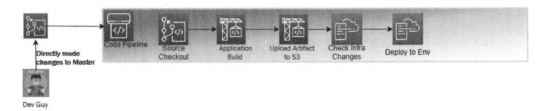

Figure 1.29 – Current CodePipeline steps

We made changes in the master branch, which triggered the CodePipeline. Then, CodePipeline invoked CodeCommit to fetch the source code from the master branch, then invoked CodeBuild to build the application code, and then uploaded the artifact into an S3 bucket. Then, the CloudFormation stage did an infra check and then deployed into the current Elastic Beanstalk environment. At this stage, Elastic Beanstalk is based on a single EC2 instance. In the next three sections, we will be modifying the CI/CD pipeline and following the diagram shown here:

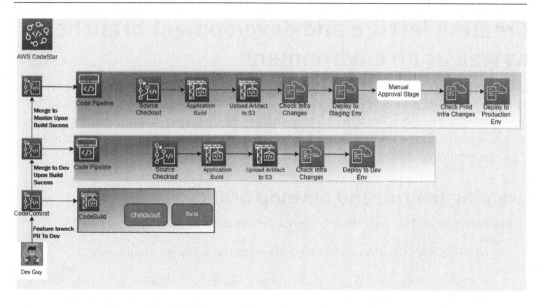

Figure 1.30 – CI/CD steps to be implemented in next three sections

Based on the preceding diagram, we will be performing the following tasks in the next three sections of the chapter:

1. Creating two extra branches—a develop branch and a feature branch.

2. Then, we will create a code pipeline with respect to the develop branch that gets triggered once code is pushed into the develop branch. This pipeline will check out the code from the develop branch, build the application, push the artifact into an S3 bucket and then spin up a separate development Elastic Beanstalk environment, and then deploy the application in the development environment.

3. We will then create a CodeBuild project that will trigger on PR.

4. Based on the PR build status, we will merge the code from the feature to the develop branch.

5. We'll then modify the existing pipeline that listens to the master branch. We will modify the existing environment name to staging and add a production stage, in which we spin up a production Elastic Beanstalk environment (two EC2 instances via an **Auto Scaling Group** (**ASG**) and an **Elastic Load Balancer** (**ELB**)), and then deploy the application in the production environment.

In the next section, we will create feature and development branches in AWS CodeCommit.

Creating feature and development branches, as well as an environment

In this section, we will be creating feature and develop branches. Post that, we will create a project in CodePipeline that triggers when there is a commit in the develop branch. In the CodePipeline project, we will also be using a stage that uses CloudFormation to spin up a new Elastic Beanstalk development environment and then deploy the application in the development environment.

Creating feature and develop branches

To create feature and develop branches in CodeCommit, follow these next steps:

1. Go to the AWS Cloud9 console shell and type the following commands:

    ```
    Nikit:~/environment/northstar (master) $ git checkout -b
    feature/image
    Switched to a new branch 'feature/image'
    Nikit:~/environment/northstar (feature/image) $ git push
    origin feature/image
    Total 0 (delta 0), reused 0 (delta 0)
    To https://git-codecommit.us-east-1.amazonaws.com/v1/
    repos/northstar
     * [new branch]        feature/image -> feature/image
    ```

2. Once you perform the steps, you will be able to see a **feature branch** in the CodeCommit Branches section, as illustrated in the following screenshot:

Figure 1.31 – CodeCommit console with the feature branch

3. Similarly, we need to create a develop branch by running the following commands:

```
Nikit:~/environment/northstar (feature/image) $ git
checkout -b develop
Switched to a new branch 'develop'
Nikit:~/environment/northstar (develop) $ git push origin
develop
Total 0 (delta 0), reused 0 (delta 0)
To https://git-codecommit.us-east-1.amazonaws.com/v1/
repos/northstar
 * [new branch]         develop -> develop
```

4. Again, you can go to the CodeCommit console to verify the presence of a develop branch. Both the develop branch and feature branch contain the latest code from the master branch.

We have created two branches: a feature branch and a develop branch. Now, let's create a development environment and pipeline.

Creating a development environment and pipeline

Since CodeStar uses a CloudFormation template to create an environment, we need to modify the existing CloudFormation template to create a development environment. Perform the following steps to replace the existing CloudFormation template:

1. Go to the AWS Cloud9 shell, navigate to the `northstar` folder, and make sure you are in the develop branch. Now, copy a file named `codestar-EBT-cft.yaml` present in the `AWS-CodeStar` folder to the current `northstar` directory by running the following commands:

```
Nikit:~/environment/northstar (develop) $ cp ../Modern-
CI-CD-on-AWS/chapter-01/codestar-EBT-cft.yaml .
Nikit:~/environment/northstar (develop) $ mv codestar-
EBT-cft.yaml template.yml
```

2. Now, push the new file into CodeCommit, as follows:

```
Nikit:~/environment/northstar (develop) $ git add
template.yml
Nikit:~/environment/northstar (develop) $ git commit -m
"adding development environment"
[develop 20dd426] adding development environment
 Committer: nikit <ec2-user@ip-172-31-2-208.ec2.internal>
```

```
 1 file changed, 235 insertions(+), 95 deletions(-)
Nikit:~/environment/northstar (develop) $ git push origin
develop
Enumerating objects: 5, done.
Counting objects: 100% (5/5), done.
Compressing objects: 100% (3/3), done.
Writing objects: 100% (3/3), 1.59 KiB | 1.59 MiB/s, done.
Total 3 (delta 1), reused 0 (delta 0)
To https://git-codecommit.us-east-1.amazonaws.com/v1/
repos/northstar
   aca723e..20dd426  develop -> develop
```

You must be wondering which changes we have made that in that `template.yml` CloudFormation template. During the start of the CodeStar project, the `template.yml` CloudFormation template includes the resource configuration of Elastic Beanstalk. But to add a new environment, you must add those new environment resource configurations to this template file.

> **Important Note**
>
> At this point, if you compare the `template.yml` file of the master branch and the develop branch, you will see that we are creating two different environments, `develop` and `prod`, and renaming the existing one to `staging`.

Since we have done the code changes, let's create a development pipeline that will also spin up a development environment. Follow these next steps:

1. We need to create a role that allows CloudFormation to performany action on other services. By default, CodeStar creates a `CodeStarWorkerCloudFormationRolePolicy` role through the `awscodestar-<projectname>` CloudFormation stack—in our case, `awscodestar-northstar`. We need to modify this stack so that we can allow the role to give some extra permissions to the resources that we will be creating. Proceed as follows:

    A. Copy the contents of the `permission.yaml` file in the AWS CodeStar repository. Now, go to CloudFormation console and click on **Stacks**, then search for `awscodestar-northstar`, as illustrated in the following screenshot:

Figure 1.32 – CloudFormation stack lists

B. Select `awscodestar-northstar`, and then click on **Update** on the right-hand side.

C. After that, select the **Edit template in designer** radio button and click on **View in Designer**, as illustrated in the following screenshot:

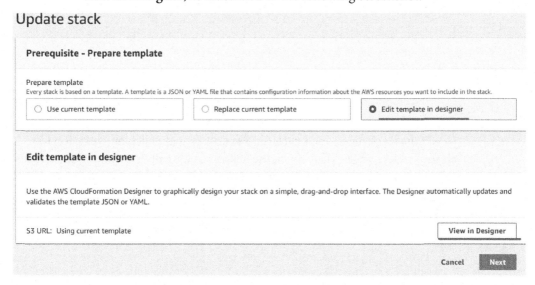

Figure 1.33 – CloudFormation stack update

D. We will be redirected to the **Template designer** page. Switch the template language from **JavaScript Object Notation (JSON)** to **YAML Ain't Markup Language (YAML)**, then replace the entire content that you copied from the `Permission.yaml` file. Then, click on the **Validate Template** icon (tick in a square box) to validate the template. If the template is valid, then click on the **Create stack** icon (upward arrow inside a cloud).

E.   You will then be redirected to the previous **Update stack** page with the S3 **Uniform Resource Locator** (**URL**), as illustrated in the following screenshot. Click on **Next** to update the changes:

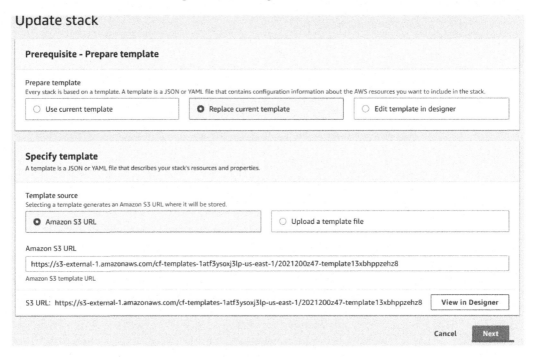

Figure 1.34 – Replacing the existing template

F.   Verify the stack details and click on **Next**, then again click on **Next**. Review all the stack changes, then check the acknowledgment box in the **Capabilities** section. After that, click on **Update stack**, as illustrated in the following screenshot:

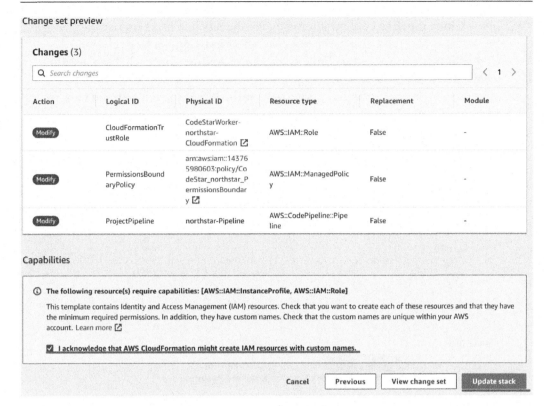

Figure 1.35 – Confirming change set

G. Carrying out the preceding steps will update the CloudFormation role with the new permission we added.

2. Once we have updated the policy inside **role**, we then need to create a pipeline by cloning the existing pipeline. Go to the CodePipeline console and click on `northstar-Pipeline` (see *Figure 1.27*), and then click on **Clone pipeline**.

3. In the **Clone pipeline** configuration, rename the pipeline `northstar-Pipeline-dev`, and under **Service role**, select **Existing Service role** and **CodeStarWorker-northstar-ToolChain**. Under **Artifact store**, choose **Custom location** and select the existing bucket name that refers to the development pipeline. Under **Encryption key**, select **Default AWS Managed Key** and click on **Clone**, as illustrated in the following screenshot:

Figure 1.36 – Pipeline clone configuration

4. You need to stop the execution of the pipeline because we need to make further changes to point the pipeline to the develop branch. To stop the execution of the pipeline, click on **Stop Execution**, mention the execution number, select **Stop and abandon**, then provide a comment, and finally, click on **Stop**.

5. Now, to make the changes to the development pipeline, we need to edit the pipeline by clicking on the **Edit** button, as illustrated in the following screenshot:

Figure 1.37 – Pipeline edit stages

6. We will be able to edit multiple stages here, and we need to modify each stage. Click on the **Edit** stage of **Source**, then click on the icon highlighted in the following screenshot:

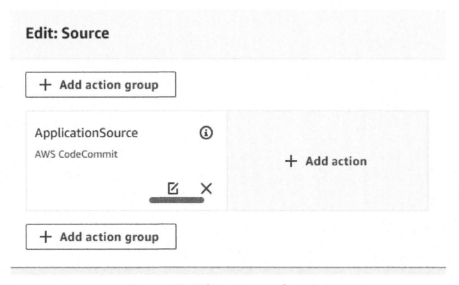

Figure 1.38 – Editing stage configuration

7. In the **Edit action** page, mention `develop` under **Branch name** and rename the **output artifact** `northstar-devSourceArtifact`, as illustrated in the following screenshot. Then, click on **Done** to save the action and click on **Done** again to save the stage:

Edit action

Action name
Choose a name for your action

ApplicationSource

No more than 100 characters

Action provider

AWS CodeCommit

Repository name
Choose a repository that you have already created where you have pushed your source code.

Q northstar

Branch name
Choose a branch of the repository

Q develop

Change detection options - *optional*
Choose a detection mode to automatically start your pipeline when a change occurs in the source code.

⊙ Amazon CloudWatch Events (recommended)
    Use Amazon CloudWatch Events to automatically start my pipeline when a change occurs

○ AWS CodePipeline
    Use AWS CodePipeline to check pe

Output artifact format - *optional*
Choose the output artifact format.

⊙ CodePipeline default
    AWS CodePipeline uses the default zip format for artifacts in the pipeline. Does not include git
    metadata about the repository.

○ Full clone
    AWS CodePipeline passes metadat
    git clone. Only supported for AWS

Variable namespace - *optional*
Choose a namespace for the output variables from this action. You must choose a namespace if you want to use the variables this action produces in your c

Output artifacts
Choose a name for the output of this action.

northstar-devSourceArtifact

No more than 100 characters

Figure 1.39 – Source action group configuration

8. Similarly, edit the build stage. In the **Edit action** page, select **northstar-devSourceArtifact** under **Input artifacts** and rename the **output artifact** `northstar-devBuildArtifact`, as illustrated in the following screenshot. Then, click on **Done** to save the action and click on **Done** again to save the stage:

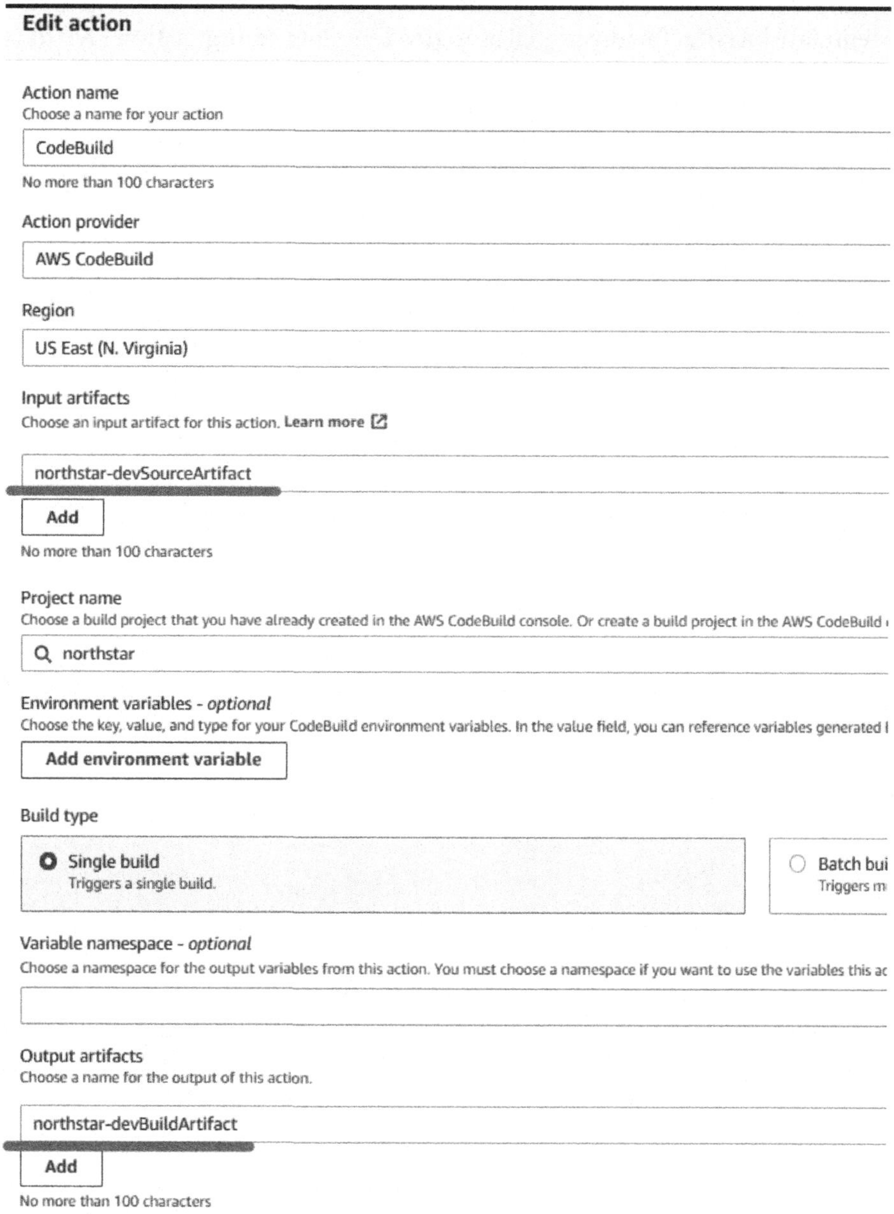

Edit action

Action name
Choose a name for your action

CodeBuild

No more than 100 characters

Action provider

AWS CodeBuild

Region

US East (N. Virginia)

Input artifacts
Choose an input artifact for this action. **Learn more** ☑

northstar-devSourceArtifact

Add

No more than 100 characters

Project name
Choose a build project that you have already created in the AWS CodeBuild console. Or create a build project in the AWS CodeBuild

Q northstar

Environment variables - *optional*
Choose the key, value, and type for your CodeBuild environment variables. In the value field, you can reference variables generated

Add environment variable

Build type

○ **Single build**
   Triggers a single build.

○ Batch bui
   Triggers m

Variable namespace - *optional*
Choose a namespace for the output variables from this action. You must choose a namespace if you want to use the variables this ac

Output artifacts
Choose a name for the output of this action.

northstar-devBuildArtifact

Add

No more than 100 characters

Figure 1.40 – Build action group configuration

9. Again, click on **Edit** for the deploy stage. There will be two action groups, **GenerateChangeSet** and **ExecuteChangeSet**. Edit **GenerateChangeSet** first. Select **northstar-devBuildArtifact** under **Input artifacts**. Modify the **stack name** to `awscodestar-northstar-infrastructure-dev`. Enter `pipeline-changeset` under **Change set name**. Select **northstar-devBuildArtifact** under **Template | Artifact name** as well as under **Template configuration | Artifact name**. Under the **Advanced** section, add a new `"Stage":"Dev"` key-value pair, then click on **Done**. The process is illustrated in the following screenshot:

Input artifacts
Choose an input artifact for this action. **Learn more** ☑

northstar-devBuildArtifact

[Add]
No more than 100 characters

Action mode
When you update an existing stack, the update is permanent. When you use a change set, the result provides a diff of the updated stack and

Create or replace a change set

Stack name
If you are updating an existing stack, choose the stack name.

Q   awscodestar-northstar-infrastructure-dev

Change set name
If you are updating an existing change set, choose the change set name.

Q   pipeline-changeset

Template
Specify the template you uploaded to your source location.

Artifact name   File name

northstar-devBuildArtifact   ▼   template-export.yml

Template configuration - *optional*
Specify the configuration file you uploaded to your source location.
🔵 Use configuration file

Artifact name   File name

northstar-devBuildArtifact   ▼   template-configuration.json

Capabilities - *optional*
Specify whether you want to allow AWS CloudFormation to create IAM resources on your behalf.

[CAPABILITY_NAMED_IAM X]

Role name

Q   arn:aws:iam::143765980603:role/CodeStarWorker-northstar-CloudFormation

▼ **Advanced**

Parameter overrides

"SubnetId":"subnet-e6251981",
"VpcId":"vpc-9d5e16e7",
"SolutionStackName":"64bit Amazon Linux 2 v5.4.2 running Node.js 12",
"EBTrustRole":"CodeStarWorker-northstar-EBService",
"EBInstanceProfile":"awscodestar-northstar-EBInstanceProfile-PL39LM998ZT3",
"Stage":"Dev"

Figure 1.41 – Generating change set action group configuration

10. Edit the `ExecuteChangeSet` action group. Just modify **Stack name** to `awscodestar-northstar-infrastructure-dev`. Under **Change set name**, keep **pipeline-changeset**, and after that, click on **Done** to save the action group. Then, click on **Done** to save the stage.

11. After that, click on **Save**. Ignore the **ValidationError** message shown in the following screenshot:

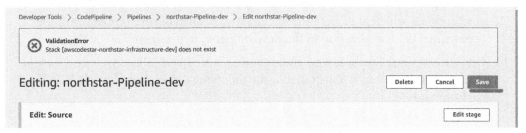

Figure 1.42 – Saving the development pipeline

12. At this stage, our development pipeline is ready to get executed. We will trigger this pipeline by modifying the code in the develop branch. Go to the Cloud9 IDE and select the `default.jade` file in `northstar/source/templates`. Edit the body page title to `AWS CODESTAR-DEV`. Save and push to the develop branch.

The process is illustrated in the following screenshot:

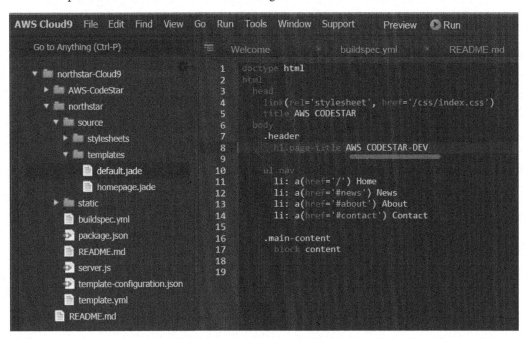

Figure 1.43 – Modifying the code for the develop branch

13. The moment code gets pushed to the develop branch, it will trigger `northstar-Pipeline-develop`. You can also see the commit message in the pipeline. This pipeline fetches the code from the develop branch, then does the build using the steps mentioned in `buildspec.yml`. After the build, it generates the artifact and pushes it to the S3 bucket. Then, at the deploy stage, it basically creates a CloudFormation change set using the parameter we passed, then it executes the change set. The change set basically includes the creation of a development environment, which is a single-instance Elastic Beanstalk environment, and the deployment of an application in the development environment.

14. Once the pipeline finishes, you can go to the Elastic Beanstalk console and look for `northstarappDev`, as illustrated in the following screenshot, then click on that environment:

Figure 1.44 – Elastic Beanstalk console showing new development environment

15. You will be redirected to the environment page, where you can access the application by clicking on the link, as illustrated in the following screenshot:

Figure 1.45 – Development environment console page

16. You will be able to see the updated application, as illustrated here:

Figure 1.46 – Development environment Node.js web application

So, we have created a feature branch, a develop branch, a development pipeline, and a development environment. In the next section, we will validate the PR raised from the feature branch to the develop branch using CodeBuild and a Lambda function.

Validating PRs/MRs into the develop branch from the feature branch via CodeBuild and AWS Lambda

In this section, we will basically implement a solution that gives the status of the build of the PR raised in CodeCommit. This helps the maintainer see that the PR raised is at least passing all the builds and tests. Let's have a look at the solution and understand the flow, as follows:

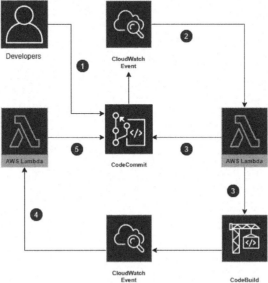

Figure 1.47 – Flow diagram of the solution

The following steps explains the flow of diagram:

1. When a developer finishes their work in the feature branch, they will then raise a PR/MR to the develop branch.

2. A CloudWatch event that is watching our repository will get triggered, and that will invoke the `TriggerCodeBuildStart` lambda function by passing some information.

3. This `TriggerCodeBuildStart` lambda function will use the CloudWatch information and trigger an AWS CodeBuild Project to our latest commit. After that, it will create a custom message that we want on our PR activity.

4. Once this CodeBuild event finishes, another CloudWatch event will send those build results and comments to another lambda function (`TriggerCodeBuildResult`).

5. This `TriggerCodeBuildResult` lambda function will comment the build result on the PR in the CodeCommit activity.

To set up the solution, perform the following steps:

1. Go to the CodeBuild section of the project and click on **Create Build Project**.

2. Enter the following information:

    A. **Project name**: `northstar-pr`

    B. **Description**: `PR-Build`

    C. **Repository**: `northstar`; **Branch**: `feature/image`

    D. **Environment Image**: `Managed Image`; **OS**: `Amazon Linux 2`; **Runtime**: `Standard`; **Image**: `aws/codebuild/amazonlinux2-x86_64-standard:3.0`; **Environment type**: `Linux`

    E. **Service Role**: `New service role`

    F. **Buildspec:** Inset build commands; **Build Commands**: `npm install && nohup npm start &`

    G. Leave the rest at their default settings and click on **Create build project**.

The CodeBuild console of the `northstar-pr` project is shown in the following screenshot:

Figure 1.48 – CodeBuild console of northstar-pr project

3. Go to the AWS Lambda console and under **Create a function**, select **Author from scratch** and give the name `TriggerCodebuildStart` and `Node.js 12.x` under **Runtime**. In the **Permissions** section, you need to select a role that has permission to access AWS CloudWatch Logs, CodeBuild, and CodeCommit. You can create a policy using the `lambdapermission.json` file and attach it to the role.

An overview of the process is shown in the following screenshot:

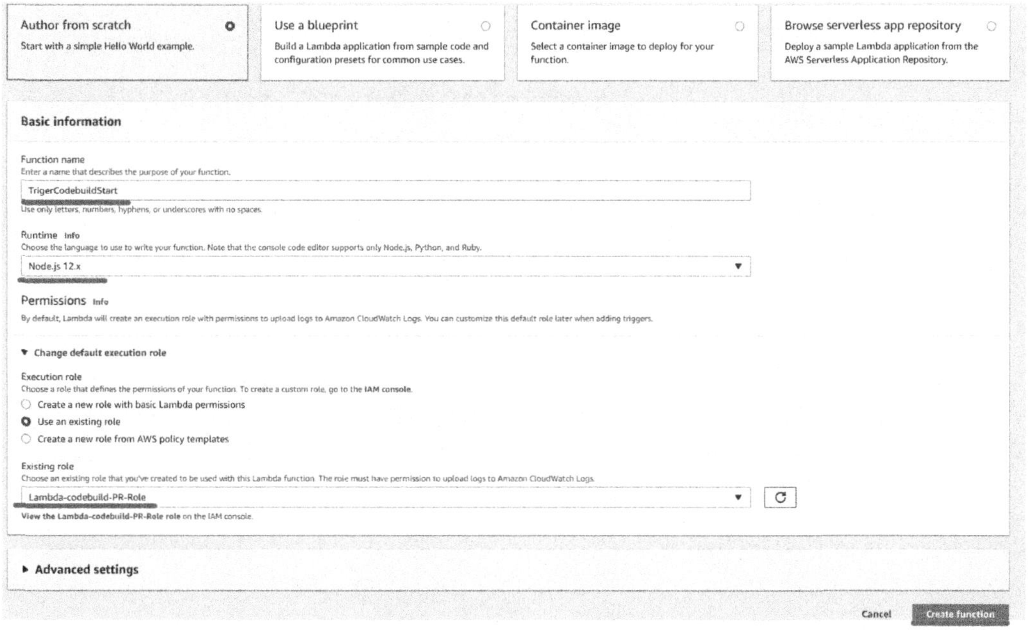

Figure 1.49 – Creating a lambda function

4. Go to the **Code Source** section and modify the index.js file. We will be using the source code present in the Accelerating-DevSecOps-on-AWS/chapter-01 folder that we downloaded for our sample application. There is a folder called TriggerCodeBuildStart that includes index.js and package.json files. Copy and paste both the files into this Lambda function and click on **Deploy**, as illustrated in the following screenshot:

Figure 1.50 – Lambda function code editor

5. After that, go to the **Configuration** section and click on **Environment variable** to add the environment variables. The lambda function code uses three environment variables shown in the following screenshot. Click on **Save** once you have entered the three environment variables:

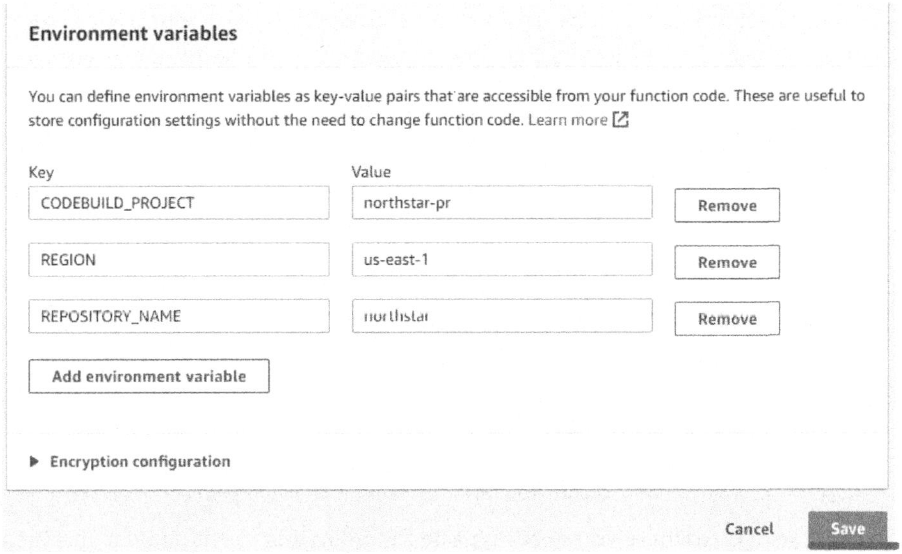

Environment variables

You can define environment variables as key-value pairs that are accessible from your function code. These are useful to store configuration settings without the need to change function code. Learn more ⤢

Key	Value	
CODEBUILD_PROJECT	northstar-pr	Remove
REGION	us-east-1	Remove
REPOSITORY_NAME	northstar	Remove

Add environment variable

▶ Encryption configuration

Cancel   Save

Figure 1.51 – Environment variables for TriggerCodebuildStart lambda function

6. Similarly, create another lambda function, `TriggerCodebuildResult`, with the code available in the `TriggerCodeBuildResult` folder. Deploy the Lambda function and go to the **Configuration** section to enter the environment variable, as illustrated in the following screenshot:

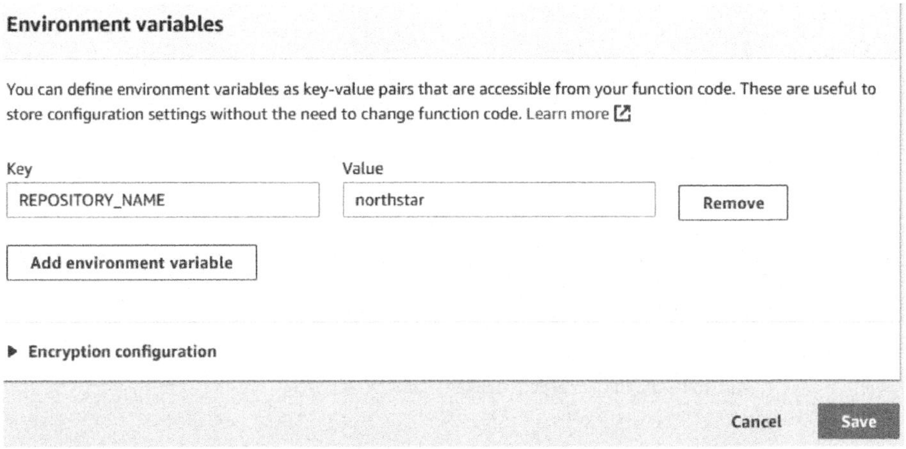

Environment variables

You can define environment variables as key-value pairs that are accessible from your function code. These are useful to store configuration settings without the need to change function code. Learn more ⤢

Key	Value	
REPOSITORY_NAME	northstar	Remove

Add environment variable

▶ Encryption configuration

Cancel   Save

Figure 1.52 – Environment variable for TriggerCodebuildResult lambda function

7. Once we have created our Lambda function, we need to create CloudWatch event rules. Go to the CloudWatch console, click on **Events** on the left-hand side, and then click on **Rule**. After that, click on **Create rule**.

8. Once you click on **Create rule**, you will be redirected to the **Event Source** section. Click on **Edit** in **Event Pattern Preview**, as illustrated in the following screenshot:

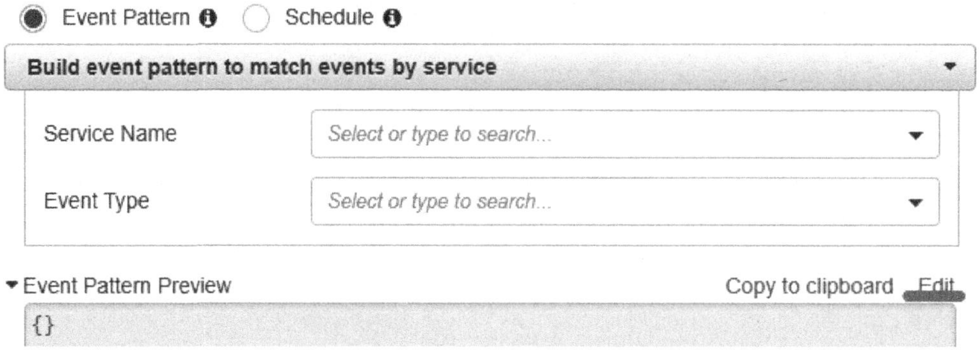

Figure 1.53 – CloudWatch rule creation with event pattern

9. You will get a box where you need to paste the following event pattern and then click **Save**:

```
{
    "source": [
      "aws.codecommit"
    ],
    "detail-type": [
      "CodeCommit Pull Request State Change"
    ],
    "resources": [
      "arn:aws:codecommit:us-east-1:<Your
accountID>:northstar"
    ],
    "detail": {
      "event": [
        "pullRequestCreated",
        "pullRequestSourceBranchUpdated"
      ]
    }
}
```

10. In the **Targets** section, select **Lambda function** in the dropdown, and then select the TriggerCodebuildStart function, as illustrated in the following screenshot:

Figure 1.54 – CloudWatch target

11. Click on **Configure details** to proceed to *Step 2*, where you need to give the rule a name and a description. Name the rule `TriggerValidatePRCodeBuildStart` and then save it.

12. Similarly, create another CloudWatch rule, naming it `TriggerValidatePRCodeBuildResult` and giving it the following event pattern, with the target being the `TriggerCodebuildResult` Lambda function:

```
{
    "source": [
        "aws.codebuild"
    ],
    "detail-type": [
        "CodeBuild Build State Change"
    ],
    "detail": {
        "project-name": [
            "northstar-pr"
        ],
        "build-status": [
            "FAILED",
            "SUCCEEDED"
        ]
    }
}
```

13. We now have two CloudWatch rules, `TriggerValidatePRCodeBuildStart` and `TriggerValidatePRCodeBuildResult`, as we can see in the following screenshot:

	Status	Name	Description
○	●	TriggerValidatePRCodeBuildResult	TriggerValidatePRCodeBuildResult
○	●	TriggerValidatePRCodeBuildStart	Validate PR Demo, Triggers Codebuild start Lambda Function

Figure 1.55 – CloudWatch rules

14. We are all set up with the solution. Now, to test this solution, we need to modify the `feature/image` branch and create a PR to the develop branch. We will modify the `northstar/source/templates/default.jade` file, save it, and push it, as illustrated in the following screenshot:

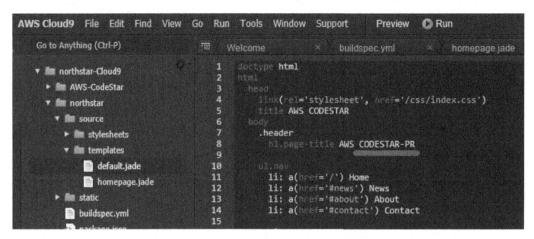

Figure 1.56 – Editing feature branch code for PR to develop branch

15. Now, let's create a PR from the CodeCommit console. Choose **feature/image** under **Source** and **develop** under **Destination**. Enter `Raising PR for Codestar-PR` for **Title** and **Description** and click on **Create pull request**, as illustrated in the following screenshot:

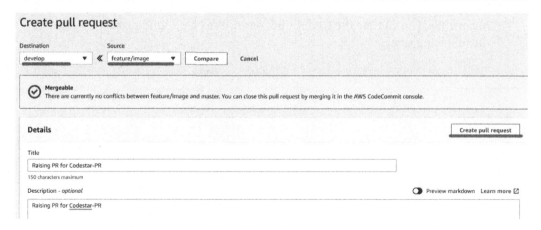

Figure 1.57 – Raising PR via CodeCommit

16. If you go to the **Activity** section of **Pull requests**, you can see a comment in **Activity history**, as illustrated in the following screenshot:

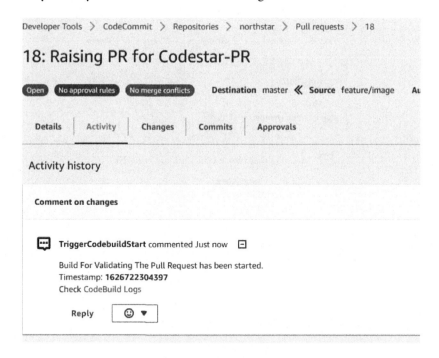

Figure 1.58 – PR status

17. Meanwhile, you can see the CodeBuild logs or the CodeBuild project by going to the following screen:

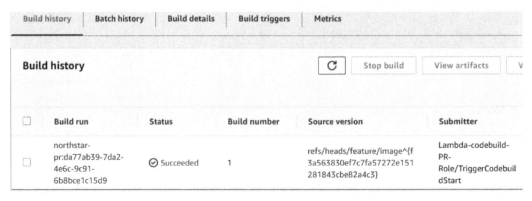

Figure 1.59 – Build status

18. Once the build is successful, you can see the build status on the **Activity** page, as illustrated in the following screenshot:

Figure 1.60 – PR build status

19. Once you see that the build related to the PR commit is successful, you can then merge the code to develop from **feature/image** by clicking on **Merge (Fast forward merge)**, which will eventually trigger a development pipeline and deploy the new changes into the development environment, as illustrated in the following screenshot:

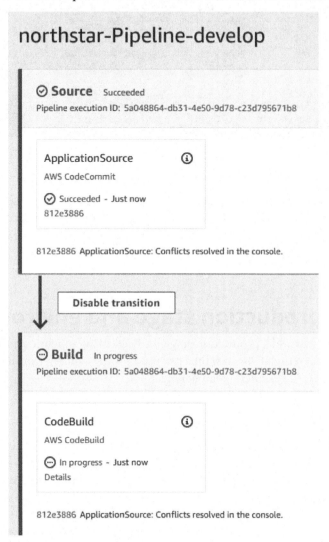

Figure 1.61 – northstar develop code pipeline

20. After that, you can go to Elastic Beanstalk and open the `northstarappdev` endpoint, and you can then see the change on the home page, as illustrated in the following screenshot:

SAMPLE NODEJS APPLICATION DEPLOYED BY AWS CODESTAR.

Figure 1.62 – Modified web application running in the development environment

So far, we have a feature branch and an associated CodeBuild project when a PR is raised and a develop branch with its own development pipeline and environment. In the next section, we will modify the existing pipeline that came by default during the start of the project. We will rename the environment as **staging** and create a new production stage and environment.

Adding a production stage and environment

In this section, we will add a production stage to the existing pipeline and will also modify the CloudFormation template to spin up a separate production environment with two EC2 instances via an ASG under a load balancer.

Modifying the pipeline

Currently, our main pipeline looks like the one shown in *Figure 1.26*. The Elastic Beanstalk environment spun up by this pipeline is named `northstarapp`, and we need to change it to `northstarappstaging`. After that, we need to add a **manual approval** stage, and then a **production deployment** stage. In the production deployment stage, we will add a configuration parameter in CloudFormation to spin up a production environment with the name `northstarappprod` and deploy the application in this new environment.

To modify the pipeline, follow these next steps:

1. Go to **northstar-Pipeline CodePipeline project** (see *Figure 1.27*) and click on **Edit**.

2. Click on **Edit stage** in the **Edit: Deploy** screen, as illustrated in the following screenshot:

Figure 1.63 – Editing exiting deploy stage of pipeline

3. Edit the **GenerateChangeSet** action group, go to **Advanced | Parameter overrides**, and add one key value in JSON format: `"Stage":"Staging"`, as illustrated in the following screenshot. Also, copy and paste the entire JSON config into a separate note because we will be using that in the production parameter. Click on **Done** to save the configuration. Click on **Done** to save the **Deploy** stage:

Figure 1.64 – Modifying parameter to be used by CloudFormation stack

4. Add a new stage by clicking on **Add stage**. Give a stage name of `Approval`, as illustrated in the following screenshot:

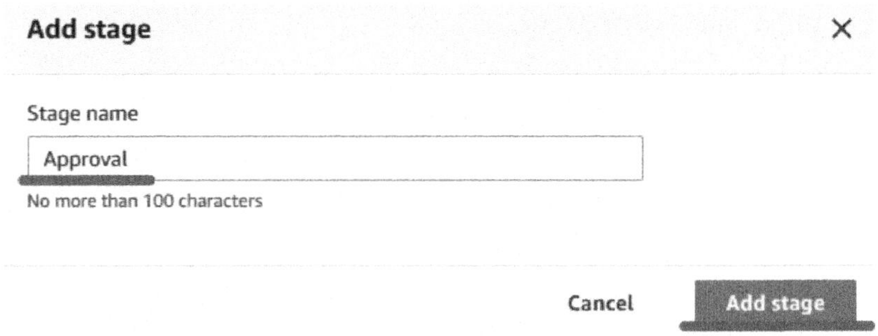

Figure 1.65 – Adding approval stage to the pipeline

5. Click on **Add action group**, then enter `ManualApproval` under **Action name** and `Manual approval` under **Action provider**, as illustrated in the following screenshot. You can configure a **Simple Notification Service (SNS)** topic, but we are skipping this here. Click on **Done** to save the action group:

Figure 1.66 – Adding approval action group

6. Click on **Add stage** to add a production deploy stage. Name the stage `ProdDeploy`. Click on **Add action group**. Enter `GenerateChangeSet` under **Action name**, `AWS CloudFormation` under **Action provider**, and `northstar-BuildArtifact` under **Input artifacts**. Then, click on **Create or replace a change set** under **Action mode** and enter `awscodestar-northstar-infrastructure-prod` under **Stack name**, `pipeline-changeset` under **Change set name**, `northstar-BuildArtifact` under **Template | Artifact name**, and `template-export.yml` under **File name**. Select **Use configuration file**, then enter `northstar-BuildArtifact` under **Template configuration | Artifact name**, `template-configuration.json` under **File name**, `CAPABILITY_NAMED_IAM` under **Capabilities**, and `CodeStarWorker-northstar-CloudFormation` under **Role name**. Click on the **Advanced** section and paste the JSON content that we copied in *Step 3*. Set the last `Stage` value to `Prod` and click on **Done**.

The process is illustrated in the following screenshot:

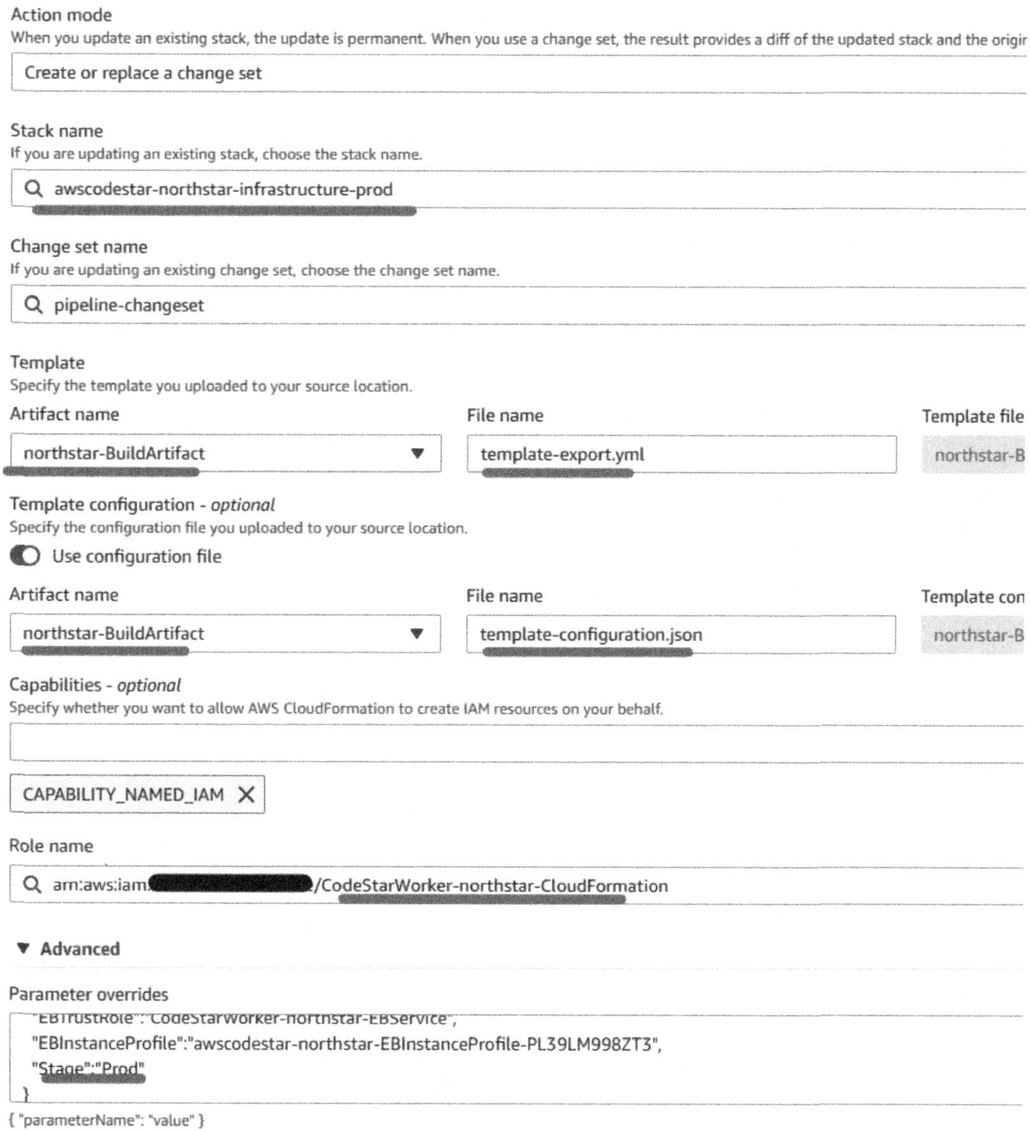

Action mode

When you update an existing stack, the update is permanent. When you use a change set, the result provides a diff of the updated stack and the origir

Create or replace a change set

Stack name

If you are updating an existing stack, choose the stack name.

Q awscodestar-northstar-infrastructure-prod

Change set name

If you are updating an existing change set, choose the change set name.

Q pipeline-changeset

Template

Specify the template you uploaded to your source location.

Artifact name	File name	Template file
northstar-BuildArtifact ▼	template-export.yml	northstar-B

Template configuration - *optional*

Specify the configuration file you uploaded to your source location.

◯ Use configuration file

Artifact name	File name	Template con
northstar-BuildArtifact ▼	template-configuration.json	northstar-B

Capabilities - *optional*

Specify whether you want to allow AWS CloudFormation to create IAM resources on your behalf.

CAPABILITY_NAMED_IAM X

Role name

Q arn:aws:iam███████████████/CodeStarWorker-northstar-CloudFormation

▼ **Advanced**

Parameter overrides

```
"EBTrustRole": "CodeStarWorker-northstar-EBService",
"EBInstanceProfile":"awscodestar-northstar-EBInstanceProfile-PL39LM998ZT3",
"Stage":"Prod"
}
```

{ "parameterName": "value" }

Figure 1.67 – GenerateChangeSet action group configuration

7. Click again on **Add action group**. For the action name, enter
    ExecuteChangeSet, and enter AWS CloudFormation under **Action
    provider**. Under **Action mode**, we need to select **Execute a change set**. Under
    Stack name, we need to enter awscodestar-northstar-infrastructure-
    prod. Under **Change set name**, we need to enter pipeline-changeset.

The process is illustrated in the following screenshot:

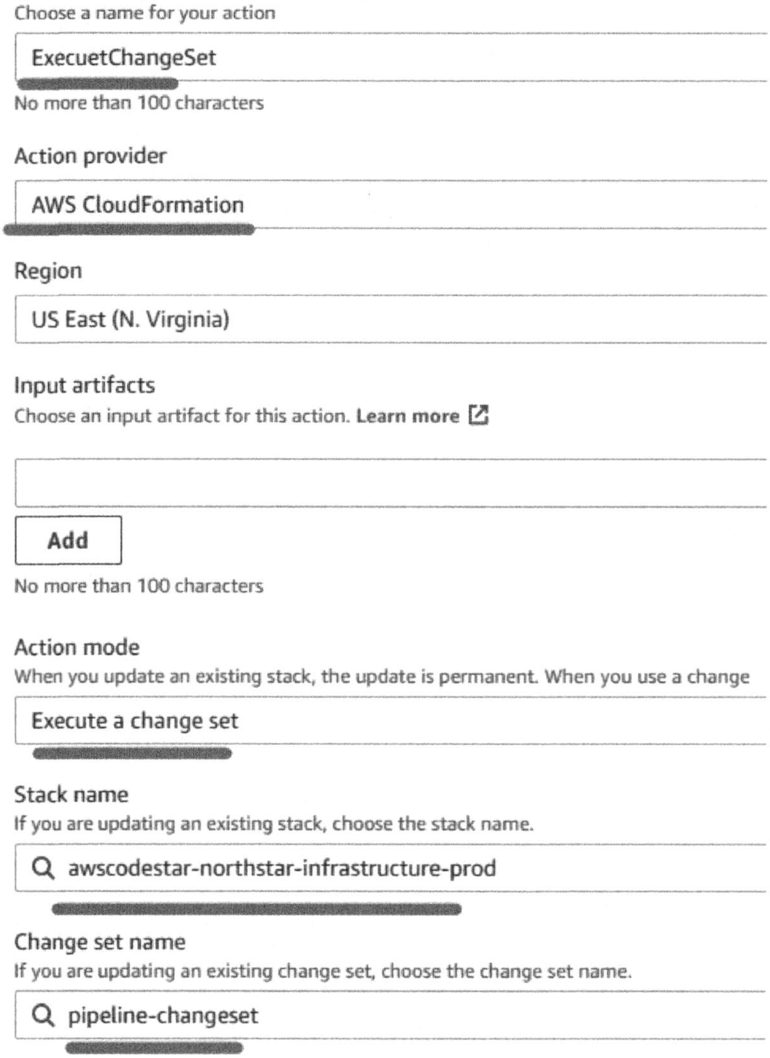

Choose a name for your action

| ExecuetChangeSet |

No more than 100 characters

Action provider

| AWS CloudFormation |

Region

| US East (N. Virginia) |

Input artifacts
Choose an input artifact for this action. **Learn more** 🗗

| |

Add

No more than 100 characters

Action mode
When you update an existing stack, the update is permanent. When you use a change

| Execute a change set |

Stack name
If you are updating an existing stack, choose the stack name.

| Q awscodestar-northstar-infrastructure-prod |

Change set name
If you are updating an existing change set, choose the change set name.

| Q pipeline-changeset |

Figure 1.68 – ExecuteChangeSet action group configuration

8. Save the pipeline. Now, raise a PR from `develop` to `master` and merge the code to `master`, which will run the `northstar-Pipeline` pipeline. This pipeline will rename the existing environment from `northstarapp` to `northstarappStaging` and deploy the application. Then, we manually need to check the application. If the application is working fine, then we need to approve it to proceed to the `ProdDeploy` stage. In the `ProdDeploy` stage, CloudFormation will spin up a `northstarappProd` Elastic Beanstalk production environment then deploy the application in the `northstarappProd` production environment.

You can see the PR being raised in the following screenshot:

Create pull request

Destination			Source				
master	▼	«	develop	▼	Compare	Cancel	

✓ **Mergeable**
There are currently no conflicts between develop and master. You can close this pull request by merging it in the AWS CodeCommit console.

Details   Create pull request

Title

Develop to master

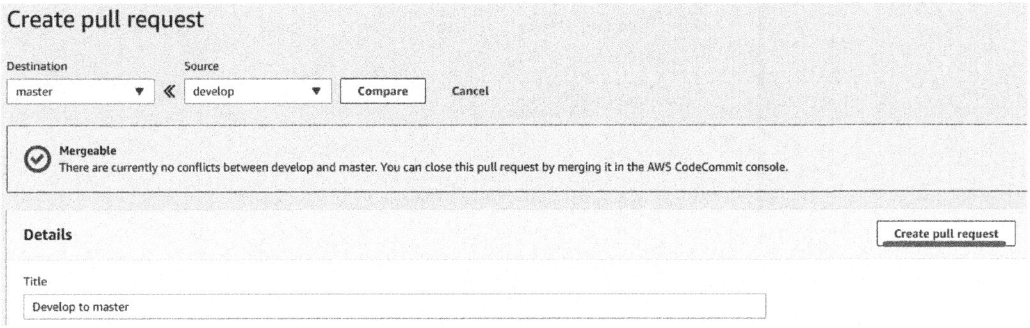

Figure 1.69 – Raising PR

9. Merge the PR from `develop` to the `master` branch, as illustrated in the following screenshot:

Developer Tools > CodeCommit > Repositories > northstar > Pull requests > 21

21: Develop to master   Close pull request   Merge

Open   No approval rules   No merge conflicts   **Destination** master « **Source** develop   **Author** Nikit   **Approvals:** 0

Details   Activity   Changes   Commits   Approvals

Figure 1.70 – Merging PR

10. The pipeline will get triggered after the merge process, as illustrated in the following screenshot:

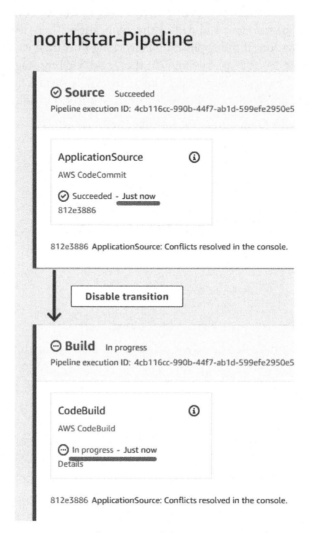

Figure 1.71 – Pipeline triggered the moment merge finishes

11. The initially created northstarapp environment will be terminated and a new northstarappStaging environment will be created, as illustrated in the following screenshot:

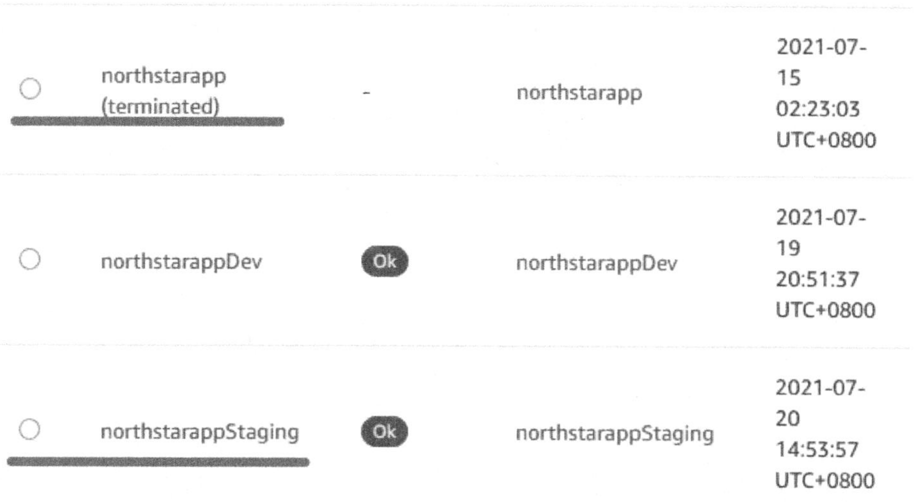

○	northstarapp (terminated)	–	northstarapp	2021-07-15 02:23:03 UTC+0800
○	northstarappDev	Ok	northstarappDev	2021-07-19 20:51:37 UTC+0800
○	northstarappStaging	Ok	northstarappStaging	2021-07-20 14:53:57 UTC+0800

Figure 1.72 – northstarapp is terminated and a new northstarappStaging environment is set up

12. You can access the staging application by navigating to the `northstarappStaging` Elastic Beanstalk environment, as illustrated in the following screenshot:

Figure 1.73 – Application running in the staging environment

13. In the pipeline, it's waiting for approval. Approve it by entering a comment, as illustrated in the following screenshot:

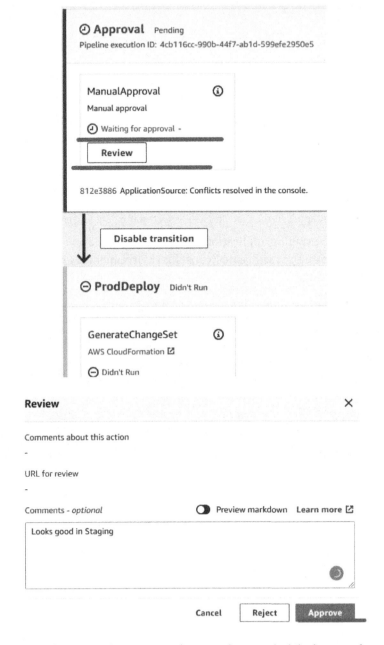

Figure 1.74 – The first screen shows waiting for manual approval while the second screen shows the approval process

14. Once the `ProdDeploy` stage is successful, you can go to Elastic Beanstalk and search for `northstarappProd`, as illustrated in the following screenshot:

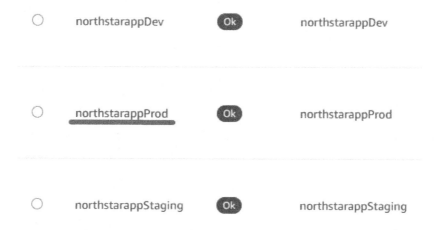

Figure 1.75 – Elastic Beanstalk console showing production environment

15. You can access the application by clicking the endpoint, as illustrated in the following screenshot:

Figure 1.76 – Application running in the production environment

16. You can also go to **Load balancer** to check the new ELB with two EC2 instances attached to it, as illustrated in the following screenshot:

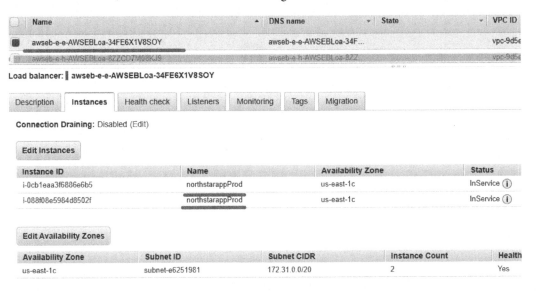

Figure 1.77 – Load balancer console showing the instances attached to it

So, we just saw how to modify a pipeline and add a production stage. You can also make it more comprehensive by creating an SNS topic during the approval stage, and also by adding an ELB **Domain Name System (DNS)** in Route 53. You can make this change via a CloudFormation template.

Summary

So, in this chapter, we learned how to use AWS CodeStar to implement a CI/CD pipeline that covers feature, develop, and master branches and their respective environments. We also learned how to modify the AWS CodePipeline stages and validate a PR using a lambda function and CodeBuild. If you are in a cloud-native company and want to create a CI/CD pipeline with cloud-native resources, you can easily do that now without worrying about the CI/CD toolchain servers. In the next chapter, we will learn how to enforce policies on infrastructure code.

2

Enforcing Policy as Code on CloudFormation and Terraform

This chapter will walk you through the concept of **policy-as-code** and how it can be helpful in terms of security and compliance. You will also learn the stage of **CI/CD** at which infrastructure policies (which is not only limited to infrastructure resources but also network access control) can be checked. After that, we will learn how to apply some policies to an **AWS CloudFormation** template using **CloudFormation Guard**. We will also learn how to use **AWS Service Catalog** across multiple development teams to spin up compliant resources. Then, we will learn how to integrate **Terraform Cloud** with **GitHub**. Finally, we will write some **HashiCorp Sentinel** policies to apply to Terraform templates to enforce the rules before Terraform spins up any cloud resources.

In this chapter, we are going to cover the following main topics:

- Implementing policy and governance as code on infrastructure code
- Using CloudFormation Guard to enforce compliance rules on CloudFormation templates
- Using AWS Service Catalog across teams with access controls and constraints
- Integrating Terraform Cloud with GitHub
- Running Terraform templates in Terraform Cloud
- Writing Sentinel policies to enforce rules on Terraform templates

Technical requirements

To get started, you will need an AWS account and a Terraform Cloud account (there is a 30-day free trial). The code examples can be found in this book's GitHub repository chapter-02:

```
https://github.com/PacktPublishing/Accelerating-DevSecOps-on-
AWS/tree/main/chapter-02
```

Implementing policy and governance as code on infrastructure code

In this section, we will learn what *policy as code* is and how it helps an organization to govern and enforce best practices when we spin up resources in a secure and compliant way. We will also learn where to place policy checks in the CI/CD pipeline.

Policy as code

A **policy** is a set of rules or a plan related to particular situations. It is a way to enforce certain rules and constraints that restrict unauthorized access to resources such as services and environments. There are three different types of policies:

- **Compliance policies**: These policies make sure the system or resources are compliant with standards such as **PCI-DSS**, **GDPR**, or **HIPAA**.
- **Security policies**: These are organizational policies for the security of infrastructure resources.
- **Operational excellence policies**: These are policies that make sure all the services or resources contain objects that make operation easy. For instance, tagging all the resources.

Policy as code basically means expressing these rules or plans in a high-level language to automate and manage the policies. It is a similar concept to **infrastructure as code** (**IaC**), where we write infrastructure resources as code. Some of the well-known policy-as-code tools available in the market are HashiCorp Sentinel, **Open Policy Agent** (**OPA**), and CloudFormation Guard.

Why use policy as code?

Policy as code is a extension of **DevSecOps**, which embraces the *shift-left culture*. DevSecOps is basically the practice of implementing *security* into each DevOps stage and activity. If we implement security at every stage, then we can identify and fix issues earlier, which helps save time, effort, and money. It's called *shift-left* because we discover issues *earlier* (to the *left*) in the timeline.

The benefits of policy as code

Policy as code provides the following benefits:

- **Codification**: When we write policy logic as code, the information and logic about the policy is directly written in code and can be commented on to add further explanation. This makes it easier to understand than relying on verbal explanations of policies.

- **Version control**: The major advantage of writing policy as code is that we can easily use and manage it in a **version control system** (**VCS**). This lets you take advantage of all the modern VCS features, such as pull requests, multiple versions, multiple commits, and more.

- **Integration with automation**: With policy as code in a text file, we can use it in our automation tools. For example, before provisioning your infrastructure, you can setup a pipeline stage that runs before to check whether the infrastructure resources meet all the conditions mentioned in the policy file.

An important use case for policy as code is to integrate it in your CI/CD plan. There are multiple ways to include it, which we will discuss in the next section.

Policy as code in CI/CD

There are multiple ways to strategize policy as code as part of your CI/CD plan. Let's look at some of these in the following figures:

Example 1:

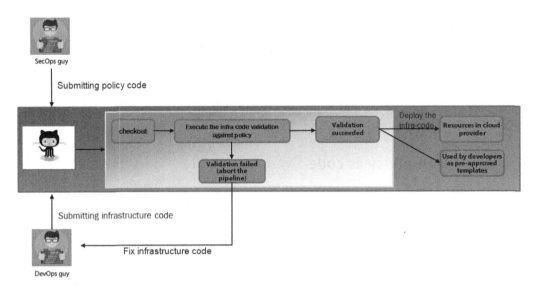

Figure 2.1 – An example of policy as code in CI/CD

In the preceding figure, the following steps are illustrated:

1. The DevOps engineer is submitting the infrastructure code in the VCS. Similarly, the SecOps engineer is submitting the policy code.

2. Then, the build system checks out the code from the VCS.

3. The build executor will run the validation command on the infrastructure code against the policy code.

4. If the validation fails, the pipeline will be aborted, and the DevOps engineer needs to fix the infrastructure code so that it will comply with the policy.

5. If the validation succeeds, then the infrastructure code will be deployed to the cloud provider.

6. This infrastructure code will also be kept as catalog/template code so that the developer can directly use it in their application CI/CD and deploy the infrastructure dynamically along with the application.

This is one way of using policy as code in CI/CD, but there is one *gotcha*, and you must be wondering what that is? It is that the pre-approved catalog code will be locked and you won't be able to change the variables in the template. For example, if the developers want to use the template but want to change a configuration slightly (such as instance type), then it won't be permitted. Otherwise, the developers can use any higher VM instance type, which might not be allowed in the organization because of high cost. But it also restricts developers, with an organizational policy, to modify configurations based on their needs. To allow the developers to modify the configuration, we can implement the CI/CD plan in the following way.

Example 2:

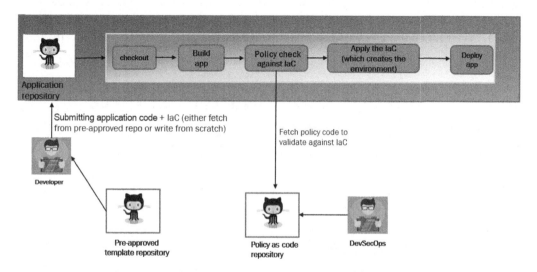

Figure 2.2 – An example of policy as code in application CI/CD

In the preceding image, we are trying to give the developers the power to spin up infrastructure resources, which saves time by cutting out the ticketing process of infrastructure provisioning, for the operation stream. But the aforementioned CI/CD pipeline also makes sure that if developers pass any value in the infrastructure code that violates the policy, then the pipeline will fail. In the preceding diagram, the following steps are illustrated:

1. The developer submits the application code along with the infrastructure code for the resources they want to create. They either write this infrastructure code from scratch or use the pre-approved template of the organization. These pre-approved templates are generally written by the DevOps team and can be used by developers.

2. The build system checks out both the application and infrastructure code.

3. The build system builds the application code.

4. The build system checks out the policy code from the policy code repository. This policy code is written by the DevSecOps team. The build system validates the policy against the infrastructure code.

5. Upon successful validation, the build system will apply the infrastructure code, which will create the environment for the application. If the validation fails, then the pipeline will fail too.

6. Once the environment is created, the application will be deployed to the environment

The policy as code not only applies to the infrastructure code, but it could also apply to **Kubernetes** definition or **access control**. There are some amazing policy engine tools available that support multiple platforms (such as AWS, Terraform, and Kubernetes) such as OPA, **Checkov**, and CloudFormation Guard. In the next section, we will explore CloudFormation Guard 2.0, which supports CloudFormation templates, Terraform, and Kubernetes.

Using CloudFormation Guard to enforce compliance rules on CloudFormation templates

In this section, we will learn about CloudFormation Guard, including how to install it, how to write rules for it, and how to validate it against CloudFormation templates.

CloudFormation Guard

CloudFormation Guard is an open source policy-as-code validation tool. It supports infrastructure configuration tools such as CloudFormation templates and Terraform JSON configuration files. It also has additional support to write rules for Kubernetes configurations. It enables developers to use a simple yet powerful **domain-specific language** (**DSL**) to write rules and validate JSON- or YAML-formatted structured data.

Installation

To install CloudFormation Guard 2.0 (the latest major version), please follow these steps:

1. Go to Terminal and enter the following command:

```
$ curl --proto '=https' --tlsv1.2 -sSf https://raw.
githubusercontent.com/aws-cloudformation/cloudformation-
guard/main/install-guard.sh | sh
$ sudo cp ~/.guard/bin/cfn-guard /usr/local/bin
```

2. Validate the installation:

```
$ cfn-guard help
```

If you get a description of `cfn-guard 2.0` and usage subcommands, that means you have installed `cfn-guard`.

Template validation

To validate your CloudFormation template with Guard rulesets, you use the following command:

```
$ cfn-guard validate -d your-cloudformation-template -r guard-rule-file
```

The `-d` (or `--data`) is for the CloudFormation template and the `-r` (or `--rules`) is for the CloudFormation Guard rules.

Writing CloudFormation Guard rules

Guard rules are used to check if resources' configurations comply with organizational policies or expectations. Guard rules are written in a DSL, and it's easy to understand. You don't need programming experience to understand or write the rules. The basic format of a Guard rule is illustrated as follows:

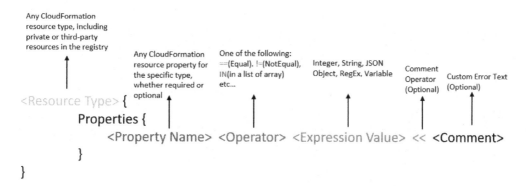

Figure 2.3 – The format of a CloudFormation Guard 2.0 rule

Let's explore this with an example. We have a CFT file, `cfntemp.yaml`, for an **Amazon EBS** volume, which can be seen as follows:

```
---
AWSTemplateFormatVersion: '2010-09-09'
Description: Sample template
```

```
Resources:
  SampleVolume:
    Type: AWS::EC2::Volume
    Properties:
      AvailabilityZone: us-west-2b
      Size: 10
      VolumeType: gp2
```

Now, suppose we want to validate that the EBS volume resources in the preceding template meet the following criteria: the encryption property is set to `true`; the size of the volume is 50 or above; the `AvailabilityZone` property's value is `ap-southeast-1a`. To do this, you will create a ruleset, shown as follows in the `cfntestpolicy` file:

```
AWS::EC2::Volume {
    Properties {
        Encrypted == true
        Size >= 50
        VolumeType == 'gp2'
        AvailabilityZone == 'ap-southeast-1a'
    }
}
```

To check whether the CFT file for the EBS volume is compliant with the policy, we need to run this command:

```
$ #cfn-guard validate -d <CloudFormationTemplate> -r
<cfn-guard-rulesetfile>
$ cfn-guard validate -d cfntemp.yaml -r cfntestpolicy
cfntest.yaml Status = FAIL
FAILED rules
cfntestrule/default    FAIL
---
Evaluation of rules cfntestrule against data cfntest.yaml
--
Property traversed until [/Resources/SampleVolume/Properties]
in data [cfntest.yaml] is not compliant with [cfntestrule/
default] due to retrieval error. Error Message [Attempting to
retrieve array index or key from map at path = /Resources/
SampleVolume/Properties , Type was not an array/object map,
Remaining Query = Encrypted]
```

```
Property [/Resources/SampleVolume/Properties/Size] in data
[cfntest.yaml] is not compliant with [cfntestrule/default]
because provided value [10] did not match expected value [50].
Error Message []
```

```
Property [/Resources/SampleVolume/Properties/AvailabilityZone]
in data [cfntest.yaml] is not compliant with [cfntestrule/
default] because provided value ["us-west-2b"] did not match
expected value ["ap-southeast-1a"]. Error Message []
```

So, the result we can see in the preceding code block is FAIL, and the reason is also mentioned in the preceding code block. If the result is FAIL, that means the infrastructure code is not compliant. Now, to make it compliant, we need to fix the preceding CloudFormation template. We will enable the encryption, increase the volume size, and also change the availability zone. The changes are as follows:

```
---
AWSTemplateFormatVersion: '2010-09-09'
Description: Sample template
Resources:
  SampleVolume:
    Type: AWS::EC2::Volume
    Properties:
      Encrypted: true
      AvailabilityZone: ap-southeast-1a
      Size: 50
      VolumeType: gp2
```

Now, to check whether the preceding CFT file is compliant with the Guard rule, we again need to run the cfn-guard validate command:

```
$ cfn-guard validate -d cfntest.yaml -r cfntestrule
cfntest.yaml Status = PASS
PASS rules
cfntestrule/default    PASS
---
Evaluation of rules cfntestrule against data cfntest.yaml
--
Rule [cfntestrule/default] is compliant for template [cfntest.
yaml]
--
```

We can see the result is PASS, and that means the CFT file is compliant with the Guard rule. This one was a simple example. Let's see another example with a different scenario that covers additional rule formats. We will use a sample template comex.yaml file that describes an **Amazon S3** bucket with server-side encryption and versioning enabled. It also describes an EBS volume with encryption set to true and AvailabilityZone set to ap-southeast-1, which is as follows:

```yaml
---
AWSTemplateFormatVersion: '2010-09-09'
Description: Sample template
Resources:
  SampleBucket:
    Type: AWS::S3::Bucket
    Properties:
      BucketEncryption:
        ServerSideEncryptionConfiguration:
          - ServerSideEncryptionByDefault:
              SSEAlgorithm: AES256
      BucketName: !Sub 'sample-bucket-${AWS::Region}-${AWS::AccountId}'
      VersioningConfiguration:
        Status: Enabled
  SampleVolume:
    Type: AWS::EC2::Volume
    Properties:
      AvailabilityZone: ap-southeast-1a
      Encrypted: true
      Size: 10
      VolumeType: gp2
```

Now, let's try to create a Guard rule file, comexrule.guard, for the preceding template:

```
let volumes = Resources.*[ Type == 'AWS::EC2::Volume' ] 1
rule sample_volume_check when %volumes !empty { 2
    %volumes.Properties.Encrypted == true 3
    %volumes.Properties.AvailabilityZone in ['ap-southeast-1a', 'ap-southeast-1b'] 4
}
```

```
let buckets = Resources.*[ Type == 'AWS::S3::Bucket' ]
rule sample_bucket_encryption when %buckets !empty {
    %buckets.Properties {
      BucketEncryption.ServerSideEncryptionConfiguration[*] {
        ServerSideEncryptionByDefault.SSEAlgorithm == 'AES256'
        }
      }
  }
}
```

You must be wondering why the rules written for this example are more complex than the first example. Let's try to understand this rule file based on the highlighted numbers in the preceding code example:

1. Here, when we are using `Resources.*[ Type == 'AWS::EC2::Volume' ]`, it means we are using a query expression to traverse hierarchical data. Inside query expressions, we can use a filter to target a subset of values. If we use `Resources.*`, then the query output will be as follows:

```
Resources:
  SampleBucket:
    Type: AWS::S3::Bucket
    Properties:
      BucketEncryption:
        ServerSideEncryptionConfiguration:
          - ServerSideEncryptionByDefault:
              SSEAlgorithm: AES256
      BucketName: !Sub 'sample-bucket-1'
      VersioningConfiguration:
        Status: Enabled
  SampleVolume:
    Type: AWS::EC2::Volume
    Properties:
      AvailabilityZone: ap-southeast-1a
      Encrypted: true
      Size: 10
      VolumeType: gp2
```

But, in our case, we are using the `Resources.*[Type ==
'AWS::EC2::Volume']` filter, so the query output will be as follows:

```
Type: AWS::EC2::Volume
Properties:
    AvailabilityZone: ap-southeast-1a
    Encrypted: true
    Size: 10
    VolumeType: gp2
```

Now, this output value will be assigned to a variable when we are using `let
volumes =`. So, in this case, `volumes` is a variable that includes the properties of
`AWS::EC2::Volume`.

2. Here, we are creating a rule block with a name. So, the format looks like the
    following:

```
rule <rule name> [when <condition>] {
    Guard_rule_1
    Guard_rule_2
    . . .
}
```

We have created a rule named `sample_volume_check`, and this rule block will
be executed only when the condition is met, meaning, when `%volumes` (the way to
call the assigned variable) is `!empty` (NOT operator). In this case, the condition is
met, because the value of volumes is *not empty*.

3. The Guard rule that we are using with (.) to traverse the data, just like in JQ utility.
    `%volumes.Properties.Encrypted`, will query the value of the `Encrypted`
    property mentioned in the CFT file and compare this with the value mentioned in
    the rule using the equal to (==) binary operator.

4. The Guard rule that uses the `IN` operator will return `true` if the value retrieved
    from the CFT file matches the value mentioned in the rule array.

If we validate the CFT file against the Guard rule, we will get the status that it is compliant
with the Guard rule:

```
$ cfn-guard validate -d comex.yaml -r comexrule
comex.yaml Status = PASS
PASS rules
comex/sample_volume_check          PASS
```

```
comex/sample_bucket_encryption        PASS
---
Evaluation of rules comex against data comex.yaml
--
Rule [comex/sample_bucket_encryption] is compliant for template
[comex.yaml]
Rule [comex/sample_volume_check] is compliant for template
[comex.yaml]
--
```

The previous two examples give you an overview of how to write a Guard rule. Now, let's try to write a Guard rule for another scenario.

We need to write a Guard rule for a CFT file, which enforces the following conditions in an **Amazon EC2** instance:

- If the EC2 instance is tagged with key Environment and value Dev, then the instance type must be t2.micro.

- If the EC2 instance is tagged with key Environment and value Prod, then the instance type must be t2.xlarge.

- The EBS volume attached to the EC2 instance must be encrypted, its volume type must be gp2, and its size must be either 100 or 200 GB.

- The EBS volume and EC2 instance must be in the availability zone ap-southeast-1a.

- The security group ports should not be open for 0.0.0.0/0.

The ruleset that covers all of the preceding conditions is as follows:

```
let volumes = Resources.*[ Type == 'AWS::EC2::Volume' ]
rule VOLUME_CHECK when %volumes !empty {
    %volumes.Properties {
        Encrypted == true
        Size in [50,100,120]
        VolumeType == 'gp2'
        AvailabilityZone in ['ap-southeast-1a']
    }
}

let sg = Resources.*[ Type == 'AWS::EC2::SecurityGroup' ]
```

```
rule SECURITYGROUP_CHECK when %sg !empty {
    %sg.Properties {
        SecurityGroupIngress[*]{
        CidrIp != '0.0.0.0/0'
                }
        }
}

let ec2_instance = Resources.*[ Type == 'AWS::EC2::Instance' ]
let ec2_instance_dev = %ec2_instance [ Properties.Tags[1].Value
== 'Dev' ]
let ec2_instance_prod = %ec2_instance [ Properties.Tags[1].
Value == 'Prod' ]
rule EC2INSTANCE_DEV_CHECK {
        when %ec2_instance_dev !empty {
        %ec2_instance.Properties.InstanceType == 't2.micro'
        %ec2_instance.Properties.AvailabilityZone == 'ap-
southeast-1a'
        }
}
rule EC2INSTANCE_PROD_CHECK {
        when %ec2_instance_prod !empty {
        %ec2_instance.Properties.InstanceType == 't2.xlarge'
        %ec2_instance.Properties.AvailabilityZone == 'ap-
southeast-1a'
        }
}
```

Now, we will test this rule on the CFT file. The commands to validate the CFT file against
the Guard rule are as follows:

```
$ git clone https://github.com/PacktPublishing/Modern-CI-CD-on-
AWS.git
$ cd chapter-02
$ cfn-guard validate -d CFT-ec2instance.yaml -r cfn-ruleset
CFT-ec2instance.yaml Status = FAIL
SKIP rules
cfn-ruleset/EC2INSTANCE_DEV_CHECK      SKIP
```

```
PASS rules

cfn-ruleset/VOLUME_CHECK                    PASS

cfn-ruleset/EC2INSTANCE_PROD_CHECK          PASS

FAILED rules

cfn-ruleset/SECURITYGROUP_CHECK             FAIL

---

Evaluation of rules cfn-ruleset against data CFT-ec2instance.
yaml

--

Property [/Resources/InstanceSecurityGroup/Properties/
SecurityGroupIngress/0/CidrIp] in data [CFT-ec2instance.
yaml] is not compliant with [cfn-ruleset/SECURITYGROUP_CHECK]
because provided value ["0.0.0.0/0"] did match expected value
["0.0.0.0/0"]. Error Message []

--

Rule [cfn-ruleset/EC2INSTANCE_PROD_CHECK] is compliant for
template [CFT-ec2instance.yaml]

Rule [cfn-ruleset/VOLUME_CHECK] is compliant for template
[CFT-ec2instance.yaml]

--

Rule [cfn-ruleset/EC2INSTANCE_DEV_CHECK] is not applicable for
template [CFT-ec2instance.yaml]
```

We can see that EC2INSTANCE_DEV_CHECK has been skipped because the EC2 instance is tagged with Prod. Also, SECURITYGROYP_CHECK has failed, because inside the CFT template, the security group port 22 is open to 0.0.0.0/0.

The next question you might ask yourself is how will we use the cloudformation guard checkin automation? The answer is the exit status. If the Guard rule execution result is PASS, then the exit status is 0, and if it is FAIL, then the exit status is 5.

Note

You can read the blog at https://aws.amazon.com/blogs/
devops/integrating-aws-cloudformation-guard/ to learn
how to use Guard rules in the AWS Developers tools. Keep one thing in mind:
the blog or the repository link mentioned in the blog is using CloudFormation
Guard 1.0 instead of 2.0. You need to change the Guard rule from v1.0 to
v2.0, as well as the Buildspec.yaml file used in **CodeBuild**.

So, in this section, we learned how to check a CloudFormation template compliance status using CloudFormation Guard rules. We can imbed this process in an automation pipeline very easily. If you want to provide a compliant CloudFormation template via user interface to developers for their own use, we can do that using AWS Service Catalog, which we will cover in the next section.

Using AWS Service Catalog across teams with access controls and constraints

In this section, we will explore how to use AWS Service Catalog to give different teams access to resources. We will learn how to enforce rules using constraints, and we will find out how to manage access with access controls.

AWS Service Catalog

AWS Service Catalog is a service managed by AWS that allows organizations to provision and manage pre-approved catalogs of IT services. IT services include any AWS resources, such as servers, databases, software, and more. This service allows IT administrators/ DevOps teams to create a service catalog and allow other teams to access it from a central portal. This way, IT administrators or DevOps teams ensure that other teams are provisioning compliant infrastructure resources. Some of the terminology used in Service Catalog is explained in the following subsections.

Users

AWS Service Catalog supports two types of *users*:

- **Catalog administrators**: Catalog administrators can be your IT administrator or DevOps engineers, whose responsibilities include the preparation of CloudFormation templates, configuring constraints, and configuring access management for sharing the catalog.

- **End users**: End users could be your developers or sales team, or any team member who wants to use the catalog to provision the resources. End users receive the details of catalogs from catalog administrators.

Products

A *product* is an IT service that is a set of AWS resources, such as Amazon EC2 instances, **Amazon RDS** instances, monitoring configurations, or networking components. For example, a CloudFormation template of **LAMP** stack can be considered a *product*.

Portfolios

A *portfolio* is a collection of *products* that contains configuration information. Portfolios help manage who can use specific products and how they can use them. With Service Catalog, you can create a customized portfolio for each type of user in your organization and selectively grant them access to the appropriate portfolio.

Constraints

Constraints control the way the *user* deploys the *product*. They allow governance over the products. For example, if the user's environment is set to `Dev`, then the EC2 instance type must be `t2.medium`.

The workflow for a *catalog administrator* is illustrated in the following figure:

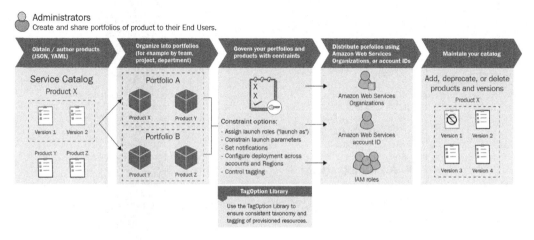

Figure 2.4 – The AWS Service Catalog administrator workflow

The workflow for an *end user* is illustrated in the following figure:

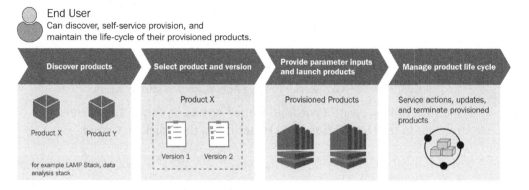

Figure 2.5 – The AWS Service Catalog end user workflow

This is a basic overview of AWS Service Catalog. Now, we will explore a scenario to understand the AWS Service Catalog in action:

We will act as a *catalog administrator*, create a *product* and organize it in a *portfolio*, and then apply some *constraints* and access controls. After that, we will log in as an *end user* and try to access the product. We will enter noncompliant parameters in the **service catalog** page and check whether it stops us from provisioning the product. The steps to implement the scenario are as follows:

1. Log in to the **AWS Management Console** and navigate to **AWS service catalog** service. You will see the home page of AWS Service Catalog. In the left-hand section, you will see the **Administration** settings menu:

Figure 2.6 – The AWS Service Catalog Administration settings menu

2. Click on **Portfolios**, create a portfolio named Application Team, enter your details in the **Description** and **Owner** fields, then click on **Create**:

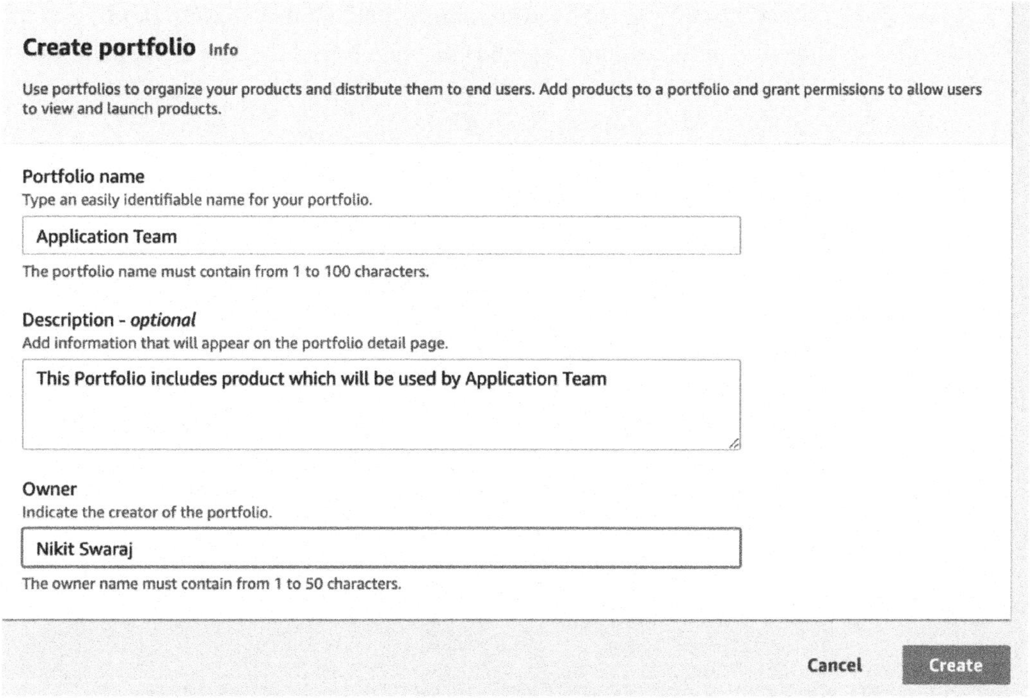

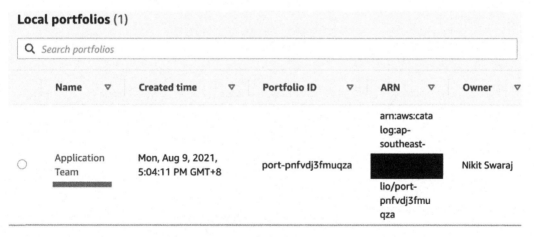

Figure 2.7 – Creating a portfolio

3. Once you have created a portfolio, click on the **Application Team** hyperlink to add the product:

Local portfolios (1)

Name	Created time	Portfolio ID	ARN	Owner
○ Application Team	Mon, Aug 9, 2021, 5:04:11 PM GMT+8	port-pnfvdj3fmuqza	arn:aws:cata log:ap-southeast-▮▮▮▮▮▮▮ lio/port-pnfvdj3fmu qza	Nikit Swaraj

Figure 2.8 – Local portfolios page

4. Click on **Upload new product** to upload a CloudFormation template. We will use the same CFT file from the repository that we cloned for CloudFormation Guard.

5. Enter `SVC-CAT-CFT-EC2` in the **Product name** field. Under **Version details**, we need to choose a method to provide the CFT File. Select the **Use a template file** radio button. Click on **Choose file** to upload the CFT file from your local machine. Enter a version name, `v0.1`, then click on **Review**:

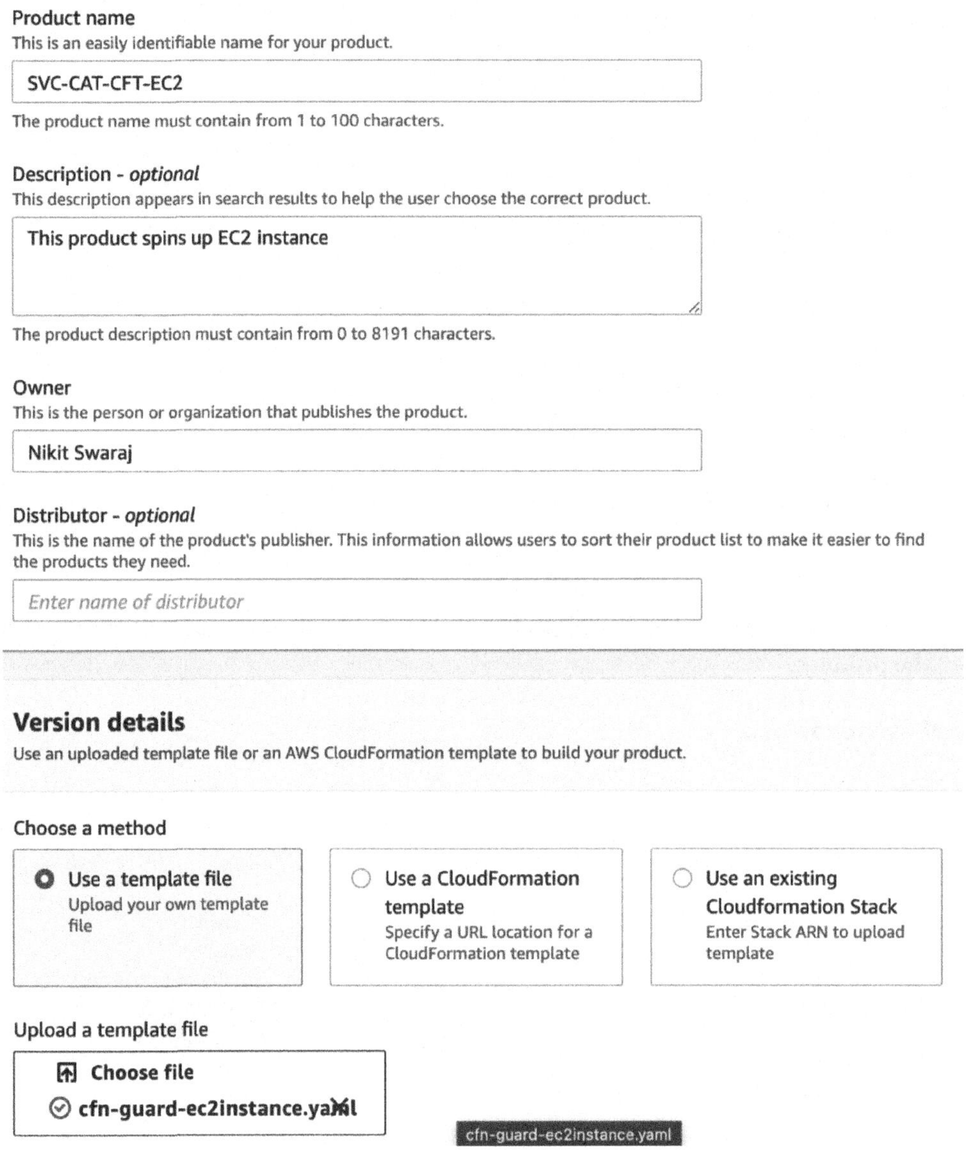

Product name

This is an easily identifiable name for your product.

```
SVC-CAT-CFT-EC2
```

The product name must contain from 1 to 100 characters.

Description - *optional*

This description appears in search results to help the user choose the correct product.

```
This product spins up EC2 instance
```

The product description must contain from 0 to 8191 characters.

Owner

This is the person or organization that publishes the product.

```
Nikit Swaraj
```

Distributor - *optional*

This is the name of the product's publisher. This information allows users to sort their product list to make it easier to find the products they need.

```
Enter name of distributor
```

Version details

Use an uploaded template file or an AWS CloudFormation template to build your product.

Choose a method

⦿ **Use a template file**	◯ **Use a CloudFormation**	◯ **Use an existing**
Upload your own template file	**template**	**Cloudformation Stack**
	Specify a URL location for a CloudFormation template	Enter Stack ARN to upload template

Upload a template file

```
⊞ Choose file
⊘ cfn-guard-ec2instance.yaml
```

cfn-guard-ec2instance.yaml

Figure 2.9 – Filling in product details

6. Click on **Create product** to create the product and associate it with the `Application Team` portfolio:

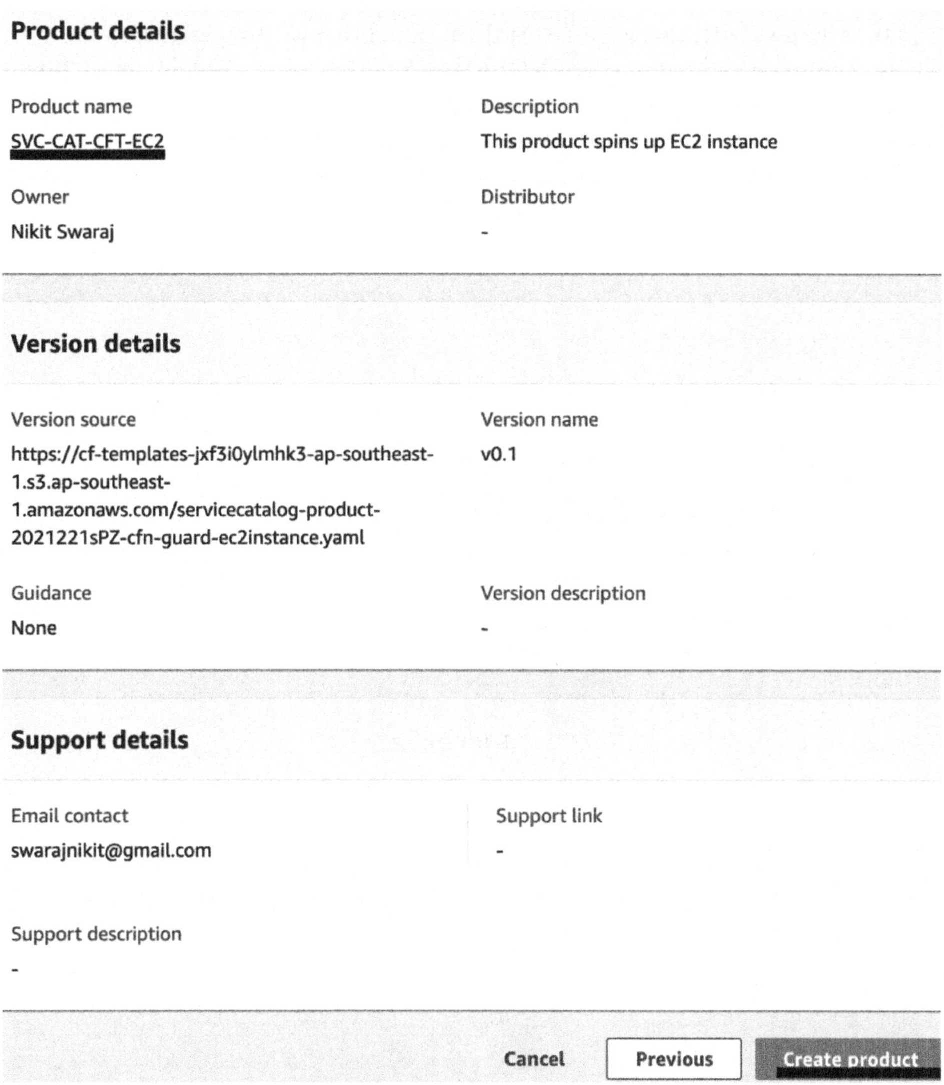

Product details

Product name
SVC-CAT-CFT-EC2

Description
This product spins up EC2 instance

Owner
Nikit Swaraj

Distributor
-

Version details

Version source
https://cf-templates-jxf3i0ylmhk3-ap-southeast-1.s3.ap-southeast-1.amazonaws.com/servicecatalog-product-2021221sPZ-cfn-guard-ec2instance.yaml

Version name
v0.1

Guidance
None

Version description
-

Support details

Email contact
swarajnikit@gmail.com

Support link
-

Support description
-

Cancel   Previous   Create product

Figure 2.10 – Creating a product

7. At this point, we will be able to see the product in the Application Team portfolio. Click on the **Constraints** tab and then on **Create constraint**:

| Products (1) | Constraints (0) | Groups, roles, and users (0) | Share (0) | Tags (0) | TagOptions (0) |

Constraints (0)   ↻   Edit constraint   Delete constraint   **Create constraint**

Q Search constraints   < 1 > ⚙

Figure 2.11 – The Constraints tab

8. In the **Create constraint** page, select the product that we just created. In the constraint type, select **Template**. In the template constraint method, select **Text editor**, where you can write the constraint rule. Copy the following JSON content and paste it into your text editor for the template constraint. Click on **Create** to create the constraint. The following rule restricts the end user to create a product with EC2 instance type of t2.medium or m3.medium:

```
{
    "Rules": {
      "Rule1": {
        "Assertions": [
          {
            "Assert": {
              "Fn::Contains": [
                [
                  "t2.medium",
                  "m3.medium"
                ],
                {
                  "Ref": "InstanceType"
                }
              ]
            },
            "AssertDescription": "Instance type should be
either t2.micro or m3.medium"
          }
        ]
      }
    }
}
```

9. To allow end users to access this product, we need to configure the **Identity and Access Management (IAM)** settings. To do this, click on the **Groups**, **Roles**, and **Users** tabs. Click on **Add groups, roles, and users**. You will be able to see all the groups, roles, and users in the groups, roles and users list. Select the identity that you will use to log in to access the product, and click on **Add access**:

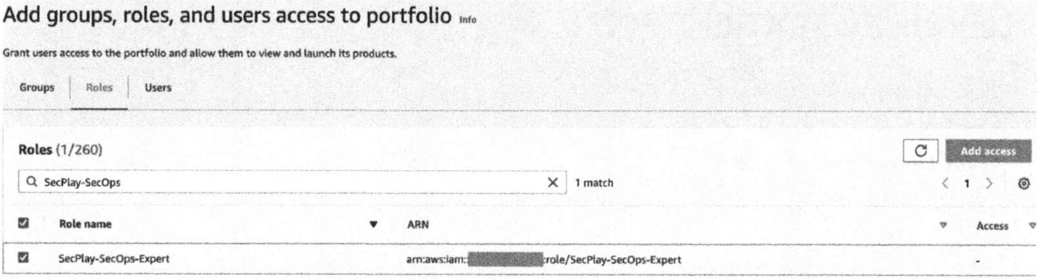

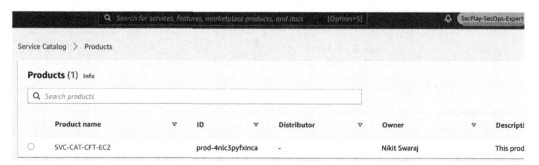

Figure 2.12 – Granting users access to the portfolio

10. We can also share this product with another AWS account by clicking on the **Share** tab and entering the details in the **AWS Account Id** field. But we are not covering that here.

11. Now, try to log in as the user you have given access to, navigate to **AWS Service Catalog**, and click on **Products**. In this case, I had given access to a *role*. I switched to the role, navigated to the product, and was able to see it:

Figure 2.13 – Product page view by end user

12. Select the **SVC-CAT-CFT-EC2** product and click on **Launch Product**. You will be redirected to a **Launch** page. Enter `App-starfish` into the **Provisioned product name** field. Select the version. Enter `t2.xlarge` in the **Instance Type** field. Here, you will get a prompt that says **Instance type should be either t2.medium or m3.medium**. This is because of constraints rule:

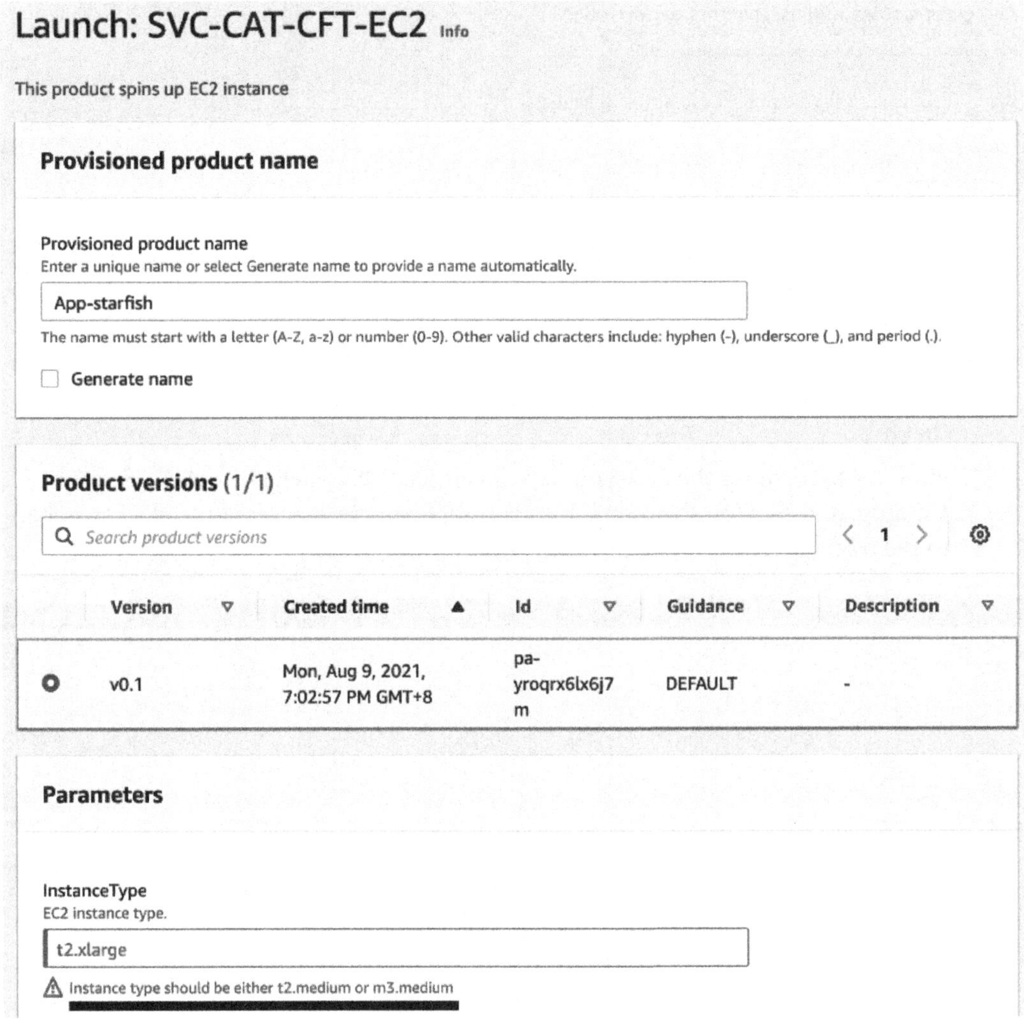

Launch: SVC-CAT-CFT-EC2 Info

This product spins up EC2 instance

Provisioned product name

Provisioned product name
Enter a unique name or select Generate name to provide a name automatically.

App-starfish

The name must start with a letter (A-Z, a-z) or number (0-9). Other valid characters include: hyphen (-), underscore (_), and period (.).

☐ Generate name

Product versions (1/1)

Q Search product versions   〈 1 〉 ⚙

	Version ▽	Created time ▲	Id ▽	Guidance ▽	Description ▽
◉	v0.1	Mon, Aug 9, 2021, 7:02:57 PM GMT+8	pa-yroqrx6lx6j7m	DEFAULT	-

Parameters

InstanceType
EC2 instance type.

t2.xlarge

⚠ Instance type should be either t2.medium or m3.medium

Figure 2.14 – Product Launch page

13. You can still click on **Launch product** by ignoring the parameter errors:

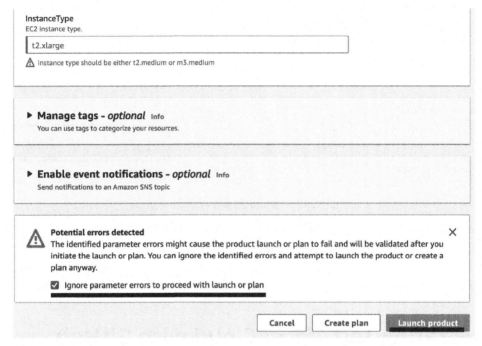

Figure 2.15 – Launching the product

14. You will be redirected to the provisioned products page, from where you can navigate to the CloudFormation page to see the actual resource that is getting provisioned.

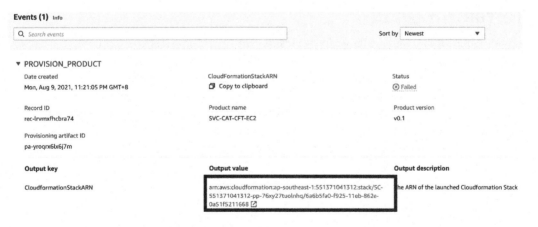

Figure 2.16 – Status page of the product

15. But from *Figure 2.16*, we can also see that the status of provisioned product is **Failed**. We can retrieve the reason for the status by clicking on the **CloudFormationStackArn** value. In this case, the reason is because of the EC2 instance type. The EC2 instance type that we provided above was t2.xlarge, but the allowed values are only t2.medium or m3.medium.

Timestamp		Logical ID	Status	Status reason
2021-08-09 23:21:10 UTC+0800	▼	SC-551371041312-pp-76xy27tuolnhq	⊗ ROLLBACK_COMPLETE	-
2021-08-09 23:21:08 UTC+0800		SC-551371041312-pp-76xy27tuolnhq	⊗ ROLLBACK_IN_PROGRESS	Parameter validation failed: assertion error: Instance type should be either t2.medium or m3.medium. Rollback requested by user.
2021-08-09 23:21:06 UTC+0800		SC-551371041312-pp-76xy27tuolnhq	ⓘ CREATE_IN_PROGRESS	User Initiated

Figure 2.17 – CloudFormation Event page

This way, we can enforce the end user to only provision the compliant resources..

In the next section, we will learn about Terraform Cloud and HashiCorp Sentinel. There is no doubt that Terraform is heavily used by developers and DevOps. So, policy as code in Terraform will be covered in the next section.

Integrating Terraform Cloud with GitHub

In this section, we will dive deep into Terraform Cloud and how we can integrate it with GitHub.

Terraform Cloud

Terraform is an IaC tool available from HashiCorp. Terraform lets you define infrastructure resources as human-readable and declarative configuration files. Terraform supports multiple cloud platforms and comes with lots of provider plugins. It also maintains a state file to track resource changes. Terraform comes in three different editions – **Terraform OSS**, **Terraform Cloud**, and **Terraform Enterprise**. Terraform OSS is free and comes with basic features. Terraform Cloud has free and paid versions. And Terraform Enterprise is a paid service with additional features.

A chart showing the differences between the Terraform versions can be seen in Table 2.1:

	OSS	Cloud			Self-Hosted
		Free	*Team & Governance*	*Business*	*Enterprise*
IaC	Yes	Yes	Yes	Yes	Yes
Workspaces	Yes	Yes	Yes	Yes	Yes
Variables	Yes	Yes	Yes	Yes	Yes
Runs (plan and apply)	Yes	Yes	Yes	Yes	Yes
Resource graph	Yes	Yes	Yes	Yes	Yes
Providers	Yes	Yes	Yes	Yes	Yes
Module	Yes	Yes	Yes	Yes	Yes
Public module library	Yes	Yes	Yes	Yes	Yes
Remote state		Yes	Yes	Yes	Yes
VCS connection		Yes	Yes	Yes	Yes
Workspace management		Yes	Yes	Yes	Yes
Secure variable storage		Yes	Yes	Yes	Yes
Remote runs		Yes	Yes	Yes	Yes
Private module registry		Yes	Yes	Yes	Yes
Team management			Yes	Yes	Yes
Sentinel policy as code management			Yes	Yes	Yes
Cost estimation			Yes	Yes	Yes
SSO				Yes	Yes
Audit logging				Yes	Yes
Self-hosted agents				Yes	

Table 2.1 – Terraform version features

Terraform Cloud is a SaaS platform that manages Terraform executions in a reliable environment instead of a local machine. It basically stores all necessary information (such as secrets and shared state files) and connects to a VCS so that a team can collaborate. Terraform executions in Terraform Cloud can take place in the following three ways:

- **Local CLI**: For this method, we need to install the Terraform **command-line interface (CLI)** on our local machine, and we need to log in to Terraform Cloud with a Terraform `login` command, where we will authenticate and generate a token. After that, we need to provide backend *remote* configurations in a `backend.tf` file, which will allow you to run the command locally but make the Terraform execution take place in Terraform Cloud.

- **UI/VCS**: For this method, the branch from the VCS is integrated with the workspace of Terraform Cloud by a webhook, so whenever there is a commit, it will automatically trigger Terraform Cloud for execution.

- **API**: For this method, Terraform Cloud is dependent on one of your organization tools like any build server. An organization tool oversees the change in the Terraform configurations, and based on that, it makes a series of calls to Terraform Cloud's **Runs** and configuration versions.

VCS-driven workflow (GitHub)

The steps to integrate Terraform Cloud with GitHub are as follows:

1. Create two repositories in GitHub, one for a Terraform config file and the other for a Sentinel policy, which will be used in the next section. Make sure the repositories have a `READ.Me` file.

2. Log in to Terraform Cloud (you need to create an account first) by clicking on this link `https://app.terraform.io/`.

3. If your account is new, then you will see the **Choose your setup workflow** page. We will go with **Start from scratch** because we need to integrate the VCS and get to know file that triggers a remote execution in Terraform Cloud:

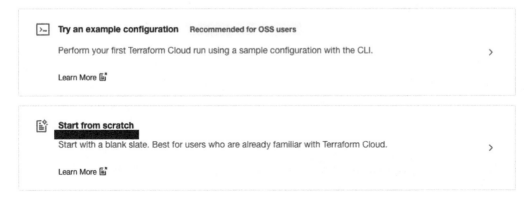

Figure 2.18 – Terraform workflow setup page

4. Enter the *organization* name as `stella` and click on **Create organization**. Organization names in Terraform Cloud are a unique name. Organizations are private shared spaces for teams to collaborate on infrastructure configuration:

Create a new organization

Organizations are privately shared spaces for teams to collaborate on infrastructure.Learn more ☑ about organizations in Terraform Clou

Organization name

e.g. company-name

| stella |

Organization names must be unique and will be part of your resource names used in various tools, for example `stella/www-prod` .

Email address

| ████rj@gmail.com |

The organization email is used for any future notifications, such as billing alerts, and the organization avatar, via gravatar.com ☑.

Create organization

Figure 2.19 – Creating an organization in Terraform Cloud

5. Once you create your organization, you will be asked to create a *workspace*. A workspace in Terraform contains all the Terraform configuration files. Select **Version Control Workflow** to integrate Terraform Cloud with your VCS.

6. Now, you need to choose your VCS. In our case, we are proceeding with GitHub. You need to authorize Terraform Cloud to access GitHub:

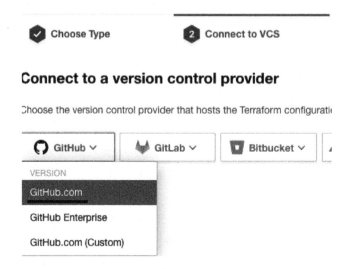

Figure 2.20 – Connecting a VCS with Terraform Cloud

7. After that, select your code repository (that is, the one we created in *Step 1* for Terraform configurations, as illustrated in following screenshot, I created policy-as-code-CFT-TF repository which will contain terraform template):

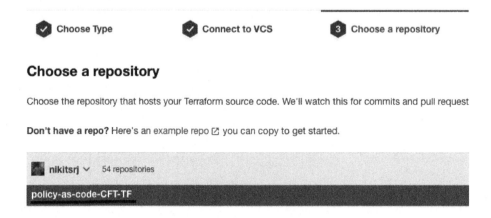

Figure 2.21 – Selecting the repository for Terraform configurations

8. After that, in **Configure settings**, you can click on **Advanced options** to set the branch on which Terraform Cloud listens to trigger runs. In our case, we are keeping the default branch. Then, click on **Create workspace**.

9. You will be able to see that Terraform Cloud is now integrated with GitHub:

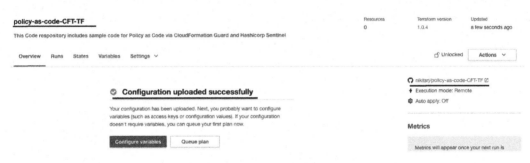

Figure 2.22 – The VCS integration status

In this section, we saw how to integrate a VCS (GitHub) with Terraform Cloud. In the next section, we will write some Terraform configurations for an AWS EC2 instance and run the configuration via Terraform Cloud.

Running a Terraform template in Terraform Cloud

In this section, we will write a Terraform configuration to spin up an EC2 instance in AWS and push that configuration to the repository that we configured in the previous section. We will also learn how to store AWS credentials Terraform Cloud. Follow the next steps to get started:

1. Go to the new GitHub repository that you integrated with Terraform Cloud and commit the content of the `ec2-instance.tf` file from folder chapter-02.

2. Now, we need to add an authentication token (access key and secret key) of AWS to Terraform Cloud. Go to the **Variables** tab of your workspace and select **Add environment variables**, as shown in the following figure:

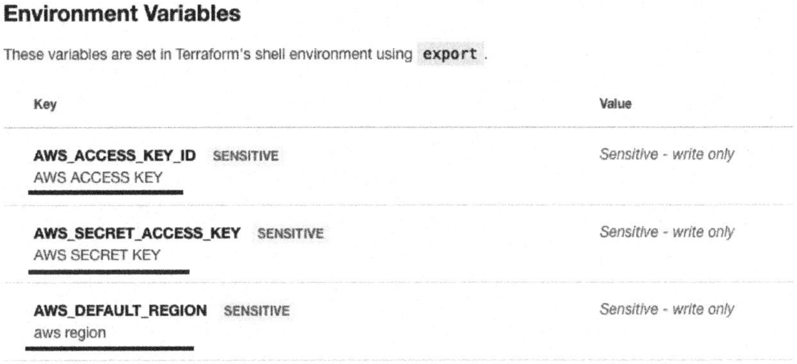

Environment Variables

These variables are set in Terraform's shell environment using `export` .

Key	Value
AWS_ACCESS_KEY_ID SENSITIVE AWS ACCESS KEY	Sensitive - write only
AWS_SECRET_ACCESS_KEY SENSITIVE AWS SECRET KEY	Sensitive - write only
AWS_DEFAULT_REGION SENSITIVE aws region	Sensitive - write only

Figure 2.23 – Adding AWS environment variables

3. During the first commit to the GitHub repository, Terraform Cloud will not run the plan. We need to start the plan manually by clicking on **Actions**, then selecting **Start new plan**:

Figure 2.24 – A Terraform plan action via the UI

4. Since we triggered the plan via the UI, in the **Runs** tab, you can see that the Terraform plan executed and after that, it will ask you to confirm to apply the changes. You need to enter a meaningful comment for the record and click on **Confirm & Apply** to create an EC2 instance in AWS:

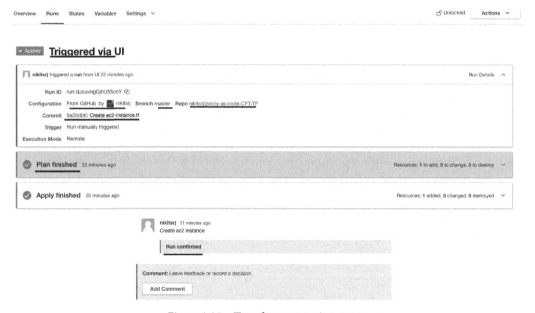

Figure 2.25 – Terraform execution status

5. You can verify the EC2 instance in your AWS account.

6. Now, let's make the changes in the Terraform code of `ec2-instance.tf` in GitHub. Replace the tag name value from `Hashicorp_Sentinel` to `Hello<your name>`. In my case, I changed it to `HelloNikit`. Commit the changes by entering a commit message of changing the tag, and then go to Terraform Cloud. Now, you will see that the Terraform plan has been started automatically. Since this time the trigger takes place on a `git commit` hook, we will see the commit message (**changing the tag**) as a run:

Figure 2.26 – The Terraform Cloud runs page

7. You can check the applied changes in the AWS **Instances** list:

Figure 2.27 – EC2 Instance name change

Up until now, we have seen how to run Terraform configurations in Terraform Cloud via a VCS. In the next section, we will learn how to enforce policies on Terraform template using Sentinel.

Writing Sentinel policies to enforce rules on Terraform templates

In this section, we will learn about HashiCorp Sentinel and how we can enable it in Terraform Cloud. After that, we will write a Sentinel policy to enforce rules on Terraform templates.

HashiCorp Sentinel

Sentinel is a framework for policy and language, built in software to enforce fine-grained, logic-based policy decisions. It is an enterprise feature of **Terraform**, **Vault**, **Nomad**, and **Consul**. Sentinel is easy to learn and needs minimal programming experience. Sentinel policies are written in a text file using the Sentinel language with the `.sentinel` file extension. The Sentinel language has a `main` function, whose value decides whether a policy *passes* or *fails*. Here's an example:

```
main = 9 > 3
```

When you execute this policy using a Sentinel command, the result will be `true`. Sentinel handles the result of the execution in levels known as an enforcement level. Sentinel has three enforcement levels:

- **Advisory**: At this level, if policies are failed, still the execution of `terraform apply` will take place. Execution will give a warning and it will be logged into the system.

- **Soft mandatory**: At this level, if policies are failed, then the rest of the execution will stop. However, it can be resumed with a comment.

- **Hard mandatory**: At this level, policies must be passed.

Enforcement levels are defined in the `sentinel.hcl` file. Enforcement levels are also tied to the name of the policy file. For example, if a policy file is named `restrict-ec2-tag.sentinel`, then the content of the `sentinel.hcl` file will be like the following JSON example:

```
policy "restrict-ec2-tag" {
enforcement_level = "hard-mandatory"
}
```

By default, Sentinel is not enabled in Terraform Cloud, as it is only available in the **Team and Governance** package. To enable Sentinel in Terraform Cloud, follow these steps:

1. Go to **Settings** tab of organization(at the top), then click **Plan & billing**, then click **here to get started**, then click **Trial plan**, and then click **Start your free trial**:

Figure 2.28 – Terraform Cloud Plan & Billing page

2. After that, Terraform Cloud will enable the paid features (including Sentinel policies) for a free trial period (30 days):

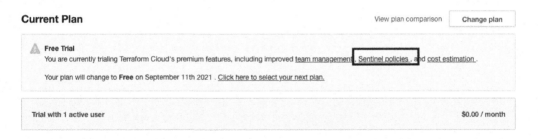

Figure 2.29 – Enabling paid features in Terraform Cloud

3. Now, we will use the second repository to store the Sentinel policies. It is not advisable to put Terraform configurations and policies in the same repository, as policy repositories are handled by the security team. Copy the content from the `enforce-mandatory-tag.sentinel` and `sentinel.hcl` from chapter-02 folder and paste it into your repository. The policy contains a rule for the configuration to have three tags (`Name`, `Owner`, and `Environment`). The enforcement level of the policy is `soft-mandatory`.

4. After that, you need to create a policy set and attach it to the workspace where our Terraform runs are taking place. Go to **Settings** of the organization and click on **Policy sets**. Click on **Connect a new policy set**. Click on the **GitHub** button and then select your policy repository.

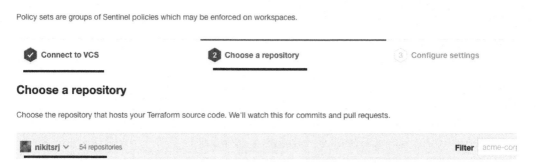

Connect a Policy Set

Policy sets are groups of Sentinel policies which may be enforced on workspaces.

✓ Connect to VCS   ② Choose a repository   ③ Configure settings

Choose a repository

Choose the repository that hosts your Terraform source code. We'll watch this for commits and pull requests.

nikitsrj ⌄   54 repositories   Filter acme-con

Figure 2.30 – Connecting a policy repository to Terraform Cloud

5. In the **Configure settings** tab, change the **Scope of Policies** option to **Policies enforced on selected workspaces**, then select the workspace that you want to run the policy on. Then click on **Connect policy set**.

6. Now, go to the repository where the Terraform configuration file (to create the EC2 instance) is located and change the value of the EC2 instance type to c3.xLarge, remove one of the tags, and commit the changes in GitHub so that the Terraform run executes automatically. Go to the **Runs** section of Terraform Cloud, and there you will see that the policy check has failed:

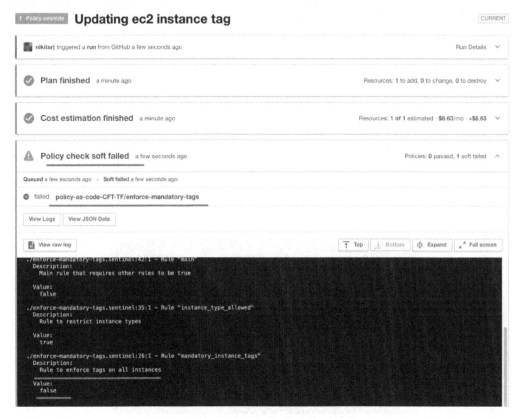

Figure 2.31 – A Sentinel policy check failure

7. Since the enforcement level is `soft-mandatory`, the **Override & Continue** option is available:

Figure 2.32 – The Override & Continue option to continue the execution

8. The policy check didn't pass because the Terraform configuration has only one tag. Let's add the additional mandatory tags and commit the code in GitHub to pass the policy check:

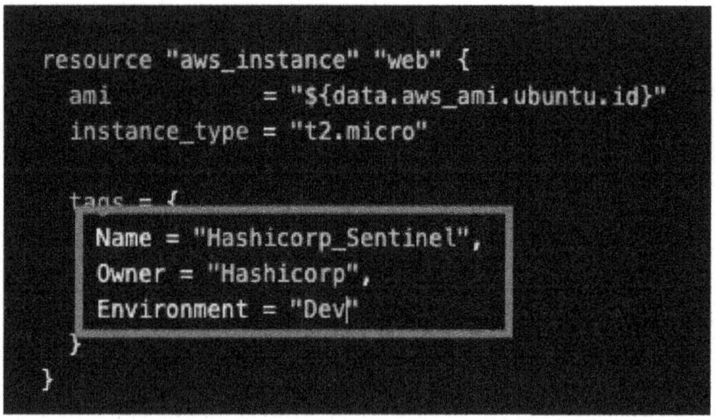

```
resource "aws_instance" "web" {
    ami           = "${data.aws_ami.ubuntu.id}"
    instance_type = "t2.micro"

    tags = {
        Name = "Hashicorp_Sentinel",
        Owner = "Hashicorp",
        Environment = "Dev"
    }
}
```

Figure 2.33 – Adding new tags to the ec2-instance.tf file

9. Once you commit the changes in the Terraform configuration file, Terraform Cloud executes the run, which will give you the status of the policy check, which is now passed.

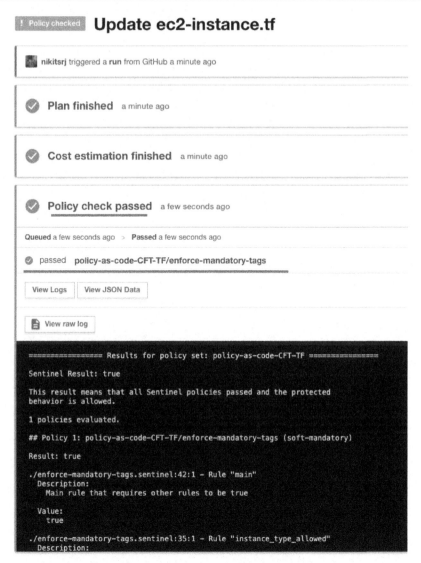

Figure 2.34 – Passed Sentinel policy check

We can also integrate Sentinel policy checks into our CI/CD toolchain, but in that case, you would need to execute the Terraform commands using a remote backend. You can read more about integrating Sentinel with **Jenkins** at the following link: https://www.hashicorp.com/resources/securing-infrastructure-in-application-pipelines.

Summary

In this chapter, we learned how we can implement policy and governance as code. We showed where we can fit our policy-as-code checks in the CI/CD pipeline. We also learned how to write AWS CloudFormation Guard rules. We implemented access controls in AWS Service Catalog to share Service Catalog *products* with *constraints*. We also subscribed to Terraform Cloud to execute Terraform configuration and we applied policies using HashiCorp Sentinel. Now, you can integrate policy checks in your CI/CD stages. In the next chapter, we will learn how to spin up application containers smoothly with the **AWS Proton** service, and we'll use **AWS Code Guru** to review the application code.

3

CI/CD Using AWS Proton and an Introduction to AWS CodeGuru

This chapter will introduce the new **AWS Proton** service and the need for it within the developer community. You will understand how AWS Proton helps both the developers and DevOps/infrastructure engineers with their work in the **Software Development Life Cycle (SDLC)**. Then, we will look at the basic blocks of the Proton service, which helps create the environment and service template. We will learn how to use environment templates to spin up multiple infrastructure environments, and how to deploy container instances on those environments. This chapter will also walk you through the code review process in case any pull requests are raised, as well as how to scan the source code and find any vulnerabilities and secret leaks. We will use **AWS CodeGuru Reviewer** to review and perform static code analysis.

In this chapter, we are going to cover the following main topics:

- Introduction to the AWS Proton service
- Creating the environment template component
- Creating the service template component
- Deploying a containerized application by creating a service instance in Proton
- Introduction to AWS CodeGuru
- Integrating CodeGuru with AWS CodeCommit and analyzing the pull request report

Technical requirements

To get started, you will need an AWS account and the source code contained in the folder chapter-03-aws-proton-template, chapter-03-aws-proton, chapter-03-codeguru-sample:

- `https://github.com/PacktPublishing/Accelerating-DevSecOps-on-AWS.git`
- Create a separate repository in your github account as aws-proton and push the files present in chapter-03-aws-proton folder

Introduction to the AWS Proton service

The AWS Proton service was developed by AWS after they considered lots of feedback from customers, where the main issue was how to maintain infrastructure, build pipelines, and deploy applications at scale. Initially, when the service became generally available, it was difficult to understand the components of AWS Proton and how it is different from **AWS Service Catalog** and other developer tools. This service has a couple of components that will be a bit confusing to you if you are just reading the documentation and not looking at the template code. So, in this section, we will dive deep into how AWS Proton solves the problem of maintenance of infrastructure, as well as how it helps you build pipelines and application deployments at scale.

What is AWS Proton?

AWS Proton is a two-fork automation framework engine that does the following:

- Automates the infrastructure provisioning process using an **environment template**. This environment template includes shared infrastructure resources. A shared infrastructure means VPCs, subnets, ECS clusters, IGWs, and so on. An environment template can be used to provision multiple environments such as development, staging, and production by changing the parameters. There is a certain standard and format when it comes to creating environment templates, which will be covered in the next section.

- Automates the process of deploying container-based and serverless applications using a **service template**. The service template includes two sub-templates – one is an application that contains service-related files such as the task definition, load balancer target group, alarms, and more, while the other sub-template is a *build and deploy* pipeline template, which includes definitions related to developer tools such as **CodeBuild**, **CodeDeploy**, and **CodePipeline**. Using the service template, we can create multiple Proton services (that refer to their respective application branches), which will build the application and deploy it to a certain infrastructure environment. When the application services get deployed to an environment, they are known as **service instances**.

The following diagram simplifies these two points:

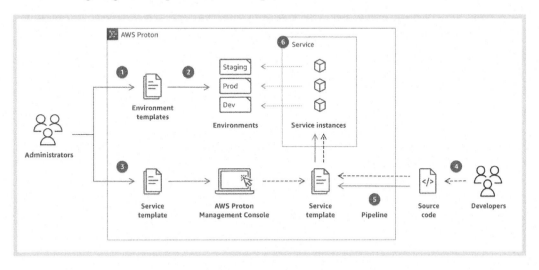

Figure 3.1 – AWS Proton workflow (from AWS Docs)

The target users for the Proton service are **Administrators/DevOps** and **Developers**. Admin/DevOps are responsible for creating environment template code (using CloudFormation). To create service template code (using CloudFormation), both DevOps and the Developers need to work together. Developer interaction is required because they will be aware of the build steps, which will be embedded into the service template code. The workflow for AWS Proton is as follows:

1. **Administrators/DevOps** create an environment template using CloudFormation. Then, They register the environment template with AWS Proton.

2. **Administrators/DevOps** get the request of spinning up three environments for a new application. They can use this environment template to create three different environments; that is, **Dev**, **Staging**, and **Prod**.

3. Now, as **DevOps**, you will coordinate with **Developers** and prepare a service template using CloudFormation. As we mentioned previously, this service template will include a definition related to the application instance and the build pipeline. Once the service template has been prepared, then DevOps need to register it with AWS Proton.

4. Next, **Developers** log into the AWS Proton service, and they need to deploy a container-based application in the development environment. The development environment that's launched from the environment template is ECS. The developer wants to deploy the container using AWS Fargate, so they also need to provide the size of the task. Their application source code is in GitHub in the development branch. Now, to deploy the application in the development ECS cluster, as a Fargate container, they need to create a service using the service template; for example, **service-dev**.

5. The moment **Developers** create the **service-dev** service, CI/CD pipeline resources will start spinning up.

6. The CI/CD pipeline will now pull the code from the development branch and deploy it into the development environment.

Now, suppose the developer needs to deploy the application in the staging environment. Here, the code should be from the staging branch. Then, the developer just needs to create another service using the same service template and configure it with the staging environment. This way, you don't need to create another pipeline manually; the service template will create another staging CI/CD resource for you, and then deploy it to the staging environment.

The following diagram shows a flow representation of the preceding steps.

We will see the preceding stages in action in the next section. Based on the aforementioned points, you may have gotten the idea as to how Proton resolves the issue of maintaining infrastructure, building pipelines, and deploying applications at scale.

There are some additional features in AWS Proton that make it more robust to use in terms of its capabilities, such as **version management** and **cross-account** support. You can manage multiple versions of the environment template and update all the environments with the latest version with a single click. AWS Proton also supports cross-account access, which means that if an admin wants to, they can use the environment template of account A (**Management account**) and create an environment infrastructure in account B (**Environment account**). Similarly, a developer can also deploy the services from account A to the environment infrastructure of account B:

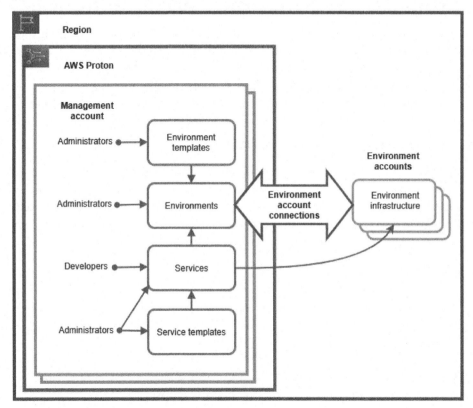

Figure 3.2 – AWS Proton cross-account connections (from AWS Docs)

Apart from writing templates in CloudFormation and template versioning, there are some new features in the roadmap of AWS Proton that adds more capabilities, such as the following:

- Defining templates in Terraform

- Template sync with a source code repository (at the time of writing, we manually upload it to an AWS S3 bucket and Proton picks the template from there)

- Template modules
- Custom infrastructure

Now that we've gotten an idea of what AWS Proton is and its components, as well as the environment template and the service template, let's look at the Proton environment template.

Creating the environment template bundle

In this section, we will learn how to create an environment template bundle for a standard environment and the tips we should use while writing an effective template. After that, we will register an environment template in AWS Proton and create multiple environments using an environment template. We will be using the `aws-proton-template` repository, which was mentioned in the *Technical requirements* section.

Writing an environment template

As we mentioned previously, in AWS Proton, the environment template defines the shared infrastructure that's used by multiple resources. With an environment template, we can create multiple environment infrastructures. An environment template typically includes resources related to compute, storage, and network. In our case, the environment template that we will be registering contains the following resources:

- A VPC and subnets
- Internet gateway and route
- An ECS cluster and security group
- The ECS TaskExecution role

To register an environment template, we need to create an environment template bundle. The environment template directory structure looks like this:

```
/infrastructure
    cloudformation.yaml
    manifest.yaml
/schema
    schema.yaml
```

As you can see, the infrastructure directory includes two files – `cloudformation.yaml` and `manifest.yaml`. The `Cloudformation.yaml` file defines the compute, storage, and network resources. If you go to the chapter-03-aws-proton-template folder, you will see an `environment` folder. If you navigate to `infrastructure/cloudformation.yaml`, then you will be able to see the content inside `cloudformation.yaml`, which defines the infrastructure resources, as shown here:

```
AWSTemplateFormatVersion: '2010-09-09'
Description: AWS Fargate cluster running containers in a public
subnet. Only supports
              public facing load balancer, and public service
discovery namespaces.
Mappings:
  # The VPC and subnet configuration is passed in via the
environment spec.
  SubnetConfig:
    VPC:
      CIDR: '{{environment.inputs.vpc_cidr}}'
    PublicOne:
      CIDR: '{{environment.inputs.subnet_one_cidr}}'
    PublicTwo:
      CIDR: '{{environment.inputs.subnet_two_cidr}}'
Resources:
  VPC:
    Type: AWS::EC2::VPC
    Properties:
      EnableDnsSupport: true
      EnableDnsHostnames: true
      CidrBlock: !FindInMap ['SubnetConfig', 'VPC', 'CIDR']
```

There are certain processes you must follow to create an environment template bundle that defines infrastructure resources. These processes are as follows:

- We need to identify which infrastructure resources will be used to create environments. For example, in our case, we need to deploy a containerized app, so we need any resources that can help us run containers, such as ECS, and other resources, such as a VPC and subnets.

- We need to identify *customization parameters*. Customization parameters are parameters that will be required by the end user as input while creating the environment. For example, in the following template, the VPC and subnet configuration will be passed in via the user input. To reference a customization parameter in the CloudFormation infrastructure, you must attach a *namespace* to it. The format for the environment namespace is as follows:

Infrastructure File	Namespace	Format
environment	environment.inputs	{{ environment.inputs.env-input }}
	environment.name	{{ environment.name }}

Table 3.1 – Environment namespace mapping

The following code explains how to use the customization parameter.

The following are the necessary mappings:

```
  # The VPC and subnet configuration is passed in via the
environment spec.
  SubnetConfig:
    VPC:
      CIDR: '{{environment.inputs.vpc_cidr}}' #customization
param
    PublicOne:
      CIDR: '{{environment.inputs.subnet_one_cidr}}'
    PublicTwo:
      CIDR: '{{environment.inputs.subnet_two_cidr}}'
```

Now, we need to identify the *resource-based parameters*. Resource-based parameters are those parameters that reference output parameters from other infrastructure template files. For example, the output values of the infrastructure template can be used in the service template as resource parameters. The following snippet can explain more:

```
Outputs:
  ClusterName:
    Description: The name of the ECS cluster
    Value: !Ref 'ECSCluster'
  ECSTaskExecutionRole:
    Description: The ARN of the ECS role
    Value: !GetAtt 'ECSTaskExecutionRole.Arn'
```

The preceding snippet contains the output values of the infrastructure template. The values of the preceding outputs (`ClusterName`) can be used in the following service template as resource parameters:

```
Service:
  Type: AWS::ECS::Service
  DependsOn: LoadBalancerRule
  Properties:
    Cluster: '{{service_instance.environment.outputs.
ClusterName}}' # imported resource parameter
    LaunchType: FARGATE
    DeploymentConfiguration:
      MaximumPercent: 200
      MinimumHealthyPercent: 75
```

Once you have identified the resources and parameters, you can define a *schema*, which serves as the customization parameter interface between AWS Proton and the infrastructure template files. AWS Proton uses the *Jinja* templating engine to handle parameters values in the schema file and the cloudformation file. The following diagram explains how the AWS Proton backend works. After this, we will have a look at the relationship between the schema file and the cloudformation file:

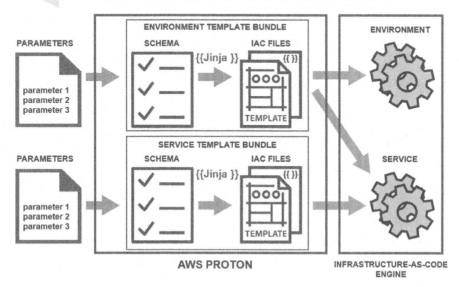

Figure 3.3 – AWS Proton engine workflow (from AWS Docs)

The schema file, which is shown on the left, shows one input property, vpc_cidr, which is used in the cloudformation file in the Mappings section:

```
schema:
  format:
    openapi: "3.0.0"
  environment_input_type: "PublicEnvironmentInput"
  types:
    PublicEnvironmentInput:
      type: object
      description: "Input properties for my environment"
      properties:
        vpc_cidr:
          type: string
          description: "This CIDR range for your VPC"
          default: 10.0.0.0/16
          pattern: ([0-9]{1,3}\.){3}[0-9]{1,3}($|/(16|24))
```

```
AWSTemplateFormatVersion: '2010-09-09'
Description: AWS Fargate cluster running containers in a public
                           public facing load balancer, and public service dis
Mappings:
  # The VPC and subnet configuration is passed in via the enviro
  SubnetConfig:
    VPC:
      CIDR: '{{ environment.inputs.vpc_cidr}}'
```

Figure 3.4 – Schema file (on the left) and CloudFormation file (on the right)

Once you have your infrastructure CloudFormation and schema files, you must organize them into directories. You also need to create a *manifest file* that lists the infrastructure files and needs to adhere to the format and the content, as shown in the following snippet:

```
infrastructure:
  templates:
    - file: "cloudformation.yaml"
      rendering_engine: jinja
      template_language: cloudformation
```

Figure 3.5 – Manifest file

The preceding points will help you create an environment template bundle that includes the cloudformation.yaml, manifest.yaml, and schema.yaml files. To use the environment template bundle in AWS Proton, we need to perform the following steps:

1. Clone the GitHub repository, which contains the environment template in the chapter-03-aws-proton-template folder:

   ```
   $git clone https://github.com/PacktPublishing/
   Accelerating-DevSecOps-on-AWS.git
   ```

2. Go to your Terminal and enter the following command to create an S3 bucket. This S3 bucket will contain the tarball of the environment template:

   ```
   # Assuming you already have awscli configured
   ```
   ```
   $aws s3api create-bucket -bucket "proton-cli-templates-
   ${account-id}"
   ```

3. Create the tarball of the environment folder and upload it to the S3 bucket:

```
$ cd Accelerating-DevSecOps-on-AWS/chapter-03-aws-proton-
template
```
```
$ tar -zcvf env-template.tar.gz environment/
```
```
$ aws s3 cp env-template.tzr.gz s3://proton-cli-
templates-${account-id}/env-template.tar.gz
```

4. Create an IAM role that will be used by AWS Proton to provision the resources:

```
# creating IAM Role
```
```
$aws iam create-role --role-name aws_proton_svc_admin
--assume-role-policy-document file://policy/proton-
service-assume-policy.json
```
```
#attaching policy to the role
```
```
$aws iam attach-role-policy --role-name aws_proton_
svc_admin --policy-arn arn:aws:iam::aws:policy/
AdministratorAccess
```
```
#Allowing Proton to use this role
```
```
$aws proton update-account-settings --pipeline-service-
role-arn "arn:aws:iam::${accountid}:role/aws_proton_svc_
admin"
```

5. Since we have an environment template in an S3 bucket and an IAM role created, go to the **AWS Proton** console and click on **Environment templates** in the **Templates** section:

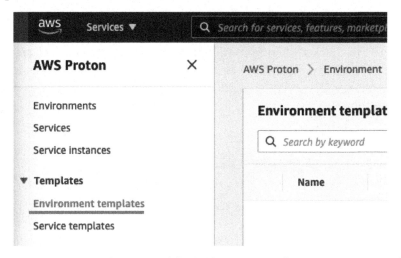

Figure 3.6 – The AWS Proton console

6. Click on **Create environment template**. For **Template options**, choose **Create a template for provisioning new environments**. For **Template bundle source**, choose **Use your own template bundle**:

Create environment template

Create an environment template so you can easily deploy an environment with your parameters baked right in.

▸ **How environment template bundles work**

Template options

Create a template that is used to provision a new environment or to import and existing environment.

◉ Create a template for provisioning new
environments

○ Create a template to use provisioned
infrastructure that you manage

Template bundle source

○ Use one of our sample template bundles
Get started right away with a sample template bundle.

◉ Use your own template bundle
Provide your own environment template bundle and upload it to S3.

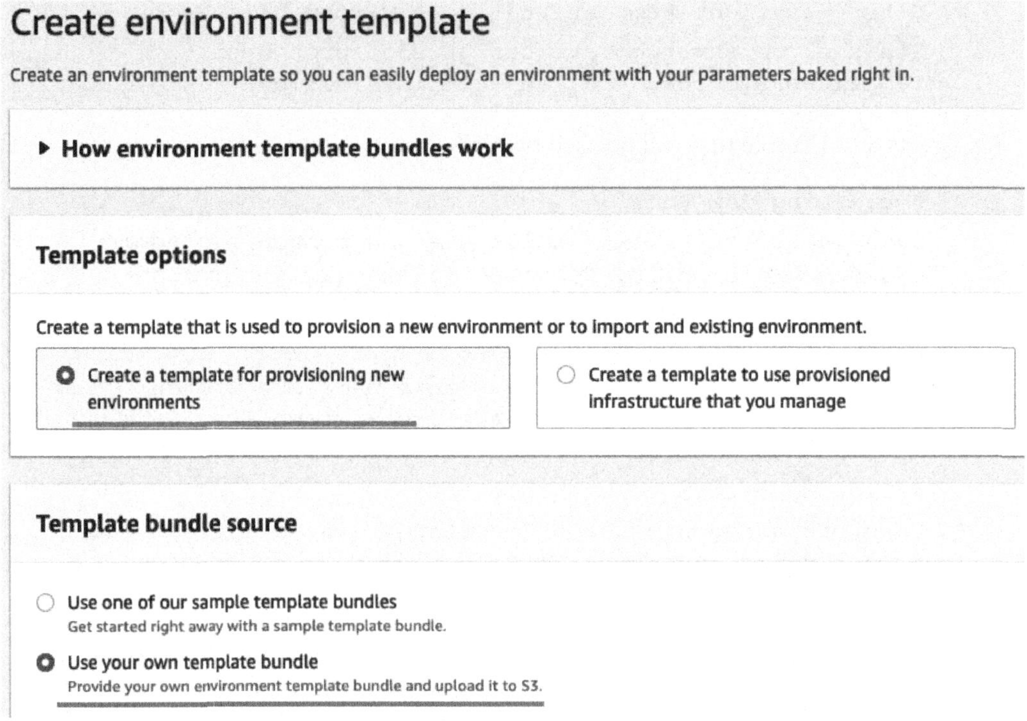

Figure 3.7 – Create environment template

7. Next, you will see **S3 bundle location**. Here, you need to click on **Browse S3** and then select the bucket where you will upload the environment template (in our case, it's `proton-cli-templates-account-id/env-template.tar.gz`):

S3 bundle location

S3 path

Figure 3.8 – Selecting the environment template via S3

8. Under **Template details**, use `stark-env-temp` for **Template name** and **Template display name**. You can fill in **Template description** as you like. Then, click on **Create environment template**:

Template details

Template name
The environment template name can't be changed after it has been created.

> stark-env-temp

Use only letters, numbers or hyphens. The maximum length is 100 characters.

Template display name - *optional*
This is the template name displayed to developers.

> stark-env-temp

The maximum length is 100 characters.

Template description - *optional*
This is the template description displayed to developers.

> ECS Fargate

The maximum length is 255 characters.

Encryption settings

Your data is encrypted by default with a key that AWS owns and manages for you. To choose a different key, customise your encryption settings. Learn more 🔗

☐ Customise encryption settings (advanced)

Tags

Customer managed tags

Add tags to help you search, filter, and track your service in AWS Proton.

No tags associated with the resource.

> **Add new tag**

You can add up to 50 more tags.

Cancel   **Create environment template**

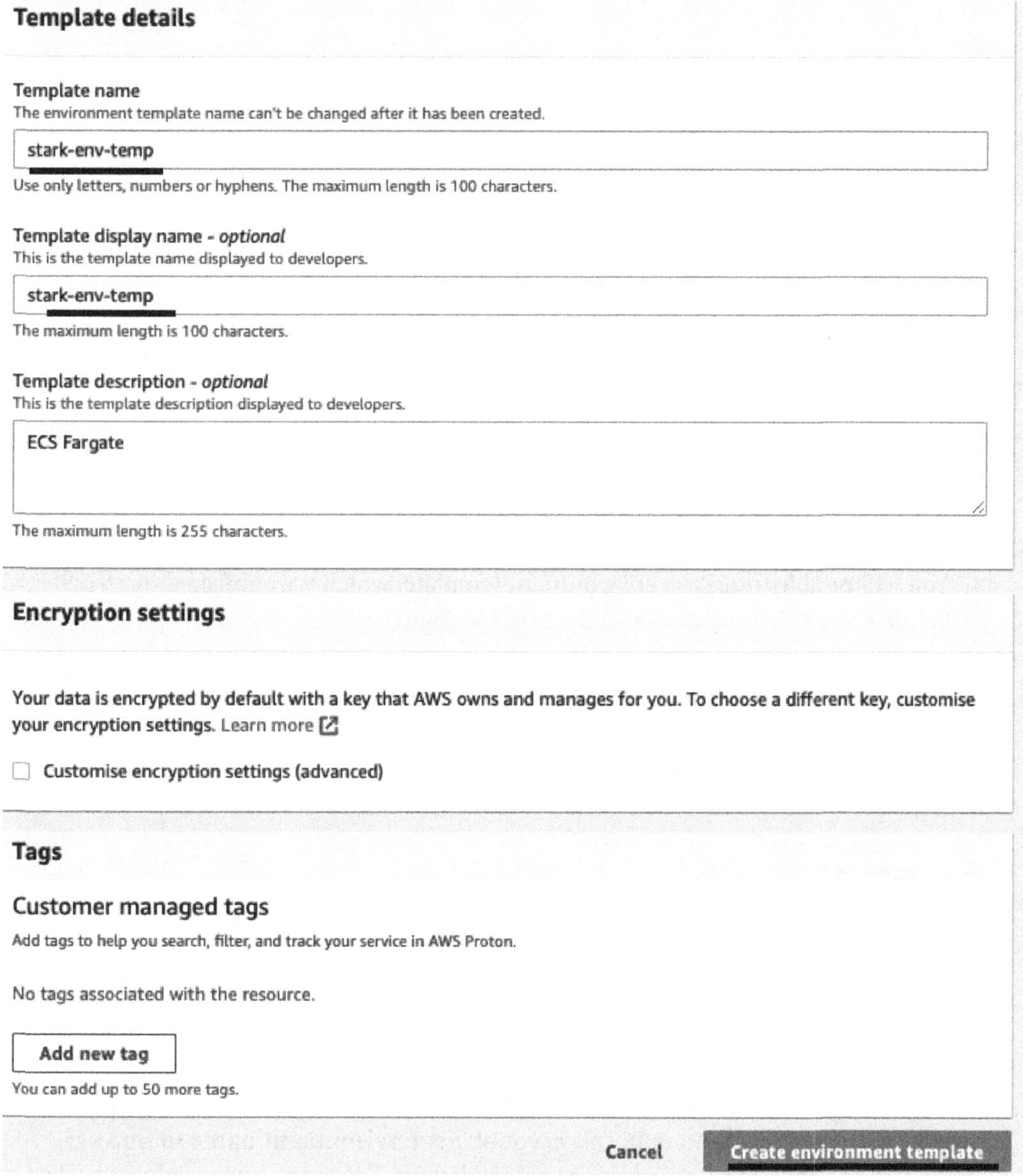

Figure 3.9 – Template details

9. Once you click on **Create environment template**, the environment template will go into draft status. To use it, we need to publish it first by clicking on **Publish v1.0**:

Figure 3.10 – Publishing the environment template

10. Once your environment template has been published, you can use it to provision two infrastructure environments (staging and dev). Click on the **Environments** section, then **Create environment**:

Figure 3.11 – The Environments console

11. You will be able to see the environment template, which we published in *Step 9*. Select stark-env-temp and click on **Configure**:

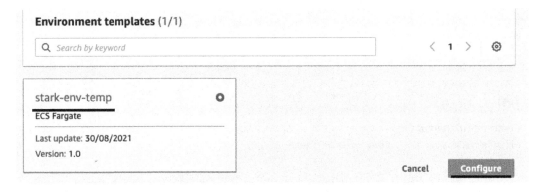

Figure 3.12 – Environment templates

12. Under **Deployment account**, click on **This AWS account** since we are going to provision the environment in this account. Set **Environment name** to stark-env-staging. For **Environment roles**, click on **Existing service role** and select the IAM role that we created in **Step 4**. Then, click **Next**:

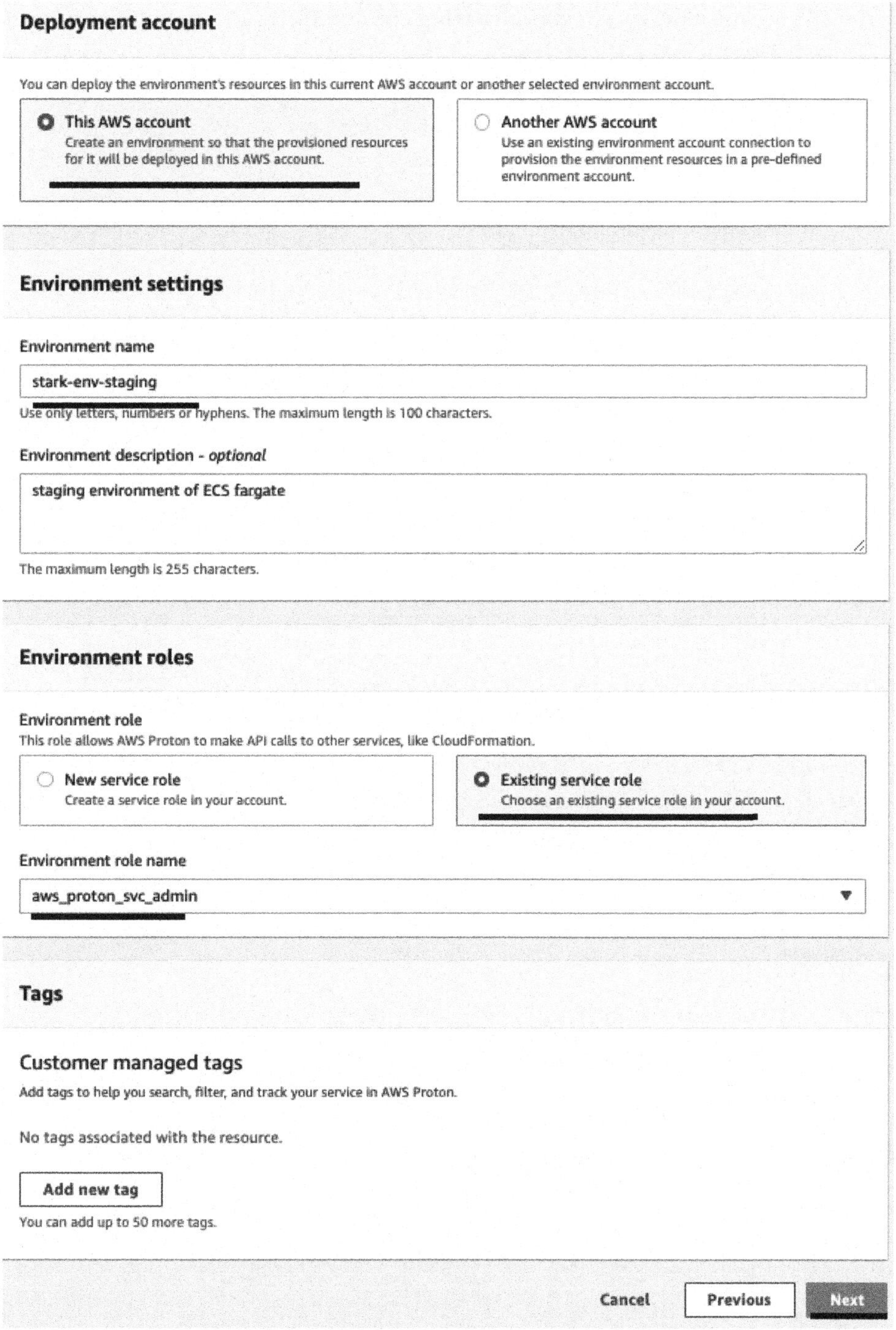

Deployment account

You can deploy the environment's resources in this current AWS account or another selected environment account.

○ **This AWS account**
Create an environment so that the provisioned resources for it will be deployed in this AWS account.

○ **Another AWS account**
Use an existing environment account connection to provision the environment resources in a pre-defined environment account.

Environment settings

Environment name

```
stark-env-staging
```

Use only letters, numbers or hyphens. The maximum length is 100 characters.

Environment description - *optional*

```
staging environment of ECS fargate
```

The maximum length is 255 characters.

Environment roles

Environment role
This role allows AWS Proton to make API calls to other services, like CloudFormation.

○ **New service role**
Create a service role in your account.

○ **Existing service role**
Choose an existing service role in your account.

Environment role name

```
aws_proton_svc_admin                                    ▼
```

Tags

Customer managed tags

Add tags to help you search, filter, and track your service in AWS Proton.

No tags associated with the resource.

[**Add new tag**]

You can add up to 50 more tags.

Cancel   Previous   **Next**

Figure 3.13 – Providing environment template information

13. You will see the **Configure custom settings** page, which came from the `schema` file. Leave it as-is and click on **Next**:

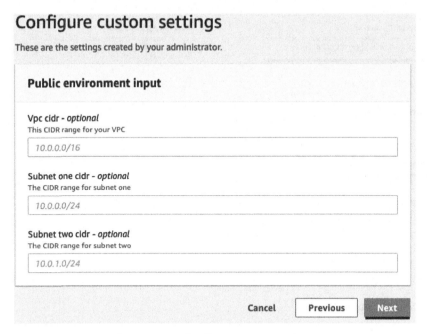

Figure 3.14 – Configure custom settings

14. You will be redirected to the **Review** page, where you need to verify all the data and then click on **Create**. Then, you will see an **Environment details** section, where you can see our **Deployment status**:

Figure 3.15 – The Environment details page

15. You can also see the provisioned environment in the ECS console:

Figure 3.16 – ECS cluster

16. Similarly, create another environment called `stark-env-dev` by performing *Step 10* to *Step 14*.

With that, we have just created two environments using the same environment template via AWS Proton. In the next section, we will learn how to create service templates and deploy services in these environments.

Creating the service template bundle

So far, we have learned how to create an environment template bundle. In this section, we will learn how to create a service template bundle and register it with AWS Proton. After that, we will learn how to create a service and service instance that will be deployed in both the staging and dev environments.

Writing the service template

At the beginning of this chapter, we provided a brief overview of the service template. The service template includes two sub-templates – one is an application-service related file that contains information regarding the task definition, load balancer target group, alarms, and so on, while the other sub-template is a *build and deploy* pipeline template that includes definitions related to developer tools such as CodeBuild, CodeDeploy, and CodePipeline. Using a service template, we can create multiple Proton services (that refer to their respective application branches), which will build the application and deploy it to a certain infrastructure environment. Application services that are deployed to an environment are known as **service instances**.

A service template bundle consists of the `cloudformation.yaml` and `manifest.yaml` files, in both the `instance_infrastructure` and `pipeline_infrastructure` folder. It also includes schema files:

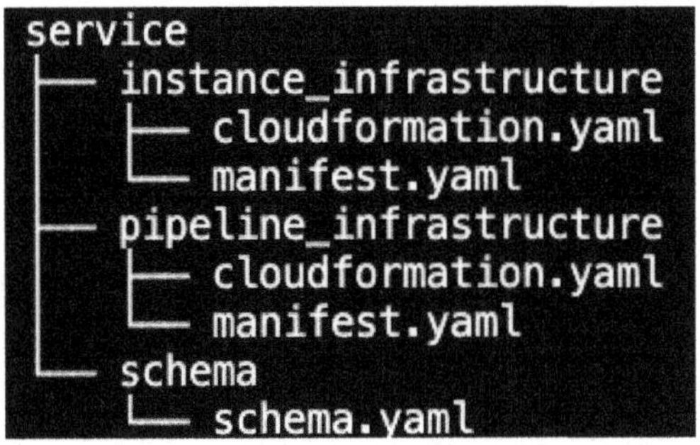

```
service
├── instance_infrastructure
│   ├── cloudformation.yaml
│   └── manifest.yaml
├── pipeline_infrastructure
│   ├── cloudformation.yaml
│   └── manifest.yaml
└── schema
    └── schema.yaml
```

Figure 3.17 – The tree structure of the service folder

The tips and recommendations for writing service templates are the same as those for writing environment templates, such as using customization and resource parameters. The service template is also in this book's GitHub repository. To use the service template bundle with AWS Proton, perform the following steps:

1. Go to the repository folder that you cloned (`chapter-03-aws-proton-template`) and create a tarball of the service folder:

    ```
    $ cd chapter-03-aws-proton-template
    $ tar -zcvf svc-template.tar.gz service/
    ```

2. Upload the tarball in the same S3 bucket that we created in the previous section (`proton-cli-templates-account-id`):

    ```
    $ aws s3 cp svc-template.tar.gz s3://proton-cli-
    templates-${account_id}/svc-template.tar.gz
    ```

3. Once you have uploaded the service template tarball into the S3 bucket, you need to register the service template by clicking on **Service templates**, then **Create service template**:

Figure 3.18 – The Service templates page

4. Under **Template bundle source**, select **Use your own template bundle**. You will then see **S3 bundle location**, where you need to click on **Browse S3** and select the bucket where you upload the service template (in our case, it's `proton-cli-templates-account-id/svc-template.tar.gz`):

Template bundle source

○ **Use one of our sample template bundles**
Get started right away with a sample template bundle.

● **Use your own template bundle**
Provide your own environment template bundle and upload it to S3.

S3 bundle location

S3 path

| 🔍 s3://proton-cli-templates-███████████svc-template.tar.gz | ✕ | | View 🗗 | | Browse S3 |

Valid format is tar.gz.

Figure 3.19 – Providing the service template's path

5. Under **Template details**, use `stark-svc-temp` as **Template name** and **Template display name**. Then, we need to associate this template with the environment it's compatible with. In our case, the service template that we are creating is compatible with the environment template we created in the previous section (`stark-env-template`). Now, click on **Create service templates**:

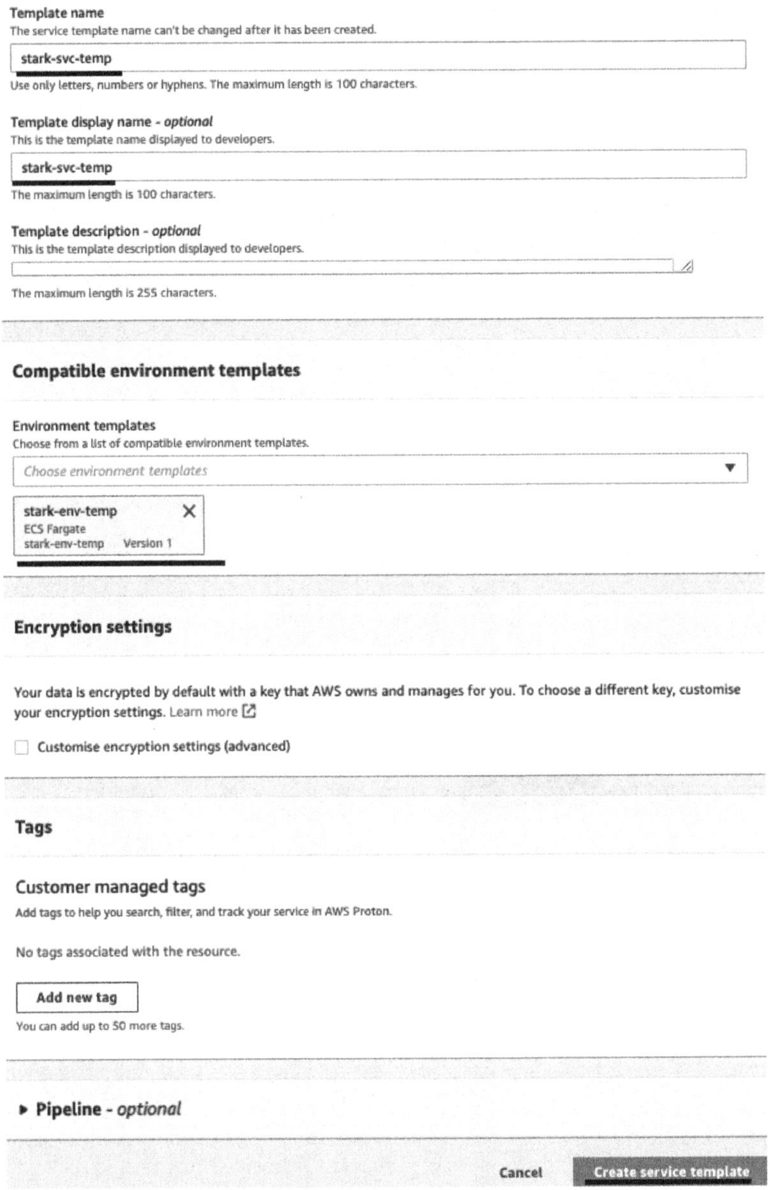

Template name
The service template name can't be changed after it has been created.

```
stark-svc-temp
```
Use only letters, numbers or hyphens. The maximum length is 100 characters.

Template display name - *optional*
This is the template name displayed to developers.

```
stark-svc-temp
```
The maximum length is 100 characters.

Template description - *optional*
This is the template description displayed to developers.

The maximum length is 255 characters.

Compatible environment templates

Environment templates
Choose from a list of compatible environment templates.

```
Choose environment templates                                        ▼
```

```
stark-env-temp                          ✕
ECS Fargate
stark-env-temp      Version 1
```

Encryption settings

Your data is encrypted by default with a key that AWS owns and manages for you. To choose a different key, customise your encryption settings. Learn more 🔗

☐ Customise encryption settings (advanced)

Tags

Customer managed tags
Add tags to help you search, filter, and track your service in AWS Proton.

No tags associated with the resource.

```
Add new tag
```
You can add up to 50 more tags.

▶ **Pipeline** - *optional*

Cancel   **Create service template**

Figure 3.20 – Providing service template details

6. Now, we need to click on **Publish** to publish the service template so that we can create a service instance:

Figure 3.21 – Publishing the service template

Once the service template has been published, the developer can use this service template to create a service instance, which helps deploy the application to the environment. We will deploy the containerized application in the next section.

Deploying the containerized application by creating a service instance in Proton

In this section, we will create a service instance to deploy the containerized application on both environments. First, we will create a source connection to the application repository (This repository you need to create in Github and push the files of chapter-03-aws-proton folder in the master branch. In my case I have created a repo aws-proton in Github) so that it can be used by AWS Proton. You also need to create a dev branch out of master branch and edit the line 93 of index.html file. You need to replace the string Staging to Dev. We will deploy the application from dev branch to `stark-env-dev` and then deploy the master branch to `stark-env-staging`.

Creating a source connection (GitHub)

To create a source connection with your VCS (GitHub, though you can use Bitbucket or GitLab as well), perform the following steps:

1. Go to the AWS Proton console and click on **Source connections** under **Settings**:

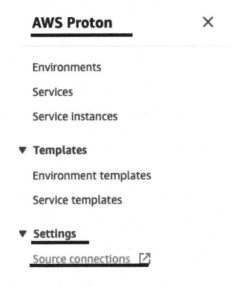

Figure 3.22 – Creating a source connection

2. Click on **Create connection** to link the VCS repository:

Figure 3.23 – Source connection page

3. Under **Select a provider**, click on **GitHub** and set github-awsproton as **Connection name**. Then, click on **Connect to GitHub**:

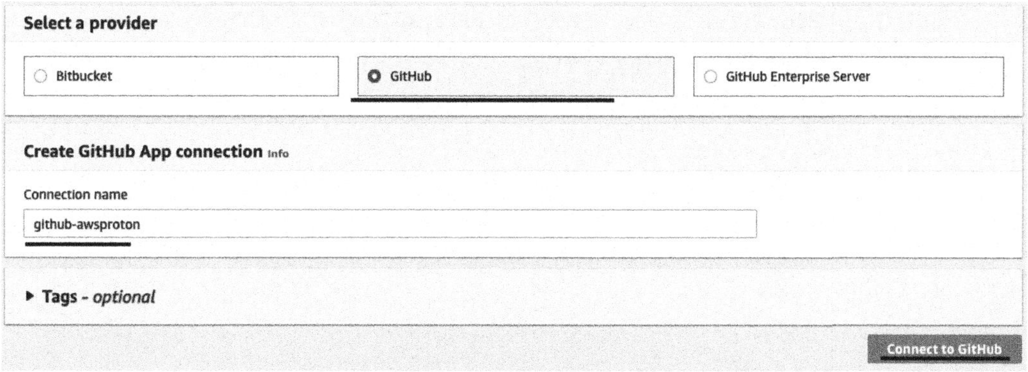

Select a provider

○ Bitbucket   ⦿ GitHub   ○ GitHub Enterprise Server

Create GitHub App connection Info

Connection name

github-awsproton

▶ **Tags** - *optional*

Connect to GitHub

Figure 3.24 – Providing a connection name

4. You will be redirected to the **Connect to GitHub** page, where you need to click on **Install a new app**:

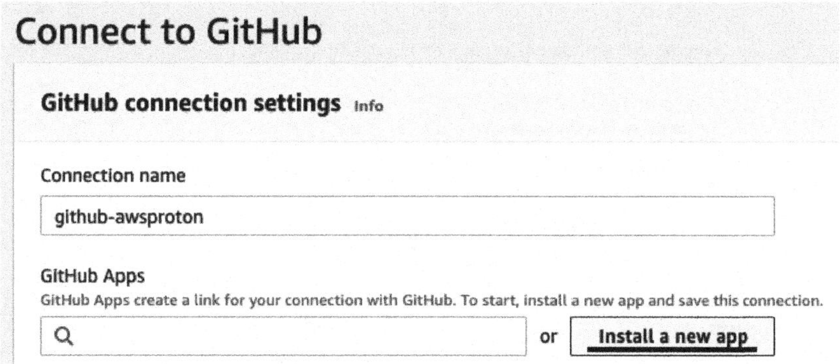

Connect to GitHub

GitHub connection settings Info

Connection name

github-awsproton

GitHub Apps

GitHub Apps create a link for your connection with GitHub. To start, install a new app and save this connection.

🔍   or   **Install a new app**

Figure 3.25 – Invoking GitHub from AWS

5. Then, you need to authorize your GitHub account to install AWS Connector and configure your account:

Figure 3.26 – Installing AWS connector in GitHub

6. Under **Repository access**, select **Only select repositories**, and then select the **aws-proton** repository. Click on **Save**:

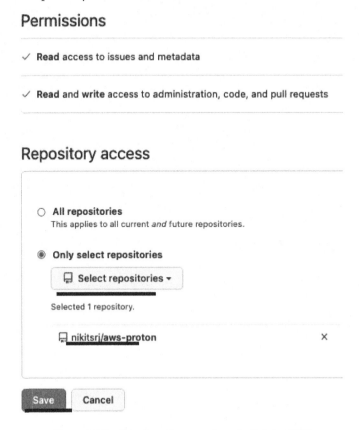

Figure 3.27 – Selecting the repository to link to AWS

7. You will be redirected to the **AWS Connection** page, which contains the GitHub Apps ID. Click on **Connect** to create your source connection:

Figure 3.28 – Source connection status

Now that we've created the source connection, let's deploy the application by creating a service instance.

Deploying the application by creating a service instance

To deploy the application on the environment, perform the following steps:

1. Go to the AWS Proton Console and click on **Services**. Then, click on **Create service**:

Figure 3.29 – The Services page

2. You will be asked to choose **Service templates**. You will see stark-svc-temp, which we created in the previous section. Select stark-svc-temp, and then click on **Configure**:

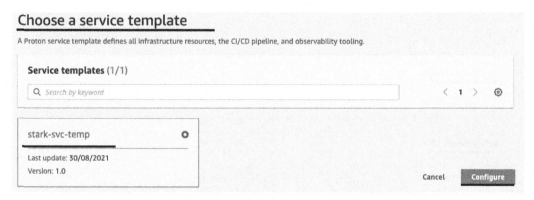

Figure 3.30 – Selecting the service template

3. Under **Service settings**, provide `neonapp-staging` as **Service name**. Give `master` as **Branch Name** and `<repo-username/repository name>` as **Repository Id**. Then, select **Repository Connection** and click on **Next**:

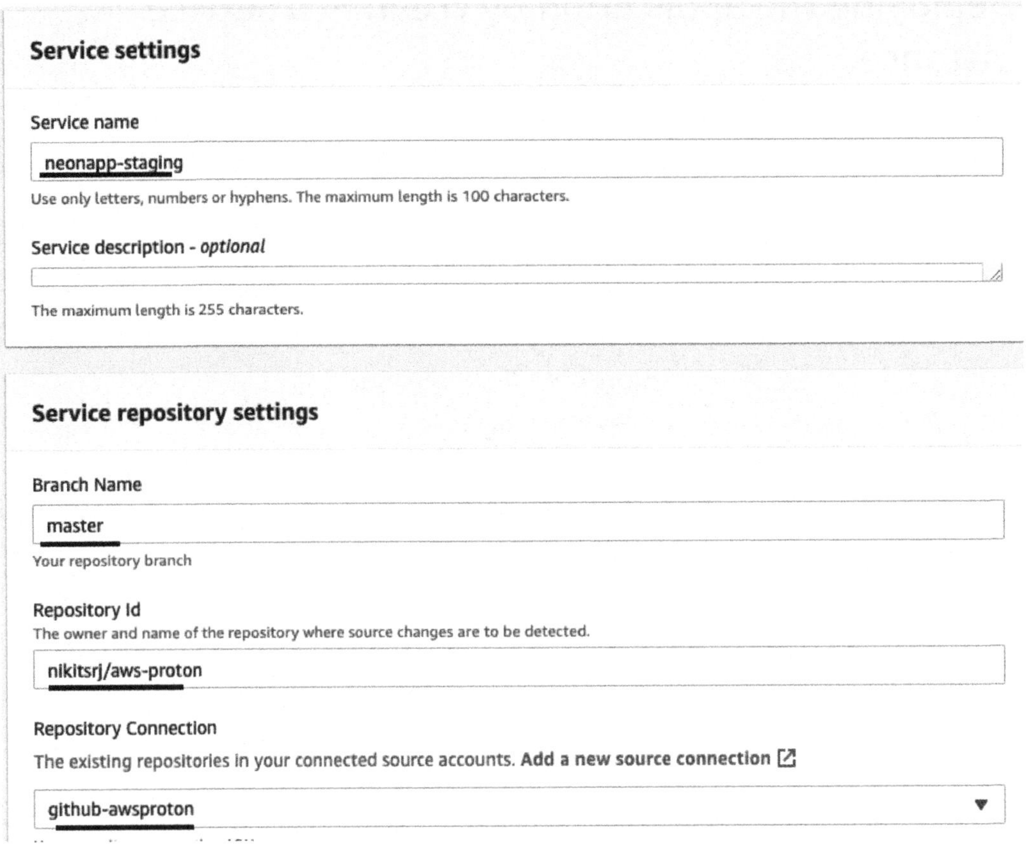

Service settings

Service name

neonapp-staging

Use only letters, numbers or hyphens. The maximum length is 100 characters.

Service description - *optional*

The maximum length is 255 characters.

Service repository settings

Branch Name

master

Your repository branch

Repository Id
The owner and name of the repository where source changes are to be detected.

nikitsrj/aws-proton

Repository Connection
The existing repositories in your connected source accounts. **Add a new source connection** [↗]

github-awsproton   ▼

Figure 3.31 – Service repository settings

4. Under **Configure custom settings**, set `neonapp-staging` as **Name**. Select `stark-env-staging` as **Environment**. Then, set **Task size** to **X small** and click on **Next**:

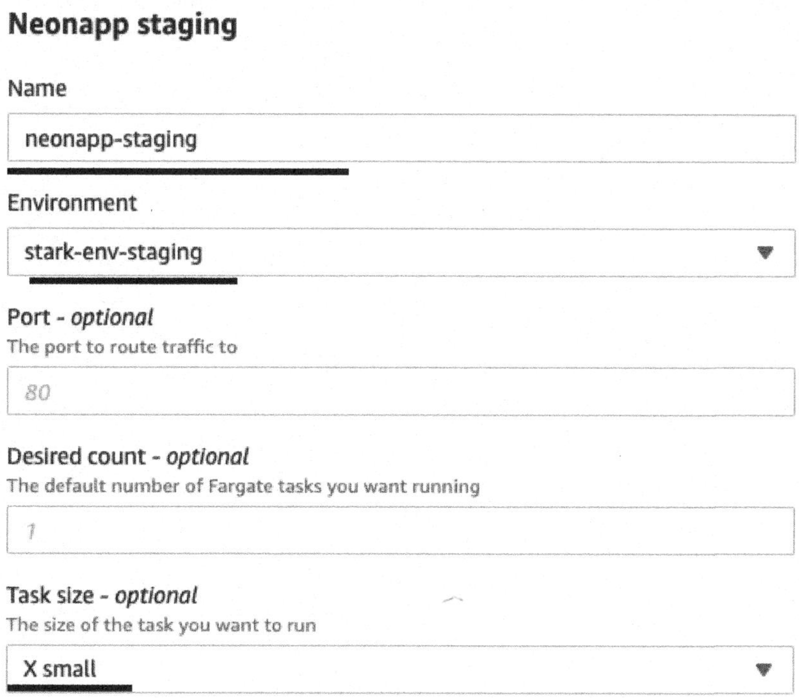

Neonapp staging

Name

neonapp-staging

Environment

stark-env-staging ▼

Port - *optional*
The port to route traffic to

80

Desired count - *optional*
The default number of Fargate tasks you want running

1

Task size - *optional*
The size of the task you want to run

X small ▼

Figure 3.32 – Providing service instance details

5. Review the service template and click on **Create**. Proton will start creating the service instance, which will run the `cloudformation` template to spin up the pipeline resources and deploy the application to the infrastructure environment. You can visit the CloudFormation Console to check the resources that have been created by the `neonapp-staging` stack.

6. You can also see the CodePipeline that was created by CloudFormation and the application's deployment flow. Go to the CodePipeline console and click on the **neonapp** pipeline:

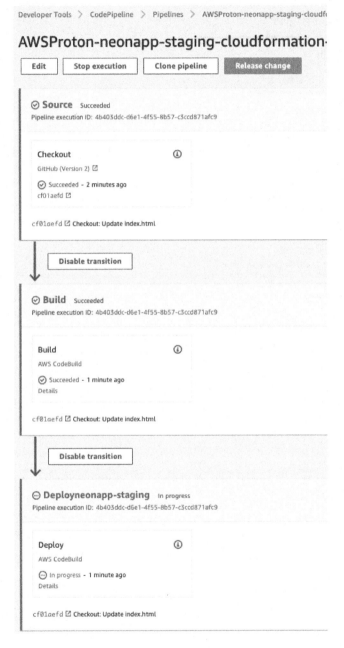

Figure 3.33 – CodePipeline created by CloudFormation

7. If you look at **Deployment status** of the `neonapp-staging` service instance, it will be **In progress**. Once **Deployment status** is **Succeeded**, you can go to the **ServiceEndpoint** link to see the application running:

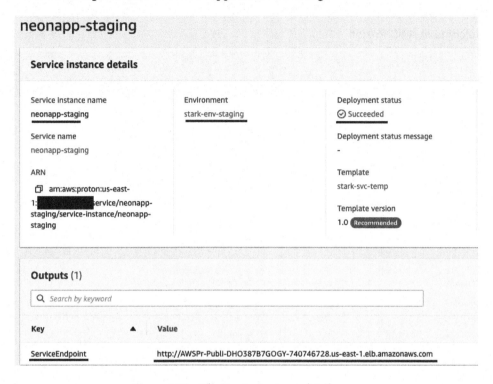

Figure 3.34 – The Service instance details page

8. Once you go to the **ServiceEndpoint** link, you will see the application, which is running in the ECS staging environment:

Figure 3.35 – Application running in the staging environment

9. Now, to deploy the dev branch in the dev environment, we need to create another service instance with the branch name dev (*Step 3*) and select stark-env-dev as the environment (*Step 4*). Once you have created the service instance, you will see that the application running in the dev environment is different:

Figure 3.36 – Application running in the dev environment

It was so straightforward to deploy the application related to the dev branch in the dev environment, without even writing a separate task definition file for ECS. Instead, we leveraged the service template. This is the power of templating and the AWS Proton service, where we can spin up multiple infrastructure environments or deploy multiple instances of the application on the environment at scale. Now, we can make this environment secure by making sure that the template we are using passes the CloudFormation guard checks. In the next section, we will learn how to scan the application code using AWS CodeGuru.

Introduction to Amazon CodeGuru

In the software development life cycle, a code review process takes place when all the developers write their code and raise a pull request to merge to an upstream branch. The code review is generally done by the team leader of the project, but it could be a slow process to eyeball the entire code. The code review process is important, but it shouldn't increase the workload for reviewers and become a bottleneck in development. By using code review tools, we can automate the process of reviewing the code. Some famous tools in the market do this magic for us, such as SonarQube. Recently, Amazon launched a new service called *Amazon CodeGuru*, which can perform code reviews as well as provide application performance. This not only helps in improving the reliability of the software but also lets us dig deep and cut down on the time spent finding difficult issues, such as sensitive data, race conditions, undefined functions, and slow resource leaks.

CodeGuru is empowered by machine learning, best practices, and a big code base. It learned from the millions of code reviews that are used in open source projects, as well as internally at Amazon.

CodeGuru provides the following two functionalities:

- **Reviewer**: Automated code analysis and reviews for static code
- **Profiler**: Visibility as well as recommendations about application performance during runtime

The following diagram shows the capabilities of Amazon CodeGuru:

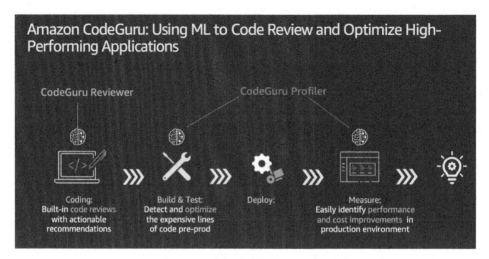

Figure 3.37 – Capabilities of CodeGuru

At the time of writing, CodeGuru supports two languages: Java and Python. It works with the following VCSes:

- AWS CodeCommit
- Bitbucket
- GitHub
- GitHub Enterprise Cloud
- GitHub Enterprise Server
- Amazon S3

We will use CodeGuru Reviewer to review the code in the CodeCommit repository in the next section.

Integrating CodeGuru with AWS CodeCommit and analyzing the pull request report

In this section, we will be creating a CodeCommit repository and pushing the code to the repository. We will associate the CodeCommit repository with CodeGuru. We will create another branch and modify the code in the new branch and raise a pull request. Then, we will look at the recommendation provided by CodeGuru on the pull request.

To get the recommendation from CodeGuru in the CodeCommit repository, perform the following steps:

1. Go to the AWS CodeCommit console to create a repository. Call it codeguru-sample-app. Click on **Enable Amazon CodeGuru Reviewer for Java and Python**. This will enable CodeGuru to review the code that we push into the repository:

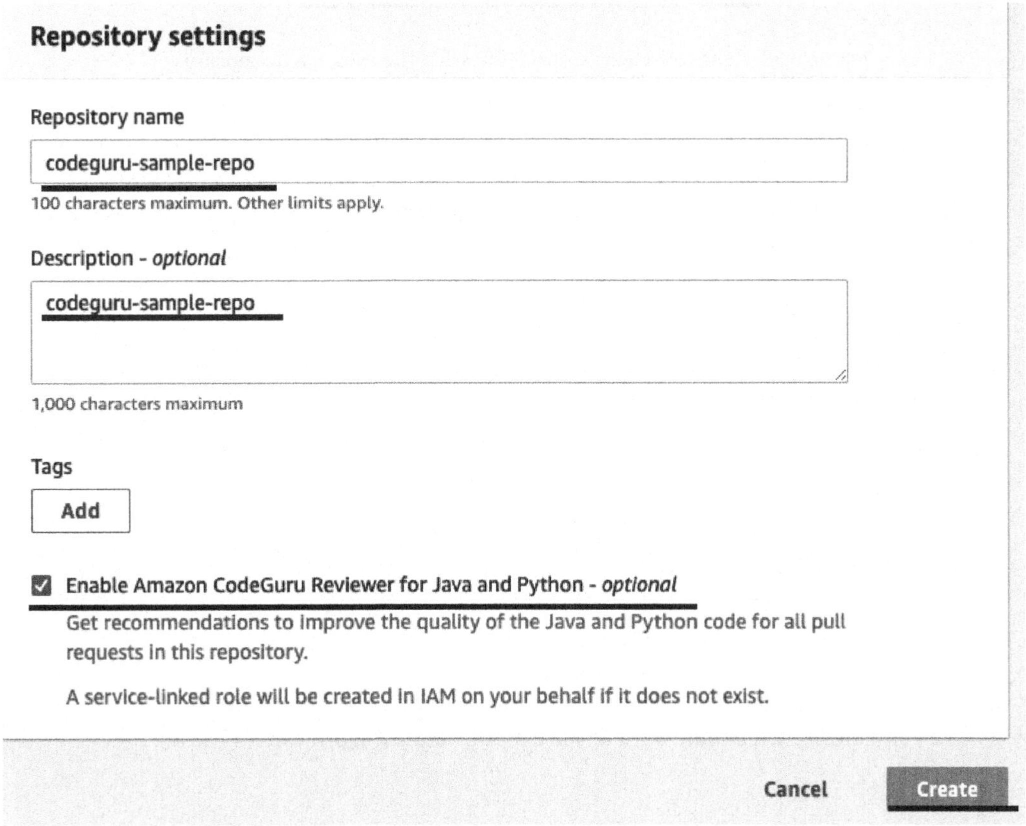

Repository settings

Repository name

codeguru-sample-repo

100 characters maximum. Other limits apply.

Description - *optional*

codeguru-sample-repo

1,000 characters maximum

Tags

Add

☑ Enable Amazon CodeGuru Reviewer for Java and Python - *optional*

Get recommendations to improve the quality of the Java and Python code for all pull requests in this repository.

A service-linked role will be created in IAM on your behalf if it does not exist.

Cancel   Create

Figure 3.38 – Creating a CodeCommit repository and enabling CodeGuru

2. Before pushing the messy code into the repository, go to the **CodeGuru** console and click on **Repositories** to see the associated repositories that we just created:

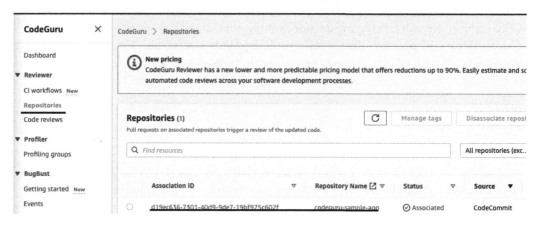

Figure 3.39 – The CodeGuru console showing the associated repository

3. Now push the files of chapter-03-codeguru-sample into the codecommit empty repository called `codeguru-sample-app`, as shown in the following code block (you will need to generate the `codecommit` HTTPS Git credential by going to `https://docs.aws.amazon.com/codecommit/latest/userguide/setting-up-gc.html`):

```
$ git clone https://git-codecommit.us-east-1.amazonaws.com/v1/repos/codeguru-sample-app
$git clone https://github.com/PacktPublishing/Modern-CI-CD-on-AWS.git
$ cd Modern-CI-CD-on-AWS/chapter-03-codeguru-sample
$ cp -rpf *codeguru-sample-app
$ cd codeguru-sample-app
$ git add .
$ git commit -m "initial push"
$ git push origin master
```

4. Now, let's create another branch, called **dev**, modify the code, and push it back to the repository. After that, we will raise a pull request from dev to master:

Create pull request

Destination   Source

| master ▼ | ≪ | dev ▼ | Compare | Cancel |

✓ **Mergeable**
There are currently no conflicts between dev and master. You can close this pull request by merging it in the AWS CodeCommit console.

Details   [Create pull request]

Title

modify the app.py

150 characters maximum

Description - *optional*   ⬤ Preview markdown   Learn more ↗

modify the app.py

Figure 3.40 – Raising a pull request

5. Once you've done this, in the **Details** section of the pull request, you will see
    a notification, stating that the CodeGuru Reviewer feature has been enabled. It will
    provide recommendations whenever you raise a pull request:

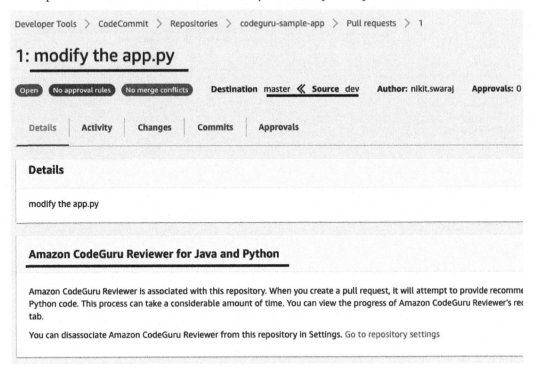

Developer Tools > CodeCommit > Repositories > codeguru-sample-app > Pull requests > 1

1: modify the app.py

(Open) (No approval rules) (No merge conflicts)   **Destination** master ≪ **Source** dev   **Author:** nikit.swaraj   **Approvals:** 0

Details   Activity   Changes   Commits   Approvals

Details

modify the app.py

Amazon CodeGuru Reviewer for Java and Python

Amazon CodeGuru Reviewer is associated with this repository. When you create a pull request, it will attempt to provide recomme
Python code. This process can take a considerable amount of time. You can view the progress of Amazon CodeGuru Reviewer's rec
tab.

You can disassociate Amazon CodeGuru Reviewer from this repository in Settings. Go to repository settings

Figure 3.41 – The status of the pull request

6. Now, go to the CodeGuru **Dashboard** page. You will see **1** under **Pull requests** in the **Service overview** section because we just raised a pull request. In the **Code Reviews** tab, **Review Status** is **Pending**. This is because CodeGuru takes 10-15 minutes to analyze the entire source code and give the recommendation:

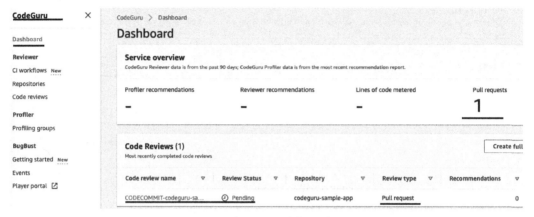

Figure 3.42 – The status of the code review

7. Once the review's status is **Completed**, you will see the recommendation provided by CodeGuru:

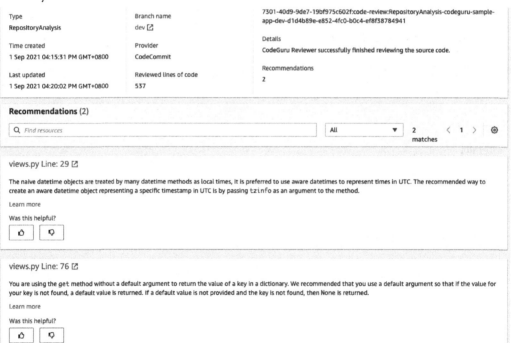

Figure 3.43 – Recommendation from CodeGuru

Based on the recommendation provided by CodeGuru, the reviewer can easily ask the person to fix the code and then raise the pull request again. This saves lots of time, as well as manual work. We will learn more about CodeGuru in *Chapter 9, DevSecOps Pipeline with AWS Services and Tools Popular Industry-Wide*, where we will be implementing a full CI/CD pipeline with security in place.

Summary

AWS Proton is an amazing service when it comes to automating the process of codifying your infrastructure and application deployment at scale. We learned how to create an environment and service template bundle and covered various writing tips. We also spun up multiple environments using a single environment template and deployed the containerized application from a different branch in the respective environment using a service instance. When it came to reviewing the code, we learned how Amazon CodeGuru can give amazing recommendations, even at the time of raising pull requests.

The next chapter will cover how we can implement a service mesh in an EKS cluster and restrict network and API communication between services and pods.

Section 2: Chaos Engineering and EKS Clusters

This part includes chapters that will walk you through implementing a secure, private production-grade EKS cluster with all the stable, necessary add-ons, such as Cluster Autoscaler, the EBS CSI driver, IRSA, Velero, and App Mesh. It covers the implementation of various features of App Mesh using examples. After that, it covers how to implement a chaos simulation using AWS FIS on EC2, RDS, and EKS worker nodes.

This section contains the following chapters:

- *Chapter 4, Working with AWS EKS and App Mesh*
- *Chapter 5, Securing Private EKS Cluster for Production*
- *Chapter 6, Chaos Engineering with AWS Fault Injection Simulator*

4

Working with AWS EKS and App Mesh

In this chapter, we will understand the architecture of an **AWS EKS cluster** and how it's different from a self-deployed **Kubernetes cluster**. Then, we will create a **single Node EKS cluster**. After that, we will understand the need for a **service mesh** and install **AWS App Mesh**. We will deploy a sample polyglot application to implement and understand features such as traffic routing and mutual TLS authentication and use the X-Ray service to trace the communication between individual services. This chapter will make you confident in deploying and managing a service mesh on an EKS cluster.

In this chapter, we are going to cover the following main sections:

- Deep diving into AWS EKS
- Deploying an EKS cluster
- Introducing AWS App Mesh
- Implementing traffic management
- Getting observability using X-Ray
- Enabling mTLS authentication between services

Technical requirements

To get started with this chapter, you will need a sample application and App Mesh definition files. You can download the following repository, which contains the folder `chapter-04` that includes necessary source code and configuration for this chapter:

`https://github.com/PacktPublishing/Accelerating-DevSecOps-on-AWS.git`

Deep diving into AWS EKS

AWS **Elastic Kubernetes Service** (**EKS**) is a managed service for Kubernetes. Even though Kubernetes has been around for a while now, in the last 2 years, it has taken the developers' world by storm. It has gained a lot of attraction among AWS customers too. **Kubernetes** (also known as **K8s**) is an open source container management framework that runs containers at scale. It's equipped with a bunch of features and functionalities that help it to do the following:

- Build or run microservices.
- Build distributed applications in the 12-factor app pattern.
- Automatic bin-packing.
- Self-healing.
- Horizontal scaling.
- Service discovery and load balancing (TCP – layer 4).
- Automated rollouts and rollbacks.
- Batch execution.
- Run anywhere (on any platform).

These features together as a package give you primitives for building modern applications. Kubernetes comprises tools that are required to solve modern application problems, which is why it is popular among the developer community.

Kubernetes has master and Node architecture patterns. Let's look at the components of Kubernetes in brief.

Kubernetes components

A Kubernetes cluster has master components (**API server**, **scheduler**, and **controller**) and Node agents (kubelet) running on either a single server or multiple servers. The following diagram gives a clear picture:

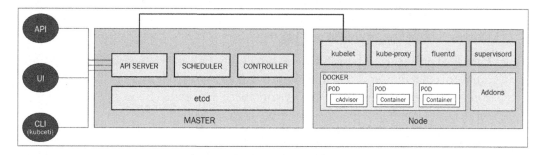

Figure 4.1 – Kubernetes components

Master components are responsible for providing the control planes. They make overall decisions about the cluster, such as scheduling, detecting, and responding to cluster events. For example, the master will start a new container whenever the CPU load becomes high and needs another resource. It has the following components:

- **API server**: This provides a frontend, or you can call it a gatekeeper. It exposes the Kubernetes API. We can access the Kubernetes cluster in three ways:

  - API call

  - UI (Kubernetes dashboard)

  - CLI (kubectl)

- **Scheduler**: This is responsible for physically scheduling Pods to Nodes and taking care of scheduling based on the resources available on hosts.

- **Controller**: This checks the health of the entire cluster. It is a coordinator that ensures Nodes are running properly.

- **etcd**: This is a key-value database developed by CoreOS. It's a central database to store the cluster state.

Node components run on every Node, maintaining running Pods and providing the Kubernetes runtime environment. The following are the components of a Node:

- **kubelet**: This is the agent responsible for talking to the API server. It returns health metrics and the current state of the Node via api-server to etcd as well as kube-master.

- **Pod**: This is a basic building block of Kubernetes where you can run an application container. A Pod can run a single container or multiple containers. Containers in the same Pod have the same hostname.

- **Docker**: This is nothing more than a runtime engine for containers. Alternatives for Docker in Kubernetes are **rkt** and **cri-0**.

- **kube-proxy**: This is responsible for maintaining the entire network configuration. It ensures that one Node communicates with another Node and one Pod communicates with another Pod. It maintains a distributed network and exposes services. It's basically a load balancer for services.

- **Supervisord**: Both Docker and kubelet are packaged into Supervisord. It's a process manager where multiple child processes can run under a master process.

- **Fluentd**: This is responsible for managing the logs.

- **Addons**: This is responsible for extra package for Kubernetes, such as UI and DNS.

Here's a walkthrough of how developers generally deploy a Kubernetes cluster on AWS. The following is a typical architecture diagram of a Kubernetes cluster on AWS:

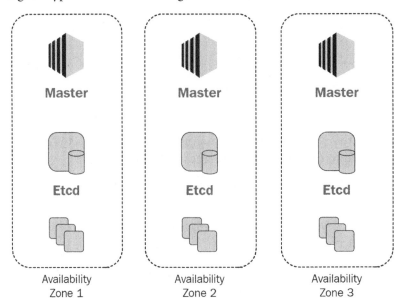

Figure 4.2 – Vanilla Kubernetes on AWS

The preceding figure shows a natural deployment pattern where you run masters and etcd across three Availability Zones for a **High-Availability** (**HA**) control panel. Each Kubernetes master essentially runs a copy of the same components. In addition to the masters, you also need to run etcd, which is the core persistence layer for Kubernetes. This is basically where all the critical metadata for your cluster lives. If you lose your etcd cluster, then an etcd lying in another Availability Zone will take care of it.

Finally, you need to run the actual worker Nodes. This is where your applications run. They are generally deployed in autoscaling groups across multiple Availability Zones. You have a lot of control over the instance type, as well as the freedom to use on-demand, reserved instances and whatever instance type suits your needs.

This whole stack is generally a source of worry. A lot of conversations that I've had with people include them saying, "Yeah! we're worried about this thing failing in the middle of the night, and we're having a hard time forecasting our growth to make sure that we can seamlessly upgrade."

We can make sure we're running the right number/instance type of Nodes, and all this doesn't come crashing down in the middle of the night. AWS received a lot of feedback in the past 6 to 12 months and here are some examples:

- Can AWS run Kubernetes for me?
- Can you provide a capability to perform native AWS integrations?

Thus, they led to AWS developing and releasing EKS.

In essence, EKS is a platform for enterprises to run production-grade workloads. It provides features and management capabilities to allow enterprises to run real workloads at scale for reliability, visibility, scalability, and ease of management.

EKS provides a native and upstream Kubernetes experience. Any modifications or improvements made on the backend, perhaps in building a service, will be transparent to the Kubernetes end user experience.

If EKS customers want to use additional AWS services, the integrations are seamless.

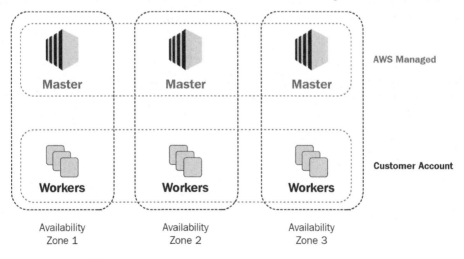

Figure 4.3 – AWS EKS model

Now, with EKS, the master and `etcd` will be managed by AWS and the worker Nodes will be taken care of by the users. So, in the end, it will look like the following figure:

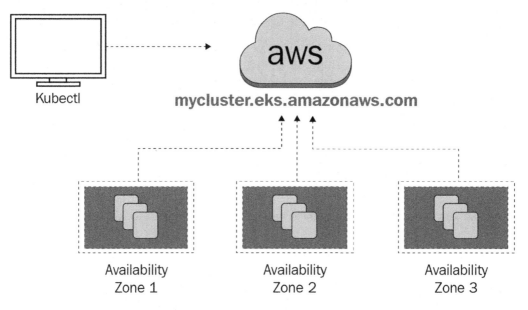

Figure 4.4 – AWS EKS endpoint access

What's nice is that the complete control panel is really simplified. So, instead of running the Kubernetes control panel in your account, you connect to the manage Kubernetes endpoint in the AWS cloud.

The endpoint abstracts the complexity of the Kubernetes control panel, and your worker Nodes check into this endpoint. You can interact with *kubectl* with this endpoint and replace all the complexity of running your Kubernetes control panel.

EKS currently supports three types of Nodes. One is **Fargate-Linux**, which allows you to run your Linux application directly as a Kubernetes resource and the underlying infrastructure is not transparent to the customer. Second is **Managed Nodes-Linux**, which allows you to spin up an EC2 instance and run your application workload on that EC2 instance. Third is **Self-Managed**, where you can also add Windows self-managed Nodes to your cluster.

In this section, we got familiar with Kubernetes and its components. In the next section, we will deploy a managed-Node EKS cluster.

Deploying an EKS cluster

In this section of the chapter, we will be deploying an EKS cluster using a CLI utility called eksctl. Then, we will access the endpoint using kubectl, which is a command-line binary to access Kubernetes resources.

To create the EKS cluster, perform the following steps:

1. We need to install the ekctl CLI binary by using the following commands:

```
$ curl --silent --location "https://github.com/
weaveworks/eksctl/releases/latest/download/eksctl_$(uname
-s)_amd64.tar.gz" | tar xz -C /tmp
$ sudo mv /tmp/eksctl /usr/local/bin
$ eksctl version
```

2. We will create an ec2 key pair so that we can use that key pair to SSH into a worker Node if required:

```
$ aws ec2 create-key-pair --key-name celestial --region
us-east-1 > celestial.pem
```

3. Once we have a key pair, we will create an EKS cluster using eksctl. For now, we are creating a public endpoint EKS cluster. We will create a private endpoint EKS cluster in the next chapter:

```
$ eksctl create cluster --name celestials --region
us-east-1 --with-oidc --ssh-access --ssh-public-key
celestial --managed
```

4. The preceding command will show the status in `stdout`, but in parallel, it will create a CloudFormation stack (shown in the following diagram), which basically spins up all the resources required for an EKS cluster, for example, a VPC, a security group, a worker Node group, and the EKS control plane:

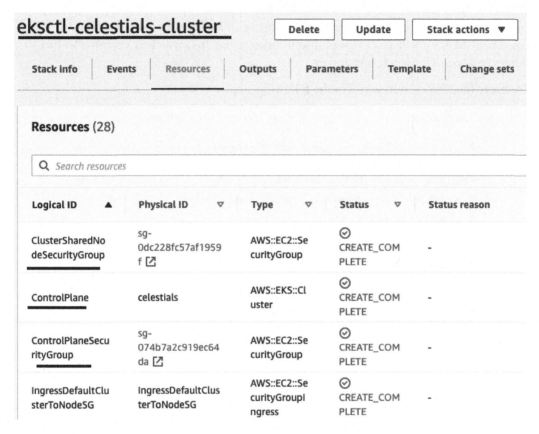

Figure 4.5 – EKS – CloudFormation stack

5. You can also navigate to the EKS console to see the status of the EKS cluster.

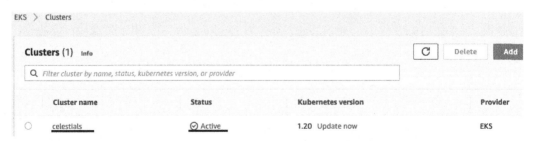

Figure 4.6 – EKS cluster in the EKS console

6. At the end of stdout in *step 3*, eksctl will create a config file in the ~/.kube folder. This config file includes the access token and endpoint of the EKS cluster. To connect to the EKS cluster, we will be using the kubectl CLI tool, which reads the config file and connects to the EKS cluster:

```
$ curl -o kubectl https://amazon-eks.s3.us-west-2.
amazonaws.com/1.20.4/2021-04-12/bin/linux/amd64/kubectl
```

```
$ chmod +x ./kubectl
```

```
$ sudo cp kubectl /usr/local/bin
```

```
$ kubectl version
```

```
Client Version: version.Info{Major:"1",
Minor:"21", GitVersion:"v1.21.1",
GitCommit:"5e58841cce77d4bc13713ad2b91fa0d961e69192",
GitTreeState:"clean", BuildDate:"2021-05-12T14:18:45Z",
GoVersion:"go1.16.4", Compiler:"gc", Platform:"darwin/
amd64"}
```

```
Server Version: version.Info{Major:"1",
Minor:"20+", GitVersion:"v1.20.7-eks-d88609",
GitCommit:"d886092805d5cc3a47ed5cf0c43de38ce442dfcb",
GitTreeState:"clean", BuildDate:"2021-07-31T00:29:12Z",
GoVersion:"go1.15.12", Compiler:"gc", Platform:"linux/
amd64"}
```

7. In the preceding kubectl version command, we got the server version information, which means we can connect to the EKS endpoint. To get the Nodes information, execute the following command:

```
$ kubectl get nodes -o wide
NAME                         STATUS    ROLES    AGE
VERSION             INTERNAL-IP       EXTERNAL-IP
OS-IMAGE        KERNEL-VERSION                CONTAINER-
RUNTIME
ip-192-168-28-162.ec2.internal   Ready     <none>    10d
v1.20.7-eks-135321   192.168.28.162   35.174.139.113
Amazon Linux 2   5.4.141-67.229.amzn2.x86_64
docker://19.3.13
ip-192-168-58-193.ec2.internal   Ready     <none>    10d
v1.20.7-eks-135321   192.168.58.193   18.207.239.87
Amazon Linux 2   5.4.141-67.229.amzn2.x86_64
docker://19.3.13
```

We have successfully created an EKS cluster. There is a possibility that you will have the latest version of EKS available in AWS. Install the correct version of `kubectl`; it must match the EKS cluster version. In the next section, we will understand the need for a service mesh and install an App Mesh controller on the EKS cluster that we just created.

Introducing AWS App Mesh

Before diving into service meshes, let's learn about the problem that they resolve. After that, we will learn about their components.

Are microservices any good?

To answer that question, we need to have a look at a traditional application, such as a monolith, where you have all your logic in one app written in one language that does all the functionality. It may be using object-orientated programming, so you have different classes that do different things, but at the end of the day, it's like one big program that does all the stuff. There are a lot of advantages of doing a monolith type of development. For example, it's easier to debug and deploy; you just need to push it out and you are done. But this is only an advantage when you have a small team and a small application. The problem with monolith comes when your app starts to grow a little bigger. If you are making a small change in the app, you must re-deploy the whole thing. There is a chance that it would be better for the frontend of your app to be written in one language and the backend to be in a second language, but in a monolith type of development, you would be stuck with using only one language. It's also hard to manage a monolithic application when it's big.

But in microservices, we break all the business logic into its own individual components that can be written in its own language and be updated and deployed independently of the others. This gives a lot more agility, flexibility, speed, and scalability. The following diagram shows what the microservices of an application looks like:

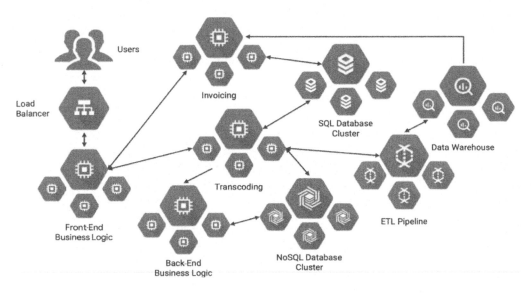

Figure 4.7 – Traffic flow between microservices

Microservices are easy to maintain when you have 20-30 microservices but what if the application becomes bigger and bigger and suddenly, your number of microservices looks like the following?

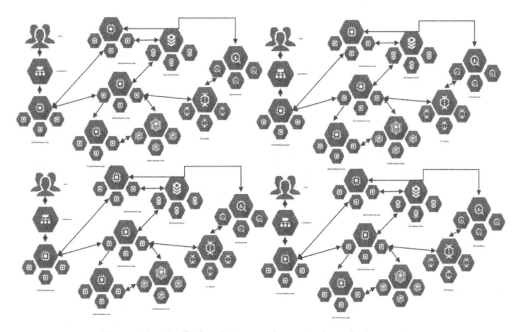

Figure 4.8 – Traffic flow between a large number of microservices

Now suppose you have 2,000 microservices: how do you know which service is talking to which one and how the intricate spider's web of connection works?

You have a single request that comes into a load balancer, gets sent to 2,000 microservices, and then is sent all the way back to the load balancer. If the chains break anywhere, the whole application looks broken. Debugging this is super hard. It becomes very difficult to manage this huge stack of services

So again, coming back to the question, are microservices any good?

Well, to be competitive in the market and provide the business features faster, we certainly use microservice, and we can solve the preceding mentioned problems of managing large numbers of microservices using service mesh tools such as Istio and App Mesh.

A service mesh is used to describe the network of microservices that make up such an application and the interactions between them. It has more complex operational requirements, such as the following:

- **Traffic control**: Intelligently control the flow of traffic and API calls between services, for example, **path-based routing**, **canary**, and **retries**.

- **Security and policies**: Secure your services through managed authorization, authentication, and encryption of communication between the services, for example, **end-user authentication** (with **JWTs**), **mTLS**, or **Role-Based Access Control** (**RBAC**).

- **Observability**: Automatic tracing, monitoring, and logging of services using tools such as **AWS X-Ray**, **Kiali**, **Jaeger**, **Prometheus**, and **Grafana**. This feature gives visibility to service communication.

Istio was one of the first service meshes developed by *IBM*, *Lyft*, and *Google*. App Mesh is a managed service mesh provided by AWS.

A service mesh has two components (a **control plane** and **data plane**), which you need to deploy in an orchestration platform and then start using the features. In this case, you must take care of the control plane as well as the data plane. But with a managed service such as App Mesh, the control plane is taken care of by AWS, and the data plane will be created by you. Since you have got an idea of what a service mesh is and what problem it solves, let's dig deep into AWS App Mesh.

AWS App Mesh

AWS App Mesh is a managed service mesh based on the **Envoy proxy**, which makes it easy to monitor and control containerized microservices. An envoy is a side container that handles the traffic directly and then transfers it to microservice containers. To understand it better, have a look at the following diagram, where the communication between microservices takes place directly:

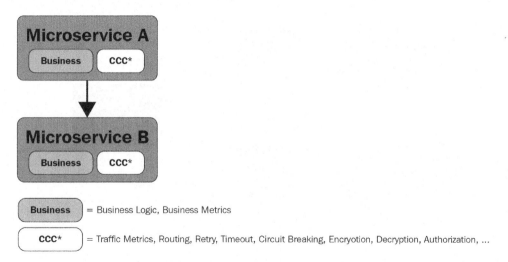

Figure 4.9 – Communication between services without a service mesh

The preceding diagram shows the communication between service A and service B directly. Both the services include business logic as well as cross-cutting concerns such as traffic metrics, routing, and encryption. So basically, a developer needs to write business logic as well as operational logic, which may slow down the release of the feature. But with the introduction of a service mesh in the platform, the developer can focus only on the business logic and the service mesh will take care of operational logic with a bit of help from configuration files. A service mesh does that by using a sidecar container called an Envoy proxy. The following diagram shows that if service A wants to communicate with service B, then the Envoy proxy of service A will first communicate with the Envoy proxy of service B, then transfer the request to service B. But there are a few more steps that take place in between that we will understand in detail when we get familiar with the data plane and control plane:

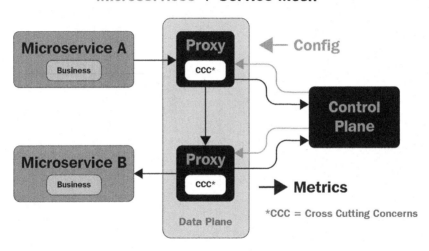

Figure 4.10 – Communication between services with a service mesh

App Mesh has two core components, a control plane and a data plane. The data plane is deployed as a Envoy proxy as a sidecar container along with the application container/ services Pod, whereas the control plane is managed by AWS.

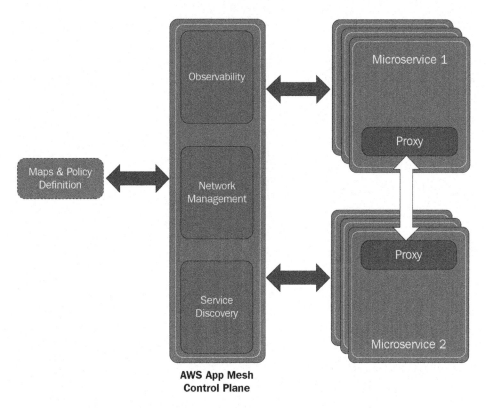

Figure 4.11 – App Mesh core components

The App Mesh control plane takes the cross-cutting concern policies in a set of `yaml` config files and applies the rule mentioned in policy on the data plane. For example, if service 1 wants to send 60% of traffic to service 2, then the DevOps team needs to write the `yaml` rule (which looks like a Kubernetes deployment file) and then apply it to the App Mesh controller. The App Mesh control plane will then govern the data plane Envoy proxy and the Envoy proxy will do the weight-based traffic control. App Mesh supports Kubernetes and **Elastic Container Service** (ECS) as well as VMs. The following diagram shows the flow of traffic between services and configurations fetched from the control and data planes:

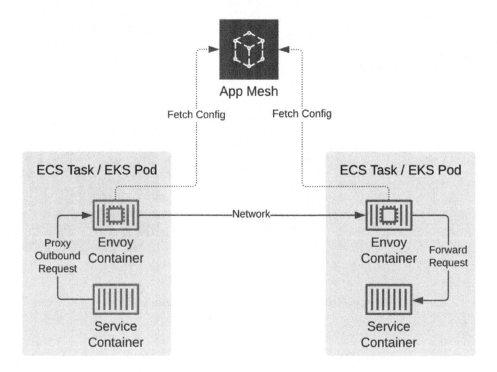

Figure 4.12 – App Mesh workflow

App Mesh follows a taxonomy of its own that is different from Kubernetes or ECS terminology. Let's take a closer look at the building blocks, which we will apply as a `yaml` file in the App Mesh control plane.

App Mesh is composed of the following building blocks, which we will understand with the following diagram:

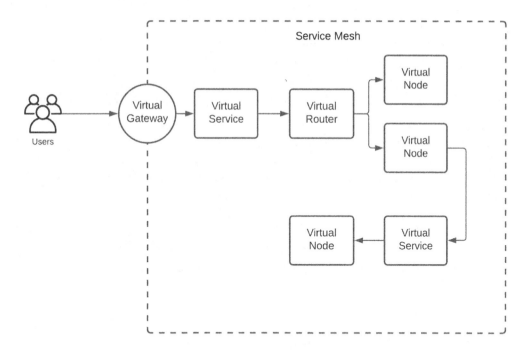

Figure 4.13 – App Mesh resources workflow

Let's take a look at the App Mesh resources:

- **Mesh**: A mesh is a logical boundary for network traffic of the microservices. We create a mesh on a platform such as EKS/ECS/VM using the AWS CLI or a mesh definition file. Once we create a mesh, we can create another component of App Mesh, through which we can use the App Mesh features.

- **Virtual service**: A virtual service is an abstraction of a real service. A virtual service calls to a virtual node or virtual router to reach out to another service. A virtual service will be reached out to via either a **virtual gateway** or a **virtual node**.

- **Virtual router**: A virtual router routes the traffic from the virtual service to the virtual Node depending on the request details, for example, a route-based transfer or weight-based request.

- **Virtual node**: A virtual Node is a pointer to the EKS/ECS service. It has three main parameters: the **listener**, **backend**, and **service discovery**. In the listener section, you must mention where the request is coming from and in the backend section, you must mention where the request will go. In service discovery, you must mention which EKS/ECS service it will point to.

- **Virtual gateway**: A virtual gateway allows any resources that are outside the mesh that wants to communicate with resources inside the mesh to access the data.

These are the main concepts of App Mesh using which we can use its features. Since we understand the basic concepts of App Mesh, let's now deploy a sample application on the EKS cluster that we created in the previous section, and then we'll enable a mesh on top of it.

Deploying an application (Product Catalog) on EKS

We will be deploying an application that comprises three microservices. These three services has been written in different languages. The main objective of deploying this application is to demonstrate how to use the features of App Mesh along with microservices. To understand App Mesh better, we need to understand the application. The three microservices are as follows:

- **Frontend**: This service (frontend-Node) shows the UI for the Product Catalog functionality. It has been developed in **Node.js** with **ES templating**.

- **Backend**: The backend is a REST API service (prodcatalog), developed in Python Flask, that does the following operations:

  - Adds a product to the catalog

  - Gets the product from the catalog

  - Gets the catalog details from the proddetail service

- **Catalog details backend**: This is also a REST API service (proddetail), developed in Node.js, and is used to get the catalog details.

The communication flow between these three services is as follows:

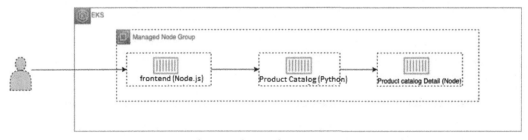

Figure 4.14 – Product Catalog application communication flow

Perform the following steps to deploy the application on EKS:

1. Clone the following repository to your terminal, from where you can also access EKS cluster:

```
$ git clone https://github.com/PacktPublishing/
Accelerating-DevSecOps-on-AWS.git
```
```
$ cd Accelerating-DevSecOps-on-AWS/chapter-04
```

2. Export the variable so that they're available when we execute AWS related commands:

```
$ export ACCOUNT_ID=<YOUR AWS ACCOUNT ID>
$ export AWS_REGION=us-east-1
$ export PROJECT_NAME=celestials
```

3. Now we need to create a namespace where we will deploy our services. We also need to create an **Identity and Access Management (IAM)** role and a service account for this namespace so that any resources in this namespace will have permission to provide the data to AWS X-Ray:

```
$ kubectl create namespace prodcatalog-ns
$ aws iam create-policy --policy-name
ProdEnvoyNamespaceIAMPolicy --policy-document file://
deployment/envoy-iam-policy.json
$ eksctl create iamserviceaccount --cluster celestials --
namespace prodcatalog-ns --name prodcatalog-envoy-proxies
--attach-policy-arn arn:aws:iam:$ACCOUNT_ID:policy/
ProdEnvoyNamespaceIAMPolicy --override-existing-
serviceaccounts --approve
# You can see the detail of service account
$ kubectl describe sa prodcatalog-envoy-proxies -n
prodcatalog-ns
```

4. The next thing we need to do is to build the services and create a Docker image, and after that, push it into **Elastic Container Registry (ECR)**. We will tag the Docker image with the application version:

```
$ aws ecr get-login-password --region $AWS_REGION |
docker login --username AWS --password-stdin $ACCOUNT_
ID.dkr.ecr.$AWS_REGION.amazonaws.com
$ export APP_VERSION=1.0
# This command is For Loop And incase you use docker
command with sudo pls add sudo in front of docker
command.
$ for app in catalog_detail product_catalog frontend_
node;  do
aws ecr describe-repositories --repository-name $PROJECT_
NAME/$app >/dev/null 2>&1 || \
aws ecr create-repository --repository-name $PROJECT_
NAME/$app >/dev/null TARGET=$ACCOUNT_ID.dkr.ecr.$AWS_
REGION.amazonaws.com/$PROJECT_NAME/$app:$APP_VERSION
```

```
docker build -t $TARGET apps/$app
docker push $TARGET
done
```

5. Once you are done with the preceding steps, you will be able to see the Docker images in ECR.

Figure 4.15 – Product Catalog container images

6. Now deploy the application in an EKS cluster:

```
$ envsubst < ./deployment/deploy_app.yaml | kubectl apply
-f -
deployment.apps/prodcatalog created
service/prodcatalog created
deployment.apps/proddetail created
service/proddetail created
deployment.apps/frontend-Node created
service/frontend-Node created
```

7. Once all the services are deployed, you can verify that using the following commands:

```
$ kubectl get deployments -n prodcatalog-ns
NAME                                  READY    UP-TO-
```

```
DATE     AVAILABLE    AGE    CONTAINERS       IMAGES
SELECTOR

deployment.apps/frontend-node    1/1     1
1          44h    frontend-Node    $ACCOUNT_ID.dkr.
ecr.us-west-2.amazonaws.com/frontend-node:4.6
app=frontend-node

deployment.apps/prodcatalog      1/1     1
1          22h    prodcatalog      $ACCOUNT_ID.dkr.
ecr.us-west-2.amazonaws.com/product-catalog:1.2
app=prodcatalog

deployment.apps/proddetail       1/1     1
1          44h    proddetail       $ACCOUNT_ID.dkr.
ecr.us-west-2.amazonaws.com/product-detail:1.1
app=proddetail
```

```
$ kubectl get pods -n prodcatalog-ns
```

```
NAME                                       READY
STATUS    RESTARTS    AGE    IP             NODE
NOMINATED nODE    READINESS GATES

pod/frontend-node-77d64585d4-xxxx    1/1      Running    0
13h    192.168.X.6      ip-192-168-X-X.us-west-2.compute.
internal          <none>          <none>

pod/prodcatalog-98f7c5f87-xxxxx         1/1      Running    0
13h    192.168.X.17    fargate-ip-192-168-X-X.us-west-2.
compute.internal    <none>          <none>

pod/proddetail-5b558df99d-xxxxx         1/1      Running    0
18h    192.168.24.X    ip-192-168-X-X.us-west-2.compute.
internal              <none>          <none>
```

```
$ kubectl get services -n prodcatalog-ns
```

```
NAME                    TYPE
CLUSTER-IP        EXTERNAL-IP
PORT(S)           AGE    SELECTOR

service/frontend-node
ClusterIP         10.100.X.X     <none>
9000/TCP          44h    app=frontend-node

service/prodcatalog       ClusterIP      10.100.X.X    <none>
5000/TCP          41h    app=prodcatalog

service/proddetail        ClusterIP      10.100.X.X    <none>
3000/TCP          44h    app=proddetail
3000/TCP          103m
```

8. To verify that the application is working fine, we can do a remote session inside the frontend Pod and try to access the `prodcatalog` service:

```
$ frontendpod=$(kubectl get pods -n prodcatalog-ns -l
app=frontend-node -o jsonpath='{.items[].metadata.name}')
$ kubectl exec -it $frontendpod -c frontend-node -n
prodcatalog-ns bash
root@frontend-node-5cb6d556f5-9hthx:/usr/src/app# curl
http://prodcatalog.prodcatalog-ns.svc.cluster.local:5000/
products/
{
    "products": {},
    "details": {
        "version": "1",
        "vendors": [
            "ABC.com"
        ]
    }
}
```

9. To test the connectivity from the `prodcatalog` service to `proddetail`, connect to the `prodcatalog` Pod and curl to `proddetail`:

```
$ prodcat=$( kubectl get pods -n prodcatalog-ns -l
app=prodcatalog -o jsonpath='{.items[].metadata.name}')
$ kubectl exec -it $prodcat -c prodcatalog -n
prodcatalog-ns bash
root@prodcatalog-f94b67f59-nkgpf:/app# curl http://
proddetail.prodcatalog-ns.svc.cluster.local:3000/
catalogDetail
{"version":"1","vendors":["ABC.com"]}
```

We deployed an application with three services. In the next section, we will enable App Mesh, port the application to App Mesh, and do weight-based traffic control with the new version of the service.

Implementing traffic management

In this section of the chapter, we will enable a mesh in the EKS cluster. After that, we will create an App Mesh component, virtual service, virtual node, virtual router, and virtual gateway. We will also create another version of a service and perform weight-based traffic routing.

Installing the App Mesh controller

The following diagram shows the traffic flow if we enable App Mesh and create all of its components:

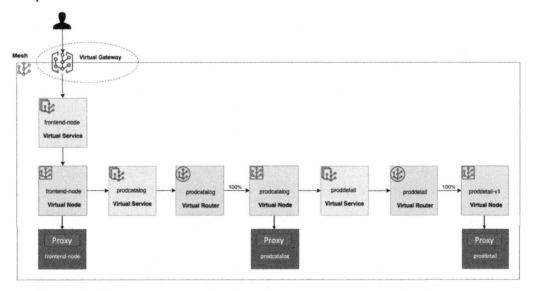

Figure 4.16 – Product Catalog application with service mesh enabled

Perform the following steps to create an App Mesh controller in an EKS cluster:

1. We will install the App Mesh controller on the EKS cluster using the Helm CLI. So, we need to install the Helm binary:

    ```
    $ curl -sSL https://raw.githubusercontent.com/helm/helm/
    master/scripts/get-helm-3 | bash
    $ helm version --short
    ```

2. Once Helm is installed, add the EKS charts repository:

    ```
    $ helm repo add eks https://aws.github.io/eks-charts
    ```

3. We will create a namespace where will install the App Mesh controller, then after that, we will do some pre-configuration, which includes creating **Custom Resource Definitions (CRDs)**, creating an IAM role, and tying it to the service account with the namespace, so that the App Mesh controller has the required permissions to interact with other AWS services:

    ```
    # Create the namespace
    $ kubectl create ns appmesh-system
    # Install the App Mesh CRDs
    ```

```
$ kubectl apply -k "github.com/aws/eks-charts/stable/
appmesh-controller//crds?ref=master"
# Download the IAM policy for AWS App Mesh Kubernetes
Controller
$ curl -o controller-iam-policy.json https://raw.
githubusercontent.com/aws/aws-app-mesh-controller-for-
k8s/master/config/iam/controller-iam-policy.json


# Create an IAM policy called
AWSAppMeshK8sControllerIAMPolicy
$ aws iam create-policy \
    --policy-name AWSAppMeshK8sControllerIAMPolicy \
    --policy-document file://controller-iam-policy.json
# Create an IAM role for the appmesh-controller service
account
$ eksctl create iamserviceaccount --cluster celestials \
    --namespace appmesh-system \
    --name appmesh-controller \
    --attach-policy-arn arn:aws:iam::$ACCOUNT_ID:policy/
AWSAppMeshK8sControllerIAMPolicy \
    --override-existing-serviceaccounts \
    --approve
```

4. Install the App Mesh controller using helm chart. We are also enabling X-Ray tracing, which we will learn more about in the next section:

```
$ helm upgrade -i appmesh-controller eks/appmesh-
controller \
--namespace appmesh-system \
--set region=$AWS_REGION \
--set serviceAccount.create=false \
--set serviceAccount.name=appmesh-controller \
--set tracing.enabled=true \
--set tracing.provider=x-ray
```

5. Confirm all the CRDs and resources are created in the appmesh-system namespace:

```
$ kubectl get crds | grep appmesh
gatewayroutes.appmesh.k8s.aws
```

```
2021-09-11T12:43:36Z
meshes.appmesh.k8s.aws
2021-09-11T12:43:38Z
virtualgateways.appmesh.k8s.aws
2021-09-11T12:43:40Z
virtualnodes.appmesh.k8s.aws
2021-09-11T12:43:42Z
virtualrouters.appmesh.k8s.aws
2021-09-11T12:43:44Z
virtualservices.appmesh.k8s.aws
2021-09-11T12:43:46Z
$ kubectl -n appmesh-system get all
NAME                                         READY      STATUS
RESTARTS     AGE
pod/appmesh-controller-6f57998dfb-jcs24      1/1        Running
0            9d
NAME                                              TYPE
CLUSTER-IP       EXTERNAL-IP     PORT(S)     AGE
service/appmesh-controller-webhook-service       ClusterIP
10.100.149.19    <none>          443/TCP     9d
NAME                                       READY     UP-TO-DATE
AVAILABLE     AGE
deployment.apps/appmesh-controller         1/1       1
1             9d
NAME                                                  DESIRED
CURRENT     READY     AGE
replicaset.apps/appmesh-controller-6f57998dfb         1
1           1         9d
```

At this stage, we have successfully installed an App Mesh controller on the EKS cluster. Now we port the Product Catalog application on App Mesh. But before that, we should understand the challenge that we are facing with the application and how App Mesh can overcome that challenge.

Currently, the Product Catalog application's frontend-node service is hardwired to make requests to the prodcatalog service and the prodcatalog service is hardwired to make requests to proddetail. So, every time we have to release a new version of the proddetail service, we have to release a new version of the prodcatalog service too to support both the new and old versions to point to its version-specific service endpoints. This works, but it's not optimal to maintain for the long term.

A more optimal way is to use a virtual service of the `proddetail` service and deploy the new version of `proddetail` (v2 being the new and v1 being the currently deployed one), and then route the traffic from `prodcatalog` to `proddetail` v1 incrementally to `proddetail` v2. Once we see that traffic flow is happening properly and the application is working fine with `proddetail` v2, then we will delete `prodetail` v1.

We will port the application on App Mesh by creating App Mesh resources, and then perform the previously mentioned configuration by taking the following steps:

1. Create the mesh in an EKS cluster. We also need to label the `prodcatalog-ns` namespace with annotations:

```
$ Kubectl apply -f deployment/mesh.yaml
namespace/prodcatalog-ns configured
mesh.appmesh.k8s.aws/prodcatalog-mesh created
```

2. You can confirm the mesh creation using the CLI as well as the UI:

```
$ kubectl describe mesh prodcatalog-mesh
```

You can see that the mesh is available in the AWS App Mesh console.

Figure 4.17 – App Mesh console showing the prodcatalog-mesh configuration

3. Create the App Mesh resources (virtual service, virtual node, and virtual router):

```
$ kubectl apply -f deployment/meshed_app.yaml
$ kubectl get virtualnode,virtualservice,virtualrouter -n
prodcatalog-ns
```

```
NAME                                                    ARN
AGE
```

```
virtualnode.appmesh.k8s.aws/frontend-node
arn:aws:appmesh:us-east-1:YOUR_ACCOUNT:mesh/prodcatalog-
mesh/virtualnode/frontend-node_prodcatalog-ns    10d
```

```
virtualnode.appmesh.k8s.aws/prodcatalog
arn:aws:appmesh:us-east-1:YOUR_ACCOUNT:mesh/prodcatalog-
mesh/virtualnode/prodcatalog_prodcatalog-ns       10d
```

```
virtualnode.appmesh.k8s.aws/proddetail-v1
arn:aws:appmesh:us-east-1:YOUR_ACCOUNT:mesh/prodcatalog-
mesh/virtualnode/proddetail-v1_prodcatalog-ns    10d
```

```
virtualnode.appmesh.k8s.aws/proddetail-v2
arn:aws:appmesh:us-east-1:YOUR_ACCOUNT:mesh/prodcatalog-
mesh/virtualnode/proddetail-v2_prodcatalog-ns    10d
```

```
NAME                                                    ARN
AGE
```

```
virtualservice.appmesh.k8s.aws/frontend-node
arn:aws:appmesh:us-east-1:YOUR_ACCOUNT:mesh/prodcatalog-
mesh/virtualService/frontend-node.prodcatalog-ns.svc.
cluster.local    10d
```

```
virtualservice.appmesh.k8s.aws/prodcatalog
arn:aws:appmesh:us-east-1:YOUR_ACCOUNT:mesh/prodcatalog-
mesh/virtualService/prodcatalog.prodcatalog-ns.svc.
cluster.local       10d
```

```
virtualservice.appmesh.k8s.aws/proddetail
arn:aws:appmesh:us-east-1:YOUR_ACCOUNT:mesh/prodcatalog-
mesh/virtualService/proddetail.prodcatalog-ns.svc.
cluster.local        10d
```

```
NAME                                                    ARN
AGE
```

```
virtualrouter.appmesh.k8s.aws/prodcatalog-router
arn:aws:appmesh:us-east-1:YOUR_ACCOUNT:mesh/prodcatalog-
mesh/virtualRouter/prodcatalog-router_prodcatalog-ns
10d
```

```
virtualrouter.appmesh.k8s.aws/proddetail-router
arn:aws:appmesh:us-east-1:YOUR_ACCOUNT:mesh/prodcatalog-
mesh/virtualRouter/proddetail-router_prodcatalog-ns
10d
```

The following figure shows all three resources are also visible in the App Mesh console:

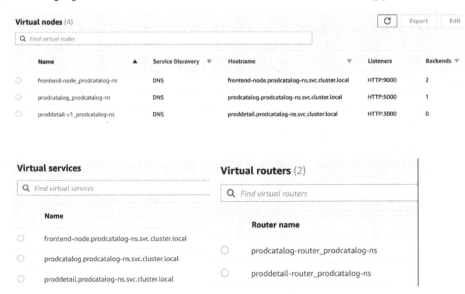

Figure 4.18 – App Mesh resources

4. Since we have already enabled the mesh and created the mesh resources, any workload resource that gets spun up in the `prodcatalog-ns` namespace will have a proxy sidecar along with it. But since we created our resources before we enabled the service mesh, we have to restart the deployment to get the proxy sidecar along with the application Pods:

```
$ kubectl -n prodcatalog-ns rollout restart deployment
prodcatalog
```

```
$ kubectl -n prodcatalog-ns rollout restart deployment
proddetail
```

```
$ kubectl -n prodcatalog-ns rollout restart deployment
frontend-node
```

5. We can verify the number of Pods in a deployment. Before restarting, the number of Pods would be 1/1, but after restarting the deployment will have three Pods, where one is the application Pod, one is the Envoy proxy, and one is the X-Ray agent:

```
NAME                                      READY
STATUS      RESTARTS    AGE     IP                NODE
NOMINATED NODE     READINESS GATES
pod/frontend-node-77d64585d4-xxxx    3/3        Running      0
13h    192.168.X.6        ip-192-168-X-X.us-west-2.compute.
internal             <none>                  <none>
```

```
pod/prodcatalog-98f7c5f87-xxxxx        3/3        Running    0
13h    192.168.X.17    fargate-ip-192-168-X-X.us-west-2.
compute.internal    <none>              <none>
```

```
pod/proddetail-5b558df99d-xxxxx        3/3        Running
0            18h    192.168.24.X    ip-192-168-X-X.us-west-2.
compute.internal                <none>              <none>
3000/TCP        44h    app=proddetail,version=v1
```

6. We need to create a virtual gateway, which will create an ingress service and expose it as the load balancer type. We will use the AWS network load balancer to route the external internet traffic:

```
$ kubectl apply -f deployment/virtual_gateway.yaml
virtualgateway.appmesh.k8s.aws/ingress-gw created
gatewayroute.appmesh.k8s.aws/gateway-route-frontend
created
service/ingress-gw created
deployment.apps/ingress-gw created
```

7. We can access the application via `loadbalancer` created through the ingress service:

```
export LB_NAME=$(kubectl get svc ingress-gw -n
prodcatalog-ns -o jsonpath="{.status.loadBalancer.
ingress[*].hostname}")
echo $LB_NAME
```

8. Access the `loadbalancer` endpoint in the browser and you will be able to access the application.

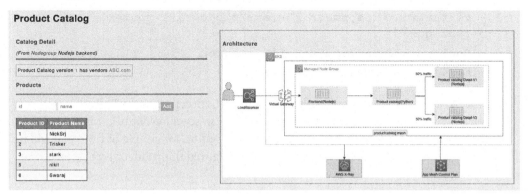

Figure 4.19 – Product Catalog application web page

9. Now let's deploy v2 of the `proddetail` service and distribute 50% of the traffic from v1 to v2. Go to the same folder where our application exists and run the following command to create a v2 Docker image and push it to ECR so that we can deploy on an EKS cluster:

```
$ aws ecr get-login-password --region $AWS_REGION |
docker login --username AWS --password-stdin $ACCOUNT_
ID.dkr.ecr.$AWS_REGION.amazonaws.com

$ PROJECT_NAME=celestials

$ export APP_VERSION_2=2.0

$ for app in catalog_detail; do
    aws ecr describe-repositories --repository-name
$PROJECT_NAME/$app >/dev/null 2>&1 || \
    aws ecr create-repository --repository-name $PROJECT_
NAME/$app >/dev/null
    TARGET=$ACCOUNT_ID.dkr.ecr.$AWS_REGION.amazonaws.
com/$PROJECT_NAME/$app:$APP_VERSION_2
    cd apps/$app
    docker build -t $TARGET -f version2/Dockerfile .
    docker push $TARGET
done
```

10. You can deploy the `proddetail-v2` service as well as the `appmesh` canary configuration to distribute the traffic:

```
$ envsubst < ./deployment/canary.yaml | kubectl apply -f
-
virtualnode.appmesh.k8s.aws/proddetail-v2 created
virtualrouter.appmesh.k8s.aws/proddetail-router
configured
deployment.apps/proddetail2 created
service/proddetail2 created
```

11. Now we can verify the equal traffic distribution between v1 and v2 by again refreshing the `loadbalancer` endpoint. You can see a new button for the canary deployment. Click on the Canary Deployment button for couple of time you will be able to see different vendor name which is configured in proddetail-v2 service.

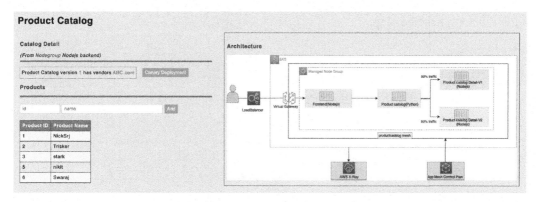

Figure 4.20 – Product Catalog application with proddetail-v2

In this section, we have installed an App Mesh controller and ported an application into App Mesh. We then deployed v2 of the `proddetail` service and distributed half of the traffic between v1 and v2. Now, to trace the traffic flow between all the services, we can use the **AWS X-Ray** service, which we will explore in the next section.

Getting observability using X-Ray

One of the main advantages of using a service mesh is to get observability of the communication between the services. It helps for troubleshooting as well as visibility purposes. The AWS X-Ray service is responsible for helping developers and DevOps engineers quickly understand how application services are performing. When it's integrated with AWS App Mesh, it makes for a more powerful analytical tool.

We use the X-Ray SDK to instrument our application code and share all the incoming and outgoing requests to the X-Ray daemon, which is running as the third container of the deployment. We already installed App Mesh with the X-Ray feature in *step 4* of the previous section. We can see the service mapping by performing the following steps:

1. Log in to the AWS console and go to the X-Ray service page.

2. Click on **Service map**.

Figure 4.21 – Service map of Product Catalog application services in AWS X-Ray

The preceding service graph shows the traffic in the following manner when the request comes to `loadbalancer`:

1. When the request comes to `loadbalancer`, it routes the traffic to the `ingress-gw` Envoy proxy of the virtual gateway, and then it gets routed to the Envoy proxy of `frontend-Node`.

2. Then, the Envoy proxy of `frontend-Node` routes the traffic to the `frontend-Node` service.

3. The `frontend-node` service would like to talk to the `prodcatalog` service, so instead of going directly, the Envoy proxy of `frontend-node` will connect to the Envoy proxy of the `prodcatalog` service.

4. The Envoy proxy of the `prodcatalog` service will route the traffic to the `prodcatalog` service.

5. Then, the `prodcatalog` service makes a request to `proddetail v1` to retrieve the catalog detail information for version 1.

6. Instead of directly reaching out to the `proddetail v1` service, the request goes to the `prodcatalog` Envoy proxy and the proxy routes the call to the `proddetail` Envoy proxy.

7. Then, the Envoy proxy of `prodetail v1` receives the request and routes it to the `proddetail v1` service.

8. Similar steps of the workflow happen when `proddetail v2` is accessed when we click on the **Canary Deployment** button.

You can get trace details from the service by clicking on the circular **prodcatalog-mesh/frontend-node_prodcatalog-ns** field and then clicking on **View traces**.

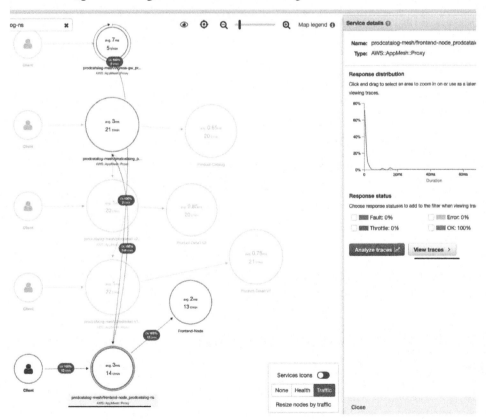

Figure 4.22 – Service details of frontend-node service

Once you click on **View traces**, you will see the whole request list routed from
`frontend-node`.

URL	AVG RESPONSE TIME	% OF TRACES	RESPONSE
http://prodcatalog.prodcatalog-ns.svc.cluster.local:5000/products/	12.1 ms	19.15%	9 OK, 0 Throttled, 0 Errors, 0 Faults
http://frontend-node.prodcatalog-ns.svc.cluster.local/	18.5 ms	17.02%	8 OK, 0 Throttled, 0 Errors, 0 Faults
http://frontend-node.prodcatalog-ns.svc.cluster.local/css/styles.css	2.3 ms	12.77%	6 OK, 0 Throttled, 0 Errors, 0 Faults
http://frontend-node.prodcatalog-ns.svc.cluster.local/architecture.png	2.3 ms	12.77%	6 OK, 0 Throttled, 0 Errors, 0 Faults
http://frontend-node.prodcatalog-ns.svc.cluster.local/stats/prometheus	3.0 ms	8.51%	4 OK, 0 Throttled, 0 Errors, 0 Faults

Trace list

ID	AGE	METHOD	RESPONSE	RESPONSE TIME	URL	CLIENT IP	ANNOTATIONS
0f160af24b04874993c8	2.1 min	GET	200	14.0 ms	http://prodcatalog.prodcatalog-...	192.168.71.41	6
daa5f6445309572aaGb	2.3 min	GET	200	19.0 ms	http://frontend-node.prodcatalo...	192.168.86.197	6
8d9f21fa496d9a79da09	5.0 min	GET	200	11.0 ms	http://prodcatalog.prodcatalog-...	192.168.71.41	6
ecbf7752f519df95de8h	2.4 min	POST	200	5.0 ms	http://prodcatalog.prodcatalog-...	192.168.71.41	6
8352f07643c5805309b9	2.6 min	GET	200	12.0 ms	http://prodcatalog.prodcatalog-...	192.168.71.41	6
9ba2b6534f0af5866d7f	5.0 min	GET	200	18.0 ms	http://frontend-node.prodcatalo...	192.168.86.197	6
72eff050464ca71c09a6	5.0 min	GET	200	12.0 ms	http://prodcatalog.prodcatalog-...	192.168.71.41	6
c6b0823d4b9b2f683115	2.1 min	GET	200	19.0 ms	http://frontend-node.prodcatalo...	192.168.39.121	6
8902f49b4c76b10B164c	5.0 min	GET	200	18.0 ms	http://frontend-node.prodcatalo...	192.168.86.197	6
c6c56094Bdda2f53dad6	6.0 min	GET	200	12.0 ms	http://prodcatalog.prodcatalog-...	192.168.71.41	6

Figure 4.23 – Trace list of frontend-node service

Click on `http://prodcatalog.prodcatalog-ns.svc.cluster.`
`local:5000/products/` and then click on any trace list to see the details of the trace.
The details of the trace look something like the following:

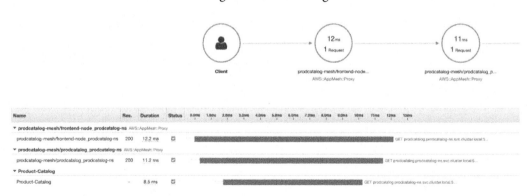

Figure 4.24 – Trace details of frontend-node service

We saw how to trace the request between services in this section. In the next section,
we will implement mTLS authentication between services.

Enabling mTLS authentication between services

In this last section, we will enable TLS encryption with mutual authentication between
service endpoints in App Mesh using X.509 certificates. We will be using a separate
application called **colorapp** and deploying it on the same EKS cluster. Before we start
enabling mTLS, let's understand what mTLS is and why we need it.

You must have encountered TLS almost 100 times today. Whenever you are visiting a website with HTTPS as the protocol, it uses TLS. TLS is mostly used whenever your web server is in the public domain and a client wants to request the data from the web server. Then, the client will ask the server to identify itself, and the server provides a certificate, which is signed by a **Certificate Authority (CA)**, and the client trusts the CA. This way, a TLS handshake takes place and the client can identify the server and create a secure HTTPS transfer.

What if the server also wants to verify the identity of the client? In most cases, the public server doesn't bother to verify the identity of the client, because they are an internet-facing server anyway. But if your server is not internet facing, stays within the enterprise network, and needs only a selected client to request its services, then in this case, the server needs to verify the identity of the client before making any HTTP transaction. That's why there is an *m*, which stands for *mutual*, in mTLS, meaning both the server and client need to verify each other's identities.

mTLS is mostly used when you need to expose your API so that some of your partner companies can use your data on a subscription basis. For example, you might encounter an application (*App A*) that compares the charges of all taxi companies, such as Uber and Lyft, and gives recommendations for the one to use that is cheapest. *App A* subscribes to use the API of Uber and Lyft and uses its own algorithm to recommend the best taxi. Uber and Lyft must have set the mTLS to only provide the data to *App A*. This is one example of an inter-company data transaction. Most of the time, mTLS is used during east-west data transactions, meaning between services deployed in Kubernetes or any other microservice orchestrator.

In the previous section, we learned how App Mesh works. We saw how in App Mesh the traffic is mediated and terminated via an Envoy proxy, which means our application code is not responsible for handling and negotiating a TLS-encrypted connection. An Envoy proxy negotiates and terminates the TLS on behalf of the application. This feature also helps developers by removing the headache of managing certificates in application code.

There are two possible certificate sources for mTLS authentication:

- **Filesystem**: Certificates will be in the local filesystem of the Envoy proxy. To provide certificates to the Envoy proxy, you need to provide the file path of the certificate chain and a private key to the App Mesh API.

- **Envoy's Secret Discovery Service (SDS)**: You need to bring your own sidecar container that implements SDS and sends the certificates to the envoy.

We will configure an envoy to use the file-based strategy via Kubernetes Secrets to set up certificates by performing the following steps:

1. We will be deploying four services (`frontend`, `blue`, `green`, and `red`) to demonstrate mTLS between the services. We will try to call the `blue` and `green` services from the frontend and verify the mTLS authentication between them. To verify the mTLS, we need to create two separate CAs. The first CA will be used to sign the certificate for the `blue` app and the frontend. The second CA will be used to sign the certificate for the `green` app:

    ```
    $ export AWS_ACCOUNT_ID=<Your account id>
    $ export AWS_DEFAULT_REGION=us-east-1
    $ cd mtls-file-based
    $ ./mtls/certs.sh
    ```

2. This script will generate some files:

    -   `*_cert.pem`: These are the public key of the certificates.

    -   `*_key.pem`: These are the private key of the certificates.

    -   `*_cert_chain`: These files are a list of public certificates that are used to sign the private key.

    -   `ca1_1_ca_2_bundle.pem`: This contains public certificates for both CAs.

    You can verify that the `blue` and frontend certificates are signed by `CA1` and the `green` certificate is signed by `CA2`:

    ```
    $ openssl verify -verbose -CAfile ca_1_cert.pem colorapp-
    blue_cert.pem
    colorapp-blue_cert.pem: OK
    $ openssl verify -verbose -CAfile ca_1_cert.pem front_
    cert.pem
    front_cert.pem: OK
    $ openssl verify -verbose -CAfile ca_2_cert.pem colorapp-
    green_cert.pem
    colorapp-green_cert.pem: OK
    ```

3. Now we will store these certificates as a Kubernetes Secret so that we can mount them in the Envoy proxy containers:

    ```
    $ ./mtls/deploy.sh
    $ kubectl get secrets -n mtls
    ```

NAME	TYPE
DATA AGE	
colorapp-blue-tls	Opaque
3 4s	
colorapp-green-tls	Opaque
3 3s	
default-token-jtd47	kubernetes.io/service-account-token
3 5s	
front-ca1-ca2-tls	Opaque
3 4s	
front-ca1-tls	Opaque
3 4s	

4. Once we have the certificates stored in a Kubernetes Secret, we need to deploy the application services, create a service mesh, then create four virtual nodes (frontend, blue, green, and red), one virtual service (color), and one virtual router (color). The virtual node frontend is configured with the virtual service (color) as the backend. The color virtual service has a virtual router (color) as the provider. The color virtual router has three routes configured, which routes to the nodeblue, green, and red virtual nodes, respectively. The following script will create all the mesh resources for you:

```
$ ./mesh.sh up
```

5. The following is the specification of the blue virtual Node, where you can see how we have mentioned the certificate details:

```
apiVersion: appmesh.k8s.aws/v1beta2
kind: VirtualNode
metadata:
  name: blue
  namespace: ${APP_NAMESPACE}
spec:
  podSelector:
    matchLabels:
      app: color
      version: blue
  listeners:
    - portMapping:
        port: 8080
```

```
          protocol: http
      healthCheck:
        protocol: http
        path: '/ping'
        healthyThreshold: 2
        unhealthyThreshold: 2
        timeoutMillis: 2000
        intervalMillis: 5000
      tls:
        mode: STRICT
        certificate:
          file:
            certificateChain: /certs/colorapp-blue_cert_
chain.pem
            privateKey: /certs/colorapp-blue_key.pem
        validation:
          trust:
            file:
              certificateChain: /certs/ca_1_cert.pem
          subjectAlternativeNames:
            match:
              exact:
              - front.${APP_NAMESPACE}.svc.cluster.local
  serviceDiscovery:
    dns:
        hostname: color-blue.${APP_NAMESPACE}.svc.cluster.
local
```

6. The following is the specification of the blue app, where you can see how we have mentioned the certificate secret using the appmesh.k8s.aws/secretMounts annotation:

```
apiVersion: apps/v1
kind: Deployment
metadata:
  name: blue
  namespace: ${APP_NAMESPACE}
spec:
```

```
    replicas: 1
    selector:
      matchLabels:
        app: color
        version: blue
    template:
      metadata:
        annotations:
          appmesh.k8s.aws/secretMounts: "colorapp-blue-
tls:/certs/"
          appmesh.k8s.aws/sds: "disabled"
        labels:
          app: color
          version: blue
      spec:
        containers:
        - name: app
          image: ${COLOR_APP_IMAGE}
          ports:
            - containerPort: 8080
          env:
            - name: "COLOR"
              value: "blue"
```

7. Once we have the mesh deployed, let's get the Pod identities, which we will use in upcoming commands:

```
$ FRONT_POD=$(kubectl get pod -l "app=front" -n mtls
--output=jsonpath={.items..metadata.name})
$ BLUE_POD=$(kubectl get pod -l "version=blue" -n mtls
--output=jsonpath={.items..metadata.name})
$ RED_POD=$(kubectl get pod -l "version=red" -n mtls
--output=jsonpath={.items..metadata.name})
$ GREEN_POD=$(kubectl get pod -l "version=green" -n mtls
--output=jsonpath={.items..metadata.name})
```

8. Let's verify mTLS by making traffic from the frontend to the color application:

```
# deploying curler pod to create traffic within cluster
$ kubectl run -i --tty curler --image=public.ecr.aws/
```

```
k8ml13p1/alpine/curler:latest -rm
# curl -H "color_header: blue" front.mtls.svc.cluster.
local:8080/; echo;
Blue
###You are seeing a SUCCESSFUL response
```

9. When we tried to request the blue service via the frontend, we got a success response, as the frontend is configured with CA1 in its validation context and blue is signed by CA1. Now let's try to access the green service from the frontend:

```
# deploying curler pod to create traffic within cluster
$ kubectl run -i --tty curler --image=public.ecr.aws/
k8ml13p1/alpine/curler:latest -rm
# curl -H "color_header: green" front.mtls.svc.cluster.
local:8080/; echo;
Connection refused
###You are seeing an error response
```

10. The frontend service is unable to read or respond to the green service because the green service certificate is signed by CA2, which is not configured in the frontend service.

11. Let's change the frontend client policy to allow the certificates from both CA1 and CA2:

```
$ SKIP_IMAGES=1 ./mesh.sh addGreen
# deploying curler pod to create traffic within cluster
$ kubectl run -i --tty curler --image=public.ecr.aws/
k8ml13p1/alpine/curler:latest -rm
# curl -H "color_header: green" front.mtls.svc.cluster.
local:8080/; echo;
Green
###You are seeing a SUCCESSFUL response
```

12. You can see how to enable mTLS between services using a file-based method. In this example, we generated the certificates and CAs by ourselves. But there will be a management issue when you need to rotate the certificate and the secrets. That's why the recommended way is to use **Amazon Certificate Manager (ACM)** as a private certificate provider and manager. You can refer to the following link: https://aws.amazon.com/blogs/security/how-to-use-acm-private-ca-for-enabling-mtls-in-aws-app-mesh/ to dig deep.

Summary

App Mesh is an important component when we are deploying our services in an orchestration system such as EKS. In this chapter, we saw the architecture of App Mesh and understood all the terminologies and its functionality. We deployed an EKS cluster and enabled App Mesh in it. After that, we deployed a polyglot application on EKS and then visualized the trace details using X-Ray. We also enabled mTLS between the services to secure the communication. We did all these things in a non-production EKS cluster. In the next chapter, we will learn how to deploy a fully private production-grade EKS cluster.

5

Securing Private EKS Cluster for Production

This chapter will walk you through all the planning you require to create a production-grade private EKS cluster. It will cover most of the necessary topics, such as the **Container Network Interface (Virtual Private Cloud CNI)**, **network policy**, **logging**, **security**, and **observability** for EKS clusters. It includes the implementation of a service mesh, and some must-have add-ons, such as **Cluster Autoscaler, IAM Role for Service Accounts (IRSA)**, and the **Elastic Block Store-Container Storage Interface (EBS-CSI)** driver. We will verify whether Kubernetes is deployed securely using **kubescape** and **kube-bench**. We will apply policy and governance using **Open Policy Agent (OPA) Gatekeeper**. After that, we will perform the backup and restore of a StatefulSet using **Velero**.

In this chapter, we are going to cover the following main sections:

- Planning your fully private EKS cluster

- Creating your EKS cluster

- Deploying add-ons

- Enabling the App Mesh sidecar injector

- Kubernetes hardening guidance using kubescape

- Policy and governance using OPA Gatekeeper

- Deploying a stateful application using Helm

- Backup and restore using Velero

Technical requirements

To get started, you will need an AWS account and admin-level privileges for that account, because we will be interacting with IAM services. You will find all the definitions and source code in the `chapter-05` folder of this repository here: `https://github.com/PacktPublishing/Accelerating-DevSecOps-on-AWS.git`.

Planning your fully private EKS cluster

In this section of the chapter, we will outline the points that are required to create a secure, scalable, and highly available production-grade EKS cluster. We created an EKS cluster using `eksctl` in the previous chapter, which was a two-node Kubernetes cluster. We can't use that cluster to deploy a production workload. Let's understand the requirements for an EKS cluster that can support a production workload. The following considerations need to be made, which will be covered in planning:

- **Networking**: Network planning will be the backbone of your EKS cluster. You need to understand all the pain points related to VPC CNI and VPC endpoints. We use VPC CNI because it has wonderful IP address management with the IP address available within the VPC. This means even the Pods get the IP address of the subnet. VPC endpoints will be used for the private cluster, where the worker nodes sitting in the private subnet need to talk to the EKS cluster and other AWS services.

- **Node management and tenancy**: Suppose you have an application that needs a high **Graphics Processing Unit (GPU)** but the rest of the application doesn't need that. How can you isolate the application running from the GPU-based worker node or non-GPU-based worker node? You can use a node group and tag it. Using the node group tag, you can restrict an application to schedule in a specific node. You can use a namespace for the tenancy.

- **Authentication and authorization**: For authentication purposes, you can associate IAM **OpenID Connect (OIDC)** and for authorization, you can use RBAC. For service account permission, **IRSA** is recommended.

- **Security and policies**: It is highly recommended to implement network policies in which one Pod can be restricted to only talking to non-necessary Pods. We can leverage tools such as kubescape and kube-bench to get recommendations on the security vulnerabilities of the cluster.

- **Logging and observability**: You should enable control plane logging, which is written in the AWS CloudWatch service. The worker node logs can be exported via a Fluentd agent and passed to Kibana for visibility purposes. You can also leverage the AWS X-Ray service via App Mesh to get visibility of the service communication flow.

- **Design for failure**: You should always make sure that if the worker nodes go down, the application is still available by scheduling another worker node or creating a new worker node via an **Auto Scaling Group (ASG)**. You should always test the chaos engineering concept before rolling it out in production.

- **DR strategy/backup and restore**: This is one of the critical components and you should always keep a backup of the production cluster. You can leverage tools such as **Velero** to create a backup and restore.

In the next section of the chapter, we will be creating a fully private EKS cluster.

Creating your EKS cluster

In this section of the chapter, we will be creating a fully private EKS cluster manually so that we will become aware of each small component integration. Let's get started.

VPC, subnet, and endpoint creation

The first thing to do is to create a network backbone for the EKS infrastructure. You need to create a VPC, three private subnets, and one public subnet. The three private subnets will be dedicated to the EKS-managed worker node. We will spin up a bastion server in the public subnet to connect to the private EKS cluster endpoint. Perform the following steps to create a VPC and public subnet:

1. Go to the VPC console. You will be at the VPC dashboard. Click on **Your VPCs** on the left-hand side. Then click on **Create VPC** on the right-hand side.

Figure 5.1 – VPC console

2. You will see the **Create VPC** page. In **VPC settings**, provide the following details:

    I.   **Name tag**: `dso-eks-vpc`.

    II.   **IPv4 CIDR block**: `10.0.0.0/22`.

    III.   Select **No IPv6 CIDR block**.

    IV.   **Tenancy: Default**.

Then click on **Create VPC**.

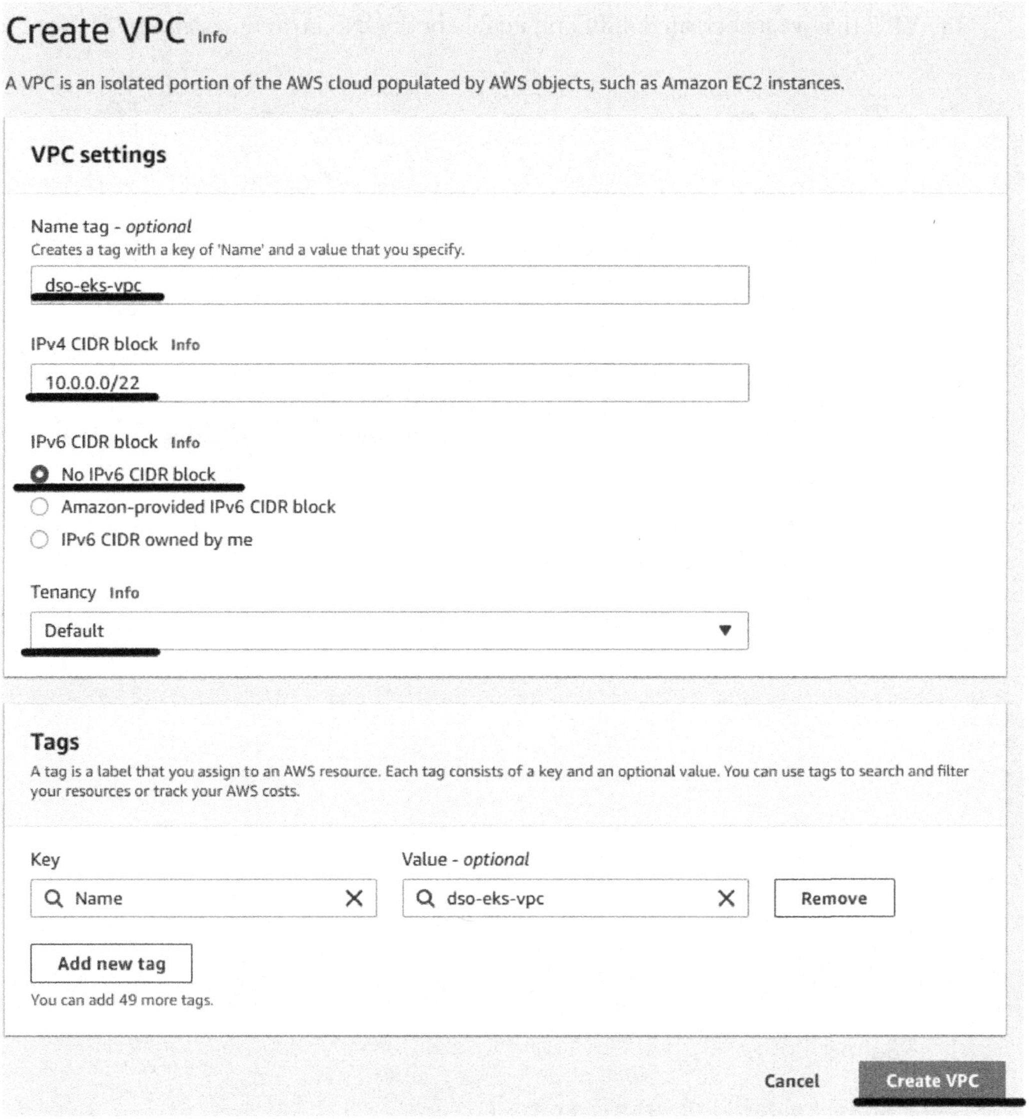

Create VPC Info

A VPC is an isolated portion of the AWS cloud populated by AWS objects, such as Amazon EC2 instances.

VPC settings

Name tag - *optional*
Creates a tag with a key of 'Name' and a value that you specify.

dso-eks-vpc

IPv4 CIDR block Info

10.0.0.0/22

IPv6 CIDR block Info
● No IPv6 CIDR block
○ Amazon-provided IPv6 CIDR block
○ IPv6 CIDR owned by me

Tenancy Info

Default ▼

Tags

A tag is a label that you assign to an AWS resource. Each tag consists of a key and an optional value. You can use tags to search and filter your resources or track your AWS costs.

Key | Value - *optional* |
Q Name ✕ | Q dso-eks-vpc ✕ | Remove

Add new tag

You can add 49 more tags.

Cancel   Create VPC

Figure 5.2 – Creating a VPC

3. Once your VPC is created, then you need to create four subnets. But before that, we need to enable DNS support and DNS hostnames for the VPC. Right-click on the VPC that we just created. Edit and enable both DNS hostnames and resolution.

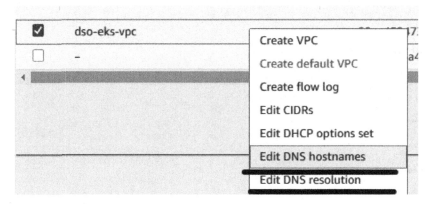

Figure 5.3 – Enabling DNS for hostnames and resolution

4. Now proceed to create subnets in the VPC that we just created. Click on **Subnets** on the left-hand side. Then click on **Create subnet**.

Figure 5.4 – Subnet list

5. On the **Create subnet** page, select **dso-eks-vpc** for the VPC ID. In **Subnet settings**, we can enter multiple subnet details to create in one go. Enter the subnet settings details as follows:

I.   Subnet 1 of 1

ii.   **Subnet name**: dso-eks-pvtsnet-1a

iii.   **Availability Zone**: us-east-1a

iv.   **IPv4 CIDR block**: 10.0.1.0/24

You can click on **Add new subnet** to enter the settings of other subnets.

   V.   Subnet 2 of 2

       i. **Subnet name**: `dso-eks-pvtsnet-1b`

      ii. **Availability Zone**: `us-east-1b`

    iii. **IPv4 CIDR block**: `10.0.2.0/24`

  IV.   Subnet 3 of 3

       i. **Subnet name**: `dso-eks-pvtsnet-1c`

      ii. **Availability Zone**: `us-east-1c`

    iii. **IPv4 CIDR block**: `10.0.3.0/24`

  IV.   Subnet 4 of 4

       i. **Subnet name**: `dso-eks-pubsnet-1a`

      ii. **Availability Zone**: `us-east-1a`

    iii. **IPv4 CIDR block**: `10.0.0.0/28`

6.   Click on **Create subnet** and the subnet will be created.

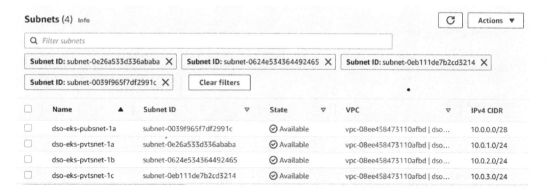

Figure 5.5 – New subnet list

7. We have created the `dso-eks-pubsnet-1a` subnet to use it as a public subnet. But to make it a public subnet, you need to create an **Internet Gateway (IGW)** and then modify the route table. Go to **Internet Gateways** on the left-hand side and click on **Create internet gateway**.

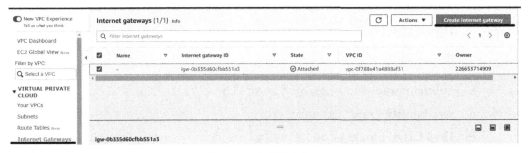

Figure 5.6 – IGWs list

8. Give it the name `dso-eks-igw` and click on **Create internet gateway**.

Figure 5.7 – Creating an IGW

9. Go to the **dso-eks-igw** page and click on **Actions**, then **Attach to VPC**.

VPC > Internet gateways > igw-0cb2bce907c6240d9
igw-0cb2bce907c6240d9 / dso-eks-igw
Actions
Attach to VPC
Detach from VPC
Manage tags
Delete
Details Info
Internet gateway ID
igw-0cb2bce907c6240d9
State
Detached
VPC ID
-
Owner
226653714909

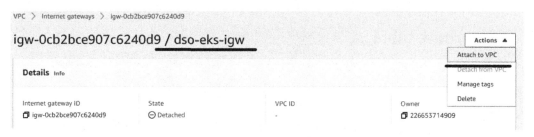

Figure 5.8 – Newly created IGW

10. Select **dso-eks-vpc** in **Available VPCs**. Click on **Attach internet gateway** so that the VPC's subnet will be able to use the IGW.

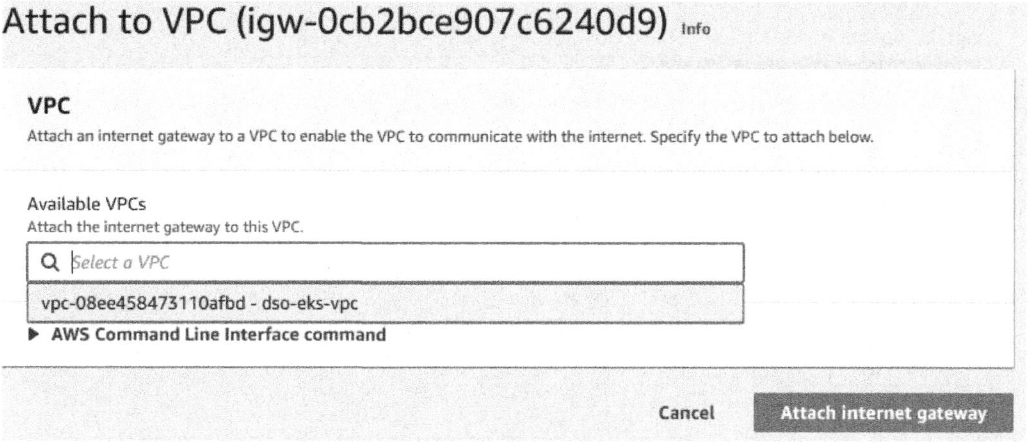

Attach to VPC (igw-0cb2bce907c6240d9) Info
VPC
Attach an internet gateway to a VPC to enable the VPC to communicate with the internet. Specify the VPC to attach below.
Available VPCs
Attach the internet gateway to this VPC.
Select a VPC
vpc-08ee458473110afbd - dso-eks-vpc
AWS Command Line Interface command
Cancel
Attach internet gateway

Figure 5.9 – Attaching an an IGW to VPC

11. Now you need to create a route table and edit the routes by adding **IGW**, and then associate the public subnet with the route. Go to **Route Tables** on the left-hand side. Click on **Create route table**.

12. Enter the route table name as `dso-eks-rtb` and select **dso-eks-vpc**. Click on **Create route table**.

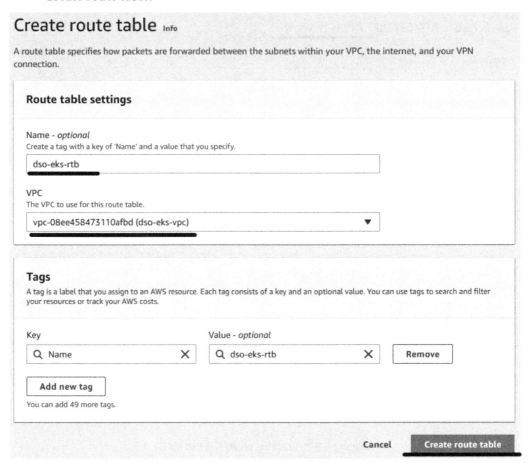

Figure 5.10 – Creating a route table

13. Once you are on the **dso-eks-rtb** page, click on **Edit routes**.

Figure 5.11 – Route table routing list

14. On the **Edit routes** page, click on **Add route**. Enter 0.0.0.0/0 in **Destination** and select the IGW in **Target**.

Figure 5.12 – Editing route table routes

15. Once you have modified the route, go to the **Subnet associations** tab and click on **Edit subnet associations**. Select **dso-eks-pubsnet-1a** and click on **Save associations**.

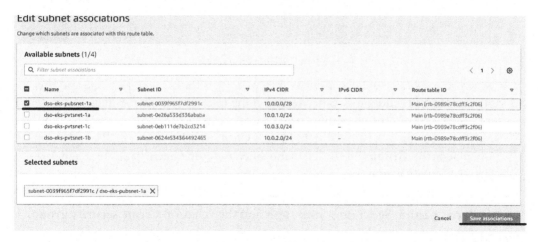

Figure 5.13 – Associating a subnet in the route table

16. Now tag all three private subnets – `dso-eks-pvtsnet-1a`, `dso-eks-pvtsnet-1b`, and `dso-eks-pvtsnet-1c` – with **Key** as `kubernetes.io/role/internal-elb` and **Value** as 1.

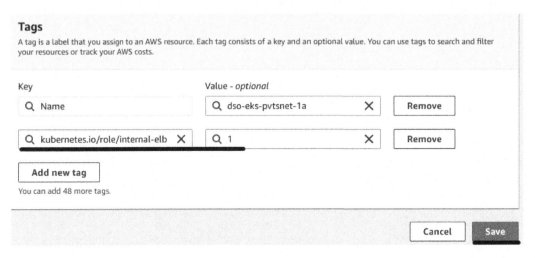

Figure 5.14 – Tagging the subnet

17. Now you need to create two security groups. One is for the control plane and the other is for VPC endpoints. Since we are going to create a fully private EKS cluster, we need to create VPC endpoints using an EKS cluster that can integrate with other AWS services such as CloudWatch, **Elastic Container Registry (ECR)**, and so on. Go to **Security Groups** on the left-hand side, under the **Security** section. Click on **Create security group**.

18. On the **Create security group** page, give the security group name as `dso-eks-controlplane`. Select `dso-eks-vpc` and then click on **Create security group**.

19. You need to create another security group and give the name as `dso-eks-endpoint`, in `dso-eks-vpc`. After that, click on **Edit inbound rules**. Click on **Add rule** to add a firewall rule. Select **HTTPS** in **Type**, mention the self-security group ID, as shown in the following figure, and click on **Save rules**.

Figure 5.15 – Editing a security group inbound rule

20. Once we have both security groups in place, we need to create VPC endpoints for the following services:

   I.   EC2

   II.   ECR.api

   III.   ECR.dkr

   IV.   S3 Gateway

   V.   Logs

   VI.   Sts

   VII.   ElasticloadbalancingAutoscaling

   VIII. Appmesh-envoy-management

   IX.   X-Ray

21. These steps will only show how to create an endpoint for EC2. You need to follow the same steps to create an endpoint for the rest of the remaining services. Go to **Endpoints** on the left-hand side of the VPC console and click on **Create Endpoint**.

Figure 5.16 – VPC endpoint console

22. On the **Create Endpoint** page, you need to search for ec2 under **Service Name**. Select the EC2 service name and then select the VPC that we created, dso-eks-vpc. Then select all the private subnets (dso-eks-pvtsnet-1a, dso-eks-pvtsnet-1b, and dso-eks-pvtsnet-1c) that we created in the VPC. In **Security group**, select the **dso-eks-endpoint** security group. You can give the Key: Name and have value as EC2-VPCE. Then click on **Create endpoint**.

Figure 5.17 – Creating an endpoint for the EC2 service

23. After a few minutes, your endpoint status will be available. Now you need to create the endpoint for the rest of the services mentioned in the list in *Step 20*.

Figure 5.18 – EC2-VPCE

24. Once you have all the endpoints created, your endpoint console should look like the following figure:

☐	EC2-VPCE	vpce-00b96da847...	vpc-0e8021b6fa8...	com.amazonaws.us-east-1.ec2	Interface	available
☐	ECR-API-V...	vpce-0197f2ba6bf...	vpc-0e8021b6fa8...	com.amazonaws.us-east-1.ecr....	Interface	available
☐	ECR-DKR-...	vpce-059d385233f...	vpc-0e8021b6fa8...	com.amazonaws.us-east-1.ecr....	Interface	available
☐	S3-VPCE-G...	vpce-02320e4efa8...	vpc-0e8021b6fa8...	com.amazonaws.us-east-1.s3	Gateway	available
☐	LOGS-VPCE	vpce-0473284408...	vpc-0e8021b6fa8...	com.amazonaws.us-east-1.logs	Interface	available
☐	STS-VPCE	vpce-062cc25607...	vpc-0e8021b6fa8...	com.amazonaws.us-east-1.sts	Interface	available
☐	ELSBAL-V...	vpce-0a24ff8511c...	vpc-0e8021b6fa8...	com.amazonaws.us-east-1.ela...	Interface	available
☐	ASG-VPCE	vpce-01a61cf383e...	vpc-0e8021b6fa8...	com.amazonaws.us-east-1.aut...	Interface	available
☐	APPMESH-...	vpce-01953b0c5f2...	vpc-0e8021b6fa8...	com.amazonaws.us-east-1.app...	Interface	available
☐	XRAY-VPCE	vpce-070b38a5f66...	vpc-0e8021b6fa8...	com.amazonaws.us-east-1.xray	Interface	available

Figure 5.19 – VPCE list

So far, you have only set up the network backbone for the EKS cluster. Now let's go ahead and spin up a bastion server, in **dso-eks-vpc** in the public subnet, through which we will be accessing the private EKS cluster.

Bastion server

You need to spin up a bastion server in the same VPC where your private EKS cluster exists. Since we have created **dso-eks-vpc** for the private EKS cluster, we will launch a bastion server in the same VPC in one of the public subnets. Perform the following steps to launch a bastion server:

1. Go to the **EC2 Dashboard** and click on **Launch instance**.

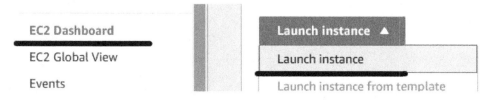

Figure 5.20 – EC2 console

2. On the AMI page, select **Amazon Linux 2 AMI (HVM)**. Choose **t2.micro** as the instance type and click **Next**. For **Network**, select **dso-eks-vpc**, and for **Subnet**, select **dso-eks-pubsnet-1a**. In **Auto-assign Public IP**, select **Enable** and then click on **Next**. In **Storage**, give the root volume as **15 GB** and click on **Next**. In **Tag**, give **Key** as **Name** and **Value** as **dso-eks-bastion** and then click on **Next**. Give **Security group name** as **dso-eks-bastionSG** and provide the firewall rule as **SSH** to your home/office IP. After that, click on **Review and Launch**. Then create a new key pair to access your bastion server via SSH. Give the name as **dso-eks-servkey** and click on **Download Key Pair**, then on **Launch instances**. After a few minutes, you will be able to see the bastion server in the **Instances** list.

Figure 5.21 – EC2 instance list

3. Now connect to this server via SSH. Go to your terminal and navigate to the folder where `dso-eks-servkey` exists and run the following command:

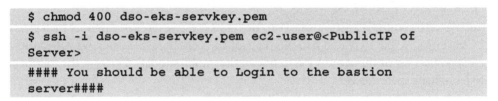

```
$ chmod 400 dso-eks-servkey.pem
$ ssh -i dso-eks-servkey.pem ec2-user@<PublicIP of
Server>
#### You should be able to Login to the bastion
server####
```

Since we have spun up our bastion server and have the server's private IP, we are good to spin up an EKS cluster.

Creating a cluster

We have created a bastion server first because we will be needing its private IP to whitelist in the control plane security group so that we can access the EKS cluster via the bastion server. To create a private cluster, perform the following steps:

1. Go to the IAM console to create an EKS cluster control plane role and EKS worker node role. Click on **Roles** on the left-hand side under **Access management** in the IAM console. Then click on **Create role**.

Figure 5.22 – IAM Roles console

2. In the **Choose a use case** section, select **EKS** at the bottom of the page and then click on **EKS-Cluster**. Then click on **Next** to attach the permission. Make sure you see **AmazonEKSClusterPolicy** present in the policy list. Then click on **Next** to add a tag. Click on **Next** to review it. Give the role name as dso-eks-cluster-role, then click on **Create**.

3. Similarly, create an IAM role for the worker node and give the name as dso-eks-node-role. Also attach the AmazonEKSWorkerNodePolicy, AmazonEC2ContainerRegistryReadOnly, and AmazonEKS_CNI_Policy policies.

4. Now go to the Amazon EKS console and go to **Clusters**, then click on **Create cluster**.

Figure 5.23 – Creating an EKS cluster

5. You will see the **Cluster configuration** page, where you need to provide the name of the cluster as `dso-eks-cluster`. Select **1.21** for **Kubernetes version**. Select the **dso-eks-cluster-role cluster IAM role**, which you created in *Step 2*, for **Cluster Service Role**. Click on **Next** to provide networking details.

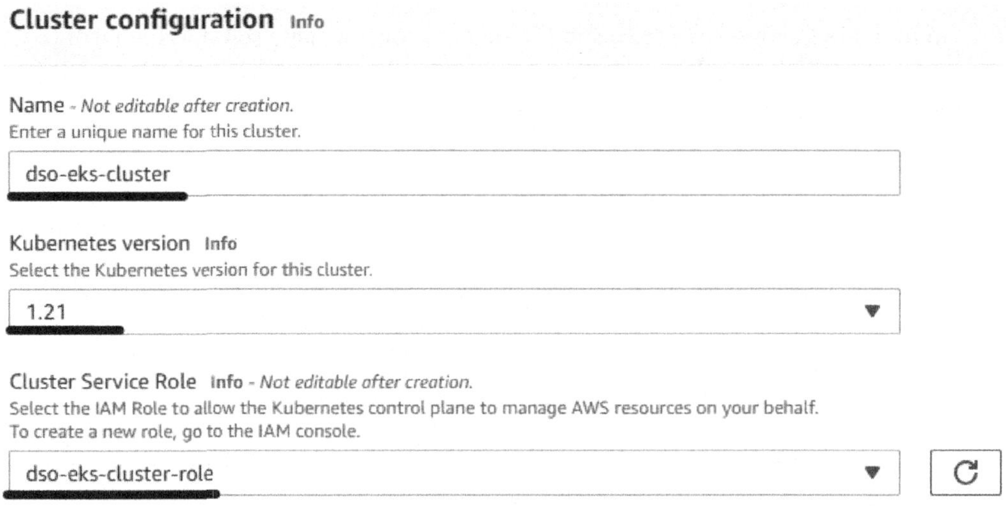

Cluster configuration Info

Name - *Not editable after creation.*
Enter a unique name for this cluster.

> dso-eks-cluster

Kubernetes version Info
Select the Kubernetes version for this cluster.

> 1.21   ▼

Cluster Service Role Info - *Not editable after creation.*
Select the IAM Role to allow the Kubernetes control plane to manage AWS resources on your behalf.
To create a new role, go to the IAM console.

> dso-eks-cluster-role   ▼   ⟳

Figure 5.24 – Providing cluster information

6. In the **Networking** section, you need to select **dso-eks-vpc** for **VPC** and then select only three subnets, which are private. In **Security Group**, select **dso-eks-controlplane**. In **Cluster endpoint access**, select **Private**. Select all the latest versions of networking add-ons and click on **Next**. Enable all **Control Plane Logging**, click on **Next** to review it, and then click on **Create** to create the EKS cluster.

7. It takes almost 15-20 minutes to create an EKS cluster. After that, you will be able to see the configuration and details of the cluster.

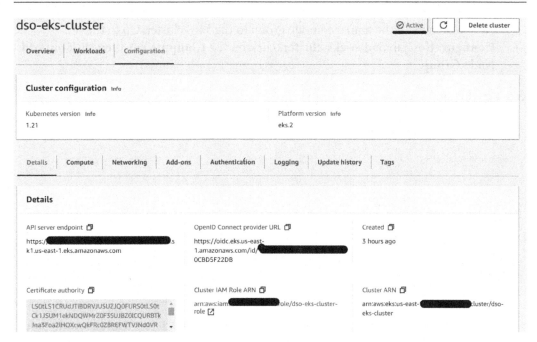

Figure 5.25 – dso-eks-cluster configuration details

8. After the cluster creation, and before creating a worker node and attaching it to the EKS cluster, we need to do two things. One is to edit the security group of the **dso-eks-controlplane** control plane and add an HTTPS rule to the private IP of the bastion server. The second is to edit the security group of the **dso-eks-endpoint** endpoint by providing all traffic to all three subnet IP ranges. For this exercise, you can provide the CIDR range of VPC which is `10.0.0.0/16` as source in dso-eks-endpoint security group. This basically lets your worker node communicate with the EKS control plane via a private endpoint interface.

9.   Now you can add the managed node group to the EKS cluster. Go to the
     Configuration tab of **dso-eks-cluster**, click on the **Compute** tab, then click on **Add
     Node Group**.

Figure 5.26 – Adding a worker node in the EKS cluster

10. Provide the name of the node group as dso-eks-node. Select **dso-eks-node-role**
     for **Node IAM role**. Give the tag key as **Name** and **Value** as **dso-eks-node**. Keep
     the rest of the settings the same in **Node Group Compute configuration** for this
     exercise. In **Node Group scaling configuration**, provide 3 for all the sizes, then
     click on **Next**. In **Subnet**, select all three private subnets, then click on **Next** and
     then **Create**. After a few minutes, you will see the status of **dso-eks-node** as **Active**.

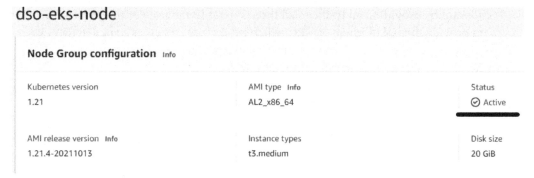

Figure 5.27 – EKS worker node status

Since we have deployed an EKS cluster and added a worker node in the cluster, now let's
access the cluster from the bastion server.

Verifying the cluster access

To access the private EKS cluster via the bastion server, perform the following steps:

1. Log in to the bastion server (see *Step 3* under the *Bastion server* heading) and then install the necessary command-line binary:

    ```
    ### Install kubectl binary via which you can interact
    with kubernetes cluster
    $ curl -LO https://dl.k8s.io/release/v1.21.0/bin/linux/
    amd64/kubectl
    $ chmod +x kubectl
    $ sudo cp kubectl /usr/local/bin
    ### Install docker cli to download the docker image and
    push it to ECR
    $ sudo amazon-linux-extras install epel
    $ sudo yum install docker
    $ sudo systemctl start docker
    $ sudo usermod -aG docker $USER
    ### CTRL+D to logout and ssh again
    ### Verify the installation of docker
    $ docker ps -a
    ```

2. Now generate the IAM user credentials (access key and secret) and then configure them in the bastion server. Make sure you use the same user credentials with which you created the EKS cluster:

    ```
    $ aws configure
    Access_key: <Your Access Key>
    Secret_key:<Your Secret Key>
    Region: us-east-1
    Output: text
    ```

3. Now you can fetch the kubeconfig file, which is like an authentication file to the EKS cluster, via the following command and access the cluster:

    ```
    $ aws eks --region us-east-1 update-kubeconfig --name
    dso-eks-cluster
    # You can find the auth file in $USER/.kube/config
    $ kubectl version
    # To see the connected worker nodes
    ```

```
$ kubectl get nodes
```

NAME VERSION	STATUS	ROLES	AGE
ip-10-0-1-98.ec2.internal v1.21.4-eks-033ce7e	Ready	\<none\>	39m
ip-10-0-2-175.ec2.internal v1.21.4-eks-033ce7e	Ready	\<none\>	39m
ip-10-0-3-29.ec2.internal v1.21.4-eks-033ce7e	Ready	\<none\>	39m

So far, we have created a fully private EKS cluster in this section. But still, there are a lot of things required to make it ready to deploy an application. In the next section, we will deploy some add-ons that will help the EKS cluster to be fault-tolerant.

Deploying add-ons

In the previous section, we created a fully private EKS cluster, but to deploy an application or add-on, we need to understand and implement the following things:

- Since this is a private EKS cluster, the cluster can only pull images from Amazon ECR via an endpoint. So, to deploy anything on the EKS cluster, we need to push the Docker images in ECR.

- We need to set up IRSA via OIDC, which is an important component to configure the service account with permissions defined in the IAM role.

- We need to install **Cluster Autoscaler** to scale the worker node in case the number of Pods increases, due to more traffic to existing Pods, and needs extra worker nodes to run on.

- We need to configure the **Amazon EBS CSI** driver for the storage class, which manages the life cycle of Amazon EBS volumes for persistent volumes.

So, in this section, we will implement the preceding points in sequence.

Creating copies of container images in ECR

Since our cluster is private and doesn't have internet access, it can't pull the images from the public registry. Instead, we need to pull the public images in the bastion server and push them to ECR. We have created the ECR VPC endpoint, via which the EKS cluster can communicate with ECR and pull the Docker images to run the Pod.

To create a local copy of images in ECR, perform the following steps:

1. Go to the ECR service console, select the **Private** tab, and click on **Create repository** (or **Get Started** if you are creating an ECR repository for the first time).

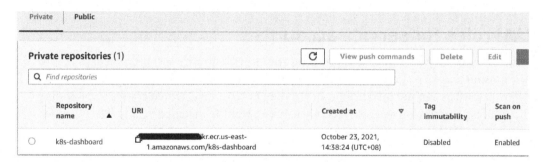

Figure 5.28 – Creating an ECR repository

2. You will see a **Create Repository General settings** page. Select the **Private** visibility setting. For **Repository name**, add k8s-dashboard. Enable image scan settings by clicking on **Scan on push**. Then click on **Create repository**. You will see the created ECR repository.

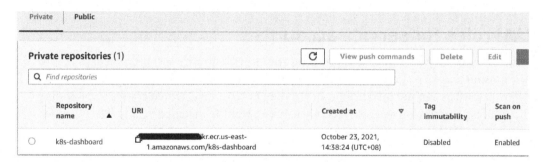

Figure 5.29 – ECR repository list

3. Now connect your bastion server using SSH and download the two Docker images, which will be used to spin up Kubernetes dashboard Pods:

```
$ docker pull kubernetesui/metrics-scraper:v1.0.6
```

```
$ docker pull kubernetesui/dashboard:v2.3.0
```

```
$ aws ecr get-login-password --region us-east-1 | docker
login --username AWS --password-stdin <accountid>.dkr.
ecr.us-east-1.amazonaws.com
```

```
$ docker tag kubernetesui/dashboard:v2.3.0 <accountid>.
dkr.ecr.us-east-1.amazonaws.com/dso-eks-dashboard:ui
```

```
$ docker tag kubernetesui/metrics-scraper:v1.0.6
<accountid>.dkr.ecr.us-east-1.amazonaws.com/dso-eks-
dashboard:scraper
```

```
$ docker push <accountid>.dkr.ecr.us-east-1.amazonaws.
com/dso-eks-dashboard:ui
```

```
$ docker push <accountid>.dkr.ecr.us-east-1.amazonaws.
com/dso-eks-dashboard:scraper
```

```
$ wget https://raw.githubusercontent.com/kubernetes/
dashboard/v2.3.0/aio/deploy/recommended.yaml
```

```
#### Modify the docker image URI with <accountid>.dkr.
ecr.us-east-1.amazonaws.com/dso-eks-dashboard:ui and
<accountid>.dkr.ecr.us-east-1.amazonaws.com/dso-eks-
dashboard:scraper In both the deployment Image spec.
```

```
$ vi recommended.yaml
```

```
$ kubectl create -f recommended.yaml
```

```
### You can verify your pod by
```

```
$ kubectl get pods -n kubernetes-dashboard
```

We need to keep repeating the `pull`, `tag`, and `push` steps every time we need to deploy anything on the EKS cluster.

IAM roles for service accounts

In the traditional way, when an application running on an EC2 instance needs access to AWS resources, we just create an instance profile and attach the required permission to it. After that, we assign the instance profile to the EC2 instance, which results in providing the running application access to AWS resources. But the instance profile fails when we are running Pods on an EC2 instance.

We will understand this by looking at a use case. Suppose you have two Pods, A and B. Pod A needs access to bucket Y and Pod B needs access to bucket Z. Now if these two Pods are running on the same EC2 instance, then you will create an instance profile (an IAM role for an EC2 instance) and add permission to it. Now, the tricky part is if you add permission to both buckets in the IAM role, then both Pod A and B will have access to both buckets, which is a security concern. To assign pod-level permission, we can use **kube2iam** and **kiam**. But we will learn about the native AWS solution, IRSA.

IRSA allows Pods to be first-class citizens in IAM. Rather than intercepting the requests to the EC2 metadata API to perform a call to the STS API to retrieve temporary credentials, changes were made in the AWS identity APIs to recognize Kubernetes Pods. By combining an OIDC identity provider and Kubernetes service account annotations, you can now use IAM roles at the Pod level.

To enable IRSA on the EKS cluster, perform the following steps:

1. Retrieve the OIDC provider URL of the EKS cluster from the UI. Go to the **Cluster configuration** page and click on **Details** and copy the OIDC provider URL.

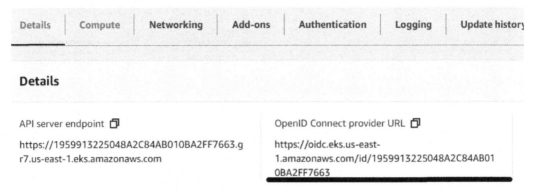

Figure 5.30 – OIDC details of the EKS cluster

2. Go to the IAM console, click on **Identity providers**, and in **Configure provider**, select **OpenID Connect**. In **Provider URL**, paste the OIDC URL that we copied in *Step 1*. Click on **Get thumbprint**. In **Audience**, you need to mention `sts.amazonaws.com`, then click on **Add provider**.

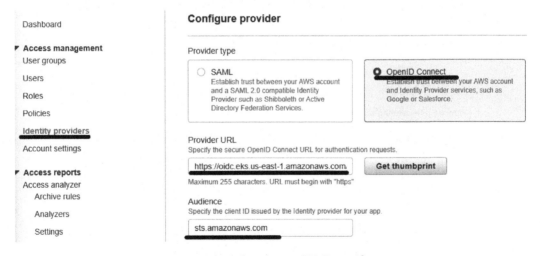

Figure 5.31 – Creating an OIDC provider

3. You will have the OIDC created for the EKS cluster.

oidc.eks.us-east-1.amazonaws.com/id/1959913225048A2C84AB010BA2FF7663

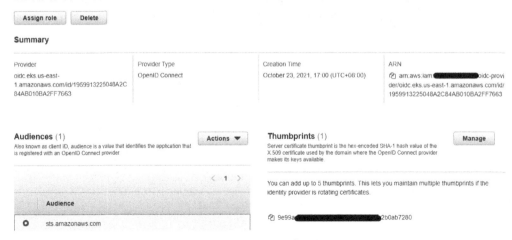

Figure 5.32 – OIDC details

We will verify IRSA is working in the next subsection by implementing **Cluster Autoscaler**, which uses AWS EC2 Auto Scaling API permission tied to a service account.

Cluster Autoscaler

Cluster Autoscaler on AWS EKS scales worker nodes within any specified autoscaling group. It is deployed as the deployment type in EKS. Cluster Autoscaler works as in the following diagram:

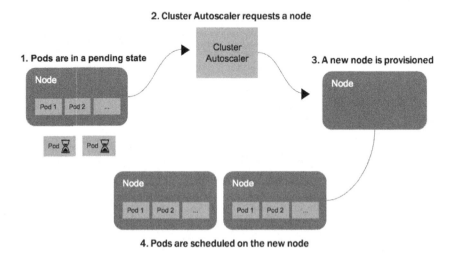

Figure 5.33 – Cluster Autoscaler workflow

To deploy Cluster Autoscaler in AWS EKS, perform the following steps:

1. The first thing we need to do is to create an IAM policy and role, which has all the permission required to perform the autoscaling operation. Go to the IAM console. Click on **Policies** on the left-hand side, then click on **Create Policy**. Choose the **JSON** tab. Paste the following JSON content and click on **Next** to provide a tag. Then provide the name of the policy as `dso-eks-autoscaler-policy` and click on **Create Policy**:

```json
{
    "Version": "2012-10-17",
    "Statement": [
        {
            "Action": [
                "autoscaling:DescribeAutoScalingGroups",

 "autoscaling:DescribeAutoScalingInstances",

 "autoscaling:DescribeLaunchConfigurations",
                "autoscaling:DescribeTags",
                "autoscaling:SetDesiredCapacity",

 "autoscaling:TerminateInstanceInAutoScalingGroup",
                "ec2:DescribeLaunchTemplateVersions"
            ],
            "Resource": "*",
            "Effect": "Allow"
        }
    ]
}
```

2. Once your policy is created, you need to create an IAM role. Go to the IAM console, click on **Roles**, then click on **Create Role**. In the **Select type of trusted entity** section, select **Web identity**. In the **Choose a web identity provider** section, select the URL for your EKS cluster, and for **Audience**, choose **sts.amazonaws.com**. Then click on **Next** to add the permission.

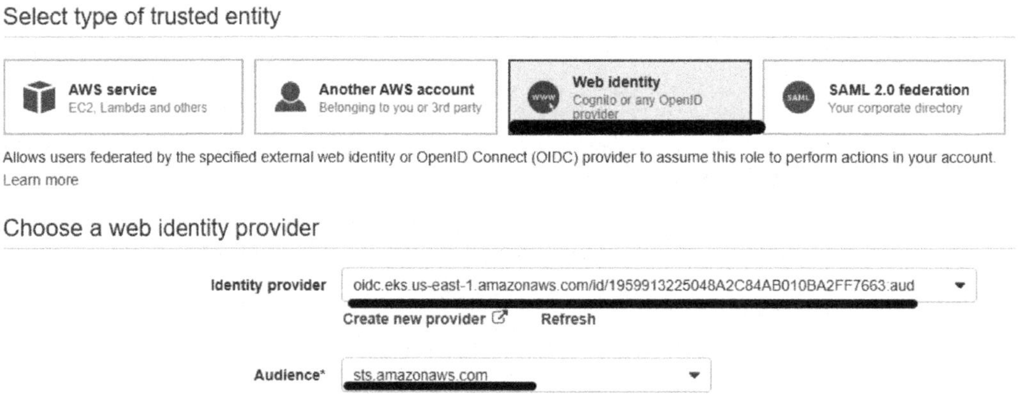

Select type of trusted entity

Choose a web identity provider

Identity provider	oidc.eks.us-east-1.amazonaws.com/id/1959913225048A2C84AB010BA2FF7663.aud ▼
	Create new provider ☐ Refresh
Audience*	sts.amazonaws.com ▼

Figure 5.34 – Creating a Web identity IAM role

3. In **Attach permission policies**, search for `dso-eks-autoscaler-policy` and select it. After that, click on **Next** to provide tags. Then, click on **Next** to give the role name as `dso-eks-autoscaler-role` and click on **Create role**.

4. Click on **dso-eks-autoscaler-role** and go to **Trust relationships**. Click on **Edit trust relationship**. You need to modify the policy document. Find the line that looks like the following:

```
"oidc.eks.us-east-2.amazonaws.com/id/
EXAMPLED539D4633E53DE1B716D3041E:aud": "sts.amazonaws.
com"
```

Replace that line with the following:

```
"oidc.eks.<region-code>.amazonaws.com/
id/<EXAMPLED539D4633E53DE1B716D3041E>:sub":
"system:serviceaccount:<namespace>:<serviceaccountname>"
```

Here's an example:

```
"oidc.eks.<region-code>.amazonaws.com/
id/<EXAMPLED539D4633E53DE1B716D3041E>:sub":
"system:serviceaccount:kube-system:cluster-autoscaler"
```

5. Click on **Update Trust Policy**.

6.   Now connect to the bastion server using SSH and perform the following command:

```
$ curl -o cluster-autoscaler-autodiscover.yaml https://
raw.githubusercontent.com/kubernetes/autoscaler/master/
cluster-autoscaler/cloudprovider/aws/examples/cluster-
autoscaler-autodiscover.yaml
```

```
##Pull the Docker image and push it to your ECR
```

```
## You need to create an ECR repository for Autoscaler.
Perform the step 1  and 2 of first heading (Creating
copies of container images in ECR) and provide the name
of repository as autoscaler.
```

```
$ docker pull k8s.gcr.io/autoscaling/cluster-
autoscaler:v1.21.0
```

```
$ aws ecr get-login-password --region us-east-1 | docker
login --username AWS --password-stdin <your account id>.
dkr.ecr.us-east-1.amazonaws.com
```

```
$ docker tag k8s.gcr.io/autoscaling/cluster-
autoscaler:v1.21.0 <accountid>.dkr.ecr.us-east-1.
amazonaws.com/autoscaler:latest
```

```
$ docker push <your account>.dkr.ecr.us-east-1.amazonaws.
com/autoscaler:latest
```

7.   Once you have pushed the cluster-autoscaler image in ECR, then you need to edit the cluster-autoscaler-autodiscover.yaml file that we curled in *Step 6*:

```
$ vi cluster-autoscaler-autodiscover.yaml
```

```
### Go to deployment container spec, replace the current
image to <your account>.dkr.ecr.us-east-1.amazonaws.com/
autoscaler:latest
```

```
### Edit the cluster-autoscaler command --node-group-
auto-discover and mention the cluster name which is
dso-eks-cluster
```

```
### Add these three commands of cluster autoscaler
```

```
- --balance-similar-node-groups
```

```
- --skip-nodes-with-system-pods=false
```

```
- --aws-use-static-instance-list=true
```

```
### You must modify the mountPath of volumeMounts to
following because we are using Amazon Linux 2
```

```
/etc/ssl/certs/ca-bundle.crt
```

```
### You also need to add environment variable
```

```
          env:
            - name: AWS_REGION
              value: us-east-1
            - name: AWS_STS_REGIONAL_ENDPOINTS
              value: regional
### Add the service account section annotation like
below.This is the place where IRSA plays role
apiVersion: v1
kind: ServiceAccount
metadata:
  annotations:
    eks.amazonaws.com/role-arn: "arn:aws:iam::<account-
id>:role/dso-eks-autoscaler-role"
  labels:
    k8s-addon: cluster-autoscaler.addons.k8s.io
    k8s-app: cluster-autoscaler
  name: cluster-autoscaler
  namespace: kube-system
```

8. Once you have modified your file, you can apply that to the EKS cluster to deploy `cluster-autoscaler`:

```
$ kubectl create -f cluster-autoscaler-autodiscover.yaml
serviceaccount/cluster-autoscaler created
clusterrole.rbac.authorization.k8s.io/cluster-autoscaler
created
role.rbac.authorization.k8s.io/cluster-autoscaler created
clusterrolebinding.rbac.authorization.k8s.io/cluster-
autoscaler created
rolebinding.rbac.authorization.k8s.io/cluster-autoscaler
created
deployment.apps/cluster-autoscaler created
```

9. Once you have deployed `cluster-autoscaler`, you can view the Pods and its logs:

```
$ kubectl get pods -n kube-system
NAME                                 READY    STATUS
RESTARTS    AGE
aws-node-8pz7p                        1/1      Running    0
```

30h			
aws-node-khd4r 30h	1/1	Running	0
aws-node-vl6mc 30h	1/1	Running	1
cluster-autoscaler-599f85fb4b-zdfx9 18m	1/1	Running	0
coredns-66cb55d4f4-7dtw9 31h	1/1	Running	0
coredns-66cb55d4f4-fq88k 31h	1/1	Running	0
kube-proxy-8pk61 30h	1/1	Running	0
kube-proxy-knt8w 30h	1/1	Running	0
kube-proxy-sngj2 30h	1/1	Running	0

```
$ kubectl logs -f cluster-autoscaler-599f85fb4b-zdfx9 -n
kube-system
```

```
I1024 10:00:30.182655       1 auto_scaling.go:199] 1
launch configurations already in cache
```

```
I1024 10:00:30.182693       1 auto_scaling_groups.go:136]
Registering ASG eks-dso-eks-node-d4be55ae-247e-c215-2a86-
f5c8de3ad10e
```

```
I1024 10:00:30.182705       1 aws_manager.go:269]
Refreshed ASG list, next refresh after 2021-10-24
10:01:30.18270237 +0000 UTC m=+80.050566269
```

```
I1024 10:00:30.182830       1 main.go:291] Registered
cleanup signal handler
```

```
I1024 10:00:30.182857       1 node_instances_cache.go:156]
Start refreshing cloud provider node instances cache
```

```
I1024 10:00:30.182867       1 node_instances_cache.
go:168] Refresh cloud provider node instances cache
finished, refresh took 4.236µs
```

```
I1024 10:00:40.183085       1 static_autoscaler.go:228]
Starting main loop
```

```
W1024 10:00:40.183447       1 clusterstate.go:432]
AcceptableRanges have not been populated yet. Skip
checking
```

```
I1024 10:00:40.183589        1 filter_out_schedulable.
go:65] Filtering out schedulables
```

```
I1024 10:00:40.183610        1 filter_out_schedulable.
go:132] Filtered out 0 pods using hints
```

```
I1024 10:00:40.183619        1 filter_out_schedulable.
go:170] 0 pods were kept as unschedulable based on
caching
```

```
I1024 10:00:40.183625        1 filter_out_schedulable.
go:171] 0 pods marked as unschedulable can be scheduled.
```

```
I1024 10:00:40.183720        1 filter_out_schedulable.
go:82] No schedulable pods
```

```
I1024 10:00:40.183747        1 static_autoscaler.go:401]
No unschedulable pods
```

```
I1024 10:00:40.183764        1 static_autoscaler.go:448]
Calculating unneeded nodes
```

```
I1024 10:00:40.183782        1 pre_filtering_processor.
go:66] Skipping ip-10-0-3-78.ec2.internal - node group
min size reached
```

```
I1024 10:00:40.183792        1 pre_filtering_processor.
go:66] Skipping ip-10-0-2-206.ec2.internal - node group
min size reached
```

```
I1024 10:00:40.183801        1 pre_filtering_processor.
go:66] Skipping ip-10-0-1-148.ec2.internal - node group
min size reached
```

If the output of the `cluster-autoscaler` Pods looks like the preceding code block, that means it's running fine. In the next subsection, we will configure the **Amazon EBS CSI driver** for the storage class.

The Amazon EBS CSI driver

When we deploy any microservices and they need persistent storage, Kubernetes provides storage classes to provision an EBS volume and attach it to the Pods running on the instance. The storage class uses drivers to interact with the native storage. AWS provides the EBS CSI driver to provide support to the Kubernetes storage class to provision an EBS volume and manage the life cycle of the volume. To configure the EBS CSI driver in the EKS cluster, perform the following steps:

1. Go to IAM and create the `dso-eks-ebs-policy` policy using the JSON content from the URL `https://raw.githubusercontent.com/kubernetes-sigs/aws-ebs-csi-driver/release-1.3/docs/example-iam-policy.json`, which provides necessary permission to do operations on EBS.

2. Create the `dso-eks-ebs-role` IAM role of the Web identity type and use the same OIDC provider as your EKS cluster, as we created in Cluster Autoscaler. Attach the **dso-eks-ebs-policy** policy to the role.

3. Go to the **dso-eks-ebs-role** trust relationships. Edit the trust relationship policy document. Modify the following:

```
"oidc.eks.us-east-1.amazonaws.com/id/
EXAMPLEDC84AB010BA2FF7663:aud": "sts.amazonaws.com"
```

This is what you should modify it to:

```
"oidc.eks.us-east-1.amazonaws.com/id/
EXAMPLEIDA2C84AB010BA2FF7663:sub":
"system:serviceaccount:kube-system:ebs-csi-controller-sa"
```

4. Click on **Update Trust Policy**.

5. Now you need to connect to the bastion server and install the **Helm CLI**, which is like a package manager for Kubernetes. And using Helm, we will install the AWS EBS CSI driver:

```
$ wget https://get.helm.sh/helm-canary-linux-amd64.tar.gz
$ tar -xvf helm-canary-linux-amd64.tar.gz
$ cd linux-amd64/
$ sudo cp helm /usr/bin/
$ helm version
$ helm repo add aws-ebs-csi-driver https://kubernetes-sigs.github.io/aws-ebs-csi-driver
$ helm repo update
$ helm fetch aws-ebs-csi-driver/aws-ebs-csi-driver
$ tar -xvf aws-ebs-csi-driver-2.4.0.tgz
$ cd aws-ebs-csi-driver/
```

6. Create an ECR repository called `ebs-csi-driver` and push the following images into ECR after downloading and tagging them in the bastion server:

```
$ docker pull k8s.gcr.io/provider-aws/aws-ebs-csi-driver
$ docker pull k8s.gcr.io/sig-storage/csi-provisioner:v2.1.1
$ docker pull  k8s.gcr.io/sig-storage/csi-attacher:v3.1.0
$ docker pull k8s.gcr.io/sig-storage/csi-snapshotter:v3.0.3
$ docker pull k8s.gcr.io/sig-storage/livenessprobe:v2.2.0
```

```
$ docker pull k8s.gcr.io/sig-storage/csi-resizer:v1.0.0

$ docker pull k8s.gcr.io/sig-storage/csi-node-driver-
registrar:v2.1.0

$ docker tag k8s.gcr.io/provider-aws/aws-ebs-csi-driver
<accountid>.dkr.ecr.us-east-1.amazonaws.com/ebs-csi-
driver:main

$ docker tag k8s.gcr.io/sig-storage/
csi-provisioner:v2.1.1 <accountid>.dkr.ecr.us-east-1.
amazonaws.com/ebs-csi-driver:provisioner

$ docker tag k8s.gcr.io/sig-storage/csi-attacher:v3.1.0
<accountid>.dkr.ecr.us-east-1.amazonaws.com/ebs-csi-
driver:attacher

$ docker tag k8s.gcr.io/sig-storage/
csi-snapshotter:v3.0.3 <accountid>.dkr.ecr.us-east-1.
amazonaws.com/ebs-csi-driver:snapshotter

$ docker tag k8s.gcr.io/sig-storage/livenessprobe:v2.2.0
<accountid>.dkr.ecr.us-east-1.amazonaws.com/ebs-csi-
driver:livenessprobe

$ docker tag k8s.gcr.io/sig-storage/csi-resizer:v1.0.0
<accountid>.dkr.ecr.us-east-1.amazonaws.com/ebs-csi-
driver:resizer

$ docker tag  k8s.gcr.io/sig-storage/csi-node-driver-
registrar:v2.1.0 <accountid>.dkr.ecr.us-east-1.amazonaws.
com/ebs-csi-driver:driverregistrar

$ docker push <accountid>.dkr.ecr.us-east-1.amazonaws.
com/ebs-csi-driver:main

$ docker push <accountid>.dkr.ecr.us-east-1.amazonaws.
com/ebs-csi-driver:provisioner

$ docker push <accountid>.dkr.ecr.us-east-1.amazonaws.
com/ebs-csi-driver:attacher

$ docker push <accountid>.dkr.ecr.us-east-1.amazonaws.
com/ebs-csi-driver:snapshotter

$ docker push <accountid>.dkr.ecr.us-east-1.amazonaws.
com/ebs-csi-driver:livenessprobe

$ docker push <accountid>.dkr.ecr.us-east-1.amazonaws.
com/ebs-csi-driver:resizer

$ docker push <accountid>.dkr.ecr.us-east-1.amazonaws.
com/ebs-csi-driver:driverregistrar
```

7. Once you have all the images that are required to spin up `ebs-csi-driver`, then you need to modify the `values.yaml` file of the Helm Chart and replace all the image repositories and tags as in the following screenshot:

```yaml
image:
  repository:            2.dkr.ecr.us-east-1.amazonaws.com/ebs-csi-driver
  # Overrides the image tag whose default is v{{ .Chart.AppVersion }}
  tag: "main"
  pullPolicy: IfNotPresent

sidecars:
  provisioner:
    env: []
    image:
      pullPolicy: IfNotPresent
      repository:            .dkr.ecr.us-east-1.amazonaws.com/ebs-csi-driver
      tag: "provisioner"
    logLevel: 2
    resources: {}
  attacher:
    env: []
    image:
      pullPolicy: IfNotPresent
      repository:            dkr.ecr.us-east-1.amazonaws.com/ebs-csi-driver
      tag: "attacher"
    logLevel: 2
    resources: {}
  snapshotter:
    env: []
    image:
      pullPolicy: IfNotPresent
      repository:            dkr.ecr.us-east-1.amazonaws.com/ebs-csi-driver
      tag: "snapshotter"
    logLevel: 2
    resources: {}
  livenessProbe:
    image:
      pullPolicy: IfNotPresent
      repository:            .dkr.ecr.us-east-1.amazonaws.com/ebs-csi-driver
      tag: "livenessprobe"
    resources: {}
  resizer:
    env: []
    image:
      pullPolicy: IfNotPresent
      repository:            dkr.ecr.us-east-1.amazonaws.com/ebs-csi-driver
      tag: "resizer"
    logLevel: 2
    resources: {}
  nodeDriverRegistrar:
    env: []
    image:
      pullPolicy: IfNotPresent
      repository:            .dkr.ecr.us-east-1.amazonaws.com/ebs-csi-driver
      tag: "driverregistrar"
    logLevel: 2
```

Figure 5.35 – Replacing images in the Helm Chart values.yaml file

8. Then you need to install `ebs-csi-driver` using the Helm CLI by using the following command. In this command, you also need to provide the ARN of `dso-eks-ebs-role` in the service account annotation:

```
$ cd ..
$ helm upgrade -install aws-ebs-csi-driver aws-ebs-csi-driver \
    --namespace kube-system \
    --set controller.serviceAccount.create=true \
    --set controller.serviceAccount.name=ebs-csi-controller-sa \
    --set controller.serviceAccount.annotations."eks\.amazonaws\.com/role-arn"="arn:aws:iam::<YourAccountid>:role/dso-eks-ebs-role"
```

9. You can verify the installation of `EBS-CSI-Driver` by running the following command, and you can check the status:

```
$ kubectl get pod -n kube-system -l "app.kubernetes.io/name=aws-ebs-csi-driver,app.kubernetes.io/instance=aws-ebs-csi-driver"
```

NAME RESTARTS AGE	READY	STATUS	
ebs-csi-controller-7554b8b5b9-9rb8n 61m	5/5	Running	0
ebs-csi-controller-7554b8b5b9-hhtp7 61m	5/5	Running	0
ebs-csi-node-jhq5x 61m	3/3	Running	0
ebs-csi-node-q55zt 61m	3/3	Running	0
ebs-csi-node-zjdwz 61m	3/3	Running	0

10. Edit the `ebs-csi-controller` deployment and add two environment variables:

```
$ kubectl edit deployment ebs-csi-controller -o yaml -n kube-system
### Add the environment variable and save the file###
        - name: AWS_REGION
          value: us-east-1
```

```
      - name: AWS_STS_REGIONAL_ENDPOINTS
        value: regional
```

11. Now you can create a storage class using the following YAML, and make it the default, so that any application you deploy on EKS that needs persistent volume can use the storage class, which triggers the driver and provisions the EBS volume:

```
$ vi storageclass.yaml
  kind: StorageClass
  apiVersion: storage.k8s.io/v1
  metadata:
    name: ebs-sc
  provisioner: ebs.csi.aws.com
  volumeBindingMode: WaitForFirstConsumer
$ kubectl create -f storageclass.yaml
$ kubectl get sc
NAME                PROVISIONER            RECLAIMPOLICY
VOLUMEBINDINGMODE        ALLOWVOLUMEEXPANSION    AGE
ebs-sc              ebs.csi.aws.com        Delete
WaitForFirstConsumer    false                   58s
gp2 (default)       kubernetes.io/aws-ebs  Delete
WaitForFirstConsumer    false                   38h
### Right now gp2 SC is default, to make ebs-sc as
default, hit below command.
$ kubectl patch storageclass ebs-sc -p '{"metadata":
{"annotations":{"storageclass.kubernetes.io/is-default-
class":"true"}}}'
$ kubectl patch storageclass gp2 -p '{"metadata":
{"annotations":{"storageclass.kubernetes.io/is-default-
class":"false"}}}'
$ kubectl get sc
NAME                PROVISIONER            RECLAIMPOLICY
VOLUMEBINDINGMODE        ALLOWVOLUMEEXPANSION    AGE
ebs-sc (default)    ebs.csi.aws.com        Delete
WaitForFirstConsumer    false                   4m5s
gp2                 kubernetes.io/aws-ebs  Delete
WaitForFirstConsumer    false                   39h
```

So, in this section, we made an EKS cluster ready to deploy an application by getting awareness of and creating an ECR repository, configuring OIDC for IRSA, setting up Cluster Autoscaler, and creating a storage class. But still, to make it production-ready, we must take care in terms of operational management and security. So, in the next section, we will enable App Mesh in a private cluster.

Enabling the App Mesh sidecar injector

In this section of the chapter, we will be deploying and configuring App Mesh.
If you are running a private EKS cluster, then only the App Mesh sidecar injector way supports private EKS clusters. App Mesh Controller is not supported in a private EKS cluster for now. To configure the App Mesh sidecar injector, perform the following steps:

1. Connect to the bastion server and run the following commands:

```
$ sudo yum install git

$ kubectl apply -k github.com/aws/eks-charts/stable/
appmesh-controller//crds?ref=master

$ helm repo add eks https://aws.github.io/eks-charts

$ helm fetch eks/appmesh-inject

$ tar -xvf appmesh-inject-0.14.8.tgz

#### Create an ECR repo as appmesh-injector, tag and push
the following images into ECR.

$ aws ecr get-login-password --region us-east-1 | docker
login --username AWS --password-stdin 602401143452.dkr.
ecr.us-east-1.amazonaws.com

$ docker pull 602401143452.dkr.ecr.us-east-1.amazonaws.
com/amazon/aws-app-mesh-inject:v0.5.0

$ aws ecr get-login-password --region us-east-1 | docker
login --username AWS --password-stdin 840364872350.dkr.
ecr.us-east-1.amazonaws.com

$ docker pull 840364872350.dkr.ecr.us-east-1.amazonaws.
com/aws-appmesh-envoy:v1.15.1.0-prod

$ aws ecr get-login-password --region us-west-2 | docker
login --username AWS --password-stdin 840364872350.dkr.
ecr.us-west-2.amazonaws.com

$ docker pull 840364872350.dkr.ecr.us-west-2.amazonaws.
com/aws-appmesh-proxy-route-manager:v3-prod

$ docker tag 840364872350.dkr.ecr.us-east-1.amazonaws.
com/aws-appmesh-envoy:v1.15.1.0-prod <youraccountid>.dkr.
ecr.us-east-1.amazonaws.com/appmesh-injector:envoy
```

```
$ docker push <youraccountid>.dkr.ecr.us-east-1.
amazonaws.com/appmesh-injector:envoy
```

```
$ docker tag 840364872350.dkr.ecr.us-west-2.
amazonaws.com/aws-appmesh-proxy-route-manager:v3-prod
<youraccountid>.dkr.ecr.us-east-1.amazonaws.com/appmesh-
injector:proxy-route-manager
```

```
$ docker push <youraccountid>.dkr.ecr.us-east-1.
amazonaws.com/appmesh-injector:proxy-route-manager
```

```
$ docker tag 602401143452.dkr.ecr.us-east-1.amazonaws.
com/amazon/aws-app-mesh-inject:v0.5.0 <youraccountid>.
dkr.ecr.us-east-1.amazonaws.com/appmesh-injector:injector
```

```
$ docker push <youraccountid>.dkr.ecr.us-east-1.
amazonaws.com/appmesh-injector:injector
```

```
$ cd appmesh-inject
```

```
$ vi values.yaml
```

```
##### Modify the repository image and tag in values.yaml.
```

The following screenshot shows the snippet of values.yaml:

```
image:
  repository: _____.dkr.ecr.us-east-1.amazonaws.com/appmesh-injector
  tag: injector
  pullPolicy: IfNotPresent

sidecar:
  image:
    repository:              dkr.ecr.us-east-1.amazonaws.com/appmesh-injector
    tag: envoy
  # sidecar.logLevel: Envoy log level can be info, warn, error or debug
  logLevel: info
  resources:
    # sidecar.resources.requests: Envoy CPU and memory requests
    requests:
      cpu: 10m
      memory: 32Mi
init:
  image:
    repository:              .dkr.ecr.us-east-1.amazonaws.com/appmesh-injector
    tag: proxy-route-manager
```

Figure 5.36 – Replacing the image in the values.yaml file

The following is a continuation of the preceding command:

```
$ cd ..
```

```
$ kubectl create ns appmesh-system
```

```
$ helm upgrade -i appmesh-inject appmesh-inject
--namespace appmesh-system --set mesh.name=global --set
```

```
tracing.enabled=true
Release "appmesh-inject" does not exist. Installing it
now.
NAME: appmesh-inject
LAST DEPLOYED: Mon Oct 25 12:36:12 2021
NAMESPACE: appmesh-system
STATUS: deployed
REVISION: 1
TEST SUITE: None
NOTES:
AWS App Mesh Inject installed!
### You can verify the installation of appmesh injector
$ kubectl get pods -n appmesh-system
NAME                                READY    STATUS
RESTARTS    AGE
appmesh-inject-5c7db48457-lgv78     1/1      Running    0
13s
```

Once you have the App Mesh sidecar injector installed on the EKS cluster,
you can start using it by labeling the namespace with `appmesh.k8s.aws/`
`sidecarInjectorWebhook=enabled`. Whenever any application Pod spins up in
that labeled namespace, then an envoy sidecar proxy container will spin up along with the
application Pod.

Kubernetes hardening guidance using Kubescape

In this section of the chapter, we will learn about the hardening guidance of the EKS
cluster using Kubescape. Kubescape is an open source tool, developed by *ARMO*.
Kubescape was developed in line with all of the recommendations and guidance from
the NSA and CISA. Kubescape tests whether a Kubernetes cluster is deployed securely
according to multiple frameworks: regulatory, customized company policies, and
DevSecOps best practices, such as the NSA/CISA and MITRE ATT&CK.

It not only scans Kubernetes clusters, but also YAML files and Helm Charts, and detects
misconfigurations and software vulnerabilities at early stages of the CI/CD pipeline. To get
the Kubescape recommendations for the EKS cluster, perform the following steps:

1. Connect to the bastion server and install the binary of kubescape:

```
$ curl -o kubescape.sh https://raw.githubusercontent.com/
armosec/kubescape/master/install.sh
```

```
$ vi kubescape.sh
```

```
#### Look for install_dir and modify the path according
to your need. I modified it to /usr/bin and running it as
sudo.
```

```
$ chmod +x kubescape.sh
```

```
$ sudo bash kubescape.sh
```

```
Installing Kubescape...
```

```
##############################################################
####################### 100.0%
```

```
Finished Installation.
```

```
Your current version is: v1.0.126
```

```
Usage: $ kubescape scan framework nsa
```

2. Once you have the kubescape binary installed in your bastion server, run the following command to get guidance on the hardening of the cluster and scorecard:

```
### Running kubescape with NSA framework###
```

```
$ kubescape scan framework nsa -submit
```

The following screenshot shows the stats and scorecard of your cluster security:

CONTROL NAME	FAILED RESOURCES	EXCLUDED RESOURCES	ALL RESOURCES	% SUCCESS
Allow privilege escalation	6	0	7	14%
Allowed hostPath	3	0	7	57%
Applications credentials in configuration files	6	0	21	71%
Automatic mapping of service account	45	0	45	0%
CVE-2021-25741 - Using symlink for arbitrary host file system access.	0	0	10	100%
CVE-2021-25742-nginx-ingress-snippet-annotation-vulnerability	0	0	18	100%
Cluster-admin binding	2	0	183	98%
Container hostPort	1	0	7	85%
Control plane hardening	0	0	7	100%
Dangerous capabilities	1	0	7	85%
Exec into container	2	0	183	98%
Exposed dashboard	0	0	7	100%
Host PID/IPC privileges	0	0	7	100%
Immutable container filesystem	5	0	7	28%
Ingress and Egress blocked	7	0	7	0%
Insecure capabilities	1	0	7	85%
Linux hardening	6	0	7	14%
Network policies	5	0	5	0%
Non-root containers	0	0	7	100%
Privileged container	2	0	7	71%
Resource policies	4	0	7	42%
hostNetwork access	2	0	7	71%
RESOURCE SUMMARY	65	0	260	75%

Figure 5.37 – Security scorecard of the EKS cluster with the NSA framework

3. We can also scan the EKS cluster with the MITRE ATT&CK framework:

```
$ kubescape scan framework mitre --submit
```

The following screenshot shows the stats and scorecard of your cluster security:

CONTROL NAME	FAILED RESOURCES	EXCLUDED RESOURCES	ALL RESOURCES	% SUCCESS
Access Kubernetes dashboard	0	0	84	100%
Access container service account	29	0	235	87%
Access tiller endpoint	0	0	4	100%
Applications credentials in configuration files	6	0	21	71%
CVE-2021-25741 - Using symlink for arbitrary host file system access.	0	0	10	100%
Cluster internal networking	5	0	5	0%
Cluster-admin binding	2	0	183	98%
CoreDNS poisoning	10	0	197	94%
Data Destruction	40	0	183	78%
Delete Kubernetes events	6	0	183	96%
Exec into container	2	0	183	98%
Exposed dashboard	0	0	7	100%
Exposed sensitive interfaces	0	0	10	100%
Kubernetes CronJob	0	0	0	NaN
List Kubernetes secrets	27	0	183	85%
Malicious admission controller (mutating)	3	0	3	0%
Malicious admission controller (validating)	1	0	1	0%
Mount service principal	4	0	7	42%
Network mapping	5	0	5	0%
Privileged container	2	0	7	71%
SSH server running inside container	0	0	10	100%
Writable hostPath mount	3	0	7	57%
hostPath mount	4	0	7	42%
RESOURCE SUMMARY	99	0	264	62%

Figure 5.38 – Security scorecard of EKS cluster with the MITRE framework

4. The preceding two commands scan the entire cluster based on the framework, but if you want to scan YAML files, then use the following command:

```
### Download some kubernetes YAML files for demo###
$ git clone https://github.com/armosec/kubescape.git
$ cd kubescape/examples/
$ kubescape scan framework nsa online-boutique/*.yaml
```

The following screenshot shows the security scorecard of your Kubernetes definition file:

CONTROL NAME	FAILED RESOURCES	EXCLUDED RESOURCES	ALL RESOURCES	% SUCCESS
Allow privilege escalation	12	0	12	0%
Allowed hostPath	0	0	12	100%
Applications credentials in configuration files	0	0	12	100%
Automatic mapping of service account	0	0	0	NaN
CVE-2021-25741 - Using symlink for arbitrary host file system access.	0	0	12	100%
CVE-2021-25742-nginx-ingress-snippet-annotation-vulnerability	0	0	12	100%
Cluster-admin binding	0	0	0	NaN
Container hostPort	0	0	12	100%
Control plane hardening	0	0	12	100%
Dangerous capabilities	0	0	12	100%
Exec into container	0	0	0	NaN
Exposed dashboard	0	0	24	100%
Host PID/IPC privileges	0	0	12	100%
Immutable container filesystem	12	0	12	0%
Ingress and Egress blocked	12	0	12	0%
Insecure capabilities	0	0	12	100%
Linux hardening	12	0	12	0%
Network policies	0	0	0	NaN
Non-root containers	0	0	12	100%
Privileged container	0	0	12	100%
Resource policies	0	0	12	100%
hostNetwork access	0	0	12	100%
RESOURCE SUMMARY	12	0	24	50%

Figure 5.39 – Security score of the Kubernetes YAML file

So, in this section, we learned how to use Kubescape to get the report of the EKS cluster, and we can also integrate it with CI/CD to scan the Kubernetes definition file and get the report at an early stage. In the next section, we will learn how to apply a policy on a Kubernetes cluster for governance and management.

Policy and governance using OPA Gatekeeper

In this section of the chapter, we will learn how to enforce policy and governance on EKS cluster resources using **OPA**. We will create a policy that denies the creation of resources that don't have a specific label.

OPA is an open source, general-purpose policy engine that is part of the CNCF, unifying policy enforcement across the stack. OPA is used for making policy decisions and can be run in different ways, for example, as a language library or as a service. We can write OPA policies in a domain-specific language called **Rego**.

OPA Gatekeeper provides the following functionality:

- A parameterized policy library
- Constraint templates, which use native Kubernetes CRDs for extending the policy library
- Constraints, which use native Kubernetes CRDs for instantiating the policy library
- Audit capabilities

The following diagram illustrates how OPA enforce policies on a Kubernetes cluster:

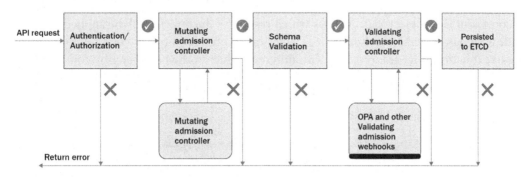

Figure 5.40 – Workflow of OPA

In Kubernetes, whenever you try to interact with the cluster to do any CRUD operation on the resource object, the request goes to the API server first before it reaches etcd. In the API server, three steps take place, which are known as **Authentication**, **Authorization**, and **Admission Control** (**AAA**). Authentication verifies the identity of the requestor. Authorization checks whether the requestor has proper permission for the particular object that has been requested. Admission controllers are plugins that govern and enforce how the cluster is used. They can change or deny a request initiated by the requestor. An admission controller consists of two phases – the **mutating phase**, which is executed first, and then the **validating phase**. The limitation of admission controllers is that they need to be compiled in `kube-apiserver` and can be enabled only when `api-server` starts up.

To overcome this rigidity of the admission controller, admission **webhooks** were introduced. Once admission webhook controllers are enabled in the cluster, they can send admission requests to external HTTP callbacks and receive admission responses. Admission webhooks are of two types: `MutatingAdmissionWebhook` and `ValidatingAdmissionWebhook`. Mutating webhooks can modify the objects that they receive but a validating webhook cannot. So, OPA Gatekeeper is installed as a validating admission webhook, which simply checks whether the request meets the defined policy or not. If it doesn't, then it will throw an error.

Before we jump to writing policy, we need to understand **constraint templates** and **constraints**.

A constraint template consists of two things: one is Rego logic, which is nothing but a program that contains the logic to enforce constraints, and the other is the schema, which includes the schema of the CRD and the parameters that can be passed into a constraint.

A constraint is an object that specifies which resources the policies will be applied to and with what parameters. Just think of it as function and function calls – constraint templates are like functions that are triggered with different values of the parameter by constraints.

To deploy Gatekeeper in our EKS cluster, perform the following steps:

1. Connect to the bastion server and download the Gatekeeper Kubernetes YAML file:

```
$ wget https://raw.githubusercontent.com/open-policy-
agent/gatekeeper/master/deploy/gatekeeper.yaml
```

2. Go into the `gatekeeper.yaml` file, search for the image, and capture the value of the image. You need to download the image and tag, and push it into your private ECR (since your cluster is private). Currently, the image value to download is `openpolicyagent/gatekeeper:v3.7.0-beta.2`. Once you replace the image URL in `gatekeeper.yaml`, then run the following command to install Gatekeeper in the EKS cluster:

```
$ kubectl apply -f gatekeeper.yaml
namespace/gatekeeper-system created
resourcequota/gatekeeper-critical-pods created
customresourcedefinition.apiextensions.k8s.io/configs.
config.gatekeeper.sh created
customresourcedefinition.apiextensions.k8s.io/
constraintpodstatuses.status.gatekeeper.sh created
customresourcedefinition.apiextensions.k8s.io/
constrainttemplatepodstatuses.status.gatekeeper.sh created
customresourcedefinition.apiextensions.k8s.io/
constrainttemplates.templates.gatekeeper.sh created
customresourcedefinition.apiextensions.k8s.io/providers.
externaldata.gatekeeper.sh created
serviceaccount/gatekeeper-admin created
Warning: policy/v1beta1 PodSecurityPolicy is deprecated
in v1.21+, unavailable in v1.25+
podsecuritypolicy.policy/gatekeeper-admin created
role.rbac.authorization.k8s.io/gatekeeper-manager-role
created
clusterrole.rbac.authorization.k8s.io/gatekeeper-manager-
role created
rolebinding.rbac.authorization.k8s.io/gatekeeper-manager-
rolebinding created
clusterrolebinding.rbac.authorization.k8s.io/gatekeeper-
manager-rolebinding created
secret/gatekeeper-webhook-server-cert created
service/gatekeeper-webhook-service created
deployment.apps/gatekeeper-audit created
deployment.apps/gatekeeper-controller-manager created
Warning: policy/v1beta1 PodDisruptionBudget is deprecated
in v1.21+, unavailable in v1.25+; use policy/v1
PodDisruptionBudget
poddisruptionbudget.policy/gatekeeper-controller-manager
created
```

```
validatingwebhookconfiguration.admissionregistration.k8s.
io/gatekeeper-validating-webhook-configuration created
```

3. You can verify the installation by running the following command:

```
kubectl get pods -n gatekeeper-system
NAME                                                  READY
STATUS     RESTARTS     AGE
gatekeeper-audit-775c6fd5b4-1j7gr                     1/1
Running    0            70s
gatekeeper-controller-manager-7f9f46948f-5xt4p        1/1
Running    0            70s
gatekeeper-controller-manager-7f9f46948f-9xxmh        1/1
Running    0            70s
gatekeeper-controller-manager-7f9f46948f-gnh2s        1/1
Running    0            70s
```

4. Now you can download the constraint template and constraints and apply them to the EKS cluster:

```
$ git clone https://github.com/PacktPublishing/
Accelerating-DevSecOps-on-AWS.git
$ cd Modern-CI-CD-on-AWS/chapter-05
$ kubectl apply -f constrainttemplate.yaml
$ kubectl apply -f constraints.yaml
```

5. At this stage, we have placed the OPA policy. Now let's test it by running a Pod that doesn't have a label. It should deny the creation of the Pod:

```
$ kubectl run nginx --image=nginx
Error from server ([label-check]
DENIED.
Reason: Our org policy mandates the following labels:
You must provide these labels: {"applicationteam",
"environment", "status"}): admission webhook "validation.
gatekeeper.sh" denied the request: [label-check]
```

6. Let's delete the constraints so that they don't interfere in the next sections of the exercise:

```
$ kubectl delete -f constratinttemplate.yaml
$ kubectl delete -f constraints.yaml
```

So, we just saw that the OPA admission controller denied creating the resource. We can use OPA Gatekeeper not only manually but also with CI/CD. In the next section of the chapter, we will deploy a stateful database application, and later we will look at backup and recovery using **Velero**.

Deploying a stateful application using Helm

In this section, we will learn about **StatefulSet** and how we can deploy and scale a stateful application using a Helm Chart.

Stateful applications are those applications that save the transaction data in persistent storage that will be used by the servers, clients, or by another application. A good example of a stateful application is a database or key-value store that stores the data, and that data is retrieved by another application or service. To deploy a stateful application on Kubernetes, we use the StatefulSet controller to deploy the application as a StatusfulSet object. StatefulSet is suitable for those applications that require the following things:

- Stable, persistent storage

- Stable, unique network identifiers

- Ordered, graceful deployment and scaling

- Ordered, automated rolling updates

Pods in StatefulSets are not interchangeable, meaning each and every Pod has its own unique identifier that is maintained, no matter where the Pod is scheduled. We will deploy a stateful application, which is MongoDB, using a Helm Chart. To deploy MongoDB, perform the following steps:

1. Connect to your bastion server, add the `mongodb` Helm repository, and fetch the chart:

```
$ helm repo add bitnami https://charts.bitnami.com/
bitnami
$ helm fetch bitnami/mongodb
$ tar -xvf mongodb-*
$ cd mongodb
```

2. Go to the `values.yaml` file and search for the image name from the top. In the current case, it's `bitnami/mongodb:4.4.10-debian-10-r11`. Pull the image in the bastion server, tag it, and push it into your ECR. Then replace the image repository in the `values.yaml` file. You also need to modify the **global image registry** and point it to the ECR repository.

3. Run the following command to install `mongodb` in the EKS cluster. We need to enable the replica architecture mode for `mongodb`, to have a primary and secondary copy:

```
$ Kubectl create ns mongodb
$ helm upgrade -i mongodb mongodb --namespace mongodb
--set architecture=replicaset --set replicaCount=3
```

4. You will see three Pods of MongoDB with the sequence number:

```
$ kubectl get pod -n mongodb
```

NAME	READY	STATUS	RESTARTS	AGE
mongodb-0	1/1	Running	0	99s
mongodb-1	1/1	Running	0	63s
mongodb-2	1/1	Running	0	36s
mongodb-arbiter-0	1/1	Running	0	99s

5. To access `mongodb`, we need to create a `mongo-client` container and `exec` inside the container, then we can access `mongodb`:

```
### Get the root password of mongodb
$ export MONGODB_ROOT_PASSWORD=$(kubectl get secret
--namespace mongodb mongodb -o jsonpath="{.data.mongodb-
root-password}" | base64 --decode)
$ kubectl run --namespace mongodb mongodb-client
--rm --tty -i --restart='Never' --env="MONGODB_ROOT_
PASSWORD=$MONGODB_ROOT_PASSWORD" --image <youraccount>.
dkr.ecr.us-east-1.amazonaws.com/mongodb:4.4 --command
bash
If you don't see a command prompt, try pressing enter.
I have no name!@mongodb-client:/$ mongo admin --host
"mongodb-0.mongodb-headless.mongodb.svc.cluster.
local:27017,mongodb-1.mongodb-headless.mongodb.svc.
cluster.local:27017,mongodb-2.mongodb-headless.mongodb.
svc.cluster.local:27017" --authenticationDatabase admin
-u root -p $MONGODB_ROOT_PASSWORD
MongoDB shell version v4.4.10
connecting to: mongodb://mongodb-0.mongodb-headless.
mongodb.svc.cluster.local:27017,mongodb-1.mongodb-
headless.mongodb.svc.cluster.local:27017,mongodb-2.
mongodb-headless.mongodb.svc.cluster.local:27017/
admin?authSource=admin&compressors=disabled&gssapiService
Name=mongodb
```

```
Implicit session: session { "id" : UUID("db199838-fad5-
4101-9650-e5ebe582d3b3") }

MongoDB server version: 4.4.10

---

The server generated these startup warnings when booting:
        2021-10-27T07:47:05.246+00:00: Using the XFS
filesystem is strongly recommended with the WiredTiger
storage engine. See http://dochub.mongodb.org/core/
prodnotes-filesystem

---

---

        Enable MongoDB's free cloud-based monitoring
service, which will then receive and display
        metrics about your deployment (disk utilization,
CPU, operation statistics, etc).

---

rs0:PRIMARY>
```

We have successfully installed MongoDB on the EKS cluster. Now let's try to validate it:

- The data is being replicated from the primary replica to the secondary replica.

- The data is still available even if we delete the ReplicaSet.

6. By default, when we install MongoDB in the replicaset, the replication mode will be enabled, but if it's not, then run the following command:

```
rs0:PRIMARY> rs.initiate({_id: "MainRepSet", version: 1,
members: [


...        { _id: 0, host : "mongodb-0.mongodb-headless.
mongodb.svc.cluster.local:27017" },
...        { _id: 1, host : "mongodb-1.mongodb-headless.
mongodb.svc.cluster.local:27017" },
...        { _id: 2, host : "mongodb-2.mongodb-headless.
mongodb.svc.cluster.local:27017" }
...  ]});
```

7. We can verify the replication mode by checking whether we have one primary replica and two secondary replicas with the output of the following query:

```
rs0:PRIMARY> rs.status();
```

8. Now let's create an admin user and use test db and populate some data:

```
rs0:PRIMARY> db.getSiblingDB("admin").createUser({
...         user : "main_admin",
...         pwd  : "abc123",
...         roles: [ { role: "root", db: "admin" } ]
...   });
rs0:PRIMARY> db.getSiblingDB('admin').auth("main_admin",
"abc123");
rs0:PRIMARY> use test;
rs0:PRIMARY> db.testcoll.insert({a:1});
rs0:PRIMARY> db.testcoll.insert({b:2});
rs0:PRIMARY> db.testcoll.find();
{ "_id" : ObjectId("61790a8ee695d2159d5c2faf"), "a" : 1 }
{ "_id" : ObjectId("61790a96e695d2159d5c2fb0"), "b" : 2 }
```

9. You can see the output of the query. Now let's log in to mongodb-1, which is a secondary Pod, and try to access the same data:

```
### Logout of the current Primary replica shell by ctrl+d
and login to mongodb-1##
I have no name!@mongodb-client:/$ mongo admin --host
"mongodb-1.mongodb-headless.mongodb.svc.cluster.
local:27017" --authenticationDatabase admin -u root -p
$MONGODB_ROOT_PASSWORD
rs0:SECONDARY> db.getMongo().setSecondaryOk()
rs0:SECONDARY> db.getSiblingDB('admin').auth("main_
admin", "abc123");
rs0:SECONDARY> use test;
rs0:SECONDARY> db.testcoll.find();
{ "_id" : ObjectId("61790a8ee695d2159d5c2faf"), "a" : 1 }
{ "_id" : ObjectId("61790a96e695d2159d5c2fb0"), "b" : 2 }
```

10. We can see that we can also retrieve the same data from the secondary replica, meaning data replication is working fine. You can scale the StatefulSet by running the following command:

```
### Logout of mongo shell and mongo-client container
$ kubectl scale statefulset mongodb -n mongodb
--replicas=5
$ kubectl get pods -n mongodb
```

NAME	READY	STATUS	RESTARTS	AGE
mongodb-0	1/1	Running	0	40m
mongodb-1	1/1	Running	0	40m
mongodb-2	1/1	Running	0	39m
mongodb-3	1/1	Running	0	2m10s
mongodb-4	1/1	Running	0	104s
mongodb-arbiter-0	1/1	Running	0	40m

11. Now let's try to remove all the Pods of mongodb:

```
$ helm del mongodb -n mongodb
```

12. You will see that PVC is still there, even after the deletion of the Pod:

```
$ kubectl get pv,pvc -n mongodb
NAME
CAPACITY      ACCESS MODES      RECLAIM POLICY      STATUS      CLAI
M                             REASON      AGE
persistentvolume/pvc-323d405c-4aae-4951-9da5-da01fd4570ca
8Gi           RWO               Delete              Bound
mongodb/datadir-mongodb-2                          67m
persistentvolume/pvc-59150af6-3ca6-478b-8635-8afbffd9cf1f
8Gi           RWO               Delete              Bound
mongodb/datadir-mongodb-3                          30m
persistentvolume/pvc-984c8e2e-54c3-4b6c-a246-e5c4fe099de3
8Gi           RWO               Delete              Bound
mongodb/datadir-mongodb-1                          68m
persistentvolume/pvc-b9009ad5-a489-4321-9487-e15ef7be7200
8Gi           RWO               Delete              Bound
mongodb/datadir-mongodb-4                          29m
persistentvolume/pvc-e75e6fbc-f07f-4a07-8547-40f61f20933e
8Gi           RWO               Delete              Bound
mongodb/datadir-mongodb-0                          68m
```

13. Now let's recreate `mongodb` using Helm:

```
$ helm upgrade -i mongodb mongodb --namespace mongodb
--set architecture=replicaset --set replicaCount=5
```

14. Connect to the `mongodb-client` container and then log in to `mongodb-0` using the admin user and password that we set before, and then try to query the data:

```
$ kubectl run --namespace mongodb mongodb-client
--rm --tty -i --restart='Never' --env="MONGODB_ROOT_
PASSWORD=abc123" --image 825031041242.dkr.ecr.us-east-1.
amazonaws.com/gatekeeper:mongo --command - bash
```
```
I have no name!@mongodb-client:/$ mongo admin --host
"mongodb-0.mongodb-headless.mongodb.svc.cluster.
local:27017" --authenticationDatabase admin -u main_admin
-p $MONGODB_ROOT_PASSWORD
```
```
rs0:PRIMARY> db.getSiblingDB('admin').auth("main_admin",
"abc123");
```
```
rs0:PRIMARY> use test;
```
```
rs0:PRIMARY> db.testcoll.find();
```
```
{ "_id" : ObjectId("61790a8ee695d2159d5c2faf"), "a" : 1 }
```
```
{ "_id" : ObjectId("61790a96e695d2159d5c2fb0"), "b" : 2 }
```

We just saw that even after the recreation of the Pod, we can still access the data. In the next section of the chapter, we will do a backup and restore using Velero.

Backup and restore using Velero

Deploying an application in a container-centric way has various advantages and perks over traditional VMs. Everything that we did on traditional VMs can be easily done on containers with greater performance, cost, and flexibility. Backup and restore is also one of the critical tasks that we perform in a traditional environment. It's always recommended to back up your production Kubernetes cluster resources. In this section, we will learn how to use Velero as a backup and restore tool for Kubernetes workloads.

Velero is an open source tool developed by VMware that helps to automate the backup and restore of Kubernetes resources. Velero can be used both on public as well as on-premises clusters (such as OpenShift). Velero helps with the following tasks:

- **Disaster recovery**: Velero takes the backup of the cluster and restores it in the event of disaster. But again, there are a couple of ways to implement it, either active-passive or hot-standby. Velero also provides a periodic backup and restore function.

- **Application migration**: Velero can migrate an application along with its data from one cluster to another.

- **Cloning**: Velero can clone all the resources of one cluster to another cluster for testing and debugging.

How does Velero work?

The following diagram explains the workflow when Velero initiates the request for a backup:

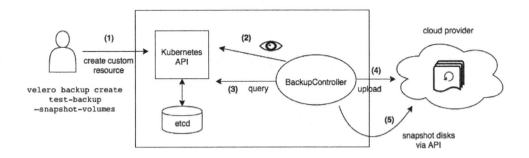

Figure 5.41 – Velero workflow

Whenever a Velero backup request is initiated in the CLI, it makes a call to the Kubernetes API server to take a backup of the object. Then the backup controller validates the type of object and then makes a call to `api-server` to query the data to be backed up. Then it starts the backup process and uploads the collected data to S3 by making an API call to the cloud provider. A similar process takes place while executing the `restore` command.

Let's install Velero on the EKS cluster by performing the following steps:

1. The first step is to download the `velero` client binary in the bastion server. In this exercise, we are downloading the current latest version:

    ```
    $ wget https://github.com/vmware-tanzu/velero/releases/
    download/v1.7.0/velero-v1.7.0-linux-amd64.tar.gz
    $ tar -xvf velero-v1.7.0-linux-amd64.tar.gz
    $ sudo cp velero-v1.7.0-linux-amd64/velero /usr/bin
    $ velero version --client-only
    ```

2. Create an S3 bucket either via the UI or CLI (make sure the bastion server has the role or AWS credentials that have the S3 permission):

    ```
    $ aws s3api create-bucket    --bucket velero-backup-
    antikythera    --region us-east-1
    ```

3. Create an IAM policy, `dso-eks-velero-policy`, using the following JSON code, then create an IAM role for the service account via the OIDC identity provider and attach this policy. Make sure to edit the trust relationship with `"oidc.eks. us-east-1.amazonaws.com/id/EXAMPLEDEF92CB2913961:sub"`: `"system:serviceaccount:velero:velerosa"`:

```
{
    "Version": "2012-10-17",
    "Statement": [
        {
            "Effect": "Allow",
            "Action": [
                "ec2:DescribeVolumes",
                "ec2:DescribeSnapshots",
                "ec2:CreateTags",
                "ec2:CreateVolume",
                "ec2:CreateSnapshot",
                "ec2:DeleteSnapshot"
            ],
            "Resource": "*"
        },
        {
            "Effect": "Allow",
            "Action": [
                "s3:GetObject",
                "s3:DeleteObject",
                "s3:PutObject",
                "s3:AbortMultipartUpload",
                "s3:ListMultipartUploadParts"
            ],
            "Resource": [
                "arn:aws:s3:::velero-*/*"
            ]
        },
        {
            "Effect": "Allow",
            "Action": [
                "s3:ListBucket"
```

```
        ],
            "Resource": [
                "arn:aws:s3:::velero-*"
            ]
        }
    ]
}
```

4. Now fetch the `velero` Helm Chart:

```
$ helm repo add vmware-tanzu https://vmware-tanzu.github.
io/helm-charts
$ helm fetch vmware-tanzu/velero
#### The current version is 2.26.1###
$ tar -xvf velero-2.26.1.tgz
```

5. If you navigate to and read its `values.yaml` file, then you will see three images that you need to download and push into your private registry. In the current scenario, the images are `velero/velero:v1.7.0` (in the topmost section), `docker.io/bitnami/kubectl:1.21.0` (in the *Kubectl* section), and `velero/velero-plugin-for-aws:v1.3.0` (in the initContainers section). Replace both images, `velero/velero:v1.7.0` and `docker.io/bitnami/kubectl:1.21.0`, with your private ECR registry image URL and leave `velero-plugin-for-aws` as it is. You will pass the `velero-plugin-for-aws` image via the Helm CLI in *Step 7*.

6. After that, search for a section where you need to configure service account details. You need to provide the same service account name as you mentioned in OIDC:

```
serviceAccount:
  server:
    create: true
    name: velerosa
    annotations:
      eks.amazonaws.com/role-arn: "arn:aws:iam::<Your
accountid>:role/dso-eks-velero-role"
    labels:
```

7. Run the `helm` command to install the `velero` server on EKS:

```
$ kubectl create ns velero
$ helm install velero velero \
--namespace velero \
```

```
--set configuration.provider=aws \
--set configuration.backupStorageLocation.name=default \
--set configuration.backupStorageLocation.bucket=velero-
backup-antikythera \
--set configuration.backupStorageLocation.config.
region=us-east-1 \
--set configuration.volumeSnapshotLocation.name=aws-
default \
--set configuration.volumeSnapshotLocation.config.
region=us-east-1 \
--set initContainers[0].name=velero-plugin-for-aws \
--set initContainers[0].image=<youraccount>.dkr.ecr.
us-east-1.amazonaws.com/velero:awsPluginImage \
--set initContainers[0].volumeMounts[0].mountPath=/target
\
--set initContainers[0].volumeMounts[0].name=plugins
```

8. Now you can check the deployment:

```
$ kubectl get pods -n velero
NAME                        READY    STATUS     RESTARTS
AGE
velero-77575f56c7-bzw6n     1/1      Running    0
36m
```

9. At this stage, your velero Pod will work if your EKS cluster is public. But our cluster is private, so we need to modify the deployment and add two environment variables:

```
$ kubectl edit deployment velero -n velero -o yaml
#### Add this two Environment Variable and save the file
#####
        - name: AWS_REGION
          value: us-east-1
        - name: AWS_STS_REGIONAL_ENDPOINTS
          value: regional
```

10. Once you save the deployment, it will take a while to terminate the older velero Pod and create a new one:

```
kubectl get pods -n velero
NAME                        READY    STATUS     RESTARTS
AGE
```

| velero-6b8df74887-kxmxr 6m59s | 0/1 | Terminating | 0 |
| velero-77575f56c7-bzw6n 45s | 1/1 | Running | 0 |

11. Once the `velero` Pod is up and running successfully, let's try to create a backup of MongoDB, which we installed in the previous section:

```
$ velero backup create mongobkp --include-namespaces
mongodb
```
```
$ velero backup describe mongobkp
```

12. The output of the preceding command will show that five snapshots have been taken and all the resources have been stored in the default location, which is the S3 bucket location. If you go to the S3 bucket and EBS snapshot console, you can verify the snapshots and backup content of MongoDB:

☐	kubernetes-dynamic-pvc-323d405c-4aae-4951-9da5-da01fd4570ca	snap-000967bfa3cbfc60c	8 GiB
☐	kubernetes-dynamic-pvc-984c8e2e-54c3-4b6c-a246-e5c4fe099de3	snap-09f182d8608847b15	8 GiB
☐	kubernetes-dynamic-pvc-59150af6-3ca6-478b-8635-8afbffd9cf1f	snap-0ae704b965509aeed	8 GiB
☐	kubernetes-dynamic-pvc-b9009ad5-a489-4321-9487-e15ef7be7200	snap-01623799233f27ea0	8 GiB
☐	kubernetes-dynamic-pvc-e75e6fbc-f07f-4a07-8547-40f61f20933e	snap-033ad4b86257603b8	8 GiB

Figure 5.42 – Snapshot of volume and S3 bucket containing the backup

13. Now let's restore the MongoDB backup, but before that, we need to delete MongoDB from the cluster:

```
$ helm del mongodb -n mongodb
### delete all 5 pvc in mongodb namespace
$ kubectl delete pvc <pvcname> -n mongodb
```

14. To restore MongoDB in the new namespace with the backup, run the following command and verify it:

```
$ velero restore create --from-backup mongobkp
--namespace-mappings mongodb:mongonew
$ kubectl get pods -n mongonew
```

NAME	READY	STATUS	RESTARTS	AGE
mongodb-0	1/1	Running	0	8m16s
mongodb-1	1/1	Running	0	8m16s
mongodb-2	1/1	Running	0	8m16s
mongodb-3	1/1	Running	0	8m16s
mongodb-4	1/1	Running	0	8m16s
mongodb-arbiter-0	1/1	Running	2	8m16s

You can see all the Pods are running in the new mongonew namespace. You can also restore this backup to another EKS cluster with some additional settings.

Summary

In this chapter, you learned how to implement a fully functional private EKS cluster, with lots of gotchas. Also, we installed some important add-ons and learned about concepts such as IRSA and the EBS CSI driver. We learned how to enforce policies using OPA and see the security recommendation using Kubescape. Once our cluster was ready to deploy an application, we deployed a StatefulSet MongoDB application, and then tried to create a backup and restoration using Velero. In the next chapter, we will learn about the important concept of chaos engineering and implement it on an EKS node with the Amazon FIS service.

6

Chaos Engineering with AWS Fault Injection Simulator

This chapter covers the concept of **chaos engineering** and when it is needed. It will walk you through the principle of chaos engineering and give insights in terms of where chaos engineering fits in concerning **Continuous Integration (CI)** / **Continuous Delivery/ Deployment (CD)**. We will implement chaos action on EC2 instances, the **Relational Database Service (RDS)**, and the **Elastic Container Service for Kubernetes (EKS)** worker node group via the **AWS Fault Injection Simulator**, and verify whether the infrastructure is fault-tolerant and the application still responsive. Performing this experiment will give you sufficient confidence to place this as part of CI/CD in your organization.

In this chapter, we are going to cover the following main topics:

- The concept of, and need for, chaos engineering
- Chaos engineering in CI/CD
- Experimenting with AWS FIS on multiple EC2 instances with a terminate action

- Experimenting with AWS FIS on EC2 instances with a CPU stress action
- Experimenting with AWS FIS on RDS with a reboot and failover action
- Experimenting with AWS FIS on an EKS cluster worker node

Technical requirements

To get started, you will require an AWS account and admin-level privileges in that account because we will be interacting with IAM services. You will also find the necessary source code used in this chapter in the `chapter-06-nodejsrestapi` and `chapter-06-starkapp` folder of the `https://github.com/PacktPublishing/Accelerating-DevSecOps-on-AWS.git`.

The concept of, and need for, chaos engineering

In the past, or still somewhere within the finance industry, software systems used to run in an on-premises or controlled environment with the help of an army of system administrators. Today, in the era of the cloud, migration to the cloud is relentless. Software systems are no longer monolithic but uncoupled in the form of microservices. The new and advanced distributed modern IT infrastructure requires robust systems thinking and reliability engineering to ensure that systems are always up and running. Downtime is no longer an option and may impact businesses. To make sure that these systems don't fail or increase the resiliency of these systems, the discipline of chaos engineering emerged.

This is how the chaos community defines chaos engineering:

> *"Chaos engineering is the discipline of experimenting on a system to build confidence in the system's capability to withstand turbulent conditions in production."*

Chaos engineering is not a new concept. Engineers think that it was introduced by *Netflix* in 2010, while there was the concept of *Game Day* in Amazon in 2000 before any big retail sale. Engineers used to simulate data center failure and test that systems were still up and running. In 2010, Netflix introduced the **Fault Injection Testing** chaos engineering framework, which resulted in disruption to, and the failure of, the distributed system where your application was running. Tools such as **Chaos Monkey** and **Chaos Kong** are famous fault injection testing tools. However, chaos engineering doesn't only mean injecting faults into the system; it's a process that is explained in its principles.

Principles of chaos engineering

The whole purpose of chaos engineering is to plan an experiment that shows us how our systems behave during failure and how we can make the system resilient:

1. **Plan an experiment**: You create a hypothesis based on the steady behavior of the system and how it will behave if something goes wrong.

2. **Contain the blast radius**: You create a real-word scenario experiment and test it on the system.

3. **Scale or squash**: You measure the impact of the failure at every stage and look for signs of failure and success.

You can create fault injection simulation by writing your own script using Bash or any programming language of your choice. AWS has introduced an amazing, fully managed chaos engineering service called **AWS Fault Injection Simulator (AWS FIS)**

AWS FIS

AWS FIS is a managed chaos engineering service that enables you to perform fault injection experiments on your AWS workloads. It provides an automated set of actions that invokes the API to perform certain operations. In this chapter, we will learn how to perform fault injection experiments on the AWS workloads using FIS, but before that, let's understand some of the terminology used in FIS:

- **Experiment template**: An experiment template includes a blueprint of your experiments. It contains the actions, target, and stop conditions for the experiment. Once you have created an experiment template, you can start the experiment and track its status.

- **Actions**: An action is a task or activity that AWS FIS applies to AWS resources during the experiment. Actions can run sequentially or in parallel. Currently, AWS FIS provides the following actions:
  - `aws:fis:inject-api-internal-error`
  - `aws:fis:inject-api-throttle-error`
  - `aws:fis:inject-api-unavailable-error`
  - `aws:fis:wait`
  - `aws:cloudwatch:assert-alarm-state`
  - `aws:ec2:send-spot-instance-interruptions`
  - `aws:ec2:reboot-instances`

- `aws:ec2:stop-instances`

- `aws:ec2:terminate-instances`

- `aws:ecs:drain-container-instances`

- `aws:eks:terminate-nodegroup-instance`

- `aws:rds:failover-db-cluster`

- `aws:rds:reboot-db-instances`

- `aws:ssm:send-command`

- `aws:ssm:start-automation-execution`

- **Targets**: A target is one or more AWS resources on which AWS FIS will perform the actions within the framework of the experiment. Currently, AWS FIS supports the following target AWS resources.

  - **Amazon Elastic Compute Cloud (Amazon EC2)**

  - **Amazon Elastic Container Service (Amazon ECS)**

  - **Amazon Elastic Kubernetes Service (Amazon EKS)**

  - **Amazon Relational Database Service (Amazon RDS)**

AWS FIS provides the chaos service using a console as well as a CLI. In the next section of this chapter, we will learn about the stage of CI/CD when chaos testing fits.

Chaos engineering in CI/CD

Chaos tests in CI/CD are well designed, carefully scripted, and automated tests that execute in runtime during the CI/CD process. They are triggered any time after the build all the way through to deployment in production

Chaos testing can be incorporated once the application has been deployed in staging and after the application has been deployed in production. The following diagram shows the chaos test steps in CI/CD:

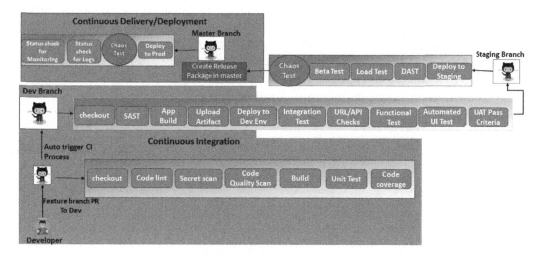

Figure 6.1 – Chaos test in CI/CD

In the preceding diagram, we are performing a chaos test after the application has been deployed in staging and is ready to be promoted to production. Before it is deployed to production, we need to monitor the behavior of the software system using a chaos test. Following that, we will implement a chaos test when the application is running in production. This test needs to be scheduled to run. During the test, we need to continuously monitor the system, too. We will actually implement a chaos test in CI/CD in *Chapter 8, DevSecOps Using AWS Native Services* and *Chapter 9, DevSecOps Pipeline with AWS Services and Tools Popular Industry-Wide*. In this chapter, we will run the FIS experiment template to first understand how chaos takes place in AWS workloads.

Experimenting with AWS FIS on multiple EC2 instances with a terminate action

In this section of the chapter, we will first deploy a sample application on EC2 instances, which will be part of the **Autoscaling group**. There will be a load balancer on top of the EC2 instance to handle the traffic. We will use FIS to terminate the EC2 instance and validate that the application is still accessible and that new EC2 instances are spinning up automatically and will serve the request shortly.

Perform the following steps to implement the experiment using AWS FIS:

1. Create an IAM role, `AmazonSSMRoleForInstanceQuickSetup`, and attach the `AmazonSSMManagedInstanceCore` AWS managed policy. Then, go to the AWS EC2 console and click on **Launch configurations** in the bottom-left corner. Then, click on **Create launch configuration**.

Figure 6.2 – Creating a launch configuration

2. Provide the configuration information to create a launch configuration, as follows:

    I.   **Name**: FIS-ASLC

    II.   **AMI**: `ami-01cc34ab2709337aa <Select AMI ID of Amazon Linux 2>` based on your region

    III. **Instance type**: **t2.micro**

    IV.   **IAM Instance profile**: **AmazonSSMRoleForInstanceQuickSetup**

    V.   In the **Additional configuration** section, under **Advanced details**, **User data**, paste the following snippet, which is a Bootstrap script that installs the Docker binary and runs a sample application. This application shows the IP address of the server on the web page:

```bash
#!/bin/bash
sudo yum update -y
sudo yum install docker -y
sudo systemctl start docker
sudo systemctl enable docker
sudo usermod -aG docker $USER
host=$(hostname)
sudo docker run -h $host --name $host -d -p 80:80 nicksrj/nova
```

VI. In **Security groups**, restrict **SSH Source type** to **Custom IP** and give your office/home IP address (you can get this from `https://www.whatismyip.com`) under **Source**, for example: `23.23.23.23/32`.

VII. Click on **Add new rule** and add an HTTP port to anywhere.

Figure 6.3 – Adding rules in security groups

VIII. In **Key pair (login)**, you can choose to select the existing key pair (make sure you have access to that key) or create a new key pair and click on **Download key pair**. Then, click on **Create launch configuration**.

Key pair (login) Info

Key pair options

Create a new key pair   ▼

Key pair name

FIS-KP

Download key pair

ⓘ You have to download the private key file (*.pem file) before you can continue. Store it in a secure and accessible location. You will not be able to download the file again after it's created.

Cancel   **Create launch configuration**

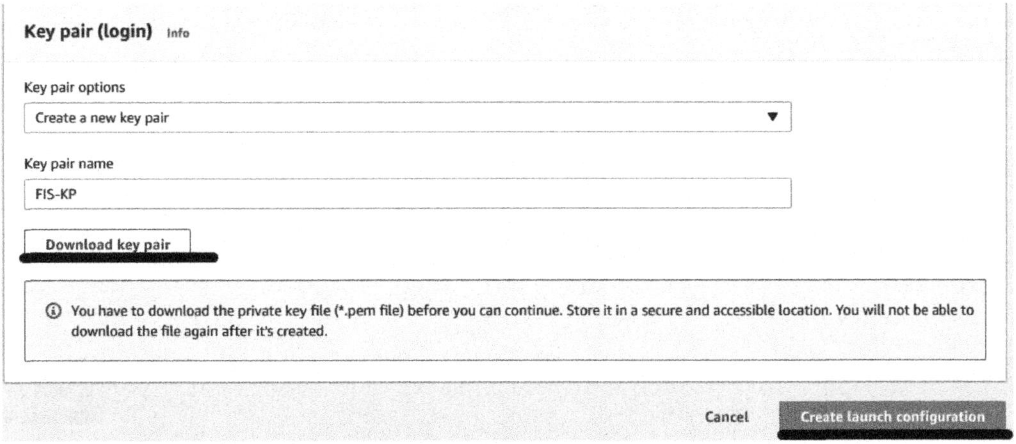

Figure 6.4 – Creating a new key pair

3. You will have created your launch configuration.

Figure 6.5 – Launch configurations list

4. Click on **Auto Scaling Groups** in the bottom-left corner and then click on **Create Auto Scaling group**.

5. Provide `FIS-ASG` in the **Auto Scaling group name** field. Then, click on **Switch to launch configuration** (if you are seeing the **Launch template section**). Select **Launch Configuration FIS-ASLC**, which we just created. Then, click on **Next** to proceed.

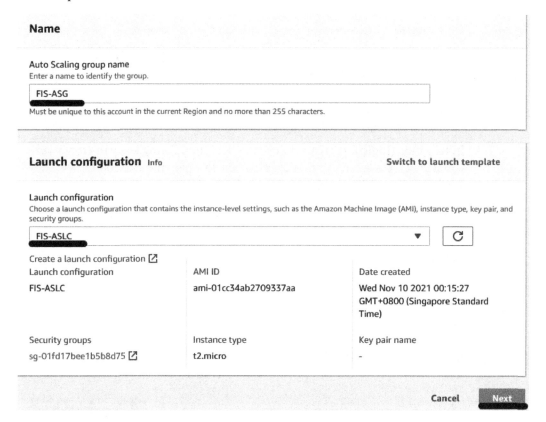

Figure 6.6 – Providing ASG information

6. In the **Network** section, select the default VPC and two/three subnets. Then, click on **Next**:

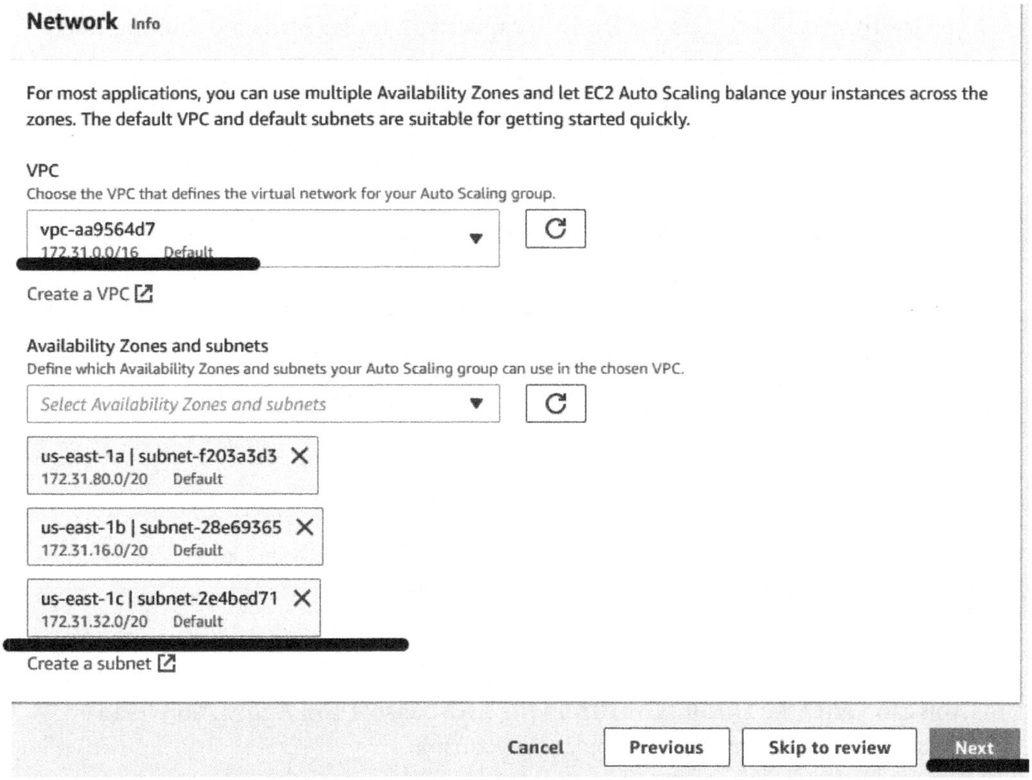

Network Info

For most applications, you can use multiple Availability Zones and let EC2 Auto Scaling balance your instances across the zones. The default VPC and default subnets are suitable for getting started quickly.

VPC
Choose the VPC that defines the virtual network for your Auto Scaling group.

| vpc-aa9564d7 | ▼ |
| 172.31.0.0/16   Default | |

Create a VPC ⟐

Availability Zones and subnets
Define which Availability Zones and subnets your Auto Scaling group can use in the chosen VPC.

| *Select Availability Zones and subnets* | ▼ |

| us-east-1a | subnet-f203a3d3 ✕ |
| 172.31.80.0/20   Default |

| us-east-1b | subnet-28e69365 ✕ |
| 172.31.16.0/20   Default |

| us-east-1c | subnet-2e4bed71 ✕ |
| 172.31.32.0/20   Default |

Create a subnet ⟐

Cancel   Previous   Skip to review   **Next**

Figure 6.7 – Providing ASG network information

7. In **Load balancing**, select **Attach to a new load balancer**. Make sure that **Application Load Balancer** has been selected as the load balancer type. Name the load balancer `FIS-ALB`. Under **Load balancer scheme**, select **Internet-facing**. In **Listeners and routing**, click on the **Default routing** dropdown and select **Create a target group**. Then, in the **New target group** field, provide a name of `FIS-ALB-TG`.

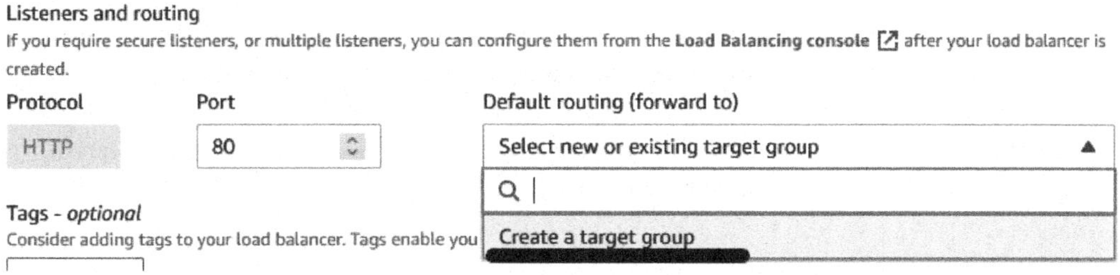

Listeners and routing
If you require secure listeners, or multiple listeners, you can configure them from the **Load Balancing console** ⟐ after your load balancer is created.

Protocol	Port	Default routing (forward to)
HTTP	80 ⌄	Select new or existing target group ▲
		Q |

Tags - *optional*
Consider adding tags to your load balancer. Tags enable you   **Create a target group**

Figure 6.8 – Creating a load balancer and target group

8. In **Health checks**, select **ELB**. Then, click on **Next**.

9. In **Group size**, insert 2 under **Desired capacity**, 2 under **Min**, and 3 under **Max**.

10. In **Scaling policies**, select **Target tracking scaling policy**. Then, select **Disable scale in** to create a scale-out policy only. Click on **Next** to proceed.

11. You can add an SNS notification, but we are skipping this step in this exercise. Click on **Next**.

12. Provide the tag details, which will be applied to EC2 instances spun up by this Auto Scaling Group (ASG). Insert Name in the **Key** field and FIS-Instance in the **Value** field. Then, click on **Next** to proceed to the review page.

13. Once you have reviewed all the information, click on **Create Auto Scaling group**. After a few minutes, you will have created an ASG with two instances.

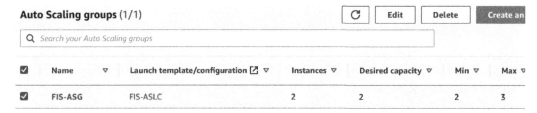

Figure 6.9 – ASG list

14. You can verify the EC2 instance from the EC2 console and Application Load Balancer (ALB) from the Load Balancers console.

Figure 6.10 – The top image shows EC2 instances and the bottom image shows the load balancer

15. Now, fetch the ALB DNS name, enter it in your browser, and you will be able to see the **Nova** application, which shows you the page getting served from which EC2 instance via the server name value. If you click on **Auto Refresh**, you will see that the **Server name** value will also change, meaning that the load balancer is transferring the request to both EC2 instances (172-31-44-121, 172-31-27-17).

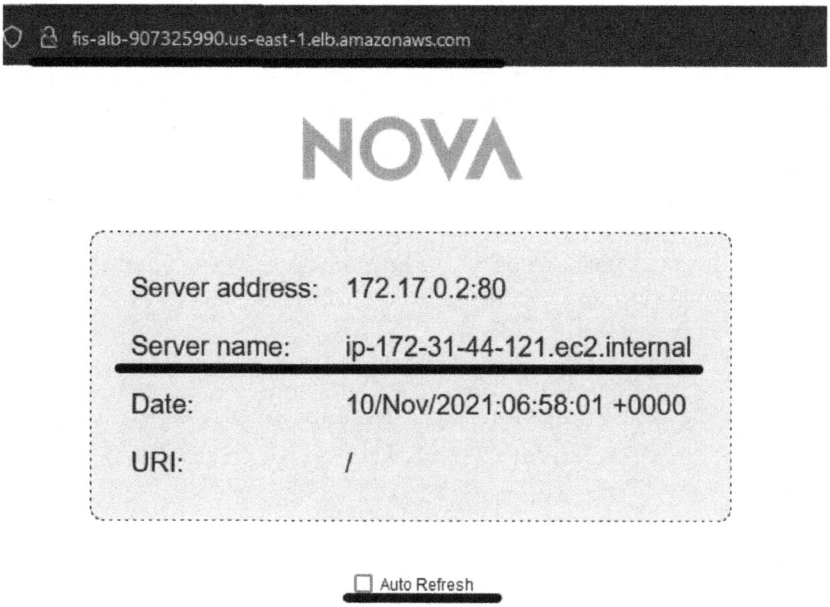

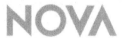

fis-alb-907325990.us-east-1.elb.amazonaws.com
NOVA
Server address: 172.17.0.2:80
Server name: ip-172-31-44-121.ec2.internal
Date: 10/Nov/2021:06:58:01 +0000
URI: /
Auto Refresh

Figure 6.11 – Nova web application

16. Once you have an app running, we need to create chaos by terminating an EC2 instance and verifying whether the application is still live and the new EC2 instance spins up and starts serving after a few minutes. You need to create an IAM role that will allow FIS to perform an action on the resources, including EC2 or RDS. Create a policy, `fis-ec2-policy`, with the following JSON snippet:

```
{
    "Version": "2012-10-17",
    "Statement": [
        {
            "Sid": "AllowFISExperimentRoleEC2ReadOnly",
            "Effect": "Allow",
            "Action": [
                "ec2:DescribeInstances"
            ],
            "Resource": "*"
        },
        {
            "Sid": "AllowFISExperimentRoleEC2Actions",
            "Effect": "Allow",
```

```
        "Action": [
                "ec2:RebootInstances",
                "ec2:StopInstances",
                "ec2:StartInstances",
                "ec2:TerminateInstances"
        ],
        "Resource": "arn:aws:ec2:*:*:instance/*"
    },
    {
        "Sid":
"AllowFISExperimentRoleSpotInstanceActions",
        "Effect": "Allow",
        "Action": [
                "ec2:SendSpotInstanceInterruptions"
        ],
        "Resource": "arn:aws:ec2:*:*:instance/*"
    }
    ]
}
```

17. Create an IAM role, `FIS-EC2-Role`, and attach the `fis-ec2-policy` policy. Then, replace the trust relationship of the role with the following snippet:

```
{
    "Version": "2012-10-17",
    "Statement": [
        {
            "Effect": "Allow",
            "Principal": {
                "Service": [
                    "fis.amazonaws.com"
                ]
            },
            "Action": "sts:AssumeRole"
        }
    ]
}
```

18. Go to the AWS FIS console and click on **Create experiment template**.

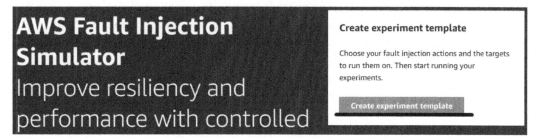

Figure 6.12 – FIS console page

19. On the **Create experiment template** page, under **Description**, provide the information related to the experiment (Experiment on ASG EC2 instance with Terminate action). Name the template EC2-Terminate-Experiment. In the **IAM role** field, select FIS-EC2-Role from the dropdown.

Description

Add a description for your experiment.

Experiment on ASG EC2 instance with Terminate action

Enter a description of up to 512 characters.

Name - *optional*

Creates a tag with a key of 'Name' and a value that you specify.

EC2-Terminate-Experiment

Enter a Name tag value of up to 256 characters.

IAM role

Select an IAM role to grant it permission to run the experiment. **Learn more**

FIS-EC2-Role ▼

Figure 6.13 – Experiment template information

20. In **Action section**, insert EC2-Teminate in both the **Name** and **Description** fields. Under **Action type**, select **aws:ec2:terminate-instances**, select and **Instances-Target-1** in the **Target** field. This is a default target name. Later, when you change the name of the target, you need to modify it here as well. Click on **Save** to save the action.

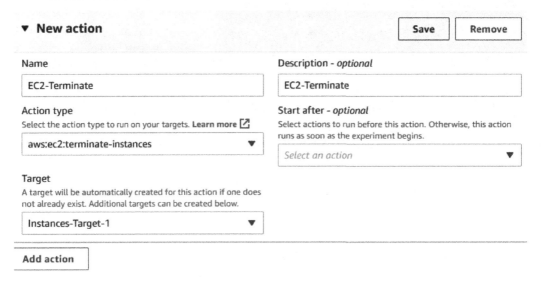

Figure 6.14 – Providing FIS Action details

21. Expand the **Instances-Target-1 (aws:ec2:instance)** field and click on **Edit**. Under **Target method**, select **Resource tags and filters**. Under **Selection mode**, choose **Percent**, and provide a value of 50. Under **Resource tags**, insert Name in the **Key** field and FIS-Instance in the **Value** field. Then, click on **Add new filter**, insert State.Name in the **Attribute path** field, and running in the **Values** field. Then, click on **Save**.

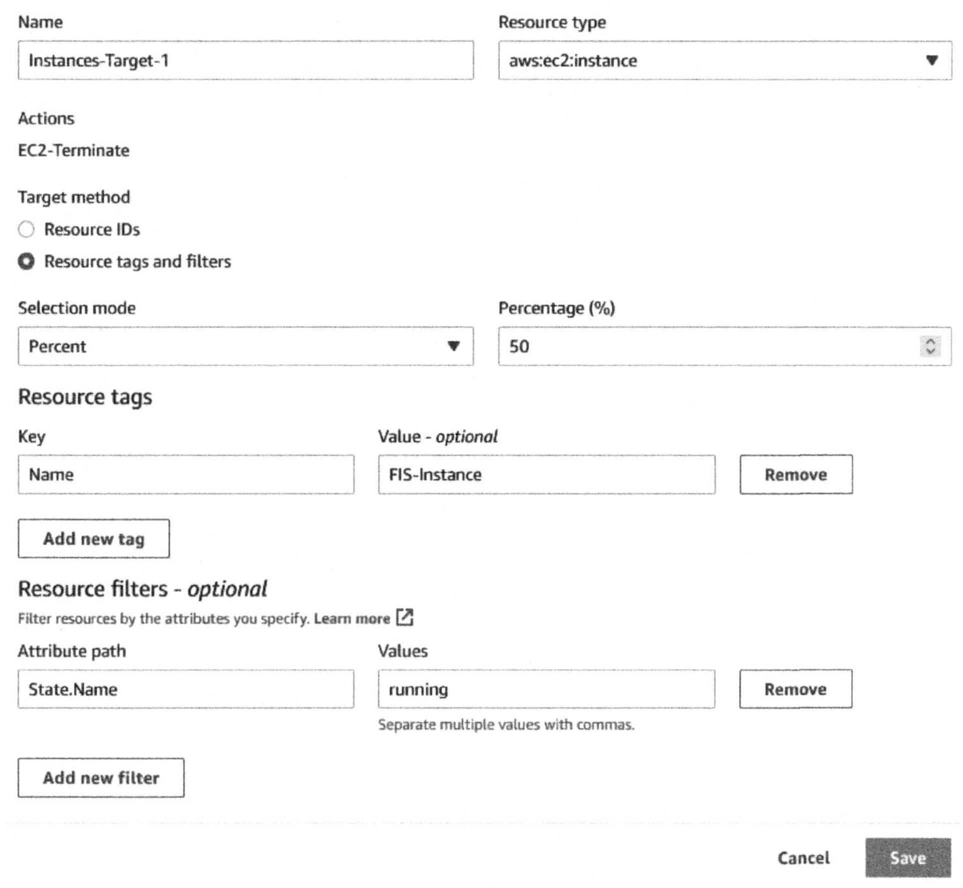

Name

Instances-Target-1

Resource type

aws:ec2:instance ▼

Actions

EC2-Terminate

Target method

○ Resource IDs

● Resource tags and filters

Selection mode

Percent ▼

Percentage (%)

50

Resource tags

Key

Name

Value - *optional*

FIS-Instance

Remove

Add new tag

Resource filters - *optional*

Filter resources by the attributes you specify. Learn more 🔗

Attribute path

State.Name

Values

running

Remove

Separate multiple values with commas.

Add new filter

Cancel   Save

Figure 6.15 – Providing FIS target details

22. Click on **Create experiment template** to create the FIS experiment template. For now, we are not creating a stop condition for the experiment, so enter the permissible string.

23. At this stage, the two instances we have are 172.31.27.17 and 172.31.44.121, which can be validated from the Nova web page. Now, go to the experiment template **Actions** dropdown and click on **Start**.

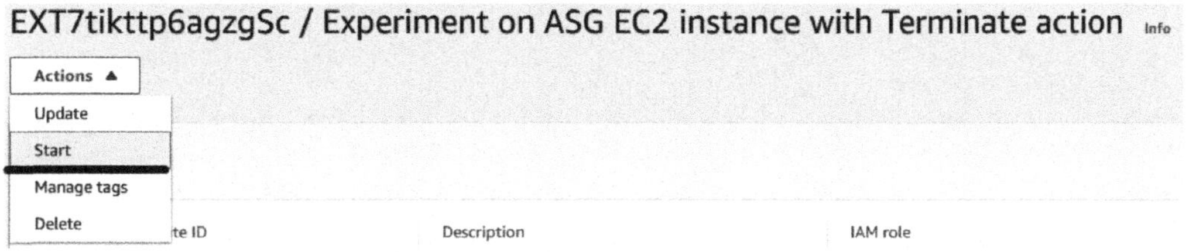

EXT7tikttp6agzgSc / Experiment on ASG EC2 instance with Terminate action Info

Actions ▲

Update

Start

Manage tags

Delete

te ID   Description   IAM role

Figure 6.16 – Starting the FIS experiment template

24. Insert Name in the **Key** field and EC2-Term-Exp-1 in the **Value** field and then click on **Start experiment**. It will ask for confirmation again because we are going to perform an experiment that will terminate your resource. Provide the confirmation string and then click on **Start experiment**.

25. Once you start the experiment, it will be in a pending and running state because it will invoke EC2 terminate action on the 50% of instances tagged with IFS-Instance.

Figure 6.17 – FIS experiment status and details

26. Once the experiment starts, you can navigate to the EC2 console, and you will see that one of the EC2 instances is in the **Terminated** state.

Figure 6.18 – Instance in a terminated state

27. Even in the Nova web application, the request is served from 172.31.27.17, and not from 172.31.44.121, because it has been terminated.

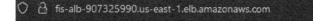

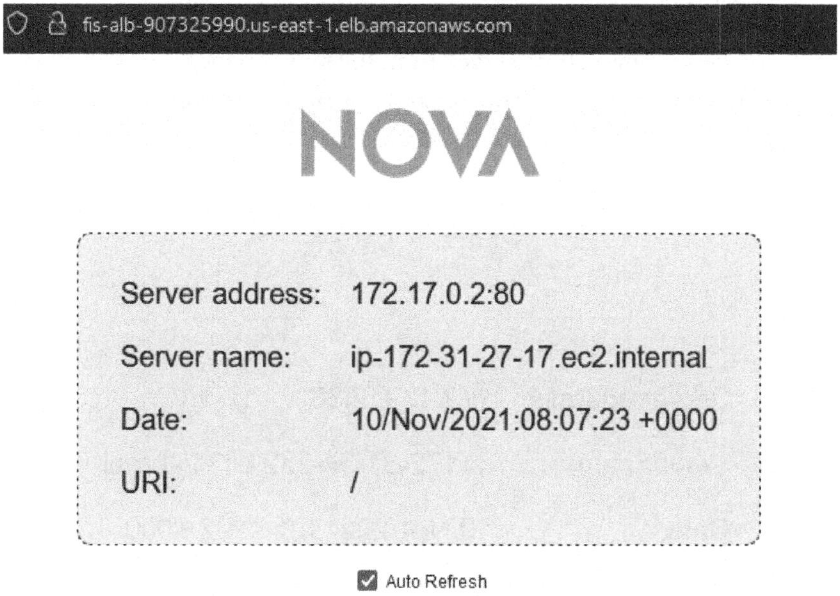

Server address: 172.17.0.2:80

Server name: ip-172-31-27-17.ec2.internal

Date: 10/Nov/2021:08:07:23 +0000

URI: /

☑ Auto Refresh

Figure 6.19 – Nova web application served by the 172.31.27.17 server only

28. At the same time, ASG will create another EC2 instance because our desired number of instances was two, and right now only one is in a running state. So, you can verify that the new instance is also spinning up.

	FIS-Instance	i-03cbff4e951710d47	⊘ Running	🔍🔍	t2.micro	🕐 Initializing	No alarms	+	us-ea
	FIS-Instance	i-025b87d437f797995	⊘ Running	🔍🔍	t2.micro	⊘ 2/2 checks passed	No alarms	+	us-ea
	FIS-Instance	i-02e89943089a98262	⊖ Terminated	🔍🔍	t2.micro	–	No alarms	+	us-ea

Figure 6.20 – New instance in a running state

29. At the same time, you can go to the Target group console and see that the new instance is being registered in the load balancer.

	Instance ID ▽	Name ▽	Port ▽	Zone ▽	Health status ▽	Health status details
	i-025b87d437f797995	FIS-Instance	80	us-east-1b	⊘ healthy	
	i-03cbff4e951710d47	FIS-Instance	80	us-east-1c	🕐 initial	Target registration is in progress

Figure 6.21 – A new instance being registered in the Target group

30. After a few minutes, once the server is registered, you can see in the Nova web app that the request is now getting served from the new instance too (172.31.34.232).

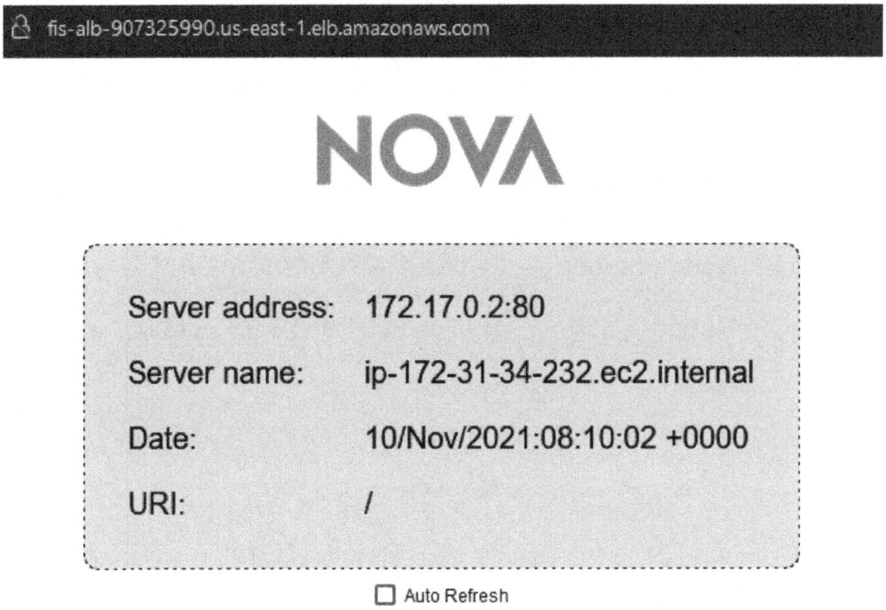

fis-alb-907325990.us-east-1.elb.amazonaws.com

Server address: 172.17.0.2:80

Server name: ip-172-31-34-232.ec2.internal

Date: 10/Nov/2021:08:10:02 +0000

URI: /

☐ Auto Refresh

Figure 6.22 – Nova web application served by a new instance

31. If you go to the experiment page again, you can see the state of the experiment is **Completed**.

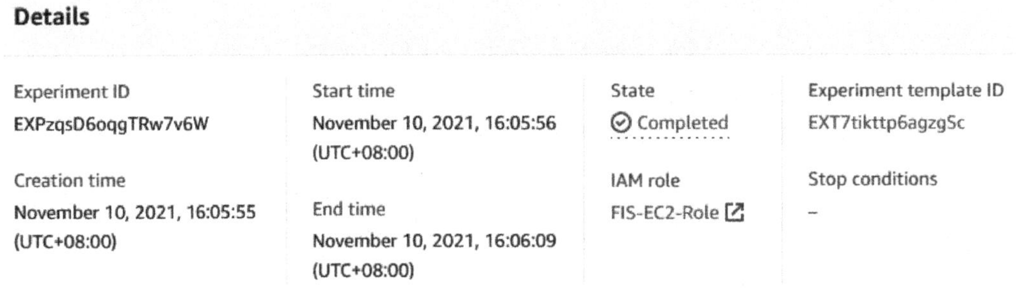

Details

Experiment ID	Start time	State	Experiment template ID
EXPzqsD6oqgTRw7v6W	November 10, 2021, 16:05:56 (UTC+08:00)	⊘ Completed	EXT7tikttp6agzgSc
Creation time		IAM role	Stop conditions
November 10, 2021, 16:05:55 (UTC+08:00)	End time	FIS-EC2-Role ⤢	–
	November 10, 2021, 16:06:09 (UTC+08:00)		

Figure 6.23 – FIS experiment completed

So, we just saw how AWS FIS created chaos in our existing running infrastructure, and since our application was running on an EC2 instance, which was backed by ASG and a load balancer, it recovered itself within a few minutes. In the next section, we will perform another experiment that is related to CPU stress on an EC2 instance.

Experimenting with AWS FIS on EC2 instances with a CPU stress action

In this section of the chapter, we will create an FIS experiment template that applies CPU stress to an EC2 instance using **Amazon Systems Manager Agent**. We will validate the fact that once the chaos experiment starts giving CPU stress to an EC2 instance and CPU utilization of the server increases by more than 50%, then ASG should automatically increase a new instance and take over the load.

Perform the following steps to implement the experiment using AWS FIS:

1. Since the AWS FIS CPU stress action uses an SSM agent on an EC2 instance, make sure that the SSM agent is installed and that the AmazonSSMRoleForInstanceQuickSetup IAM role is attached to both servers running in ASG. Amazon Linux 2 AMI comes with an SSM agent installed and in a running state. In *Step 2 | IV* of the previous section, *Experimenting with AWS FIS on multiple EC2 instances with a terminate action*, we also applied the IAM role to the launch configuration.

2. If you are using SSM for the first time, then you need to go to the AWS Systems Manager console, click on **Quick Setup** in the top-left corner, click on the required region, and then click on **Get Started**.

Figure 6.24 – AWS Systems Manager console

3. Click on **Create new configuration**, and then click on **Host Management**. Click on **Next** to proceed to the next page and then click on **Create** to complete the setup.

4. You will see that **Configuration deployment status** is in the **Running** state.

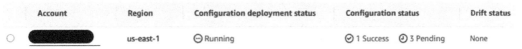

Figure 6.25 – Host management configuration deployment status

5.   After some time, you will see that the host management configuration deployment is successful.

Figure 6.26 – Success status of the configuration deployment

6.   Now you need to create an IAM policy, `fis-ssm-policy`, using the following snippet:

```
{
    "Version": "2012-10-17",
    "Statement": [
        {
            "Sid": "AllowFISExperimentRoleSSMReadOnly",
            "Effect": "Allow",
            "Action": [
                "ec2:DescribeInstances",
                "ssm:GetAutomationExecution",
                "ssm:ListCommands"
            ],
            "Resource": "*"
        },
        {
            "Sid": "AllowFISExperimentRoleSSMSendCommand",
            "Effect": "Allow",
            "Action": [
                "ssm:SendCommand"
```

```json
            ],
            "Resource": [
                "arn:aws:ec2:*:*:instance/*",
                "arn:aws:ssm:*:*:document/*"
            ]
        },
        {
            "Sid":
"AllowFISExperimentRoleSSMCancelCommand",
            "Effect": "Allow",
            "Action": [
                "ssm:CancelCommand"
            ],
            "Resource": "*"
        },
        {
            "Sid": "AllowFISExperimentRoleSSMAutomation",
            "Effect": "Allow",
            "Action": [
                "ssm:StartAutomationExecution",
                "ssm:StopAutomationExecution"
            ],
            "Resource": "*"
        },
        {
            "Sid":
"AllowFISExperimentRoleSSMAutomationPassRole",
            "Effect": "Allow",
            "Action": [
                "iam:PassRole"
            ],
            "Resource": "arn:aws:iam::<Your_Account_
ID>:role/ AmazonSSMRoleForInstanceQuickSetup"
        }
    ]
}
```

7. Create an IAM role, FIS-SSM-Role, and attach the fis-ssm-policy policy. Also, edit the trust relationship of the role with the following JSON snippet:

```
{
    "Version": "2012-10-17",
    "Statement": [
        {
            "Effect": "Allow",
            "Principal": {
                "Service": "fis.amazonaws.com"
            },
            "Action": "sts:AssumeRole"
        }
    ]
}
```

8. Now, go to the FIS console and click on **Create experiment template**.

9. Provide the following details in the **Description**, **Name**, and **IAM Role** fields:

    I.   **Description**: Experiment on ASG EC2 instance with CPU stress action

    II.   **Name**: EC2-CPU-Stress-Experiment

    III.   **IAM Role**: FIS-SSM-Role

10. Provide the following information in the **Action** section:

    I.   **Name**: CPU-Stress-Action.

    II.   **Description**: CPU-Stress-Action.

    III.   **Action type**: aws:ssm:send-command/AWSFIS-Run-CPU-Stress.

    IV.   **documentParameters**: {"DurationSeconds":"400"}.

    V.   **Duration**: 6 Minute

    VI.   Click on **Save**.

11. Edit the **Targets** field. Under **Target method**, select **Resource tags and filters**. In **Selection mode**, select **All**. Under **Resource tags**, click on **Add new tag**. Insert Name in the **Key** field and FIS-Instance in the **Value** field. Under **Resource filters**, click on **Add new filter**. Insert State.Name in the **Attribute path** field and running in the **Values** field. Then, click on **Save**.

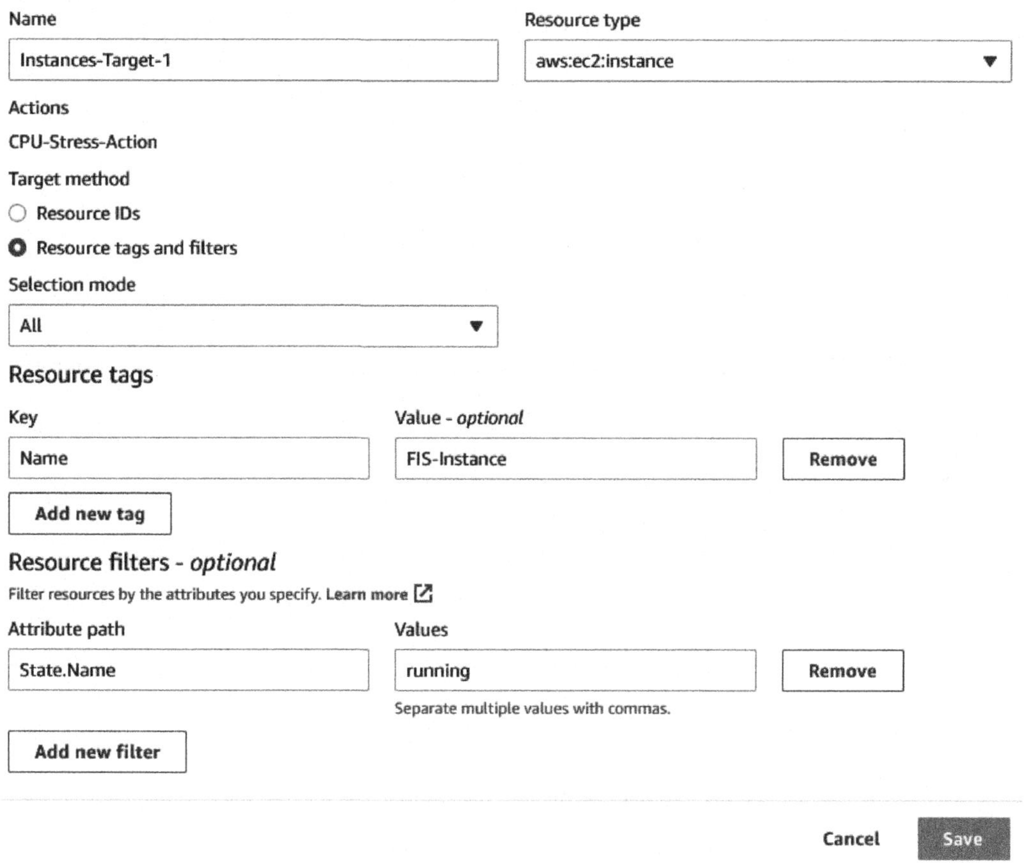

Name

Instances-Target-1

Resource type

aws:ec2:instance ▼

Actions

CPU-Stress-Action

Target method

○ Resource IDs

● Resource tags and filters

Selection mode

All ▼

Resource tags

Key

Name

Value - *optional*

FIS-Instance

Remove

Add new tag

Resource filters - *optional*

Filter resources by the attributes you specify. Learn more ☑

Attribute path

State.Name

Values

running

Remove

Separate multiple values with commas.

Add new filter

Cancel   Save

Figure 6.27 – Providing FIS target details

12. Click on **Create experiment template**. Provide a confirmation string and then click on **Create experiment template**.

13. Once you have created the template, we can start the experiment. Click in the **Actions** dropdown and then select **Start**. Provide the tag. Click on **Start experiment**. It will ask for confirmation again because we are going to perform an experiment that will impact your resource. Provide the confirmation string and click on **Start experiment**.

14. Once you start the experiment, the experiment will be in the **Running** status.

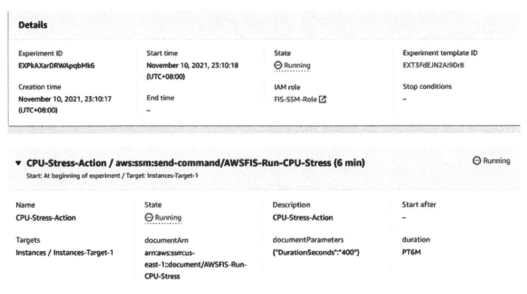

Figure 6.28 – Status of the FIS experiment

15. Go to the EC2 console, monitor one of the EC2 instances, and you will see that the CPU utilization of the server will go to more than 50%.

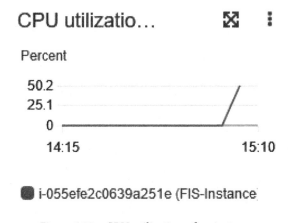

Figure 6.29 – CPU utilization of an instance

16. The moment it reaches 50% CPU utilization, the ASG scaling policy (which we set in *step 10* of the previous section, *Experimenting with AWS FIS on multiple EC2 instances with a terminate action*) will trigger, which scales the EC2 server from two to three instances.

☑	Name	▽	Launch template/configuration 🗗 ▽	Instances ▽	Desired capacity ▽	Min ▽	Max ▽	Availab
☑	FIS-ASG		FIS-ASLC	3	3	2	3	us-east-1

WaitingForI nstanceWar mup	Launching a new EC2 instance: i-06ef39defd934ecca	At 2021-11-10T15:13:51Z a monitor alarm TargetTracking-FIS-ASG-AlarmHigh-03656be5-0560-43a7-b0e8-3fbf6b6f36df in state ALARM triggered policy Target Tracking Policy changing the desired capacity from 2 to 3. At 2021-11-10T15:13:57Z an instance was started in response to a difference between desired and actual capacity, increasing the capacity from 2 to 3.
Successful	Launching a new EC2 instance: i-055efe2c0639a251e	At 2021-11-10T09:24:23Z a user request created an AutoScalingGroup changing the desired capacity from 0 to 2. At 2021-11-10T09:24:27Z an instance was started in response to a difference between desired and actual capacity, increasing the capacity from 0 to 2.

Figure 6.30 – Message upon reaching the CPU threshold and spinning a new instance

17. You can verify the new third EC2 instance in the EC2 console.

☐	Name	▽	Instance ID	Instance state	▲	Instance type	▽	Status check	Alarm status
☐	FIS-Instance		i-06ef39defd934ecca	⊘ Running ⊕⊖		t2.micro		⏱ Initializing	No alarms
☐	FIS-Instance		i-055efe2c0639a251e	⊘ Running ⊕⊖		t2.micro		⊘ 2/2 checks passed	No alarms
☐	FIS-Instance		i-0b903615a7593371f	⊘ Running ⊕⊖		t2.micro		⊘ 2/2 checks passed	No alarms

Figure 6.31 – New instance coming up

18. You can also verify that the Nova web application is also served from the new EC2 instance (172.31.38.94).

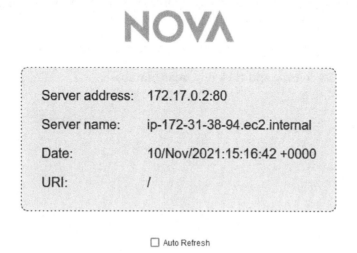

Figure 6.32 – Nova web application served from the new instance

19. After verifying this, you can see that your FIS experiment is complete.

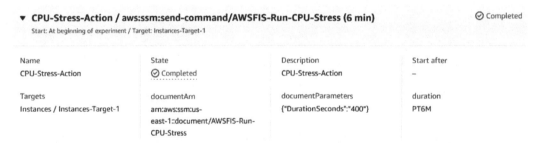

Figure 6.33 – Status of the FIS experiment

So, we just saw how AWS FIS created chaos on our existing running infrastructure, and since our application was running on an EC2 instance, which was backed by ASG with a scaling policy, it spins up another EC2 instance. In the next section, we will perform an action related to RDS master to RDS reader failover step.

Experimenting with AWS FIS on RDS with a reboot and failover action

In this section of the chapter, we will create an FIS experiment template that will invoke an API call to reboot a database cluster with failover. In failover, the read-only replica will be promoted as the primary instance (the cluster writer), and you can also see that the availability zone in use will also change. We will validate by reviewing the availability of the application during the reboot and failover of MySQL RDS. We will deploy an example Node.js REST API application with MySQL RDS.

Perform the following steps to implement the experiment using AWS FIS:

1. Go to the RDS console and click on **Create database**.

2. Select **Standard create** under **Choose a database creation method**. Select **MySQL** under **Engine type**.

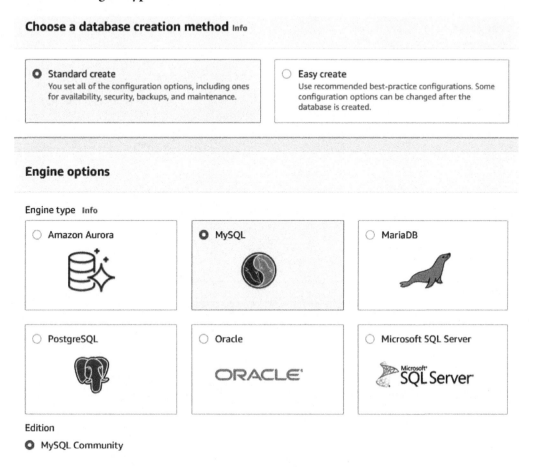

Figure 6.34 – Choosing a database engine

3. Under **Templates**, select **Dev/Test**, while under **DB instance identifier**, enter
    RDS-FIS. Complete the **Master password** and **Confirm password** fields.

Templates

Choose a sample template to meet your use case.

○ **Production**	● **Dev/Test**	○ **Free tier**
Use defaults for high availability and fast, consistent performance.	This instance is intended for development use outside of a production environment.	Use RDS Free Tier to develop new applications, test existing applications, or gain hands-on experience with Amazon RDS. **Info**

Settings

DB instance identifier Info

Type a name for your DB instance. The name must be unique across all DB instances owned by your AWS account in the current AWS Region.

```
RDS-FIS
```

The DB instance identifier is case-insensitive, but is stored as all lowercase (as in "mydbinstance"). Constraints: 1 to 60 alphanumeric characters or hyphens. First character must be a letter. Can't contain two consecutive hyphens. Can't end with a hyphen.

▼ **Credentials Settings**

Master username Info

Type a login ID for the master user of your DB instance.

```
admin
```

1 to 16 alphanumeric characters. First character must be a letter.

☐ **Auto generate a password**
    Amazon RDS can generate a password for you, or you can specify your own password.

Master password Info

```
••••••••••••
```

Constraints: At least 8 printable ASCII characters. Can't contain any of the following: / (slash), '(single quote), "(double quote) and @ (at sign).

Confirm password Info

```
••••••••••••
```

Figure 6.35 – Providing database credentials

4. Under **DB instance class**, select **Burstable classes** and **Include previous generation classes** (to enable older and cheaper instance types since this is an experiment). Deselect **Enable storage autoscaling**.

DB instance class   Info

○ Standard classes (includes m classes)

○ Memory optimized classes (includes r and x classes)

◉ Burstable classes (includes t classes)

db.t2.micro ▼
1 vCPUs   1 GiB RAM   Not EBS Optimized

🔘 Include previous generation classes

Storage

Storage type   Info

General Purpose SSD (gp2) ▼
Baseline performance determined by volume size

Allocated storage

20 ⬍	GiB

(Minimum: 20 GiB. Maximum: 16,384 GiB) Higher allocated storage **may improve** IOPS performance.

> ⓘ Provisioning less than 100 GiB of General Purpose (SSD) storage for high throughput result in higher latencies upon exhaustion of the initial General Purpose (SSD) IO credit more 🗗

Storage autoscaling   Info
Provides dynamic scaling support for your database's storage based on your application's needs.

☐ Enable storage autoscaling
Enabling this feature will allow the storage to increase once the specified threshold is exceeded.

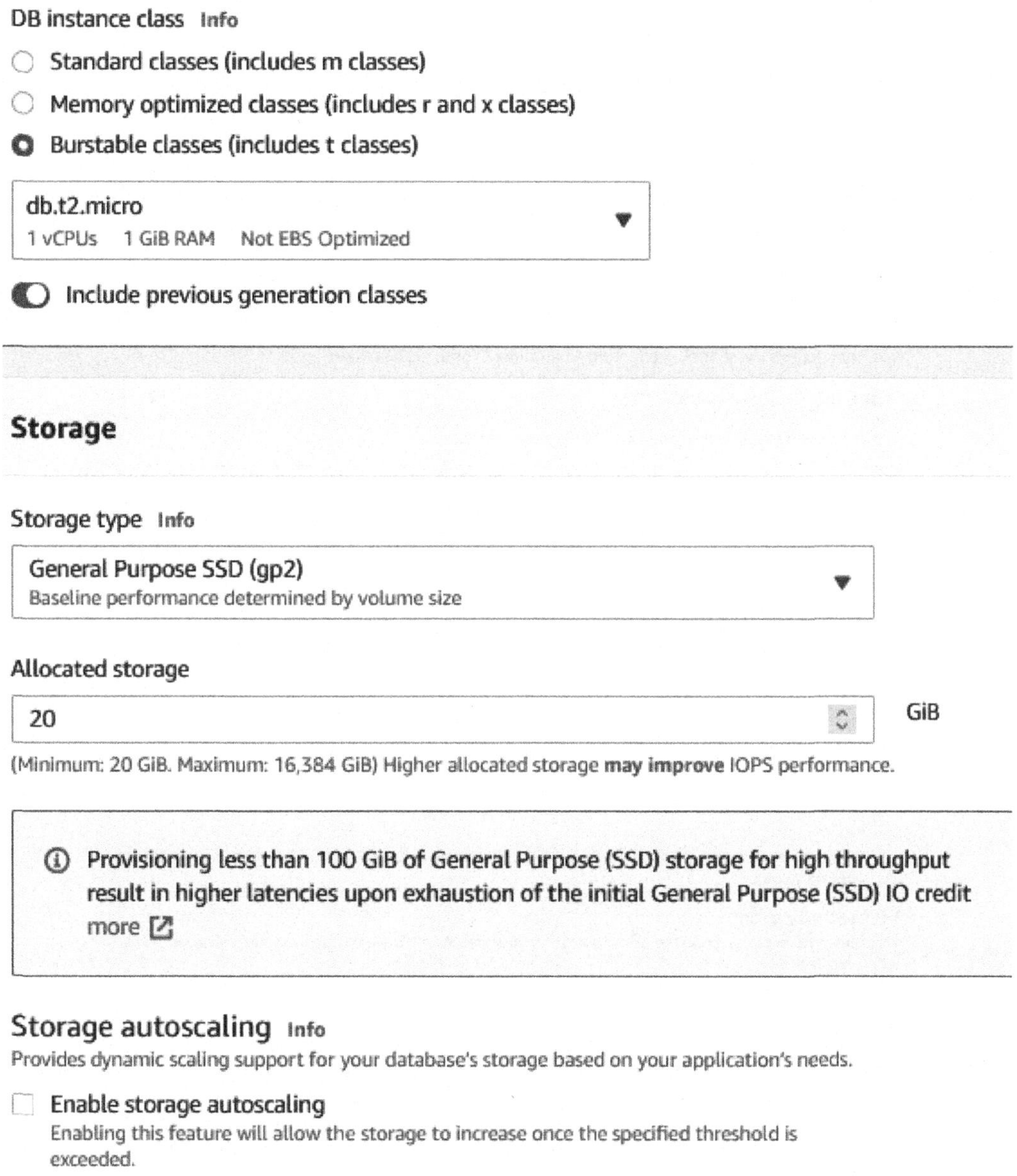

Figure 6.36 – Providing database storage details

5. Under **Multi-AZ deployment**, select **Create a standby instance**. Under **Virtual private cloud (VPC)**, select **Default VPC**. Select **Yes** under **Public access** (not recommended in production). Choose the default security group.

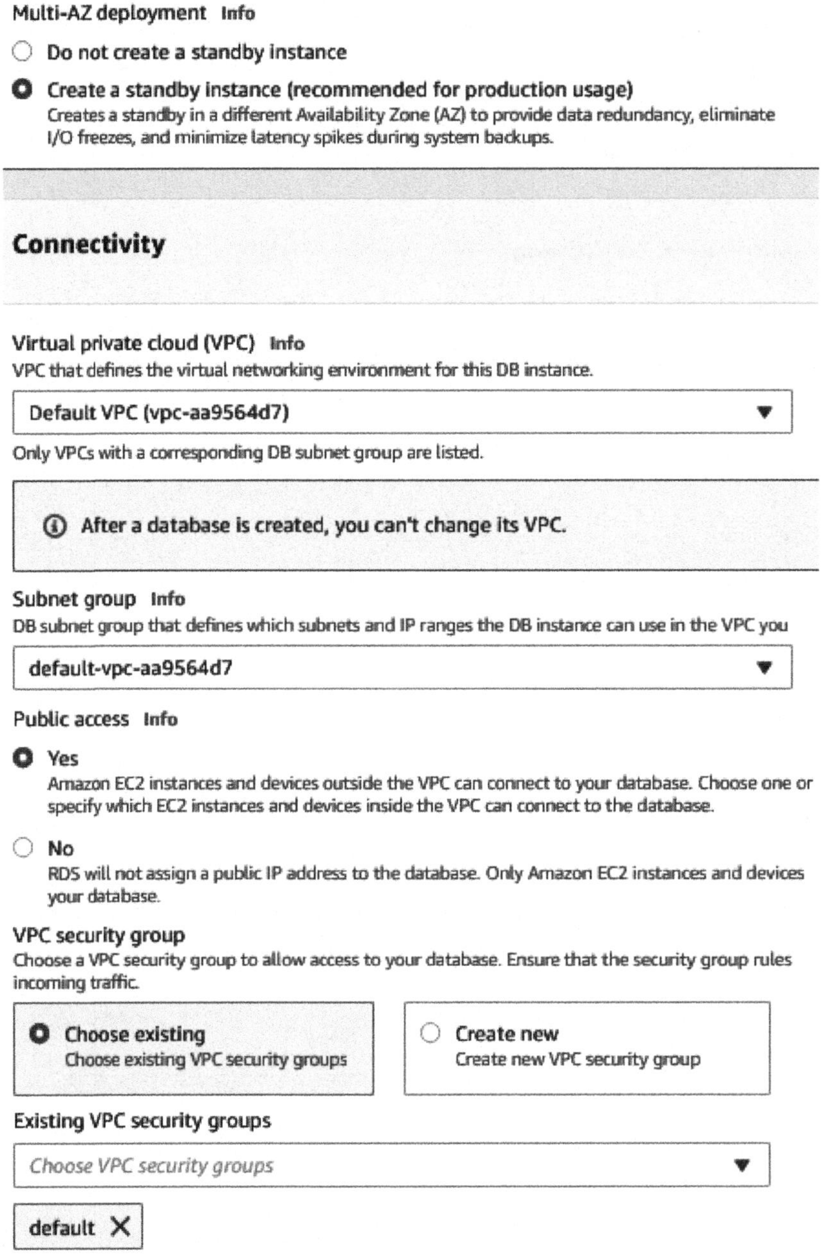

Multi-AZ deployment Info

○ Do not create a standby instance

● Create a standby instance (recommended for production usage)
Creates a standby in a different Availability Zone (AZ) to provide data redundancy, eliminate I/O freezes, and minimize latency spikes during system backups.

Connectivity

Virtual private cloud (VPC) Info
VPC that defines the virtual networking environment for this DB instance.

Default VPC (vpc-aa9564d7) ▼

Only VPCs with a corresponding DB subnet group are listed.

ⓘ After a database is created, you can't change its VPC.

Subnet group Info
DB subnet group that defines which subnets and IP ranges the DB instance can use in the VPC you

default-vpc-aa9564d7 ▼

Public access Info

● Yes
Amazon EC2 instances and devices outside the VPC can connect to your database. Choose one or specify which EC2 instances and devices inside the VPC can connect to the database.

○ No
RDS will not assign a public IP address to the database. Only Amazon EC2 instances and devices your database.

VPC security group
Choose a VPC security group to allow access to your database. Ensure that the security group rules incoming traffic.

● Choose existing	○ Create new
Choose existing VPC security groups	Create new VPC security group

Existing VPC security groups

Choose VPC security groups ▼

default ✕

Figure 6.37 – Providing database network details

6. Select **Password authentication** under the database authentication options. Expand **Additional configuration** and then, in the **Initial database** field, insert `student_ dev` and then click on **Create database**. You will see that a database instance will be in the **Creating** state. After 10-15 minutes, the database status will change to **Available**. Once you click on the database and select the **Configuration** tab, you will see the necessary information, which shows that the database is **Multi-AZ**, that the primary AZ is **us-east-1b** (in my case), while the secondary AZ is **us-east-1f**.

Figure 6.38 – RDS configuration information

7. Go to **Security group rule ID** (which is the default security group) and add a `MYSQL/Aurora` rule for the VPC CIDR (in my case, `172.31.0.0/16`) source because we will spin up an EC2 instance, which runs an application, in the same VPC.

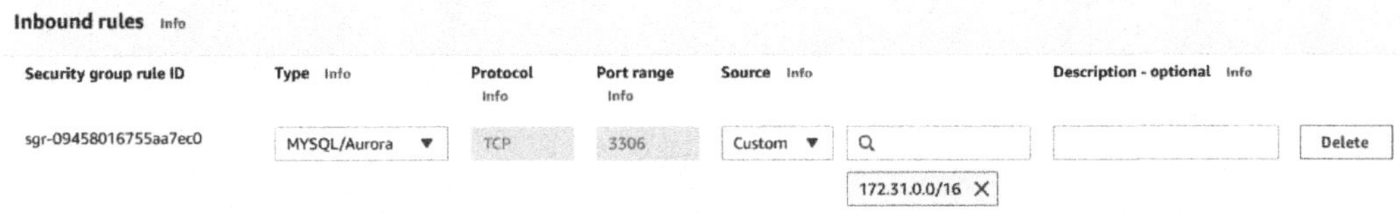

Figure 6.39 – Adding a MySQL rule to the RDS Security group

8. Now you need to spin up an EC2 instance with Amazon Linux 2 AMI and select the default VPC, enable the subnet, provide the following user data script (change the password and database endpoint in the script), provide 10 GB of storage, enable SSH and HTTP (to your home/office IP address), and select a key pair that you already have:

```bash
#!/bin/bash
sudo yum update -y
sudo yum install docker mysql telnet git jq  -y
sudo systemctl enable docker
sudo systemctl start docker
sudo amazon-linux-extras install epel -y
sudo yum install moreutils -y
git clone https://github.com/PacktPublishing/Modern-CI-CD-on-AWS.git
cd Modern-CI-CD-on-AWS/chapter-06-nodejsrestapi
jq '.development.username = "admin"' config/config.json | sponge config/config.json
jq '.development.password = "<DB_PASSWORD>"' config/config.json | sponge config/config.json
jq '.development.host = "<DB_ENDPOINT>"' config/config.json | sponge config/config.json
sudo docker build -t nodejs-express-mysql:v1 .
sudo docker run -d -p 80:3000 -p 3306:3306 --name nodejs-api-app nodejs-express-mysql:v1
```

9. Once you have your EC2 instance ready, fetch the public IP address of the server and put it in Postman (you can download Postman here: https://www.postman.com/downloads/). In my case, the public IP address is 54.91.118.188. You perform a GET request and insert the URL as http://PUBLIC_IP/students. You will get an empty array, [], as a reply, which means that database connectivity is there, just that there is no data.

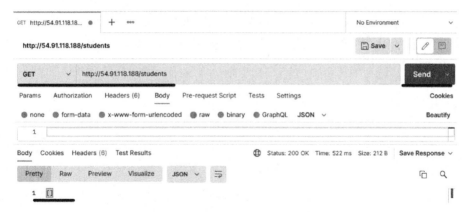

Figure 6.40 – Postman console showing the GET request result of the student record

10. We will upload a student record that will be saved in the database. Use a POST request with the following body. You will see the message Post created successfully:

```
{
    id: 1,
    firstname": "Julius",
    lastname": "Caesar",
    class: 3A,
    nationality: Rome
}
```

Figure 6.41 – Postman Console showing the POST request result of the student record

11. Now you can run the same GET request as you did in *step 9*, and you will get the student record. This means that our application is running fine and able to add and read data from the database.

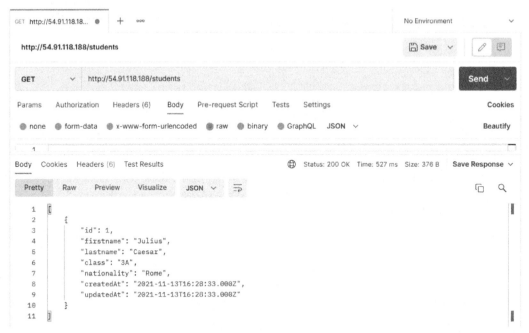

Figure 6.42 – Postman console showing the GET request result of the student record

12. Now we will create an FIS experiment template to inject a database reboot and failover, which will have an impact on the application. Before we create an experiment template, we need to create an IAM policy, `fis-rds-policy`, using the following code snippet:

```
{
    "Version": "2012-10-17",
    "Statement": [
        {
            "Sid": "AllowFISExperimentRoleRDSReadOnly",
            "Effect": "Allow",
            "Action": [
                "rds:DescribeDBInstances",
                "rds:DescribeDbClusters"
            ],
            "Resource": "*"
```

```
        },
        {
            "Sid": "AllowFISExperimentRoleRDSReboot",
            "Effect": "Allow",
            "Action": [
                "rds:RebootDBInstance"
            ],
            "Resource": "arn:aws:rds:*:*:db:*"
        },
        {
            "Sid": "AllowFISExperimentRoleRDSFailOver",
            "Effect": "Allow",
            "Action": [
                "rds:FailoverDBCluster"
            ],
            "Resource": "arn:aws:rds:*:*:cluster:*"
        }
    ]
}
```

13. Create an IAM role, `FIS-RDS-Role`, and attach `fis-rds-policy` to it. Edit the trust relationship with the following snippet:

```
{
    "Version": "2012-10-17",
    "Statement": [
        {
            "Effect": "Allow",
            "Principal": {
                "Service": [
                    "fis.amazonaws.com"
                ]
            },
            "Action": "sts:AssumeRole"
        }
    ]
}
```

14.   Once the IAM role has been created, go to the FIS console and click on **Create experiment template**. Provide the following details in the **Description**, **Name**, and **IAM Role** fields:

  I.   **Description**: RDS-Resiliency-Test

  II.   **Name**: RDS-Resiliency-Test

  III. **IAM Role**: FIS-RDS-Role

15. Provide the following information in the **Action** section. Then, click on **Save**:

  I.   **Name**: RDS-FIS-Action

  II.   **Action type**: aws:rds:reboot-db-instances

  III. **Target**: DBInstance-Target-1

  IV.   **forceFailover**: true

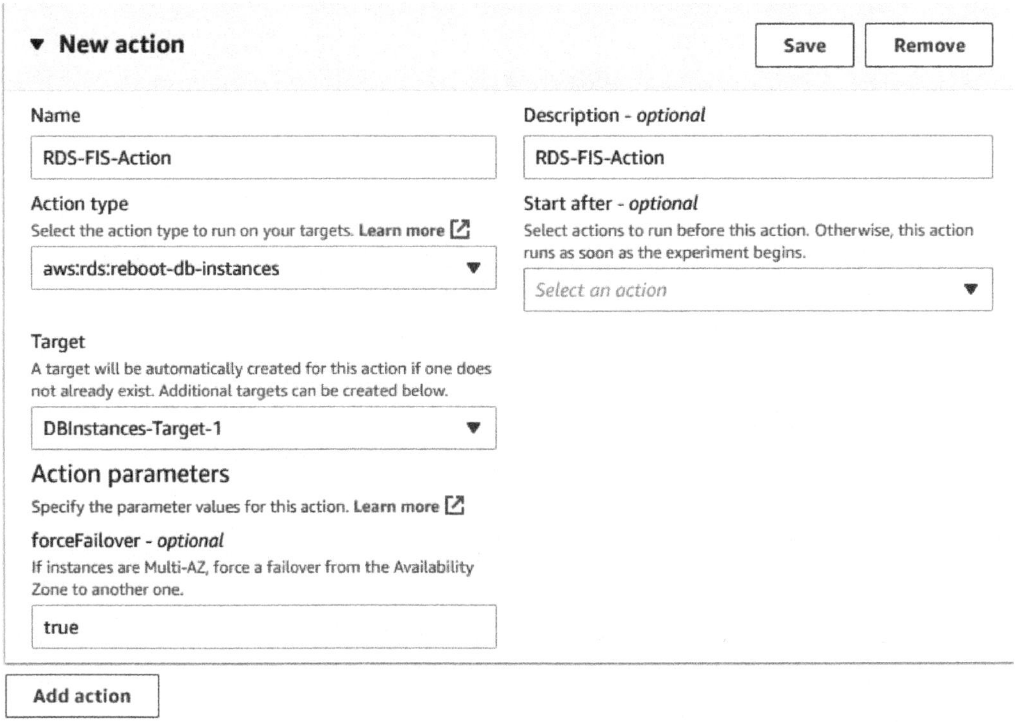

Figure 6.43 – Providing details for the FIS action

16. Click on **Edit** in **DBInstances-Target-1**. Click on the **Resource IDs** dropdown and select the **rds-fis** RDS instance, and then click on **Save**. Then, click on **Create experiment template**.

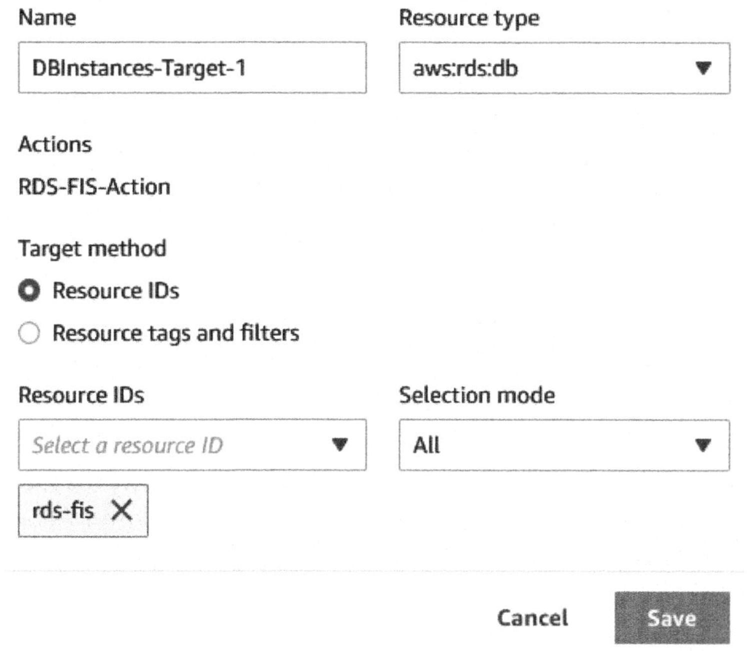

Name

DBInstances-Target-1

Resource type

aws:rds:db ▼

Actions

RDS-FIS-Action

Target method

● Resource IDs

○ Resource tags and filters

Resource IDs

Select a resource ID ▼

Selection mode

All ▼

rds-fis ✕

Cancel   Save

Figure 6.44 – Providing FIS target details

17. Once you have created an experiment template, click on the **Action** dropdown button and then click on **Start** to start the experiment. Provide a tag and give a confirmation string because you are going to perform disruptive action on your application environment.

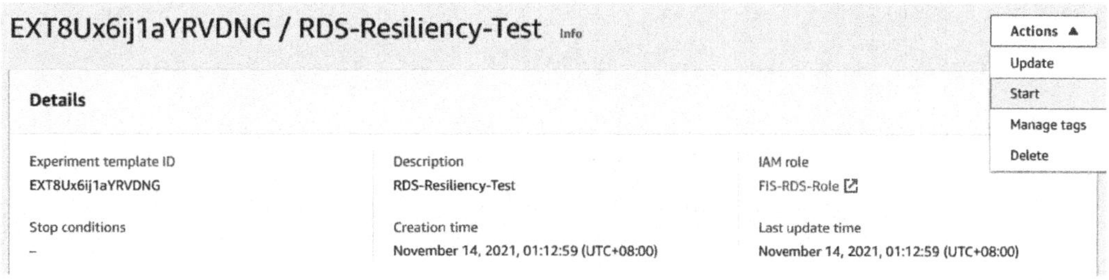

EXT8Ux6ij1aYRVDNG / RDS-Resiliency-Test Info

Actions ▲

Update

Details

Start

Manage tags

Experiment template ID
EXT8Ux6ij1aYRVDNG

Description
RDS-Resiliency-Test

IAM role
FIS-RDS-Role 🔗

Delete

Stop conditions
–

Creation time
November 14, 2021, 01:12:59 (UTC+08:00)

Last update time
November 14, 2021, 01:12:59 (UTC+08:00)

Figure 6.45 – Starting the FIS experiment

18. Once you have started the experiment, you can see that the state of the action will be **Running**.

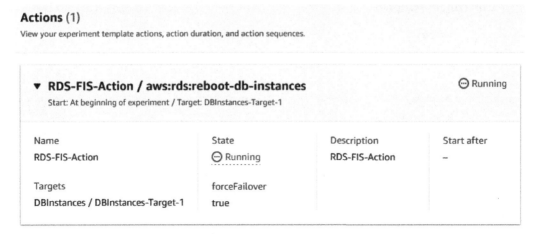

Figure 6.46 – Status of the FIS experiment template

19. After that, keep on sending GET requests in Postman to receive the student record. At a certain point, for a few seconds, you will see a 500 error message with **something went wrong**, which means that the database is rebooting (you can verify this from the RDS console) and failing over to another availability zone.

Figure 6.47 – Postman console showing an error message with the GET request

20. The GET request will show the error message only for a few seconds, and once you resend the request, you will see the student record.

Figure 6.48 – Postman console showing the GET request result of the student record

21. Since you are getting the student record, you can go to the RDS console and check the status of the database as well as the current availability. The status of the database will be **Available**, while the availability zone will be switched from **us-east-1b** to **us-east-1f**.

Figure 6.49 – RDS console

22. After that you can go to the FIS console to see the status of **RDS-FIS-Action**. It will now be **Completed**.

Figure 6.50 – FIS experiment status

So, we just did an experiment where AWS FIS is creating chaos on the Node.js application by rebooting and failing over the RDS. Since RDS is a managed service and has the capability of rebooting and automatic failover within a minute, the application downtime is less than a minute. In the next section, we will try to inject node group failure into an EKS cluster.

Experimenting with AWS FIS on an EKS cluster worker node

In this section of the chapter, we will use FIS to create a disturbance on an EKS cluster by terminating instances of worker node groups. We will deploy an application on an EKS cluster and then we will start the FIS experiment to delete instances of worker nodes and see whether the application is running fine.

Perform the following steps to implement the experiment using AWS FIS:

1. Spin up an EKS cluster by running the following command on your terminal (make sure your server or local machine has `aws cli` configured with the user who has permission to access the EKS).

```
$ ssh-keygen -y -f <$PRIVATE_KEY_FILE_PATH> public.pem
$ eksctl create cluster --name fis-cluster --region
us-east-1 --ssh-access --ssh-public-key public.pem
```

2. Check the number of worker nodes in the cluster. It should be two:

```
### Make sure .kube/config file is present.
$kubectl get nodes
```

NAME VERSION	STATUS	ROLES	AGE
ip-192-168-26-157.ec2.internal v1.21.5-eks-bc4871b	Ready	<none>	3h54m
ip-192-168-50-4.ec2.internal v1.21.5-eks-bc4871b	Ready	<none>	5h12m

3. You can go to the EKS console and see the node group of `fis-cluster`. The node group name in this case is **ng-69f2e42f** and it contains two worker nodes:

Nodes (2) Info

Node name		Instance type		Node Group		Created		Status
ip-192-168-50-4.ec2.internal	▽	m5.large	▽	ng-69f2e42f	▽	5 hours ago	▽	⊘ Ready
ip-192-168-26-157.ec2.internal		m5.large		ng-69f2e42f		4 hours ago		⊘ Ready

Figure 6.51 – EKS worker nodes

4. Now, deploy an application on an EKS cluster, which will spread across worker node instances:

```
$ curl -o kube-app.yaml https://raw.githubusercontent.
com/PacktPublishing/Accelerating-DevSecOps-on-AWS/main/
chapter-06-starkapp/kube-deployment.yml
$ kubectl create -f kube-app.yaml
```

5. Once you try to get the Pod information, you will see that Pod placement is spread in both instances (192.168.26.157 and 192.168.50.4):

```
$ kubectl get pods -o wide
NAME                         READY     STATUS
RESTARTS     AGE    IP                    NODE
NOMINATED NODE     READINESS GATES
db-79468d5ff4-zqwhk          1/1       Running   0          21s
192.168.16.205    ip-192-168-26-157.ec2.internal   <none>
<none>
web-67c6fbbfb5-hpn96         1/1       Running   0          18s
192.168.4.170     ip-192-168-26-157.ec2.internal   <none>
<none>
words-59dc77b9db-bhrtg       1/1       Running   0          19s
192.168.59.102    ip-192-168-50-4.ec2.internal     <none>
<none>
words-59dc77b9db-d454t       1/1       Running   0          19s
192.168.25.241    ip-192-168-26-157.ec2.internal   <none>
<none>
words-59dc77b9db-qjqw6       1/1       Running   0          19s
192.168.8.77      ip-192-168-26-157.ec2.internal   <none>
<none>
words-59dc77b9db-t5chq       1/1       Running   0          19s
192.168.1.90      ip-192-168-26-157.ec2.internal
```

```
<none>
words-59dc77b9db-w9q98    1/1       Running    0            19s
192.168.36.9       ip-192-168-50-4.ec2.internal       <none>
<none>
```

6. You can get the DNS endpoint of a web service that is exposed as a load balancer:

```
kubectl get svc | grep web
web            LoadBalancer    10.100.106.64
a3c0ee988db4546e7b5c9ffd86de36a2-1187254052.us-east-1.
elb.amazonaws.com    80:31738/TCP    3m20s
```

7. Copy the ELB DNS and access it in the browser. You will see a Stark word application (every time you refresh the page, you will see a different word box).

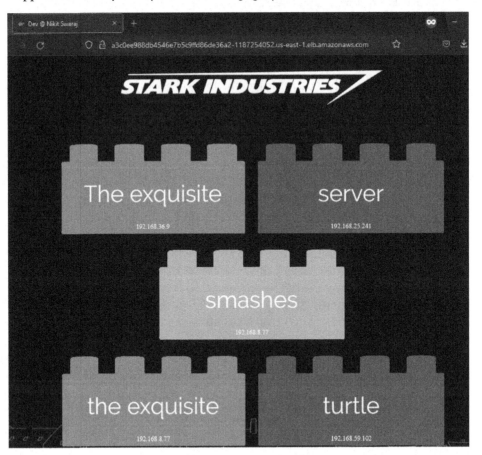

Figure 6.52 – stark-word-app

8. Since your application is running fine on an EKS cluster and spread across multiple worker nodes, let's create chaos using an FIS EKS terminate node group instance action to test the resiliency of the infrastructure. Go to IAM and create an IAM policy, `fis-eks-policy`, using the following code snippet:

```json
{
    "Version": "2012-10-17",
    "Statement": [
        {
            "Sid": "AllowFISExperimentRoleEKSReadOnly",
            "Effect": "Allow",
            "Action": [
                "ec2:DescribeInstances",
                "eks:DescribeNodegroup"
            ],
            "Resource": "*"
        },
        {
            "Sid": "AllowFISExperimentRoleEKSActions",
            "Effect": "Allow",
            "Action": [
                "ec2:TerminateInstances"
            ],
            "Resource": "arn:aws:ec2:*:*:instance/*"
        }
    ]
}
```

9. Create an IAM role, `FIS-EKS-Role`, and attach the `fis-eks-policy` policy. Edit the trust relationship of the role using the following code snippet:

```json
{
    "Version": "2012-10-17",
    "Statement": [
        {
            "Effect": "Allow",
            "Principal": {
                "Service": [
```

```
                    "fis.amazonaws.com"
              ]
          },
          "Action": "sts:AssumeRole"
        }
      ]
}
```

10. Once an IAM role is created, go to the FIS console, and click on **Create experiment template**. Provide the following details in the **Description**, **Name**, and **IAM Role** fields:

   I.   **Description**: EKS-Node-Resiliency-Test

   II.   **Name**: EKS-Node-Resiliency-Test

   III. **IAM Role**: FIS-EKS-Role

11. Provide the following information in the **Action** section:

   I.   **Name**: EKS-Node-Termination-Action.

   II.   **Action type**: aws:eks:terminate-nodegroup-instances.

   III. **Target**: Nodegroups-Target-1.

   IV.   **instanceTerminationPercentage**: 50.

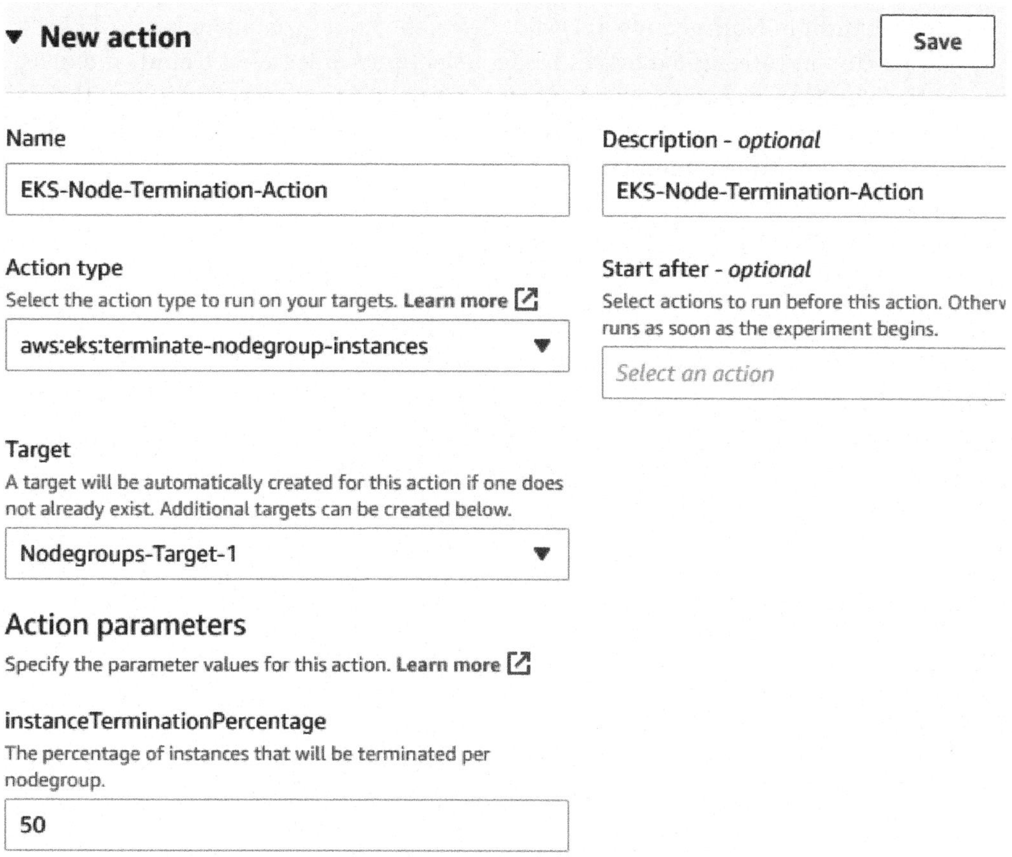

▼ **New action**   Save

Name

EKS-Node-Termination-Action

Description - *optional*

EKS-Node-Termination-Action

Action type

Select the action type to run on your targets. **Learn more** [↗]

aws:eks:terminate-nodegroup-instances   ▼

Start after - *optional*

Select actions to run before this action. Otherv
runs as soon as the experiment begins.

Select an action

Target

A target will be automatically created for this action if one does
not already exist. Additional targets can be created below.

Nodegroups-Target-1   ▼

Action parameters

Specify the parameter values for this action. **Learn more** [↗]

instanceTerminationPercentage

The percentage of instances that will be terminated per
nodegroup.

50

Figure 6.53 – Providing FIS action details

V.   Click on **Save** to save the action.

12. Click on **Edit** in **Nodegroups-Target-1**. Select the node group name of the FIS cluster (in this case, **ng-69f2e42f**). Under **Selection Mode**, select **Count**, and then, in the **Number of resources** field, insert 1. Click on **Save** to save the target. Then, click on **Create experiment template**. Provide a confirmation string and then click on **Create experiment template**.

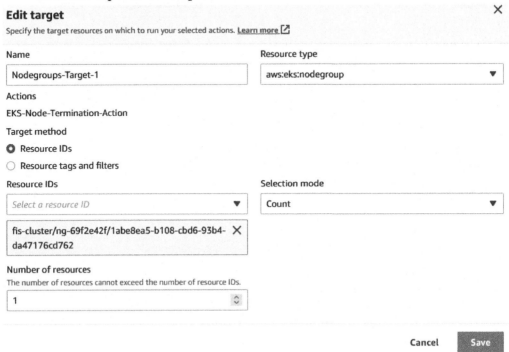

Figure 6.54 – Providing FIS target details

13. Once you have created an experiment template, click on **Actions** followed by **Start experiment** to start the experiment. Provide the tag and confirmation string.

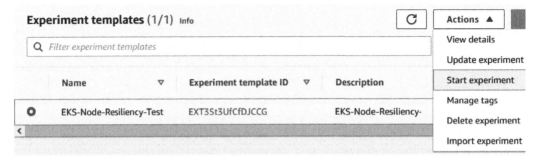

Figure 6.55 – Starting the FIS experiment

14. You will see that the experiment will be initiated and in the **Running** state.

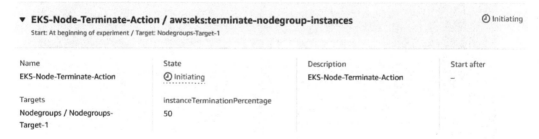

▼ EKS-Node-Terminate-Action / aws:eks:terminate-nodegroup-instances   ⏱ Initiating
Start: At beginning of experiment / Target: Nodegroups-Target-1

Name	State	Description	Start after
EKS-Node-Terminate-Action	⏱ Initiating	EKS-Node-Terminate-Action	–

Targets	instanceTerminationPercentage
Nodegroups / Nodegroups-Target-1	50

Figure 6.56 – Status of the FIS experiment

15. When the experiment starts, it invokes an API call to terminate 50% of the node group (one instance). You can go to the EC2 console to see that one of the worker nodes has been terminated (`192.168.50.4`).

Instances (2) Info   ↻   Connect   Instance state ▼

	Name	▽	Instance ID	Instance state	▽	Instance type	▽	Status check
☐	fis-cluster-ng-69f2e42f-No...		i-0d6ea20ae958524e5	⊖ Terminated ⊕⊖		m5.large		–
☐	fis-cluster-ng-69f2e42f-No...		i-0a7add81025d61f23	⊘ Running ⊕⊖		m5.large		⊘ 2/2 checks passed

Figure 6.57 – EC2 console showing one worker node terminated

16. When one of the worker nodes terminates, any Pods in the terminated worker node will move to the running worker node (`192.168.26.157`).

```
very 2.0s: kubectl get pods -o wide

AME                        READY   STATUS    RESTARTS   AGE   IP               NODE                           NOMINATED NODE   READINESS GATES
b-79468d5ff4-zqwhk         1/1     Running   0          39m   192.168.16.205   ip-192-168-26-157.ec2.internal   <none>           <none>
eb-67c6fbbfb5-hpn96        1/1     Running   0          39m   192.168.4.170    ip-192-168-26-157.ec2.internal   <none>           <none>
ords-59dc77b9db-d454t      1/1     Running   0          39m   192.168.25.241   ip-192-168-26-157.ec2.internal   <none>           <none>
ords-59dc77b9db-qjqw6      1/1     Running   0          39m   192.168.8.77     ip-192-168-26-157.ec2.internal   <none>           <none>
ords-59dc77b9db-qwstv      1/1     Running   0          26s   192.168.8.147    ip-192-168-26-157.ec2.internal   <none>           <none>
ords-59dc77b9db-t5chq      1/1     Running   0          39m   192.168.1.90     ip-192-168-26-157.ec2.internal   <none>           <none>
ords-59dc77b9db-tdsvg      1/1     Running   0          26s   192.168.14.188   ip-192-168-26-157.ec2.internal   <none>           <none>
```

Figure 6.58 – Showing all the Pods placed on one worker node; ip-192-168-26-157

17. When you try to access the application, it will still be available.

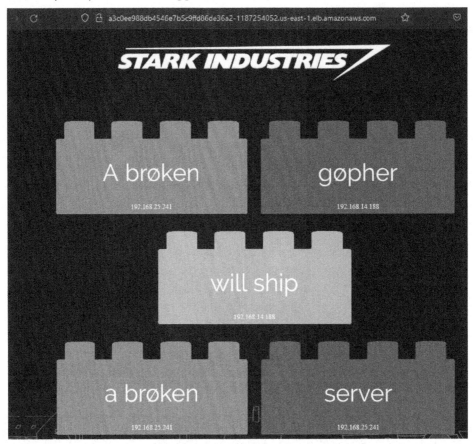

Figure 6.59 – stark-word-app

18. Since the node group is backed by ASG and the desired number of worker nodes is two, ASG will spin up another instance to meet the desired number of instances.

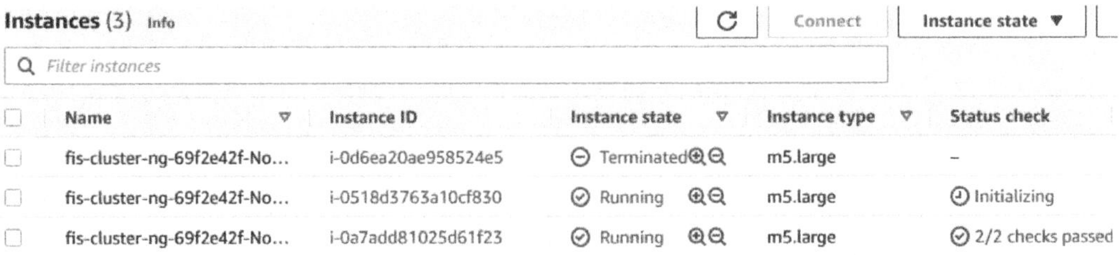

Name		Instance ID	Instance state		Instance type		Status check
fis-cluster-ng-69f2e42f-No...		i-0d6ea20ae958524e5	⊖ Terminated		m5.large		–
fis-cluster-ng-69f2e42f-No...		i-0518d3763a10cf830	⊘ Running		m5.large		⊕ Initializing
fis-cluster-ng-69f2e42f-No...		i-0a7add81025d61f23	⊘ Running		m5.large		⊘ 2/2 checks passed

Figure 6.60 – EC2 console showing a new EC2 instance spinning up

19. After a while, when you run the following command, you will see that the new worker node is available in the EKS cluster.

```
$ kubectl get nodes
```

NAME VERSION	STATUS	ROLES	AGE
ip-192-168-26-157.ec2.internal v1.21.5-eks-bc4871b	Ready	<none>	4h47m
ip-192-168-57-215.ec2.internal v1.21.5-eks-bc4871b	Ready	<none>	54s

20. When you go back to the FIS experiment state, it will be in the **Completed** state.

▼ **EKS-Node-Terminate-Action / aws:eks:terminate-nodegroup-instances**   ⊘ Completed
   Start: At beginning of experiment / Target: Nodegroups-Target-1

Name	State	Description	Start after
EKS-Node-Terminate-Action	⊘ Completed	EKS-Node-Terminate-Action	–

Targets	instanceTerminationPercentage
Nodegroups / Nodegroups-Target-1	50

Figure 6.61 – FIS experiment status

We just performed an experiment where we created a disturbance on **stark-word-application** using the AWS FIS EKS node group instance terminate action. We saw how EKS manages the application Pod by scheduling it to the available running worker node. And since the node group is backed by ASG, it spins up a new worker node to meet the desired number of instances.

Summary

Chaos engineering is one of the important steps in testing the resiliency of the infrastructure and applications running on top of it. In this chapter, we covered the principle of chaos engineering and how we can position it in the CI/CD framework to automate the chaos testing of infrastructure. We learned more about the managed chaos engineering service, Fault Injection Simulator. We performed various chaos actions on running application infrastructure and concluded the downtime. In the next chapter, we will learn how to automate the security posture in the cloud using AWS.

Section 3: DevSecOps and AIOps

This part includes chapters that cover infrastructure security automation using various AWS solutions. It also covers DevSecOps implementation using AWS native services such as CodeGuru Reviewer, ECR Scan, as well as using open source tools for code advisory, **Static Application Security Testing (SAST)**, **Dynamic Application Security Testing (DAST)**, and **Runtime Application Security Protection (RASP)**. It also shows how to use AWS DevOps Guru, which is an AIOps service to find anomalies in applications deployed on EKS clusters and serverless applications.

This section contains the following chapters:

- *Chapter 7, Infrastructure Security Automation Using Security Hub and Systems Manager*
- *Chapter 8, DevSecOps Using AWS Native Services*
- *Chapter 9, DevSecOps Pipeline with AWS Services and Tools Popular Industry-Wide*
- *Chapter 10, AIOps with Amazon DevOps Guru and Systems Manager OpsCenter*

7

Infrastructure Security Automation Using Security Hub and Systems Manager

In this chapter, we will explore AWS **Security Hub**, which is one of the security services of AWS. We will learn how to implement solutions with the integration of Security Hub and various other AWS services to achieve security automation. We will implement three solutions. The first will be related to **Elastic Container Registry** (ECR) compliance and how we can ensure that a non-compliant image does not run in an **Elastic Container Service for Kubernetes** (EKS) cluster. The second solution will be importing an AWS Config rules evaluation as a finding in Security Hub using **Lambda** and **AWS EventBridge** rule. The third solution will be about the auto-creation of an incident in **Incident Manager** when there is a critical finding in Security Hub, and remediation using an **OpsCenter** runbook. Knowing how to use Security Hub will also help in the next chapter, where we will import **Static Application Security Testing(SAST)** tool findings in Security Hub.

This chapter contains the following main sections:

- Introduction to AWS Security Hub
- Deny execution of non-compliant images on EKS using AWS Security Hub and ECR
- Importing an AWS Config rules evaluation as a finding in Security Hub
- Integrating AWS Systems Manager with Security Hub to detect issues, create an incident, and remediate automatically

Technical requirements

To implement the solutions covered in this chapter, you need to clone the GitHub repository:

`https://github.com/PacktPublishing/Accelerating-DevSecOps-on-AWS`

Navigate to the `chapter-07` folder. You also need to have an AWS account where you have permission to enable the AWS Config, AWS Systems Manager, and Security Hub services.

Introduction to AWS Security Hub

AWS Security Hub is a cloud security service that performs security best practice checks, aggregates all the security findings, and enables automated remediation. Before we dig deep into AWS Security Hub, let's understand the overall AWS cloud security strategy (shown in the following diagram), which is based on the **National Institute of Standards and Technology** (**NIST**) Cybersecurity Framework.

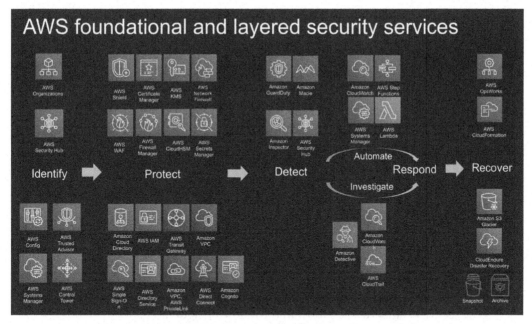

Figure 7.1 – AWS services aligned with the NIST Framework

There are five main core functions of the NIST Framework:

- **Identify**: This is all about identifying the key assets and resources in your AWS account. AWS has services such as **AWS Systems Manager** and **AWS Config** to help you understand what your resources are and how they are deployed within your AWS environment. You can't protect your resources until you properly identify them.

- **Protect**: This is about building a hard outer shell around your data, applications, users, and networks. AWS has services such as **AWS Shield**, which is an anti-DDoS service, and **AWS WAF**, which is a web application firewall that can protect your assets.

- **Detect**: This is all about detecting anomalies, unusual behaviors, and compliance issues inside your AWS environments. AWS has services such as **GuardDuty**, which is a threat detection service, and Security Hub, which helps you detect compliance drift and helps you identify what your most important alerts are, based on priority.

- **Respond**: This is about responding to alerts and findings. AWS has added two across path (see *Figure 7.1*, Automate and Investigate), which is to **Automate** the response. AWS has services such as **Lambda** and **Step Functions** to automate responses. Some alerts require human **investigation**, and for that AWS has services such as **CloudWatch** and **CloudTrail**, which helps us to see through the underlying activity to understand whether the alerts or findings that we have detected are true positives.

- **Recover**: If there are major incidents, then we need to recover using services such as **EBS snapshots**, **golden images**, and **Glacier archives**. You can quickly rebuild the resources that have been compromised.

AWS introduced AWS Security Hub because of the following issues:

- **Compliance**: Many AWS customers have both internal and external compliance requirements. Some of those are regulatory, such as the **Health Insurance Portability and Accountability Act (HIPAA)** and **Payment Card Industry (PCI)**, and some of them are just internal industry best practices. Currently, AWS provides three security standards, as shown in the following figure:

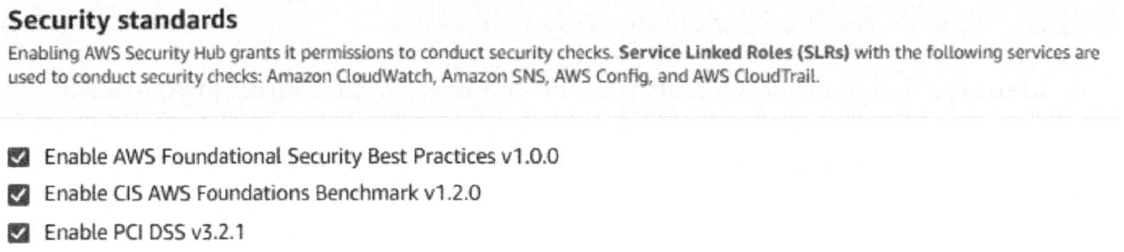

Security standards

Enabling AWS Security Hub grants it permissions to conduct security checks. **Service Linked Roles (SLRs)** with the following services are used to conduct security checks: Amazon CloudWatch, Amazon SNS, AWS Config, and AWS CloudTrail.

- ☑ Enable AWS Foundational Security Best Practices v1.0.0
- ☑ Enable CIS AWS Foundations Benchmark v1.2.0
- ☑ Enable PCI DSS v3.2.1

Figure 7.2 – Compliance standards provided by AWS Security Hub

- **Multiple formats**: When customers are using different security tools, the alert format of all those tools is different too, so the customers must parse and normalize this data into a common format so that they can start searching and analyzing the alerts. AWS Security Hub supports **AWS Security Finding Format (ASFF)**, which eliminates the need for time-consuming data conversion. ASFF consists of approximately 100 JSON-formatted fields, but most of them are optional. The most important field is **finding types**. The finding type taxonomy is what we are using to categorize the findings. The following diagram explains the categorization of findings severity:

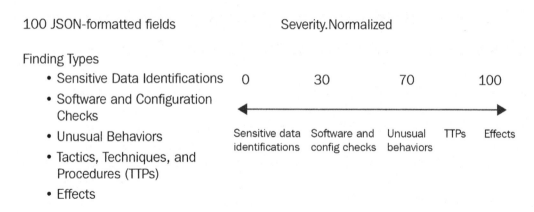

100 JSON-formatted fields

Finding Types
- Sensitive Data Identifications
- Software and Configuration Checks
- Unusual Behaviors
- Tactics, Techniques, and Procedures (TTPs)
- Effects

Severity.Normalized

0   30   70   100

Sensitive data   Software and   Unusual   TTPs   Effects
identifications   config checks   behaviors

Figure 7.3 – Relationship between ASFF findings and severity

- **Prioritization**: If we receive thousands of alerts each day, then the problem becomes to prioritize all those alerts. AWS Security Hub helps in the prioritization of alerts.

- **Visibility**: If we want a single pane of glass, which means a single place where we can find all the security and compliance states, then Security Hub provides us with that feature.

AWS Security Hub continuously aggregates all the data and findings from services such as **GuardDuty**, **Amazon Inspector**, **Amazon Macie**, and **AWS Config**, and then assesses high-priority security alerts and the compliance status. It has amazing integration with AWS Systems Manager, which helps in incident creation and the auto-remediation of findings using a runbook. This was a basic overview of AWS Security Hub. In the next section, we will learn how to enable Security Hub in your AWS account and how to deny the execution of non-compliant images in an EKS cluster.

Deny execution of non-compliant images on EKS using AWS Security Hub and ECR

As we move toward application modernization, we are more likely to work with **microservices** and **containers**. In this digital era of high-speed application development, if you miss out on any security loophole, then it will make your application vulnerable and may impact your business. In the **DevSecOps** shift-left practice, we try to find out all the vulnerabilities long before deployment. In this section, we will learn how to automate a solution that denies the creation of EKS resources with non-compliant container images. The following diagram shows the flow of the solution and how all the components integrate with each other:

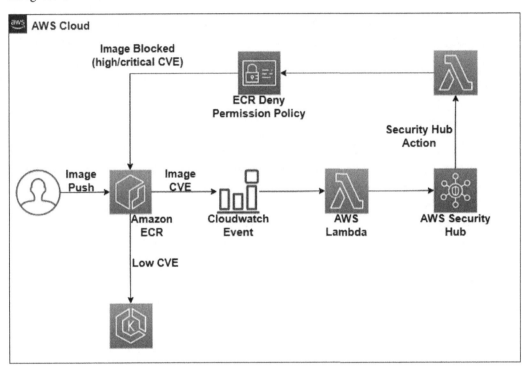

Figure 7.4 – Flow diagram of an ECR compliance solution

The preceding diagram illustrates the following steps:

1. Whenever a developer builds an image and pushes it to ECR, ECR will scan the image. The scanning of the image takes place on either image push or manual scan. It depends on how have you configured your ECR repositories.

2. Once the image scan completes, an event is created in AWS EventBridge, which triggers a Lambda function.

3. The Lambda function translates the event from the image scan into ASFF and ingests it to AWS Security Hub.

4. This solution also creates a Security Hub action, which triggers the Lambda function to attach the *ECR Repository Deny Policy* when the remediation action is invoked.

5. Once the repository is attached to the policy, EKS won't be able to pull the image.

To set up this solution, we should perform the following steps:

1. You need to enable Security Hub in the AWS account if you are using this service for the first time. Go to the AWS Security Hub console. Click on **Go to Security Hub**.

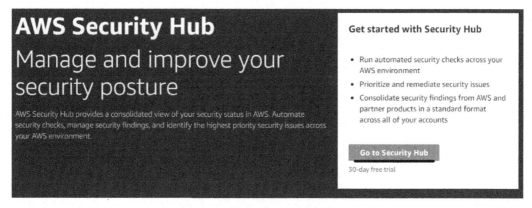

Figure 7.5 – The AWS Security Hub console

2. The next page will show **Security standards**. For this exercise, we need to make sure that we have two standards selected, which are **Enable AWS Foundation Security Best Practices v1.0.0** and **Enable CIS AWS Foundation Benchmark v1.2.0**. Then, click on **Enable Security Hub**. This will enable the Security Hub service in your AWS account. This step is shown in the following figure:

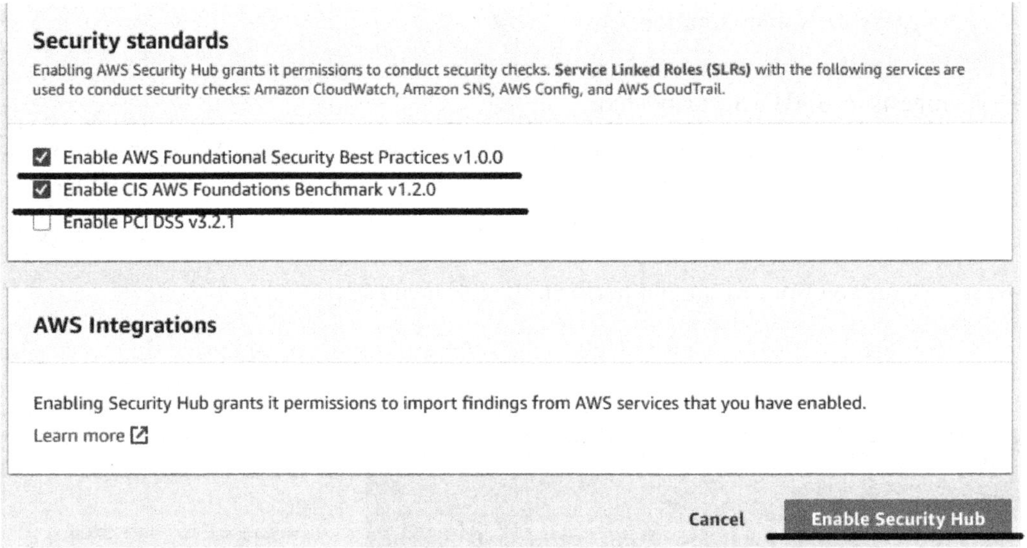

Figure 7.6 – Enabling Security Hub with security standards

3. Once the Security Hub service is enabled in your account, you will be able to see the security scores of your AWS account, as shown in the following figure:

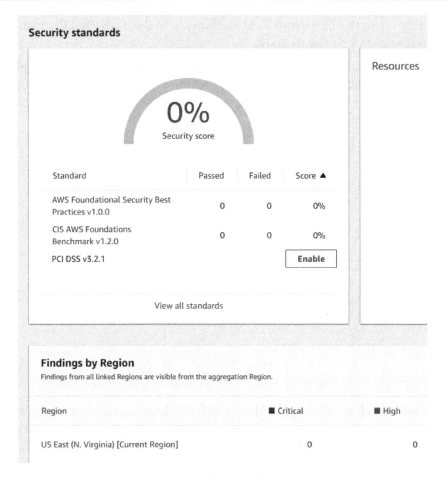

Figure 7.7 – AWS Security Hub dashboard showing the security score

4. The next step is to set up the solution. We will use the following CloudFormation template to provision the resources:

```
$ wget https://raw.githubusercontent.com/PacktPublishing/
Accelerating-DevSecOps-on-AWS/main/chapter-07/
ecr-compliance.yaml
```

5. Once you have this file in your local machine, go to the AWS CloudFormation console and click on **Create stack**.

6. In the **Create stack** page, select **Upload a template file** in the **Specify template** section. Then click on **Choose file** and select the `ecr-compliance.yaml` file available in your local machine. Then click on **Next**. This step is shown in the following screenshot:

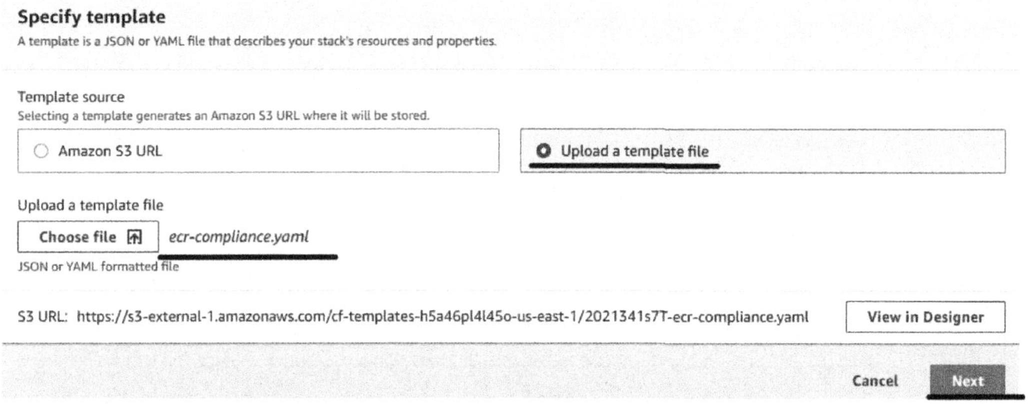

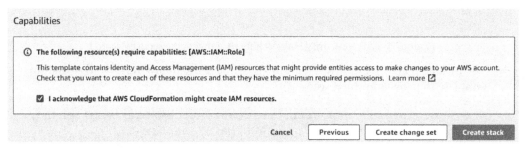

Figure 7.8 – Uploading the CloudFormation template

7. Enter the stack name as `ECR-Compliance` and click on **Next**.

8. Provide a tag to the stack and click on **Next**. On the next page, in the **Capabilities** section, check the acknowledgment box and click on **Create stack**, as shown here:

Figure 7.9 – Creating the CloudFormation stack

9. It will take 3–5 minutes to spin up all the resources required to set up the solution.

10. Once the solution setup is completed by CloudFormation, we need to verify the solution by pushing a vulnerable image into the ECR repository and trying to run that image in an EKS cluster. To create an ECR repository, go to the **AWS ECR** console. Click on **Create repository**. Set **Repository Name** to node, because we will push the node:10 Docker image, which has lots of vulnerabilities. Enable **Scan on push** and then click on **Create repository**.

11. Once the node repository is created, we will push the node:10 Docker image to the repository by running the following commands:

```
$ docker pull node:10
```

```
#######Make sure you have configured aws
keys##############
```

```
$ aws ecr get-login-password --region us-east-1 | docker
login --username AWS --password-stdin <yourAWSAccount>.
dkr.ecr.us-east-1.amazonaws.com
```

```
$ docker tag node:10 <yourAWSAccount>.dkr.ecr.us-east-1.
amazonaws.com/node:latest
```

```
$ docker push <yourAWSAccount>.dkr.ecr.us-east-1.
amazonaws.com/node:latest
```

12. Once the image is pushed into the repository, you can see **Scan status** is **In progress**. After a while, **Scan status** will change to **Complete**, and you will be able to see the number of vulnerabilities, as shown here:

	Image tag	Pushed at ▼	Size (MB) ▽	Image URI	Digest	Scan status	Vulnerabilities
☐	latest	December 07, 2021, 20:24:08 (UTC+08)	349.06	📋 Copy URI	🗂 sha256:686e0e859358f2...	In progress	-

	Image tag	Pushed at ▼	Size (MB) ▽	Image URI	Digest	Scan status	Vulnerabilities
☐	latest	December 07, 2021, 20:24:08 (UTC+08)	349.06	📋 Copy URI	🗂 sha256:686e0e859358f2...	Complete	⚠ 1 Critical + 810 others (details)

Figure 7.10 – Container image scanning status

13. Now that the image scan has been completed, it will trigger the **EventBridge** rule **CaptureECRScanEvent** (created by the CloudFormation stack), and then run the target Lambda function, which captures the vulnerability findings and passes them to Security Hub. Go to the Security Hub console and click on **Findings**; you will be able to see that the **Severity** value of the vulnerability findings of the ECR image is **CRITICAL**, as shown here:

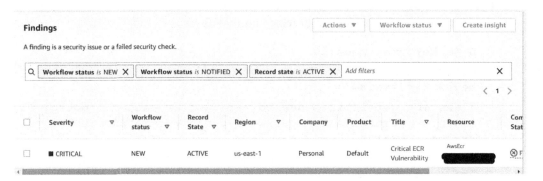

Figure 7.11 – AWS Security Hub shows the findings of the ECR vulnerability

14. When a DevOps/DevSecOps engineer sees that an image is non-compliant and has critical vulnerabilities, they will then try to configure the settings such that image doesn't get pulled in any platform. To do that, select the finding and click on **Actions**, and then click on **DENYECR**, as shown here:

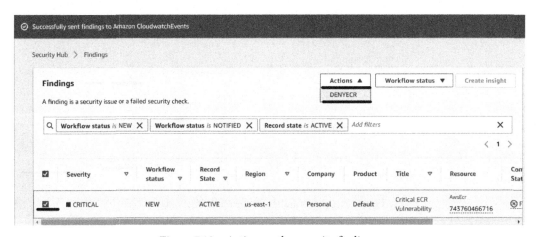

Figure 7.12 – Acting on the security findings

15. Once you click on **DENYECR**, the findings from Security Hub will be sent to CloudWatch Events, which triggers the **ECRAccessProhibitedLambda** Lambda function. This Lambda function will modify the ECR repository permission policy. You can check this by clicking on the **Permissions** tab of the repository.

Figure 7.13 – ECR permissions showing the deny effect

16. To verify the policy, we will issue a command in the EKS cluster to run the node:10 image:

```
###Spin up an EKS Cluster using eksctl
$ eksctl create cluster dsotest –region=us-east-1
$ kubectl run node --image=<yourAWSAccount>.dkr.ecr.
us-east-1.amazonaws.com/node:latest
$ kubectl describe pod node
#### The bottom Events Section###
Events:
  Type       Reason      Age    From              Message
  ----       ------      ----   ----              -------
  Normal     Scheduled   8s     default-scheduler
Successfully assigned default/node to ip-192-168-90-29.
ec2.internal
  Normal     Pulling     7s     kubelet           Pulling
image "670918263229.dkr.ecr.us-east-1.amazonaws.com/
node:latest"
  Warning    Failed      7s     kubelet           Failed to
pull image "670918263229.dkr.ecr.us-east-1.amazonaws.
com/node:latest": rpc error: code = Unknown desc =
Error response from daemon: pull access denied for
670918263229.dkr.ecr.us-east-1.amazonaws.com/node,
repository does not exist or may require 'docker login':
denied: User: arn:aws:sts::670918263229:assumed-role/
NodeIAMRole/i-0101d8fab87c00077 is not authorized to
perform: ecr:BatchGetImage on resource: arn:aws:ecr:us-
```

| east-1:670918263229:repository/node with an explicit deny in a resource-based policy |
| Warning   Failed   7s   kubelet   Error: ErrImagePull |
| Normal   BackOff   6s   kubelet   Back-off pulling image "670918263229.dkr.ecr.us-east-1.amazonaws.com/node:latest" |
| Warning   Failed   6s   kubelet   Error: ImagePullBackOff |

We can verify that the image is not able to run on EKS because access is denied on this image due to CRITICAL or HIGH CVE. So, in this section, we learned a cloud-native solution of blocking to run a non-compliant image on your EKS cluster. You can also explore other tools such as AquaSec and Prisma, which do an excellent job in container security. In the next section, we will implement a solution that collects AWS Config un-compliant status data to Security Hub.

Importing an AWS Config rules evaluation as a finding in Security Hub

In this section, we will implement a solution that imports a non-compliant AWS Config rules evaluation as a finding in Security Hub. This solution helps in showing the non-compliant resources in a single pane of the dashboard of Security Hub, which makes it easier to investigate. Once we receive the finding in Security Hub, we can also automate the taking of actions using Lambda. The following figure shows a flow diagram of the solution:

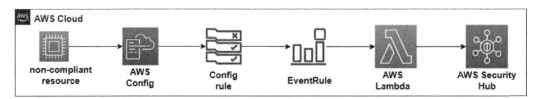

Figure 7.14 – Flow diagram of the solution

The preceding solution consists of the following steps:

1. When we deploy or provision any non-compliant resources, the AWS Config rule will detect the changes and change the state from compliant to non-compliant.

2. The moment the Config rule changes the resource state from compliant to non-compliant, the CloudWatch event rule will trigger the Lambda function.

3. The Lambda function will gather the data and convert it into ASFF, and then it will be imported into AWS Security Hub.

To set up the solution, perform the following steps:

1. You need to enable the AWS Config service if you are using it for the first time in your AWS account. Go to the AWS Config console and click on **Get started**.

Figure 7.15 – AWS Config console setup page

2. You can keep the default selection and click on **Next** to select the config rule.

3. In the **Rules** page, you will find **AWS Managed Rules**. These rules detect the changes in the resources and show the compliance status. Go to the search box and search for SSH. You will find a rule with the name **restricted-ssh**. This rule checks whether security groups that are in use disallow unrestricted incoming SSH traffic. Select the rule and click on **Next**.

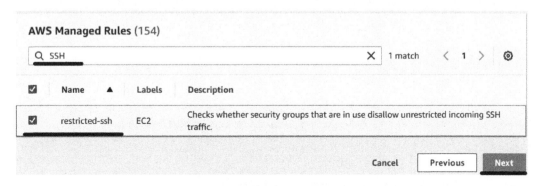

Figure 7.16 – Selecting restricted-ssh

4. Click **Confirm** to enable Config with the selected rule.

5. The next step is to enable Security Hub in your AWS account. You can refer to *Step 1* and *Step 2* of the *Deny execution of the non-compliant Image on EKS using AWS Security Hub and ECR* section to enable Security Hub.

6. Once you have enabled Security Hub, you need to create a `conf2sechubRole` IAM role for the Lambda function with a policy of `conf2sechubPolicy`. The policy will contain the following snippet:

```
{
    "Version": "2012-10-17",
    "Statement": [
        {
            "Action": [
                "securityhub:BatchImportFindings"
            ],
            "Resource": [
                "*"
            ],
            "Effect": "Allow"
        },
        {
            "Action": [
                "logs:CreateLogGroup",
                "logs:CreateLogStream",
                "logs:PutLogEvents"
            ],
            "Resource": "*",
            "Effect": "Allow"
        },
        {
            "Action": [
                "config:DescribeConfigRules"
            ],
            "Resource": "*",
            "Effect": "Allow"
        }
    ]
}
```

7. Go to the AWS Lambda console and click on **Create function**. Select **Author from scratch** to create your function. In **basic information**, provide the following details:

   I. **Function name**: `conf2SecHub`.

II. **Runtime**: `Python 3.7`.

III. In **Permissions**, select **Use an existing role** and then select **conf2sechubRole**.

IV. Click on **Create function**.

5. Once you have created the function, remove the existing code from the editor, copy the code from `https://raw.githubusercontent.com/PacktPublishing/Accelerating-DevSecOps-on-AWS/main/chapter-07/config2secHub.py`, and paste it into the editor. Then click on **Deploy**.

Figure 7.17 – Adding code in an AWS Lambda function

6. Once you click on **Deploy**, the status will change from **Changes not deployed** to **Changes deployed**.

7. The next step is to create an EventBridge rule. Go to the EventBridge console and click on **Rules** on the left side of the console. Then click on **Create rule**. Provide the following information on the **Create rule** page:

I. **Name**: `conf2sechubEvent`.

II. Select **Event pattern** in the **Define pattern** section.

III. Select **Custom pattern** and provide the following snippet in the event pattern box, then click on **Save**:

```
{
    "detail-type": ["Config Rules Compliance Change"],
    "source": ["aws.config"],
    "detail": {
        "messageType": ["ComplianceChangeNotification"]
    }
}
```

The following screenshot shows where to provide the event pattern snippet:

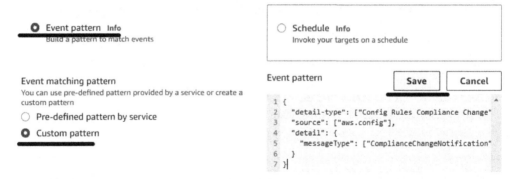

Figure 7.18 – Adding an event pattern in an EventBridge rule

IV. In **Target**, select the **conf2secHub** Lambda function. Then click on **Create**.

At this point, we have implemented the solution. Now, to test the solution, perform the following steps:

1. Spin up an EC2 instance in the same region. Open port 22 to 0.0.0.0/0, just to test the solution.

2. Go to the Config console and click on **Rules**. Select the **restricted-ssh** rule, and you will see a non-compliant resource, which is the security group in which we opened port 22 to 0.0.0.0/0.

restricted-ssh

▼ **Rule details**

Description	Trigger type	Last successful evaluation
Checks whether security groups that are in use disallow unrestricted incoming SSH traffic.	• Oversized configuration changes • Configuration changes	⊘ December 9, 2021 12:17 AM
Config rule ARN	Scope of changes	
arn:aws:config:us-east-1:652556272305:config-rule/config-rule-w5px6g	Resources	
	Resource types EC2 SecurityGroup	

▼ **Resources in scope**

Noncompliant ▼

ID	Type	Status	Annotation	Compliance
sg-0a916cf319bb93fc3	EC2 SecurityGroup	-	-	⚠ Noncompliant

Figure 7.19 – Non-compliant resource showing under the restricted-ssh rule

3.   We can see the non-compliant resources here in the Config console, but the whole point of implementing the solution is to get this data visible in Security Hub. So, go to the Security Hub console and click on **Findings**. Click on **Add filter** and then select **Title is restricted-ssh**; then you will see one entry of **restricted-ssh**, whose resource is the non-compliant security group.

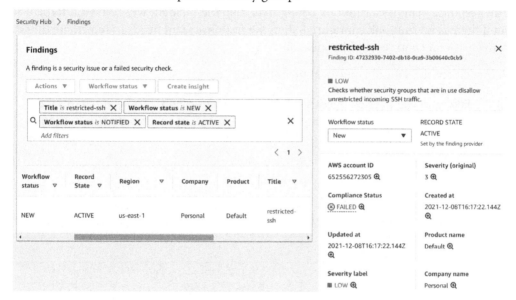

Figure 7.20 – Looking at the Config evaluation in the AWS Security Hub findings

This shows that our implemented solution works. This helps to collect all the security-related findings in a single dashboard, which helps security engineers to identify and act faster. In the next section of the chapter, we will implement a solution to auto-create a security incident in AWS Incident Manager using Security Hub and EventBridge and remediate the incident using the OpsCenter remediation runbook.

Integrating AWS Systems Manager with Security Hub to detect issues, create an incident, and remediate automatically

Based on the AWS Security Incident Response Guide, it is recommended to use security response automation, which increases both the scale and effectiveness of your security operations. With the help of automation, we can easily detect and alert the response team about an incident and, based on the specific runbook, which is an automation script, we can also remediate the incident. In this section, we will create a solution that helps us to detect security incidents and loopholes and alert the security operation team.

We will configure the AWS Systems Manager OpsCenter to aggregate all the security findings from AWS Security Hub into OpsCenter as issues. At the same time, we will configure an Event Bridge rule to check the event on the newly created finding in Security Hub and, based on that EventBridge rule, trigger the AWS incident response plan to create an incident. This incident will send an email and a message to the contact person. Now, if the response plan has a runbook configured, then the incident will resolve automatically. But if there is no runbook configured, then the response team needs to remediate the issue from OpsCenter and resolve the incident.

To implement the solution, perform the following steps:

1. Make sure you have enabled AWS Config in your region. (You can refer to the *Importing an AWS Config rules evaluation as a finding in Security Hub* section to see the steps to enable it.)

2. Make sure you have enabled AWS Security Hub in your region. (You can refer to the previous section to see the steps to enable it.)

3. Once Config and Security Hub are enabled, we need to set up AWS Systems Manager. Go to the **AWS Systems Manager** console, click on **Quick Setup**, and then click on **Create**.

Figure 7.21 – Setting up AWS Systems Manager

4. In **Configuration type**, click on **Config Recording**, which basically collects all the data from the AWS Config service, and click on **Next**.

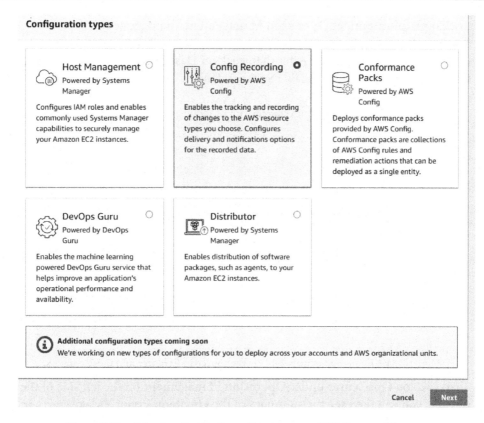

Figure 7.22 – Selecting Config Recording to set up AWS Systems Manager

5. Keep the rest of the default selections and click on **Create**. Systems Manager will then start the deployment of the **Config Recording** configuration.

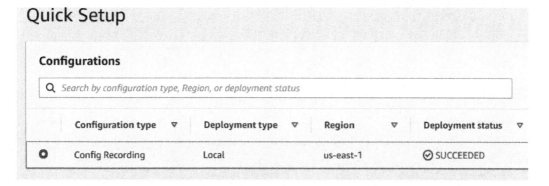

Figure 7.23 – Deployment status of the Systems Manager configuration

6. Click on **Explorer** under **Operation Management**, to integrate the Explorer dashboard with OpsCenter. You will see the **Explorer setup** page, where you need to click on **Enable Explorer**. After that, click on **Dashboard action** and then select **Configure Dashboard** and enable **Security Hub**.

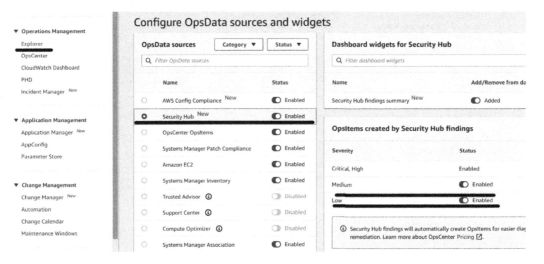

Figure 7.24 – Enabling Security Hub as the source in Explorer and OpsCenter

7. Then click on **OpsCenter** under **Operation Management** on the left side of the console; you will then see the summary of the **OpsItems** count. (Make sure you have enabled OpsCenter.) These items came from Security Hub. So, at this stage, we have integrated Security Hub and the Systems Manager OpsCenter.

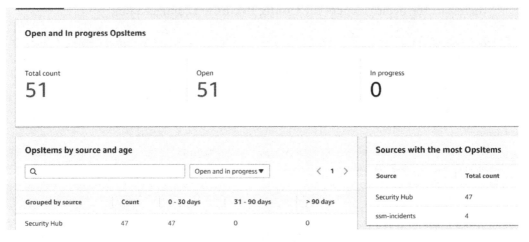

Figure 7.25 – OpsCenter showing the count of OpsItems received from Security Hub

8. Now, to get an incident details of OpsItems, click on **Incident Manager** under **Operation Management**, and click on **Get prepared**.

Figure 7.26 – The Incident Manager console

9. You will see a **Get prepared** page, where we need to set up **General settings** and **Response plan**. Click on **Set up** under **General settings**.

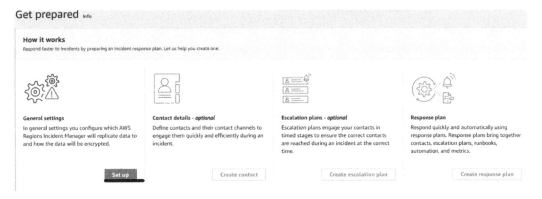

Figure 7.27 – Incident Manager setup steps

10. On the next page, accept the terms and conditions and click on **Next**. Select another AWS Region in which you want the incidents to be replicated, but since this is an exercise, we can just leave the settings as default and click on **Create**.

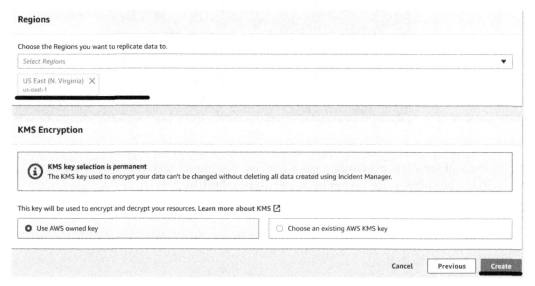

Figure 7.28 – General setup of incident replication to another region

11. You will be returned to the **Get prepared** page, where you need to click on **Create contact**.

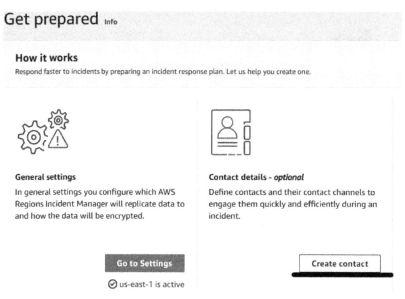

Figure 7.29 – Creating contact settings for Incident Manager

12. On the contact information page, type `SecOps Team` for **Name**, and `secops-responder-team` for **Unique alias**. In **Contact channel**, set **Type** to **Email**, set **Email** as **Channel Name**, and then provide the email address. Again, select **SMS** under **Type**, **SMS** under **Channel name**, and provide a cellphone number in **Detail**. Under **Engagement plan**, enter 0 into the **Engagement time** field for **Email**, so that if there is an incident we get an email instantly, and 2 minutes for **SMS**. Click on **Create**. These two contact details will receive an activation code, which is required to verify the details.

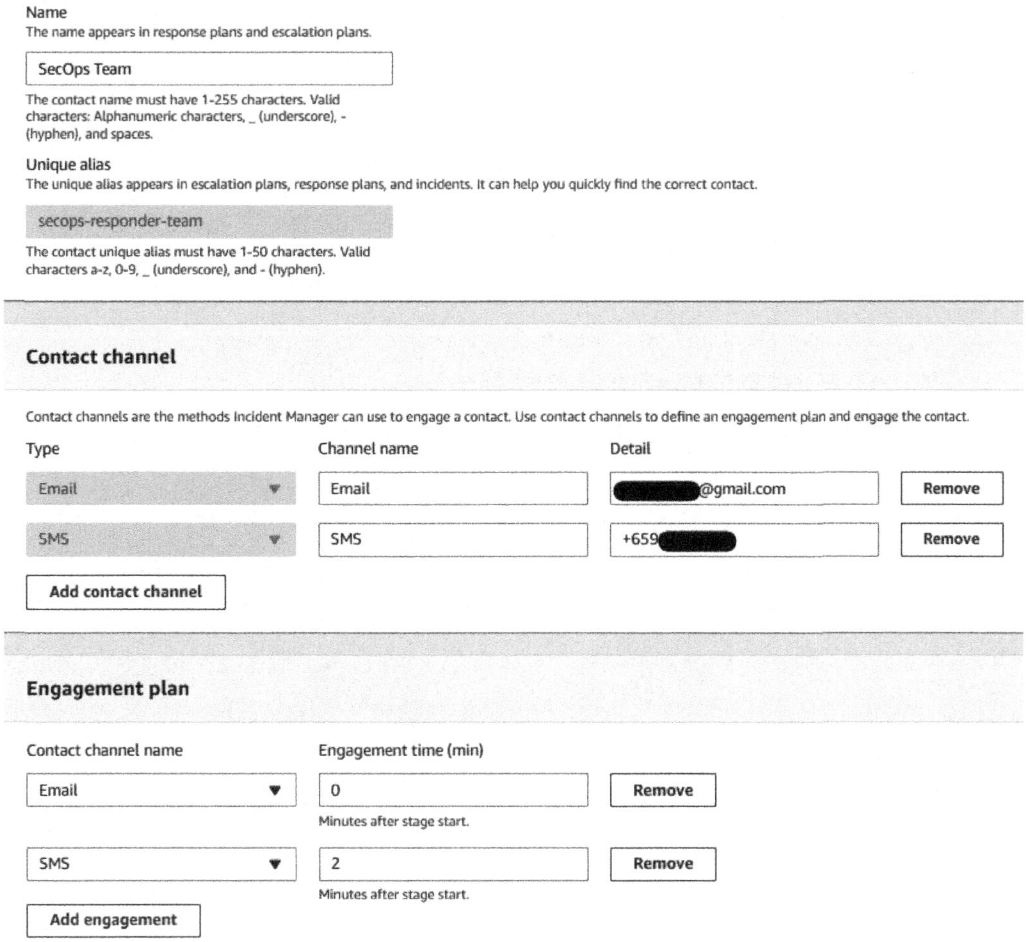

Name
The name appears in response plans and escalation plans.

```
SecOps Team
```

The contact name must have 1-255 characters. Valid
characters: Alphanumeric characters, _ (underscore), -
(hyphen), and spaces.

Unique alias
The unique alias appears in escalation plans, response plans, and incidents. It can help you quickly find the correct contact.

```
secops-responder-team
```

The contact unique alias must have 1-50 characters. Valid
characters a-z, 0-9, _ (underscore), and - (hyphen).

Contact channel

Contact channels are the methods Incident Manager can use to engage a contact. Use contact channels to define an engagement plan and engage the contact.

Type	Channel name	Detail	
Email ▼	Email	⬛⬛⬛@gmail.com	Remove
SMS ▼	SMS	+659⬛⬛⬛	Remove

Add contact channel

Engagement plan

Contact channel name	Engagement time (min)	
Email ▼	0	Remove
	Minutes after stage start.	
SMS ▼	2	Remove
	Minutes after stage start.	

Add engagement

Figure 7.30 – Providing contact details in contact settings

13. Now that the contact details have been created, click on **Create response plan**. Give `SecOpsResponsePlan` for **Display name** and `SecOpsResponsePlan` for **Incident Title**, and select **High** under **Impact**.

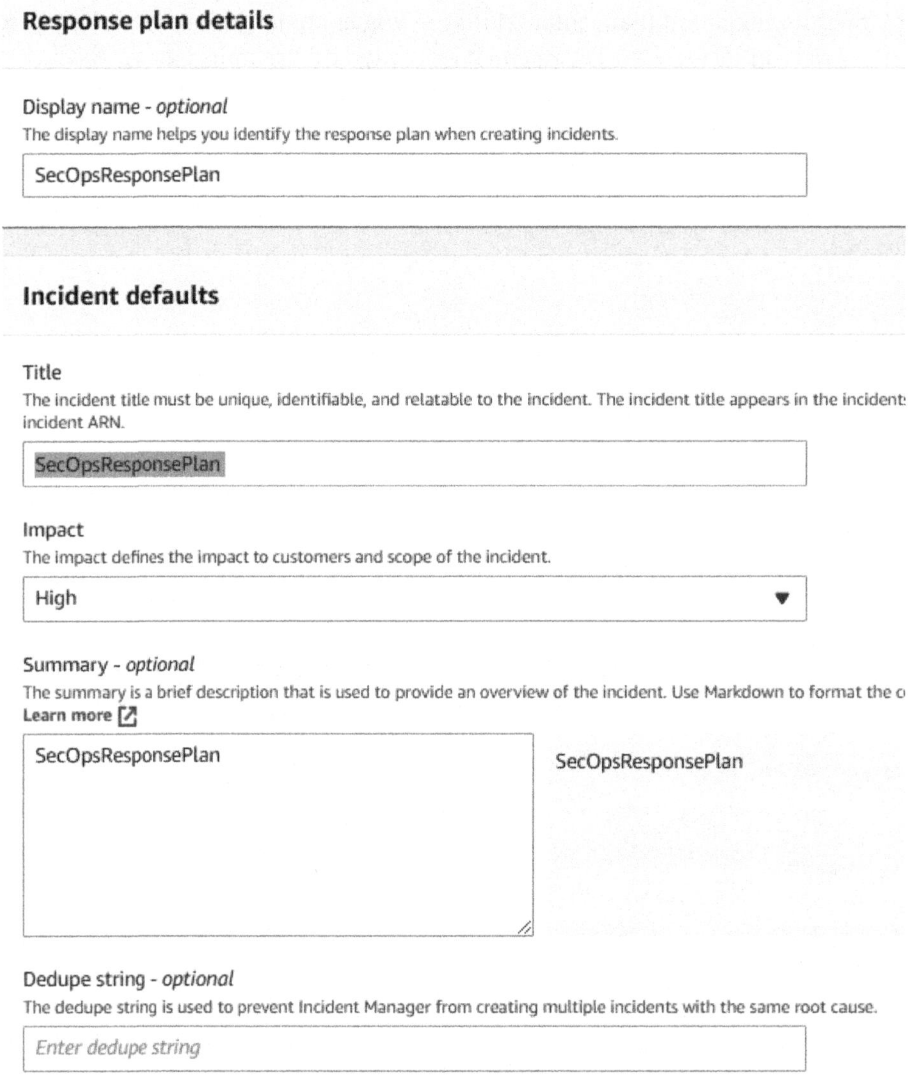

Response plan details

Display name - *optional*
The display name helps you identify the response plan when creating incidents.

```
SecOpsResponsePlan
```

Incident defaults

Title
The incident title must be unique, identifiable, and relatable to the incident. The incident title appears in the incident: incident ARN.

```
SecOpsResponsePlan
```

Impact
The impact defines the impact to customers and scope of the incident.

```
High                                                                          ▼
```

Summary - *optional*
The summary is a brief description that is used to provide an overview of the incident. Use Markdown to format the o
Learn more [↗]

```
SecOpsResponsePlan                              SecOpsResponsePlan



```

Dedupe string - *optional*
The dedupe string is used to prevent Incident Manager from creating multiple incidents with the same root cause.

```
Enter dedupe string
```

Figure 7.31 – Providing response plan details

14. In the **Engagements** section, select **SecOps Team** and then click on **Create response plan**.

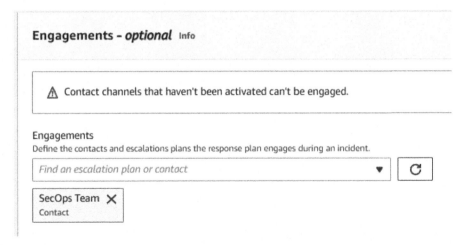

Figure 7.32 – Selecting the engagement contact team

15. Once the response plan has been created, we need to create an event rule, which triggers the incident response plan, in case there is an event in Security Hub. Go to the EventBridge console, click on **Rules**, and click on **Create rule**. Give the name of the rule as **SecurityGroupSSHRemediation**, because we will test the solution using a security group later. Select **Event pattern** and click on **Custom pattern** and paste the following snippet and save it. In the **Target** section, select **Incident Manager response plan**. In **Response plan**, select the **SecOpsResponsePlan** response plan that we just created. Click on **Create** to create the rule.

```
{
    "source": ["aws.securityhub"],
    "detail-type": ["Security Hub Findings - Imported"],
    "detail": {
      "findings": {
        "Compliance": {
          "Status": ["FAILED"]
        },
        "RecordState": ["ACTIVE"],
        "Severity": {
          "Label": ["MEDIUM", "HIGH", "CRITICAL"]
        },
        "Workflow": {
          "Status": ["NOTIFIED", "NEW"]
        }
```

```
              }
          }
      }
```

At this stage, we have implemented our solution. Now let's try to test the solution, by creating a security group, which will have port 22 open to 0.0.0.0/0. Perform the following steps to test the solution:

1. Go to the EC2 console and create a security group named IncidentSSHSG with the inbound rule port 22 open to 0.0.0.0/0.

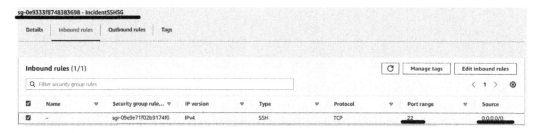

Figure 7.33 – Security group with SSH to all inbound rule

2. After a while, go to the Security Hub console and click on **Findings**. Based on the sorted data of **Updated at** field, you will see an issue related to the security group with **CRITICAL** severity. (There might be a situation where you will see this non compliant finding with another severity level, so you need to filter it out by adding a filter with the incident name)

Figure 7.34 – Security group failed the compliance status with CRITICAL severity

3. Now there will be an email notification sent to the email address given in the response plan with a code that will be used later in the incident response.

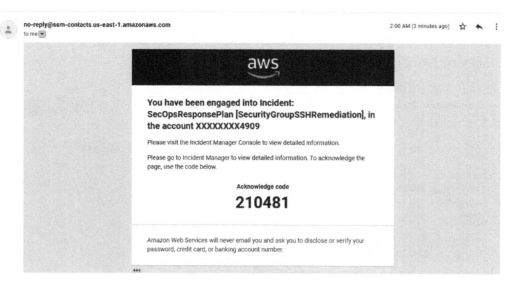

Figure 7.35 – Incident email alert

4. If the incident is not acknowledged within 2 minutes, an SMS will be sent to the contact number provided in the response plan (you can see the email was sent at 2:00 AM and the SMS was sent at 2:02 AM).

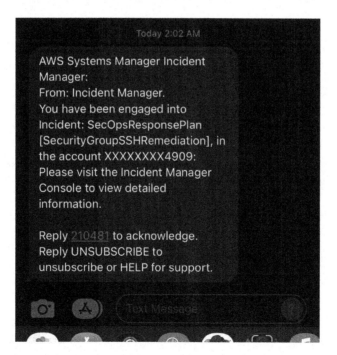

Figure 7.36 – Incident SMS alert

5.   Now go to the **Incident Manager** page; you will see an open incident about which the email was sent.

Figure 7.37 – Open incident in Incident Manager

6.   Click on the incident, then click on **Acknowledge engagement**.

Figure 7.38 – Acknowledging the incident

7.   Provide the six-digit code that was sent in the email and SMS, then click on **Acknowledge**.

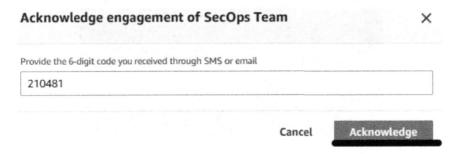

Figure 7.39 – Providing the acknowledgment code

8. This incident would be auto remediated if we had associated any runbook with the response plan, but since there is no runbook associated with this response plan, we will auto remediate it using OpsCenter. Go to the OpsCenter page and click on the number below **Open**. (This number will vary based on your AWS account.)

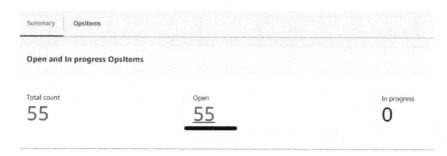

Figure 7.40 – Increased number of open OpsItems

9. We can see the latest OpsItem is related to the security group that we just created. (It may take some time to appear in the OpsItem console.) Click on the OpsItem ID.

Figure 7.41 – OpsItem related to the security group with an Open status

10. You will see an overview of the related resources. Click on the **Related resource details** tab next to **Overview**.

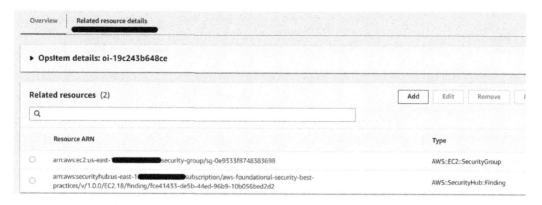

Figure 7.42 – Details of the open security group OpsItem

11. Click on **Run automation** and select **AWS-DisablePublicAccessForSecurityGroup**, then click on **Execute**, which will run the automation runbook and remove the SSH rule from the security group.

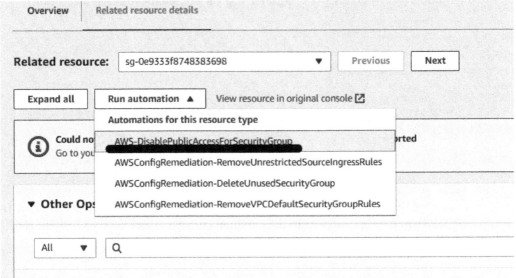

Figure 7.43 – Running the automation runbook for remediation

12. You can see the green highlight at the top of the page. Click on **View automation status**, where you will see the executed steps and the status of the execution.

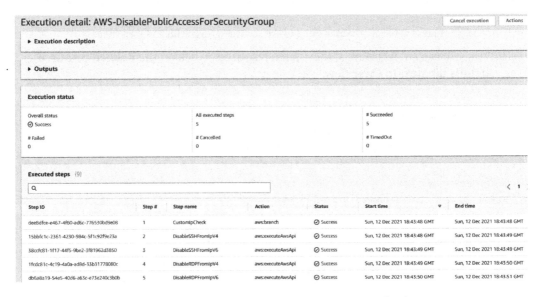

Figure 7.44 – Execution steps of the automation runbook

13. Now you can go back to Security Hub and see that the related finding compliance status will be **PASSED**.

Figure 7.45 – Security group related finding status changed to PASSED

14. Go to the security group inbound rules, and see that port 22 has been removed by the automation script.

Figure 7.46 – SSH inbound rule has been removed by the automation script

15. Even the OpsItem related to the security group will be removed. But we still need to resolve the incident. Go to the incident and click on **Resolve incident**. After that, we need to click on **Create analysis**. This is basically to give the details related to the incident. We mostly use the term **Root Cause Analysis** (**RCA**) in the industry.

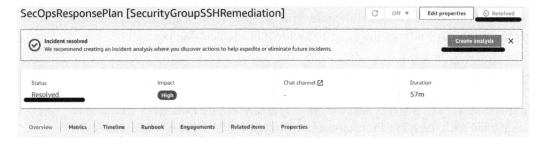

Figure 7.47 – Resolving the open incident

16. Click on **Create analysis**, select the default template, and click on **Create**. Edit **Incident summary** and **Impact,** and then click on **Complete** to close the incident with RCA.

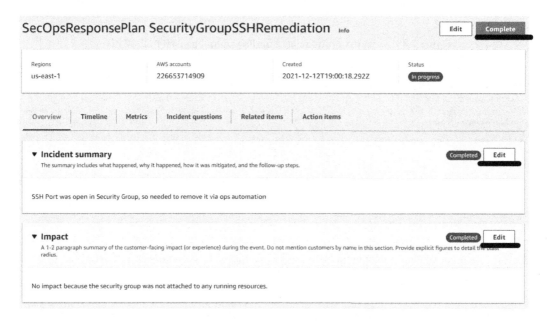

Figure 7.48 – Creating an RCA for the incident

This solution can be used and tweaked in many ways to play around with the incident response process. We can also integrate other security tools, for example, GuardDuty, to get more security findings and raise an incident in Incident Manager.

Summary

In this chapter, we learned about the NIST Framework and how AWS services are compatible with the NIST Framework core functions. We learned about how AWS Security Hub helps us with security compliance and prioritizing alerts. Then, we implemented three solutions in which we denied the execution of a non-compliant image on an EKS cluster and imported an AWS Config evaluation to the AWS Security Hub findings console. We also automated incident creation in Incident Manager whenever there were **CRITICAL** findings in AWS Security Hub. This chapter helped us get familiar with Security Hub and Systems Manager. In the next chapter, we will be ingesting SAST and DAST findings in Security Hub and deciding on the stages of the DevSecOps pipeline.

8

DevSecOps Using AWS Native Services

In this chapter, we will create a **continuous integration/continuous deployment** (CI/CD) pipeline for a microservice application. This pipeline will comprise all the native services of **Amazon Web Services** (**AWS**). In this pipeline, you will be learning all the small details that are required to set up a production-grade pipeline, with an example. We will create a pipeline by taking care of the security aspect of the application code using CodeGuru Reviewer, as well as a Docker image using an **Elastic Container Registry** (**ECR**) scan. We will use Parameter Store for storing secrets and will access it in the build stages. We will be using the AWS Developer toolchain for **version control systems** (**VCS**) and orchestration purposes. We will also test the resiliency of the application and underlying infrastructure using AWS **Fault Injection Simulator** (**FIS**) as part of the pipeline before we deploy it to production. In the end, we will configure the application with AWS DevOps Guru, which will detect any anomalies in the application. You will find basic security tools used in this chapter because we are leveraging mostly on AWS native services. In the next chapter, we will use more security tools to secure our application.

This chapter contains the following main sections:

- Strategy and planning for a CI/CD pipeline

- Creating a CodeCommit repository for microservices

- Creating **pull request** (**PR**) CodeBuild stage with CodeGuru Reviewer

- Creating a development CodePipeline with image scanning and an **Elastic Container Service for Kubernetes(EKS)** cluster

- Creating a staging CodePipeline with mesh deployment and a chaos test with AWS FIS

- Creating a production CodePipeline with canary deployment and its analysis using Grafana

Technical requirements

To implement and perform the tasks mentioned in this chapter, you will need the code and configuration mentioned in the `chapter-08` folder of the following Git repository:

`https://github.com/PacktPublishing/Accelerating-DevSecOps-on-AWS.git`

This chapter includes hands-on topics, so please perform all tasks carefully as there might be a chance that you make a typo or miss some steps. If you're not successful the first time, please troubleshoot and then raise an issue in the GitHub repository.

Strategy and planning for a CI/CD pipeline

In *Chapter 1*, *CI/CD Using AWS CodeStar*, we learned about the branching strategy and how to create a multibranch pipeline using the CodeStar service, which uses CodeCommit as a VCS, CodeBuild for the build stages, and CodePipeline to orchestrate the build stage and deploy to the environment. We were using a monolithic code application, and for that, we were using a **mono repository** (**monorepo**) approach. But in this chapter, we will deploy a polyglot microservice application that we used in *Chapter 4*, *Working with AWS EKS and App Mesh*. One advantage of microservices is that a team of developers can entirely focus on one service while another team can focus on another service. The first stage of development is creating a source code repository, but a question arises as to whether we should use a single repository (monorepo) for all microservices or create multiple repositories for each microservice. It's not necessarily true that having multiple repositories (polyrepos) is more advantageous than having a monorepo—both have their pros and cons. Let's have a look into monorepos versus polyrepos in brief.

Monorepos versus polyrepos

A **monorepo** layout consists of a single code repository where multiple services' source code exists in a hierarchical folder structure, as we see next. There are various benefits to adopting a monorepo, including the following:

- It is simple to exchange code between projects.

- Enables you to keep test suites, automation scripts, and infrastructure configurations all in one location.

Monorepos have also been used by large enterprises to manage their projects.

However, one prevalent misperception among developers is that using a monorepo creates coupling in application code. This is not true, because a monorepo is ultimately responsible for source control, not application dependencies. Have a look at the following code structure of a monorepo:

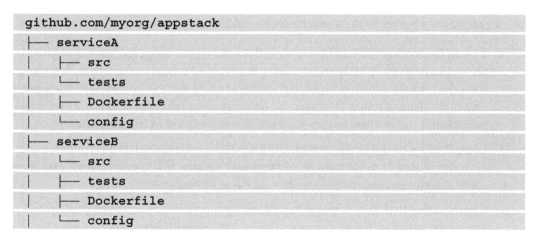

In a **polyrepo** layout, every service has its own individual repository, as shown next. Each repository focuses on specific functionality. Working using polyrepos has various advantages, such as the following:

- It makes it easier to administer access control for distinct code bases individually.

- There are fewer conflicts while "checking in" code.

- If you work with many repositories, you will have fewer changes to "pull".

Furthermore, unless they specifically allow monorepos, certain **development-operations (DevOps)** systems make it simple to build and publish using polyrepos. Have a look at the following code structure of a polyrepo:

```
github.com/myorg/app1
├── docs
├── examples
├── src
└── tests


github.com/myorg/app2
├── docs
└── src
```

It all depends on the type of project or language that you are choosing. We will discuss a few criteria for whether to use a polyrepo or a monorepo, as follows:

- **Ease of importing**: Polyrepois highly influenced by the language. Even though the language needs a package repository in the middle when accessing code from different source repositories, polyrepos appear to be more common. When adopting a monorepo architecture, it is typically better to construct unique modules for each project, and some organizations have built-in tools to aid in this process.

- **Contributing to the same project**: With a polyrepo architecture, it is simpler to trace the history of modifications per repository rather than per directory, making it easier to manage contributions within the same project.

- **Contributing to different projects**: Managing contributions across multiple projects is typically easier with a monorepo arrangement since PRs can make changes to many components at once and there is no need to continually update the referenced version of dependencies. Furthermore, integration faults are instantly visible.

- **CI/CD**: In this regard, polyrepos have a smaller overhead. It is typical for a CI server to have a build and release pipeline for each component. (Recall that one microservice concept is that they must be independently deployable.) In the instance of a polyrepo, if the entire repository is for one service, then any changes uploaded to that repository will trigger a test, build, and deploy pipeline for that service exclusively. In the monorepo world, you must set up the pipeline to only activate when the changeset contains files for that pipeline that create a certain component. Many, but not all, CI servers provide this functionality.

So, it all depends on your requirement, application, team size, and access controls to choose between a polyrepo and a monorepo.

At present, **CodeCommit** doesn't have integration with **CodePipeline** and **CodeBuild** natively to support a monorepo multi-pipeline method. GitHub with CodePipeline and CodeBuild does support a solution through which you can achieve monorepo multi-pipeline build systems. This happens because GitHub has an event `ChangeMatchExpression` event parameter that tells at which path a change has occurred and using that, we can call a lambda function to handle the logic and trigger a specific pipeline. You can read more about this here: `https://aws.amazon.com/blogs/devops/integrate-github-monorepo-with-aws-codepipeline-to-run-project-specific-ci-cd-pipelines/`.

There is an out-of-the-box solution that helps us achieve a CodeCommit monorepo multi-pipeline build. It uses the `git_differences` method to find changes in the files and, based on that, it triggers the pipeline. You can read more about this here: `https://github.com/aws-samples/monorepo-multi-pipeline-trigger`.

In this chapter, we will be going for the monorepo style, but we will learn to design the pipeline in such a way that each folder or service has its individual build and deploy stages.

Since we are using a monorepo repository style, let's have a look in detail at the branches and associated code pipeline that we will create. We are taking a bottom-to-top approach and will first dive into the feature branch. You can refer to the architecture diagram shown next to relate to this.

Feature branch

We will be using a **product catalog** application that consists of three microservices: `frontend-node`, `product catalog`, and `catalog details`. We will push the code to the CodeCommit `master` branch and create three branches—`staging`, `develop`, and `feature`—out of the `master` branch. We will also associate the repository with **CodeGuru Reviewer** to scan the source code and find any vulnerabilities or secrets.

You might have seen a scenario where a developer pushes code to the `feature` branch and an event then gets created to trigger the code pipeline, but the gotcha here is that CodePipeline only accepts the source from a specific branch. But if you will be having multiple `feature` branches, then you will end up creating multiple pipelines for those `feature` branches, which is neither feasible nor necessary. We should create a generic build pipeline for all `feature` branches.

We will tackle this problem by performing the following steps:

1. Instead of using CodePipeline, we will be using CodeBuild. But CodeBuild also accepts the source from a specific branch via the AWS console, so we will be creating a CodeBuild project via the **command-line interface** (**CLI**). Mentioning a branch name in a CodeBuild project is not mandatory via the CLI.

2. Instead of triggering CodeBuild on code push in the `feature` branch, we will create an EventBridge rule to trigger CodeBuild only when there is a PR created from the `feature` branch to the `develop` branch. This way, we can skip the issue of delayed multiple builds during code push in the `feature` branch.

The CodeBuild project associated with the `feature` branch PR to the `develop` branch will be doing the following two things:

1. It will create a CodeGuru Reviewer repository analysis, which will give us some recommendations as a result. If there are no recommendations, then the build will continue; else, the CodeBuild project fails.

2. If there are no recommendations related to any security vulnerabilities, the second step is to build the microservice code. For now, in the build step, we are building all three services (not pushing a Docker image to any registry). If the microservice build step fails, then the CodeBuild project will fail too.

The code from the `feature` branch will only get merged to the `develop` branch if the code build is successful. The following diagram shows the architecture of a CI/CD pipeline using AWS native services:

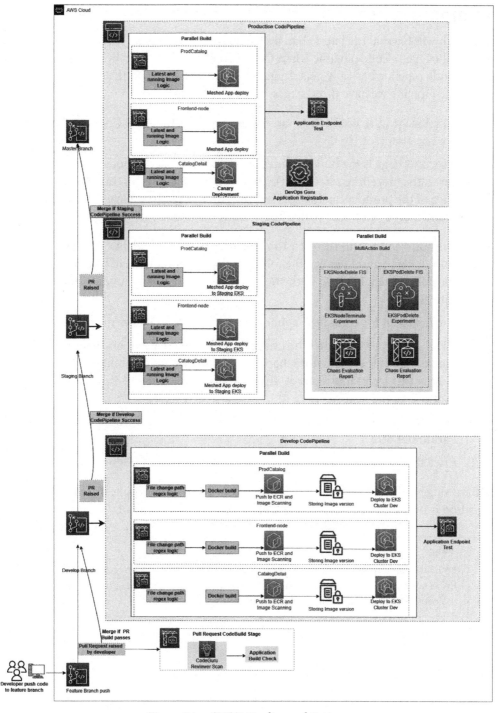

Figure 8.1 – CI/CD Pipeline architecture

Develop branch

This branch will have all the latest changes to the source code of all three services. This branch will trigger a code pipeline when the PR from the `feature` branch is merged. So, here, the code pipeline basically gets triggered on the code push to the `develop` branch. In this code pipeline we have three stages, as outlined here:

1. The first stage is, as usual, the source stage, which is the AWS CodeCommit `develop` branch.

2. The second stage is the build and deploy stage. This stage includes parallel actions (refer to the preceding screenshot). There are three actions in this stage for each service of the product catalog application. All three actions have the same steps but execute in different folder paths. The actions include the following steps:

    A. The build action will run a custom shell script that will identify the latest changes with the path and filter out the folder. If the folder name matches with the condition, then it will go to the next step; else, it will skip building and exit with status `0`.

    B. The next step is to build the application and create a Docker image.

    C. The third step is to upload the image to ECR and create an on-demand ECR image scan. If there are more than two `CRITICAL` vulnerabilities (you can modify this count in the script) in the image then the build will fail; else, it will continue to the next step.

    D. Once the image scan has been passed, it will then store the image version in **Parameter Store**.

    E. After that, it will deploy the service to the **development (Dev)** EKS cluster.

The third stage is the endpoint test stage where it will check the application's health. If the application is healthy, the code pipeline will be successful; else, it fails.

> **Note**
>
> You can also implement the *Deny execution on non-compliant images* on the EKS section on the Dev EKS cluster to make it more secure. You can refer to the previous chapter for the implementation steps.

Staging branch

This branch will have all the latest changes as well. This branch will be associated with the staging code pipeline, which will eventually deploy all the services to the staging environment where various **Chaos experiment via FIS** operations will take place and check the resiliency of the application. This environment will evaluate if the application is ready for production deployment. The staging code pipeline will execute when we merge the code to the `staging` branch from the `develop` branch PR. The code pipeline has three stages, as outlined here:

1. The first stage is, as usual, the source stage, which is the AWS CodeCommit `staging` branch.

2. The second stage is the deploy stage, which contains three parallel actions for each service. All three actions have the same steps, as described here:

   A. All three actions will execute parallelly, and the first step is to fetch the latest image version from Parameter Store and compare it with the currently running image version in the `deployment` kind in the staging EKS cluster. If the image versions are not the same, then deployment will take place with the latest image version present in Parameter Store. If the value of the currently running image is empty, then deployment will also take place with the latest image version present in Parameter Store. If the image versions are the same, then the deployment will skip, with an exit status of 0.

   B. In this pipeline, the deployment is meshed, meaning that the EKS staging environment will be configured to run the service using an **AWS AppMesh** service mesh.

3. The third stage is the chaos test stage, which contains two parallel action group builds looking something like this:

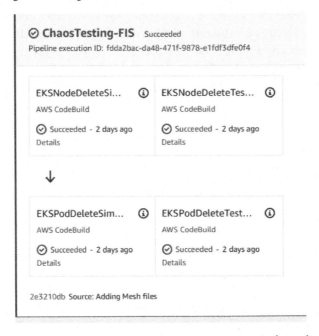

Figure 8.2 – Parallel build steps of FIS experiment in CodePipeline

The first action group contains two actions that run in parallel sequence. The first action will run the *EKS worker node deletion FIS experiment,* and the second action will check the availability of the application and generate an evaluation report. The second action group similarly has two actions, one of which will run the *EKS Pod deletion FIS experiment,* with the other checking the availability of the application and generating an evaluation report.

You can also add a manual approval stage to approve the deployment of the services to production.

Master branch

This branch will have all the latest code with a tag. This branch will be associated with the production code pipeline, which will eventually deploy all the services to the production EKS environment. The deployment strategy of the services will be **canary deployment**. The production EKS cluster will also be integrated with the DevOps Guru service from AWS AIOps. This code pipeline associated with the `master` branch will have three stages, as follows:

1. The first stage is, as usual, the source stage, which is the AWS CodeCommit `master` branch.

2. The second stage is similar to the second stage of the staging code pipeline, the only difference being in the deployment strategy. In this stage, canary deployment will take place in the production EKS cluster.

3. The third stage is application endpoint testing.

We will be using all the AWS native services in this CI/CD pipeline. The stages and steps in this pipeline are very generic, for learning purposes. You can definitely edit and add multiple stages as per your requirement. The `buildspec.yaml` file will be separated from the application repository and will be fed into the CodeBuild project via the **user interface (UI)**. This has been done to showcase that the developer won't have full control of the build steps. There might be a chance that the developer will modify the `buildspec.yaml` file and skip some steps. So, for that reason, we are putting all of the `buildspec.yaml` file inside the CodeBuild project. You can also restrict the developer access to have read-only permission for CodeBuild or CodePipeline projects. You can also make the CI/CD pipeline cross the AWS account since we are using all the native services. Every company and team has different requirements in CI/CD. This chapter is trying to cover the necessary stages with the use of all AWS native services, including **AWS CodeGuru, FIS**, and **DevOps Guru**.

We just saw the CI/CD pipeline stages and the action workflow, so let's now dive into the application infrastructure in brief.

We will be spinning up three EKS clusters for the development, staging, and production environments. The development EKS cluster will only have one worker node, and the staging and production clusters will be similar and have two worker nodes. The reason for keeping the staging and production environment the same is to test the infrastructure resiliency in staging and check if the application is still running. If staging can handle the chaos simulation, then there's a high possibility that production will also act the same. If the staging environment application is down due to chaos simulation, then we need to improve the staging environment as well as the production environment.

All the EKS clusters used in this chapter will be spun up by the `eksctl` command, and they will be accessible at a public endpoint. The focus of this chapter is more on the CI/CD pipeline. You can read *Chapter 5, Securing Private EKS Cluster for Production* to create a production-grade and secure EKS cluster.

The development EKS cluster will be simple without any additional add-ons. The staging cluster will have **App Mesh** configured. The production cluster will have both App Mesh and **Flagger** installed. Flagger is an open source tool that automates canary deployment with App Mesh configuration.

We will be performing all terminal-related activities using **AWS Cloud9**. So, let's get started and create all the necessary prerequisites before we create a repository and pipeline.

> **Note**
>
> All the activities are performed in the us-east-1 region. You can do the necessary changes if you are using another region.

Creating the prerequisite components

The first thing we need to create a Cloud9 environment where we will be doing all the operation- and terminal-related tasks. Proceed as follows:

1. Go to the **AWS Cloud9** home page and click on **Create environment**.

2. Provide a **Name** value of ProductCatalogDev and give a value for **Description**. Then, click on **Next step**.

3. In the **Environment settings** page, keep all the selections as default and click on **Next step**, where you will see a **Review** page. Click on **Create environment** to create a Cloud9 environment. It will take a few minutes to create an environment. You will see a development environment that looks like this:

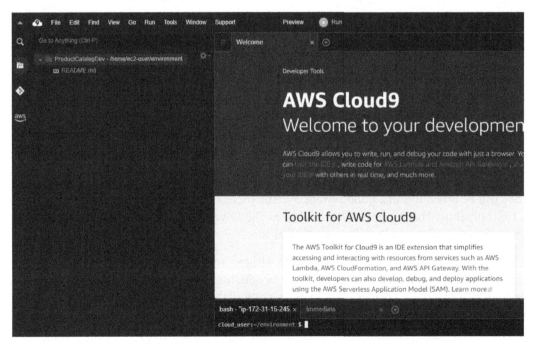

Figure 8.3 – Cloud9 integrated development environment (IDE)

4. After that, we need to increase the disk size of this environment. By default, it spins up with 10 **gigabytes (GB)** disk size. Run the following command in the cloud terminal to increase the disk size to 25 GB:

```
pip3 install --user --upgrade boto3
export instance_id=$(curl -s http://169.254.169.254/
latest/meta-data/instance-id)
python -c "import boto3
import os
from botocore.exceptions import ClientError
ec2 = boto3.client('ec2')
volume_info = ec2.describe_volumes(
    Filters=[
        {
            'Name': 'attachment.instance-id',
            'Values': [
                os.getenv('instance_id')
            ]
        }
    ]
)
volume_id = volume_info['Volumes'][0]['VolumeId']
try:
    resize = ec2.modify_volume(
            VolumeId=volume_id,
            Size=25
    )
    print(resize)
except ClientError as e:
    if e.response['Error']['Code'] ==
'InvalidParameterValue':
        print('ERROR MESSAGE: {}'.format(e))"
if [ $? -eq 0 ]; then
    sudo reboot
fi
```

5. Once the preceding command succeeds, run the following command to check the disk size—it should be 25 GB:

$ df -hT						
Filesystem	Type	Size	Used	Avail	Use%	Mounted on
devtmpfs	devtmpfs	475M	0	475M	0%	/dev
tmpfs	tmpfs	492M	0	492M	0%	/dev/shm
tmpfs	tmpfs	492M	468K	491M	1%	/run
tmpfs cgroup	tmpfs	492M	0	492M	0%	/sys/fs/
/dev/xvda1	**xfs**	**25G**	**8.1G**	**17G**	**33%**	**/**
tmpfs user/1000	tmpfs	99M	0	99M	0%	/run/

6. Once the disk resize is done, install the necessary command-line tools, such as kubectl, jq, eksctl, and awscli. You can do this by executing the following code:

```
$ sudo curl --silent --location --o /usr/local/bin/
kubectl https://amazon-eks.s3.us-west-2.amazonaws.
com/1.21.2/2021-07-05/bin/linux/amd64/kubectl
$ sudo chmod +x /usr/local/bin/kubectl
$ curl "https://awscli.amazonaws.com/awscli-exe-
linux-x86_64.zip" -o "awscliv2.zip"
$ unzip awscliv2.zip
$ sudo ./aws/install
$ sudo yum -y install jq gettext bash-completion
moreutils
$ curl --silent --location "https://github.com/
weaveworks/eksctl/releases/latest/download/eksctl_$(uname
-s)_amd64.tar.gz" | tar xz -C /tmp
$ sudo mv -v /tmp/eksctl /usr/local/bin
```

7. Now, we need to create an **identity and access management (IAM)** role with a trusted entity of **Elastic Compute Cloud (EC2)** and name it Cloud9AdminAccess. For now, please attach an AdministratorAccess policy to it.

8. Once you have created this role, go to the Cloud9 editor, click on the gray circle at the top right, and select **Manage EC2 Instance**, as illustrated in the following screenshot:

Figure 8.4 – Cloud9 IDE setting to manage the environment

9. You will be redirected to the EC2 instance page, where this environment is running. Select the EC2 instance and click on **Actions**. Select **Security** and then select **Modify IAM role**. Then, select the `Cloud9AdminAccess` IAM role from the dropdown and click on **Save**. The process is illustrated in the following screenshot:

Figure 8.5 – Attaching IAM role to Cloud9 EC2 instance

10. Once you have attached the IAM role to the EC2 instance that is running in the Cloud9 environment, you need to go to the terminal and run the following command to disable the temporary credentials. Cloud9 uses dynamic AWS managed credentials, which are not compatible with EKS IAM authentication. Once the AWS managed temporary credentials are disabled, we will generate new credentials:

```
$ aws cloud9 update-environment  --environment-id $C9_PID
--managed-credentials-action DISABLE
$ rm -vf ${HOME}/.aws/credentials
$ export ACCOUNT_ID=$(aws sts get-caller-identity
--output text --query Account)
$ export AWS_REGION=$(curl -s 169.254.169.254/latest/
```

```
dynamic/instance-identity/document | jq -r '.region')
$ export AZS=($(aws ec2 describe-availability-zones
--query 'AvailabilityZones[].ZoneName' --output text
--region $AWS_REGION))
$ echo "export ACCOUNT_ID=${ACCOUNT_ID}" | tee -a
~/.bash_profile
$ echo "export AWS_REGION=${AWS_REGION}" | tee -a
~/.bash_profile
$ echo "export AZS=(${AZS[@]})" | tee -a ~/.bash_profile
$ aws configure set default.region ${AWS_REGION}
$ aws configure get default.region
```

11. Now, you need to create two service roles that will be used by CodeBuild projects. Go to **IAM role** and create two roles (in this use case, we select CodeBuild), CodeBuildServiceRole and CodeBuildServiceRole2, as illustrated in the following screenshot. Attach an AdministratorAccess policy to both these roles:

☐	Role name ▽	Trusted entities
☐	CodeBuildServiceRole	AWS Service: codebuild
☐	CodeBuildServiceRole2	AWS Service: codebuild

Figure 8.6 – Created CodeBuild service roles

12. Create an ECR repository and name it catalogapp, then upload the following two images:

A. node:14

B. python3.9

13. Create three parameter stores to keep the latest available Docker image version, as follows:

```
$ aws ssm put-parameter --name "catalog_detail" --type
"String" --value "XYZ"
$ aws ssm put-parameter --name "frontend_node" --type
"String" --value "ABC"
$ aws ssm put-parameter --name "product_catalog" --type
"String" --value "SGR"
```

Up to now, we have done the initial configuration. In the next section, we will create a CodeCommit repository and push the sample code into it.

Creating a CodeCommit repository for microservices

In this section, we will create a CodeCommit repository that will be integrated with the CodeBuild and CodePipeline projects. We will also enable CodeGuru Reviewer on the repository to scan the source code. Perform the following steps:

1. Go to CodeCommit and click on **Create repository**. Type `CatalogApp` in the **Repository name** field and provide an entry for the **Description** field. Also, select the **Enable Amazon CodeGuru Reviewer for Java and Python** checkbox, and then click on **Create**.

2. You will be redirected to the **Repositories** page. Select `HTTPS` under the **Clone URL** section, as illustrated in the following screenshot:

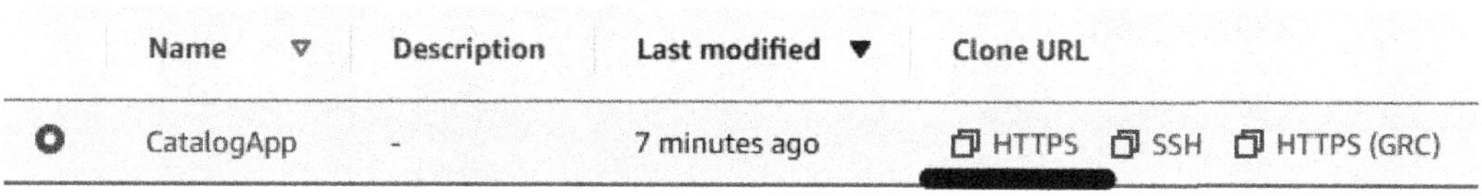

Name ▽	Description	Last modified ▼	Clone URL
⚙ CatalogApp	-	7 minutes ago	⧉ HTTPS ⧉ SSH ⧉ HTTPS (GRC)

Figure 8.7 – CodeCommit CatalogApp repository

3. Go to the Cloud9 editor terminal and paste the following command:

    ```
    $ git clone https://git-codecommit.us-east-1.amazonaws.
    com/v1/repos/CatalogApp
    ```

4. Now, clone the repository and copy `chapter-08` to the `CatalogApp` folder, as follows:

    ```
    $git clone https://github.com/PacktPublishing/
    Accelerating-DevSecOps-on-AWS.git
    $ cp -rf Accelerating-DevSecOps-on-AWS/chapter-08/
    CatalogApp/* CatalogApp/
    ```

5. Navigate to each folder (`catalog_detail`, `frontend_node`, and `product_catalog`) and replace the image version in the Dockerfile with the ECR repository image that we uploaded in *Step 12* of the previous section. Now, push this application code to the `master` branch of the CodeCommit repository and create three branches, `feature`, `develop`, and `staging`, like this:

    ```
    $ cd CatalogApp
    $ git add .
    $ git commit -m "Initial Push"
    $ git push origin master
    ```

```
$ git checkout -b staging
$ git push origin staging
$ git checkout -b develop
$ git push origin develop
$ git checkout -b feature-anothercatalog
$ git push origin feature-anothercatalog
```

6. You can go to the CodeCommit **CatalogApp** page, and you can verify the presence of microservice code and branches. Your screen should look like this:

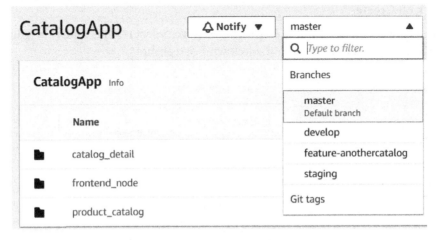

Figure 8.8 – Content inside the CatalogApp repository

7. You can also verify the association of the CatalogApp repository in CodeGuru Reviewer. Go to the **CodeGuru** page and click on **Repositories** under the **Reviewer** section. You will be able to see the repository name, as illustrated in the following screenshot:

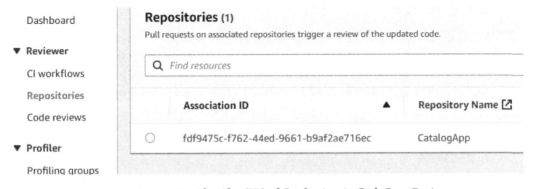

Figure 8.9 – Association identifier (ID) of CatalogApp in CodeGuru Reviewer

At this stage, we have created a microservice monorepo. In the next section, we will create a CodeBuild project that will get executed when a developer raises a PR from the `feature` branch to the `develop` branch.

Creating PR CodeBuild stages with CodeGuru Reviewer

In this section, we will create a CodeBuild project via the CLI that will get executed whenever a developer raises a PR from any `feature` branch. The CodeBuild project will not be bounded to a specific `feature` branch. It will execute the build steps for all PRs from the `feature` branch to the `develop` branch.

This CodeBuild project includes two steps—one is to scan the `feature` branch code via CodeGuru Reviewer, and the other is to execute the build steps of the microservice code. To achieve this, perform the following steps:

1. Create a **Simple Storage Service** (**S3**) bucket named `dsoawscicdbucket-<accountno>`, as follows:

```
$ aws s3api create-bucket --bucket dsoawscicdbucket-
$ACCOUNT_ID --create-bucket-configuration
LocationConstraint=us-east-1
```

2. Run the following command to create a CodeBuild project via the CLI using an input **JavaScript Object Notation** (**JSON**) file. Make sure to replace the **S3 bucket** and **IAM ServiceRole** values:

```
$ cat <<EOF > CatalogApp-Feature-PR.json
{
    "name": "CatalogApp-Feature-PR",
    "source": {
      "type": "CODECOMMIT",
       "location": "https://git-codecommit.us-east-1.
amazonaws.com/v1/repos/CatalogApp"
    },
    "artifacts": {
      "type": "S3",
      "location": "<REPLACE BUCKET NAME>"
    },
    "environment": {
```

```
      "type": "LINUX_CONTAINER",
      "image": "aws/codebuild/amazonlinux2-x86_64-
standard:3.0",
      "computeType": "BUILD_GENERAL1_SMALL"
    },
    "serviceRole": "arn:aws:iam::< Your ACCOUNT NO>:role/
CodeBuildServiceRole"
  }
EOF
$ aws codebuild create-project --cli-input-json file://
CatalogApp-Feature-PR.json
```

3. You can verify the CodeBuild project creation by going to the **CodeBuild** page. You will see a project named CatalogApp-Feature-PR, as illustrated in the following screenshot. Click on that to get more information:

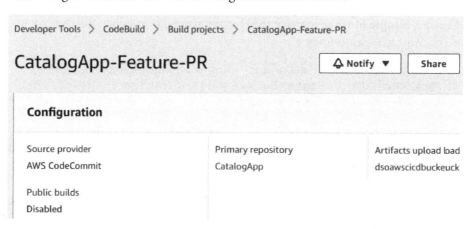

Figure 8.10 – CodeBuild project showing repository name but not any branch

4. As you can see from the preceding screenshot, only the repository name is present and there was no reference to any branches. Now, to make this project execute during the PR, we need to create an *EventBridge rule* and provide a PR *event pattern* to develop and target this CodeBuild project. Go to the **EventBridge** page, click on **Rules**, and then click on **Create rule**.

5. In the **Create rule** page, provide a **Name** value of catalogAppFeaturePREventRule. In the **Define pattern** section, click on **Event pattern** and select **Custom pattern** under **Event matching pattern**. In the **Event pattern** textbox, paste the following content and click on **Save**. Make sure you change the arn value of the CodeCommit repository:

Define pattern

Build or customize an Event Pattern or set a Schedule to invoke Targets.

Figure 8.11 – Custom event pattern in EventBridge rule

The event pattern code is shown in the following snippet:

```
{
    "detail": {
        "event": ["pullRequestCreated",
"pullRequestSourceBranchUpdated"],
        "destinationReference": ["refs/heads/develop"]
    },
    "detail-type": ["CodeCommit Pull Request State
Change"],
    "resources": ["arn:aws:codecommit:us-east-1:<Your-
Accoun-No>:CatalogApp"],
    "source": ["aws.codecommit"]
}
```

6. Under the **Select targets** section, click on the **Target** dropdown, select **Codebuild project**, and mention the CatalogApp-Feature-PR CodeBuild project **Amazon Resource Name (ARN)** in the **Project ARN** text field. You can find the CatalogApp-Feature-PR CodeBuild project ARN under the **Details** section of the CodeBuild project, as illustrated in the following screenshot:

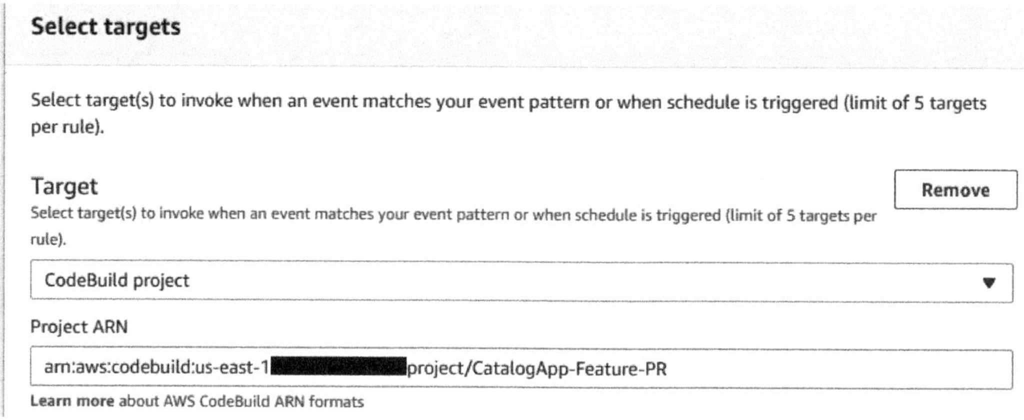

Figure 8.12 – Selecting CodeBuild project as the target of EventBridge rule

7. Expand the **Configure input** section and select **Input transformer**. In the **Input Path** box, paste the following content:

```
{"destinationCommit":"$.detail.
destinationCommit","pullRequestId":"$.
detail.pullRequestId","repositoryName":"$.
detail.repositoryNames[0]","revisionId":"$.
detail.revisionId","sourceCommit":"$.detail.
sourceCommit","sourceReference":"$.detail.
sourceReference","sourceVersion":"$.detail.sourceCommit"}
```

In the **Input Template** box, paste the following content of the InputTemplate file from the chapter08/CICD folder (this step basically gets the event pattern from CodeCommit and transforms the event pattern to a variable, making those variable values environment variables under the CodeBuild project):

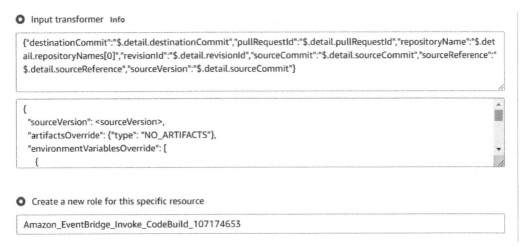

● Input transformer Info

{"destinationCommit":"$.detail.destinationCommit","pullRequestId":"$.detail.pullRequestId","repositoryName":"$.det ail.repositoryNames[0]","revisionId":"$.detail.revisionId","sourceCommit":"$.detail.sourceCommit","sourceReference":" $.detail.sourceReference","sourceVersion":"$.detail.sourceCommit"}

{
  "sourceVersion": <sourceVersion>,
  "artifactsOverride": {"type": "NO_ARTIFACTS"},
  "environmentVariablesOverride": [
    {

● Create a new role for this specific resource

Amazon_EventBridge_Invoke_CodeBuild_107174653

Figure 8.13 – Providing input transformer and input template

8. Leave the rest of the settings as they are, provide a **Tag** value, and click on **Create**.

9. Now, go to the CatalogApp-Feature-PR CodeBuild project and edit **Buildspec**, as illustrated in the following screenshot:

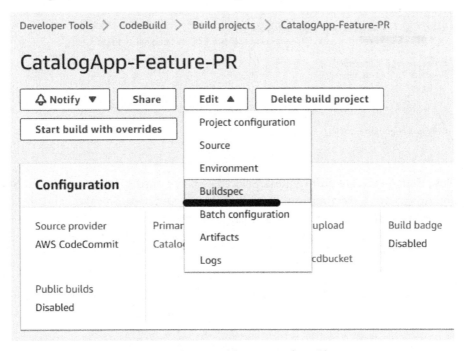

Figure 8.14 – Editing Buildspec in CodeBuild project

10. In the **Edit Buildspec** page, select **Insert build commands**. Then, click on **Switch to editor**. Paste the content of the `CatalogAppFeaturePR.yaml` file present in the `chapter-08/CICD` folder. Also, change the environment variable value. You can get the `ASSOCIATION_ID` value from the **CodeGuru Reviewer** page. Click on **Repositories** under the **Reviewer** section. You will see **Association ID**.

11. Now, let's do a minor modification in the `feature` branch and raise a PR to `develop`. Go to the `CatalogApp` CodeCommit repository. Switch the branch to `feature-anothercatalog`. Go to the `catalog_detail` folder, as illustrated in the following screenshot. Select **Dockerfile** and click on **Edit**. Remove the first line, which is a comment, since we have already pointed to the correct image path in *Step 6* of the previous section. Provide **Author name**, **Email address**, and **commit message** (`removing comment`) values and click on **Commit changes**:

Figure 8.15 – Editing Docker image

12. Now, click on **Create pull request**. Select `feature-anothercatalog` for **Source** and `develop` as **Destination**. Provide **Title** and **Description** values and click on **Create pull request**. Once you create a PR, the `CatalogApp-Feature-PR` CodeBuild project will execute, as illustrated in the following screenshot:

Figure 8.16 – CodeBuild project build run

The activity will also get updated in the **Pull Request Activity** tab. Once the build finishes, it will update the status in the **Pull Request Activity** tab. Unfortunately, the build has failed, and the status is updated in the **Pull Request Activity** tab, as illustrated in the following screenshot:

Figure 8.17 – CodeCommit Pull Request Activity tab showing build status

If you review the build logs, you will find that after the CodeGuru Reviewer scan, there have been some recommendations, as illustrated in the following screenshot. We shouldn't approve the PR if there are some recommendations:

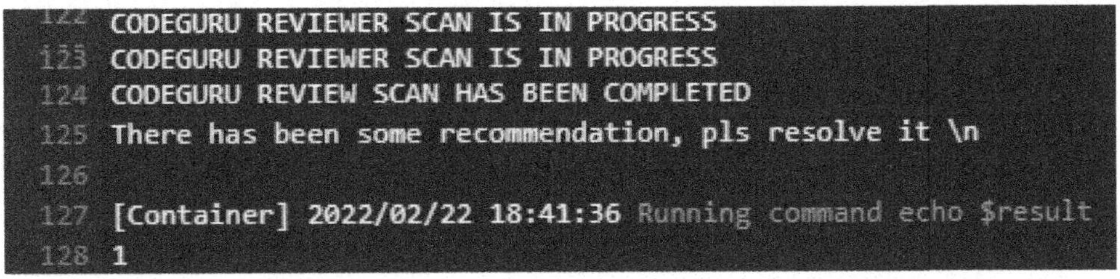

```
122  CODEGURU REVIEWER SCAN IS IN PROGRESS
123  CODEGURU REVIEWER SCAN IS IN PROGRESS
124  CODEGURU REVIEW SCAN HAS BEEN COMPLETED
125  There has been some recommendation, pls resolve it \n
126
127  [Container] 2022/02/22 18:41:36 Running command echo $result
128  1
```

Figure 8.18 – CodeBuild build logs showing CodeGuru has some recommendations

Now, go to the CodeGuru Reviewer console and find out what the recommendations are. Click on **Code reviews** under the **Reviewer** section and then click on **Full repository analysis**. Then, select the latest name, which is catalogApp-BuildNo (for example, catalogApp-1). Go to the bottom and you will find the **Security**

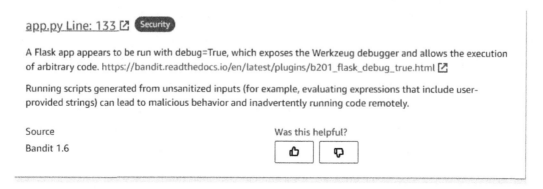

Figure 8.19 – CodeGuru recommendation in Python code

13. Now, go to the file and line number where the app.py Line:133 recommendation is pointing to and edit the file. Go to the last line of code and remove debug=True so that it looks like this: app.run(host="0.0.0.0"). Now, again raise a PR, and see that the build will be successful. Again, you will get the build status in the **Activity** tab of the PR, as illustrated in the following screenshot:

Comment on changes

AWSCodeBuild-8a24f717-c343-4bf9-9da5-d568c62f0e8e commented 4 minutes ago

Build Succesful

Reply

Figure 8.20 – CodeCommit PR Activity tab showing build status

You can also go and see the build logs to see whether the recommendations persist, as illustrated in the following screenshot:

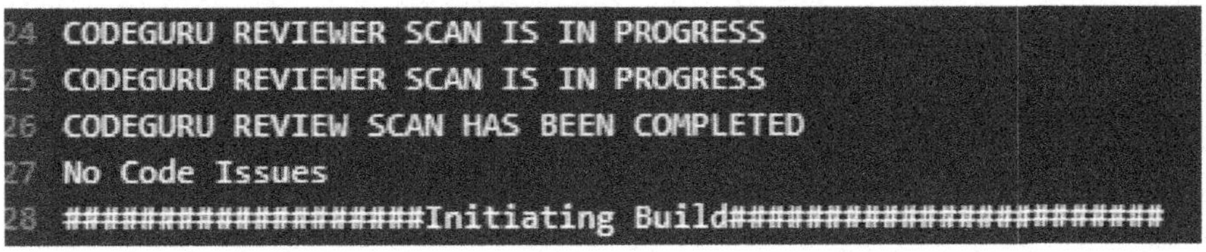

```
24  CODEGURU REVIEWER SCAN IS IN PROGRESS
25  CODEGURU REVIEWER SCAN IS IN PROGRESS
26  CODEGURU REVIEW SCAN HAS BEEN COMPLETED
27  No Code Issues
28  ###################Initiating Build####################
```

Figure 8.21 – CodeBuild build logs showing no recommendation from CodeGuru Reviewer

You can see No Code Issues displayed, and after that, the microservice code build takes place. For now, don't merge the PR to the develop branch. We will merge it into the next section so that it can trigger a develop CodePipeline project.

This CodeBuild project status helps us to analyze and make a decision quickly whether to approve the PR or reject it. You can also see the CodeGuru Reviewer recommendation during the PR, which is natively provided by AWS, but it doesn't give the full repository analysis. Also, you can pass the full repository analysis recommendation in the **Pull Request Activity** tab in a similar way to how we are passing the build status. In the next section, we will set up a development CodePipeline project and spin up a development EKS environment.

Creating a development CodePipeline project with image scanning and an EKS cluster

In the previous section, we raised a PR from feature-anothercatalog to the develop branch after fixing a security recommendation. That means the new feature is ready to get merged to the develop branch and to deploy on the **development EKS cluster**. Mostly, the development environment runs multiple builds and deployments in a day. These days, you will see most enterprises and start-ups roll out their features every day. In this section, we will create a CodePipeline project that will get triggered the moment the PR gets merged from feature-anothercatalog to the develop branch. We also need to make sure that the build and deployment should take place only to the microservice that has code changes. We discussed in the first section that either we can choose polyrepo and multiple pipelines or we can have a monorepo and path-based multi-pipeline. It was also highlighted that currently, we can't do path-based multiple pipelines with CodeCommit, but there is an out-of-the-box solution developed by AWS using the **Cloud Development Kit (CDK)**. But we are not taking that approach and are instead trying something different.

In this CodePipeline project, we will be creating a stage that will have three parallel builds that identify in which folder the change had taken place, and based on that, it acts. The logic has been written with a simple shell script that is easy to understand. You can tweak it and play around with it based on your use case and requirement. To achieve this, perform the following steps:

1. Go to the **CodePipeline** page and click on **Create pipeline**. Enter `CatalogApp-DevBuild` as the pipeline name. In **Service role**, **New service role** will have been auto-selected and will have generated a role name as well, as illustrated in the following screenshot. Click on **Next**:

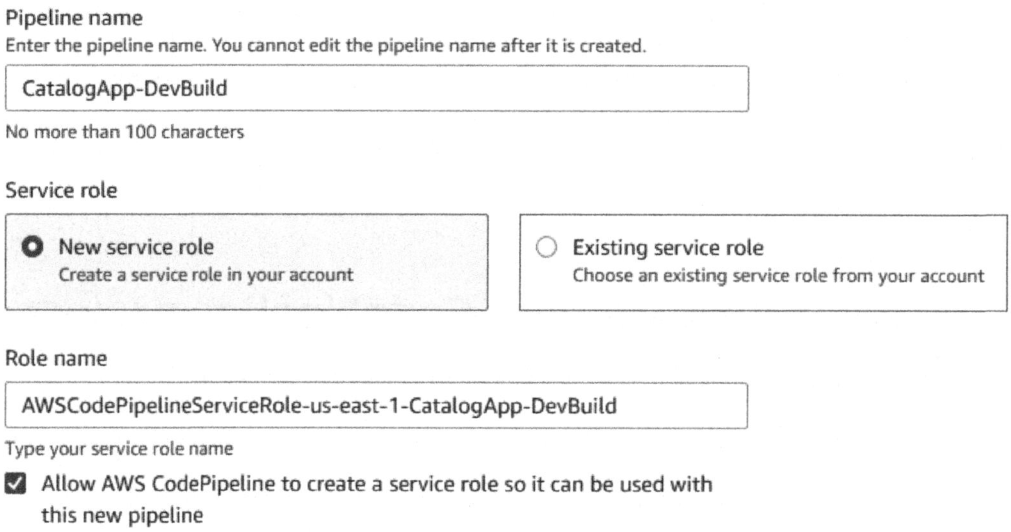

Pipeline name

Enter the pipeline name. You cannot edit the pipeline name after it is created.

> CatalogApp-DevBuild

No more than 100 characters

Service role

- ● New service role
  Create a service role in your account

- ○ Existing service role
  Choose an existing service role from your account

Role name

> AWSCodePipelineServiceRole-us-east-1-CatalogApp-DevBuild

Type your service role name

☑ Allow AWS CodePipeline to create a service role so it can be used with this new pipeline

Figure 8.22 – Creating a CodePipeline project with a new service role

2. On the **Source** page, select **AWS CodeCommit** in the **Source provider** dropdown. Select `CatalogApp` for the **Repository** name and select `develop` for the **Branch** name. In **Output artifact format**, select **full clone** and then click on **Next**.

3. On the **Build** page, select **AWS CodeBuild** in **Build provider**. Select the region—in this case, it's **US East**. Then, click on **Create project**, which will open a new pop-up browser page with **Create build project**. Enter the following details on this page:

    A. **Project name**: `CatalogApp-catalogDetail-DevBuild`

    B. **Environment image**: **Managed image**

    C. **Operating system**: **Amazon Linux 2**

    D. **Runtime**: **Standard**

E. **Image**: `aws/codebuild/amazonlinux2-x86_64-standard:3.0`

F. **Environment type**: **Linux**

G. Check the **Privileged** box, as we will be using the `docker build` command inside.

H. Select **Existing service role** and select `CodeBuildServiceRole`.

I. In **Build specifications**, select **Insert build commands**. In **Build commands**, enter `echo "Hello world!"` for now.

J. Click on **Continue to CodePipeline**.

4. You will be redirected to the CodePipeline **Build** page. Click on **Next**. Then, click on **Skip deploy stage**. Then, you will be on the **Review** page. Click on **Create pipeline**. This was the basic creation of a pipeline. Now, we need to customize it.

5. Click on **Edit** on the `CatalogApp-DevBuild` CodePipeline page. Click on the **Edit** stage of the **Build** stage. You will see an existing **Build action** group. Click on the **Edit** icon of the **Build action** group and change the **Action name** value from `Build` to `CatalogApp-catalogDetail-DevBuild`. Leave the rest of the fields as they are and click on **Done**. The following screenshot illustrates the process:

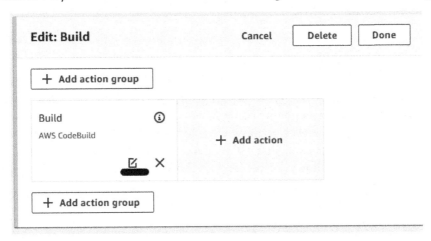

Figure 8.23 – Editing CodePipeline Build stage Build action

6. Now, click on **Add action** parallel to it and give an **Action name** value of
   `CatalogApp-productCatalog-DevBuild`. In the **Action provider**
   dropdown, select **AWS CodeBuild**. In **Input artifacts**, choose `SourceArtifact`.
   In **Project name**, click on **Create project**. Give the project name as `CatalogApp-`
   `productCatalog-DevBuild` and provide the rest of the details in the same way
   as *Step 3 | b* to *Step 3 | j*.

7. Repeat *Step 6* with the **Action name** value as `CatalogApp-frontendNode-`
   `DevBuild` and **Project name** as `CatalogApp-frontendNode-DevBuild`.
   Once you have created three actions, click on **Done** to save the **Build** stage, as
   illustrated in the following screenshot:

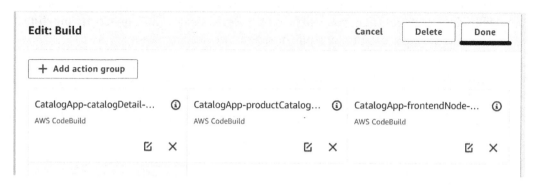

Figure 8.24 – CodePipeline Build stage having parallel actions

8. Click on **Add stage** to create a new stage. Provide a **Stage name** value of **Test** and
   click on **Add stage**. Click on **Add action group**. Do the same as in *Step 6*, with
   Action name and **Project name** being `EndpointHealthCheck`. Click on **Done**
   to save the stage. Then, click on **Save** at the top of the **CodePipeline** page. At the
   end of the process, your pipeline will look like this, and the action would be in
   Didn't Run. In the following screenshot, it shows **Succeeded** because the pipeline
   had been executed before:

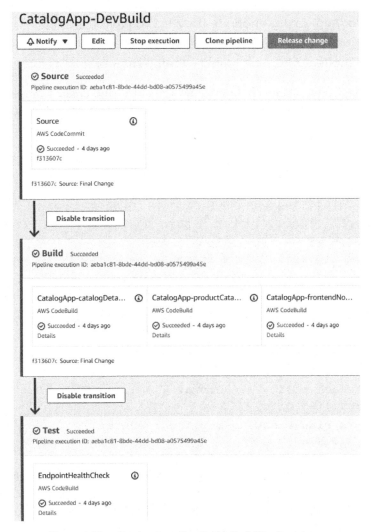

Figure 8.25 – CatalogApp-DevBuild CodePipeline stages

9. Now, edit all the following CodeBuild projects and modify the `buildspec` content. See *Step 9* of the previous section for how to edit the `buildspec` content. You need to go to the `chapter-08/CICD` folder, copy the content of the file, and paste it to the respective CodeBuild project. Also, make sure you change the necessary details inside, such as **AWS Account No**:

   A. `CatalogApp-CatalogDetail-DevBuild` project—
      `CatalogAppCatalogDetailDevBuild.yaml`

   B. `CatalogApp-productCatalog-DevBuild` project—
      `CatalogAppProductCatalogDevBuild.yaml`

C. `CatalogApp-frontendNode-DevBuild` project—
`CatalogAppFrontEndNodeDevBuild.yaml`

D. `EndpointHealthCheck` project—`EndpointHealthCheck.yaml`

Once we have the CodePipeline configured, let's go ahead and create a development environment EKS cluster. Perform the following steps to create an EKS cluster via the Cloud9 terminal:

1. Go to the Cloud9 terminal and run the following command to create a `catalogapp-dev` EKS cluster. It will take approximately 10-15 minutes to do this:

```
cd Accelerating-DevSecOps-on-AWS/chapter-08
$ eksctl create cluster --name catalogapp-dev --nodes 1
--node-type t3.small --with-oidc
$ kubectl create ns prodcatalog-ns
$ aws iam create-policy --policy-name ProdEnvoyIAMPolicy
--policy-document file://CICD/envoy-iam-policy.json
$ eksctl create iamserviceaccount --cluster catalogapp-
dev \
    --namespace prodcatalog-ns \
    --name prodcatalog-envoy-proxies \
    --attach-policy-arn arn:aws:iam::$ACCOUNT_ID:policy/
ProdEnvoyIAMPolicy \
    --override-existing-serviceaccounts \
    --approve
```

2. Edit the `aws-auth` config map of the EKS cluster to grant permission to `CodeBuildServiceRole` and `CodeBuildServiceRole2`, which are attached to CodeBuild projects to execute commands on the EKS cluster. To do so, execute the following code:

```
$ kubectl edit cm aws-auth -n kube-system -o yaml
Add the following content and save the file
- rolearn: arn:aws:iam::<YourAccNo>:role/
CodeBuildServiceRole
  username: CodeBuildServiceRole
    groups:
      - system:masters
- rolearn: arn:aws:iam::<YourAccNo>:role/
CodeBuildServiceRole2
  username: CodeBuildServiceRole2
```

```
groups:
     - system:masters
```

The following snippet screenshot shows the indentation.

```
apiVersion: v1
data:
  mapRoles: |
    - groups:
      - system:bootstrappers
      - system:nodes
      rolearn: arn:aws:iam:            role/eksctl-catalogapp-dev-nodegroup-n-NodeInstanceRole-F075G4C3A6B
      username: system:node:{{EC2PrivateDNSName}}
    - rolearn: arn:aws:iam::           :role/CodeBuildServiceRole
      username: CodeBuildServiceRole
      groups:
        - system:masters
```

Figure 8.26 – Snippet of aws-auth config map for indentation

3. Create three ECR repositories and name them catalogapp/catalog_detail, catalogapp/frontend_node, and catalogapp/product_catalog. Don't enable **Scan on push** while creating ECR repositories. You can see the repositories in the following screenshot:

Repository name ▲	Created at ▽	Tag immutability	Scan frequency	Encryption type	Pull through cache
○ catalogapp	February 17, 2022, 16:14:22 (UTC+08)	Enabled	Manual	AES-256	Inactive
○ catalogapp/catalog_detail	February 17, 2022, 17:27:13 (UTC+08)	Enabled	Manual	AES-256	Inactive
○ catalogapp/frontend_node	February 17, 2022, 17:27:36 (UTC+08)	Enabled	Manual	AES-256	Inactive
○ catalogapp/product_catalog	February 17, 2022, 17:27:57 (UTC+08)	Enabled	Manual	AES-256	Inactive

Private repositories (4) C View push commands Delete Edit **Create repository**

Q Find repositories   ‹ 1 › ⚙

Figure 8.27 – ECR repositories page showing the repositories that we created

Since your development EKS cluster is ready, let's now merge the PR that we raised in the previous section. You will notice in the following snippet that we did changes in four files:

```
CatalogApp/catalog_detail/Dockerfile
```

```
CatalogApp/frontend-node/Dockerfile
```

```
CatalogApp/product_catalog/Dockerfile
```

```
CatalogApp/product_catalog/app.py
```

Since the change has occurred in all three services, all three CodeBuild projects will build and deploy the service to the EKS cluster.

Since we have just merged the PR to the develop branch, the code pipeline will get triggered and execute the parallel build actions. If you go and see the logs of all three builds, it does the following three actions:

1.   It checks the modified file and compares it with the current microservice folder name, and based on that, it continues, as illustrated in the following screenshot:

```
59
60 =============== list modified files ===============
61 catalog_detail/Dockerfile
62 catalog_detail/deployment.yaml
63 frontend_node/Dockerfile
64 product_catalog/Dockerfile
65 product_catalog/app.py
66 ========== check paths of modified files ==========
67 catalog_detail/Dockerfile
68 catalog_detail/deployment.yaml
69 There is a change under the 'catalog_detail' folder.
70 Continuing the build
```

Figure 8.28 – CodeBuild log shows file changes in the folder path

2.   After that, it builds the Docker image, pushes it to ECR, and invokes an ECR image scan. If there are fewer than three CRITICAL vulnerabilities, then it will allow the next step; else, it will fail the build. The process is illustrated in the following screenshot:

```
241 190d40895b87: Pushed
242 9c3bb3a5a4f6: Pushed
243 202202230906-42: digest: sha256:b8e169edd92bb74fb7a29b1e83e3841f699009e98548d17fa027df63627e1957 size: 3050
244 ===============Image Scanning===============
245 {
246     "registryId": "              ",
247     "repositoryName": "catalogapp/catalog_detail",
248     "imageId": {
249         "imageDigest": "sha256:b8e169edd92bb74fb7a29b1e83e3841f699009e98548d17fa027df63627e1957",
250         "imageTag": "202202230906-42"
251     },
252     "imageScanStatus": {
253         "status": "IN_PROGRESS"
254     }
255 }
256 ECRIMAGE SCAN IS IN PROGRESS
257 ECRIMAGE SCAN IS IN PROGRESS
258 ECRIMAGE SCAN IS IN PROGRESS
259 ECR IMAGE SCAN has been completedDeploying Service to Kubernetes
```

Figure 8.29 – CodeBuild log showing ECR scan completed

3. After that, it will deploy the service to the `catalogapp-dev` EKS cluster and wait till the deployment completes, as illustrated in the following screenshot:

```
Added new context arn:aws:eks:us-east-1               :luster/catalogapp-dev to /root/.kube/config
deployment.apps/proddetail created
service/proddetail created
Waiting for deployment "proddetail" rollout to finish: 0 of 1 updated replicas are available...
deployment "proddetail" successfully rolled out
{
    "Version": 20,
    "Tier": "Standard"
}
```

Figure 8.30 – CodeBuild log showing the deployment of service in EKS cluster

4. After that, it pushes the image version to Parameter Store for the reference of the staging CodePipeline.

5. Post the build and deploy stage, the test stage gets executed. It first waits for the load-balancer endpoint to be available if you are deploying for the first time; else, it will try to do a health check on the service endpoint. The process is illustrated in the following screenshot:

```
46 Added new context arn:aws:eks:us-east-1:               :cluster/catalogapp-dev to /root/.kube/config
47 Waiting for end point...
48 End point ready:
49 ad8f1cb760efb417c9844303a26215a9-597508766.us-east-1.elb.amazonaws.com
50 Health Check Passed
```

Figure 8.31 – CodeBuild log showing the health check of endpoint

6. You can also enter the load-balancer endpoint with port 9000 in the browser, and you will be able to see the application. The following screenshot illustrates this:

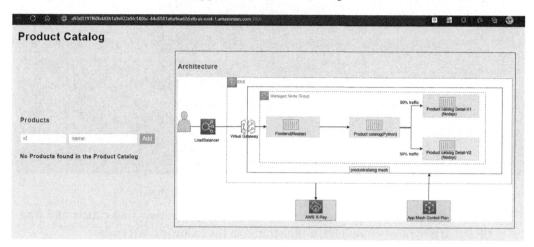

Figure 8.32 – CatalogApp UI in browser

So, we just saw how the pipeline executed and deployed the services to the development EKS cluster. You can again do some changes in a single service, try to commit the change, and see how the pipeline executes. It will skip another service build and deploy only that service in which you have made changes. In the next section, we will create a staging CodePipeline project and environment where we will deploy the application with the presence of App Mesh configuration. We will also test the resiliency of the application as well as its infrastructure.

Creating a staging CodePipeline project with mesh deployment and chaos testing with AWS FIS

In the previous section, we deployed the microservices in the `catalogapp-dev` EKS cluster using the `CatalogApp-DevBuild` CodePipeline project. This CodePipeline project also sent the latest image version to **Parameter Store**, which can be referenced in the staging CodePipeline project. The staging CodePipeline project will fetch the image version and try to compare it with the existing running image as `deployment` in the `catalogapp-staging` EKS cluster. If the image versions are different, then the image version present in Parameter Store will be updated in the deployment of the `catalogapp-staging` EKS cluster. If the image is not present in the `catalogapp-staging` EKS cluster, then it will deploy the new service with the latest image present in Parameter Store.

Once the service is up and running, then the next stage will be resiliency testing on the EKS cluster using an **AWS FIS experiment template** that will try to delete the worker node. In parallel, there will be a CodeBuild project that will monitor the status of the application and cluster. Once this test completes, then another experiment takes place that deletes the microservice pod. In parallel, there will be a CodeBuild project that will monitor the status of the application during this experiment.

So, let's create a staging CodePipeline project by performing the following steps:

1. Go to the **CodePipeline** page and click on **Create pipeline**. Enter `CatalogApp-stageBuild` for the **Pipeline name** value. In **Service role**, **New service role** will have been auto-selected and will have generated a role name as well. Click on **Next**.

2. On the **Source** page, select **AWS CodeCommit** in the **Source provider** dropdown. Select `CatalogApp` in the **Repository name** field and select `staging` in the **Branch name** field. In **Output artifact format**, select **full clone**, and then click on **Next**.

3. On the **Build** page, select **AWS CodeBuild** in **Build provider**. Select the region—in this case, it's **US East**. Then, click on **Create project**, which will open a new pop-up browser page with **Create build project**. Enter the following details on this page:

    A. **Project name**: `CatalogApp-catalogDetail-StageBuild`

    B. **Environment Image: Managed image**

    C. **Operating system: Amazon Linux 2**

    D. **Runtime: Standard**

    E. **Image**: `aws/codebuild/amazonlinux2-x86_64-standard:3.0`

    F. **Environment type: Linux**

    G. Check the **Privileged** box, as we will be using the `docker build` command inside.

    H. Select **Existing service role** and select `CodeBuildServiceRole2`.

    I. In **Build specifications**, select **Insert build commands**. In **Build commands**, enter `echo "Hello world!"` for now.

    J. Click on **Continue to CodePipeline**.

4. You will be redirected to the CodePipeline **Build** page. Click on **Next**. Then, click on the **Skip** deploy stage. Then, you will be on the **Review** page. Click on **Create pipeline**. This was the basic creation of a pipeline. Now, we need to customize it.

5. Click on **Edit** in the `CatalogApp-stageBuild` CodePipeline page. Click on **Edit stage of Build stage**. You will see an existing **Build** action group. Click on the **Edit** icon of the **Build** action group and change the **Action name** value from `Build` to `CatalogApp-catalogDetail-StageBuild`. Leave the rest of the fields as they are and click on **Done**, as illustrated in the following screenshot:

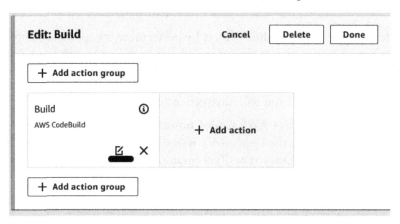

Figure 8.33 – Editing Build stage build action

6. Now, click on **Add action** parallel to it and give an **Action name** value of `CatalogApp-prodCatalog-StageBuild`. In the **Action provider** dropdown, select **AWS CodeBuild**. In **Input artifacts**, choose `SourceArtifact`. In **Project name**, click on **Create project**. Provide a **Project Name** value of `CatalogApp-prodCatalog-StageBuild`, and provide the rest of the details in the same way as *Step 3 | B* to *Step 3 | J*.

7. Repeat *Step 6*, with **Action name** as `CatalogApp-frontEndNode-StageBuild` and **Project name** as `CatalogApp-frontEndNode-StageBuild`. Once you have created three actions, click on **Done** to save the **Build** stage. You can see the stage with the parallel actions here:

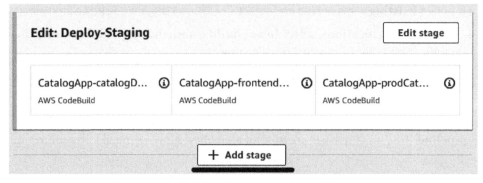

Figure 8.34 – CodePipeline stage with parallel actions

8. Now, click on **Add stage** to create a new stage. Provide ChaosTesting-FIS as the name of the stage and click on **Add stage**. After that, click on **Add action group**. Provide EKSNodeDeleteSimulation as the **Action name** value and then create a CodeBuild project named EKSNodeDeleteSimulation, similarly to *Step 6*.

9. You need to create another action parallel to it with an **Action name** value of EKSNodeDeleteTestReport and then create a CodeBuild project named EKSNodeDeleteTestReport, similarly to *Step 6*, as illustrated in the following screenshot:

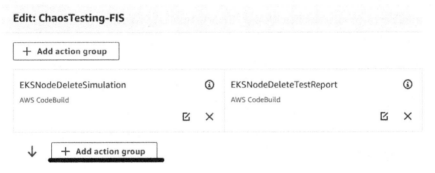

Figure 8.35 – Adding another action group in the CodePipeline stage

10. Click on + **Add action group** at the bottom of the page and create two action groups similarly to *Step 8* and *Step 9*. Name the first action EKSPodDeleteSimulation and provide a CodeBuild project name of EKSPodDeleteSimulation. Name the second action EKSPodDeleteTestReport and provide a CodeBuild project name of EKSPodDeleteTestReport, as illustrated in the following screenshot:

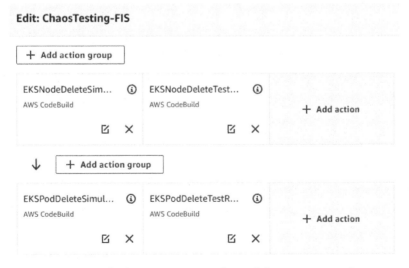

Figure 8.36 – Multiple action groups with parallel actions in a single stage

11. Click on **Done** to save the stage and **Save** to save the `CatalogApp-stageBuild` pipeline. The pipeline should look like the one shown in the next screenshot. Copy the content of the **Buildspec** file from `chapter-08/CICD` and paste it into the CodeBuild project `buildspec` editor in the following manner. Go through the content inside the `buildspec` file and make the necessary modifications such as modifying environment variables and node group ARNs:

- `CatalogApp-catalogDetail-StageBuild` project— `CatalogAppCatalogDetailStageDeploy.yaml`

- `CatalogApp-frontEndNode-StageBuild` project— `CatalogAppFrontEndNodeStageDeploy.yaml`

- `CatalogApp-prodCatalog-StageBuild` project— `CatalogAppProductCatalogStageDeploy.yaml`

- `EKSPodDeleteTestReport` project— `EKSDeletePodTestReport.yaml`

- `EKSNodeDeleteTestReport` project— `EKSDeletePodTestReport.yaml`

- `EKSNodeDeleteSimulation` project— `EKSNodeTerminateTestFIS.yaml`

- `EKSPodDeleteSimulation` project—`EKSPodDeleteTestFIS.yaml`

    You can see the complete stages here:

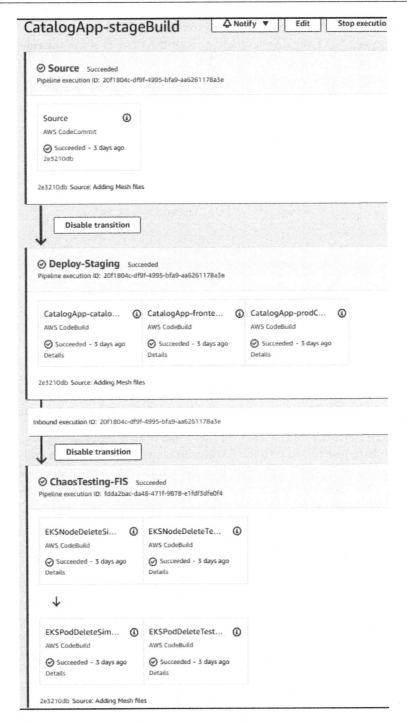

Figure 8.37 – CodePipeline project complete stages

Once the pipeline has been created, you need to create an **IAM role** name of `FISROLE`. Attach `AmazonEC2FullAccess` and `AmazonSSMFullAccess` to the role. Edit the trust relationships of the role and save it with the following code:

```
{
    "Version": "2012-10-17",
    "Statement": [
        {
            "Effect": "Allow",
            "Principal": {
                "Service": "fis.amazonaws.com"
            },
            "Action": "sts:AssumeRole"
        }
    ]
}
```

After you have created a FIS role, we need to create **SSM Document**, which will include the **EKS Pod Deletion** script. Go to the **System Manager** console and choose **Documents**. On the **Create document** menu, select **Command or Session**. Provide a name of `Delete-Pods`. In the content section, select yaml and copy the content of `chapter-08/CICD/Delete-Pods.document`, paste it, and click on **Create document**.

For `EKSNodeTerminateTestFIS.yaml` and `EKSPodDeleteTestFIS.yaml` that you have just pasted into the `EKSNodeDeleteSimulation` and `EKSPodDeleteSimulation` CodeBuild projects buildspec section, please edit the resourceArn values of `targets`, `CloudWatch`, `documentArn`, and `rolearn` of resources and the FIS IAM role.

Once you are done with these prerequisites, let's create a staging EKS cluster and install App Mesh in it. Go to the Cloud9 terminal and proceed as follows:

1. Run the following command to create a `catalogapp-stage` EKS cluster with two worker nodes and necessary configurations for services:

```
$ cd Accelerating-DevSecOps-on-AWS/chapter-08
$ eksctl create cluster --name catalogapp-stage --nodes
2 --node-type t3.small --zones us-east-1a,us-east-1b
--with-oidc
$ kubectl create ns prodcatalog-ns
$ eksctl create iamserviceaccount --cluster catalogapp-
stage \
```

```
  --namespace prodcatalog-ns \
  --name prodcatalog-envoy-proxies \
  --attach-policy-arn arn:aws:iam::$ACCOUNT_ID:policy/
ProdEnvoyIAMPolicy \
  --override-existing-serviceaccounts \
  --approve
$ kubectl describe sa prodcatalog-envoy-proxies -n
prodcatalog-ns
```

2. Edit the aws-auth EKS cluster config map to grant permission to CodeBuildServiceRole2 attached to CodeBuild projects of the CatalogApp-stageBuild CodePipeline project to execute commands on the EKS cluster, as follows:

```
$ kubectl edit cm aws-auth -n kube-system -o yaml
Add the following content and save the file
- rolearn: arn:aws:iam::<YourAccNo>:role/
CodeBuildServiceRole2
  username: CodeBuildServiceRole2
  groups:
  - system:masters
```

3. Now, install some tools that create container insights in CloudWatch and help to create CloudWatch alarms that we will use it as *stop conditions* in the FIS experiment template, as follows:

```
$ eksctl create iamserviceaccount \
  --cluster catalogapp-stage \
  --namespace amazon-cloudwatch \
  --name cloudwatch-agent \
  --attach-policy-arn  arn:aws:iam::aws:policy/
CloudWatchAgentServerPolicy \
  --override-existing-serviceaccounts \
  --approve
$ eksctl create iamserviceaccount \
  --cluster catalogapp-stage \
  --namespace amazon-cloudwatch \
  --name fluentd \
  --attach-policy-arn  arn:aws:iam::aws:policy/
CloudWatchAgentServerPolicy \
```

```
    --override-existing-serviceaccounts \
  --approve
$ curl -s https://raw.githubusercontent.com/aws-samples/
amazon-cloudwatch-container-insights/latest/
k8s-deployment-manifest-templates/deployment-mode/
daemonset/container-insights-monitoring/quickstart/
cwagent-fluentd-quickstart.yaml | sed "s/{{cluster_
name}}/catalogapp-stage/;s/{{region_name}}/us-east-1/" |
kubectl apply -f -
$ eksctl create iamserviceaccount \
  --cluster catalogapp-stage \
  --namespace amazon-cloudwatch \
  --name cwagent-prometheus \
  --attach-policy-arn  arn:aws:iam::aws:policy/
CloudWatchAgentServerPolicy \
  --override-existing-serviceaccounts \
  --approve
### Incase you are deploying to another region, download
the file, modify and then apply.
$ kubectl apply -f https://raw.githubusercontent.com/
aws-samples/amazon-cloudwatch-container-insights/latest/
k8s-deployment-manifest-templates/deployment-mode/
service/cwagent-prometheus/prometheus-eks.yaml
```

4. Now, go to the CloudWatch console and click on **In alarm**, then click on **Create alarm**. Click on **Select metric**. In the **Metrics** search box, search for node_count, as illustrated in the following screenshot:

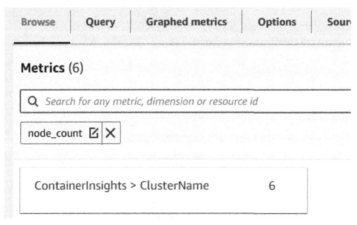

Figure 8.38 – Searching for metrics in CloudWatch

5. Click on the ContainerInsights | Clustername result box. You will see the cluster name and metric name. Select catalogapp-stage, which is in parallel with the cluster_node_count metric. Then, click on **Select metric**, as illustrated in the following screenshot:

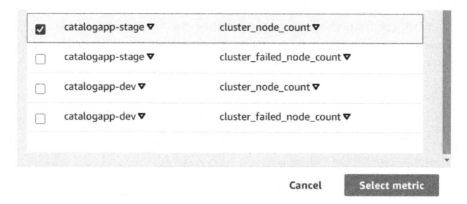

Figure 8.39 – Selecting metrics in CloudWatch

6. In the **Metric** section, select **1 minute** in the **Period** dropdown. In the **Conditions** section, choose **Lower than...** 2 and click on **Next**, as illustrated in the following screenshot:

Conditions

Threshold type

○ **Static**
Use a value as a threshold

○ Anomaly detection
Use a band as a threshold

Whenever cluster_node_count is...
Define the alarm condition.

○ Greater
> threshold

○ Greater/Equal
>= threshold

○ Lower/Equal
<= threshold

● Lower
< threshold

than...
Define the threshold value.

2

Must be a number

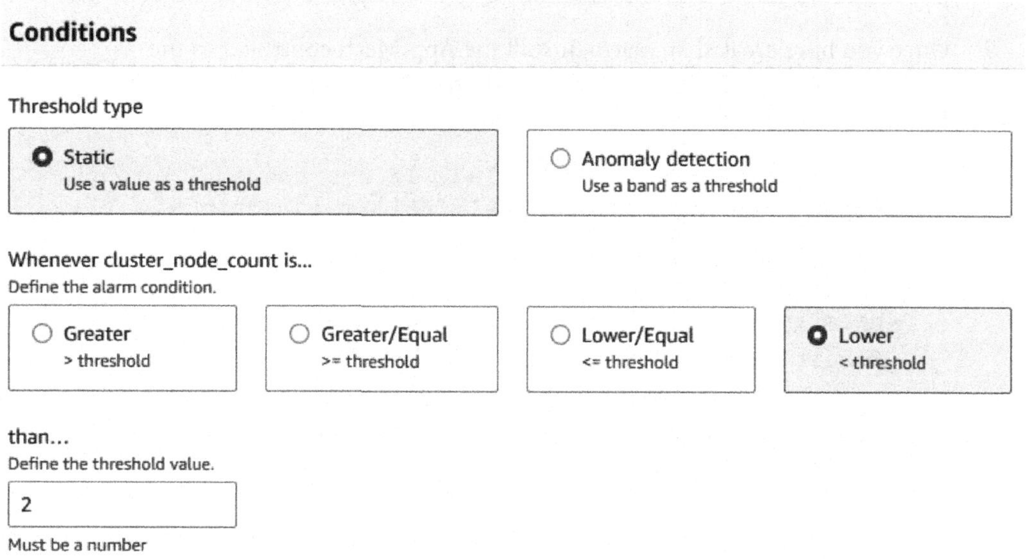

Figure 8.40 – Providing a condition for the CloudWatch alarm

7. On the **Configure action** page, select **Select an existing SNS topic, Choose your existing SNS topic,** or **Create a new one,** and provide an **email address** value. Then, click on **Next** and provide an **Alarm name** value of `EKSNodeCountFailure`, click on **Next** then **Review the alarm**, and click on **Create alarm**. The state of this alarm will be **OK in 1 minute**.

8. Similarly, create another alarm named `EKSPodDeletion`. Search for `namespace_number_of_running_pods` metrics, as illustrated in the following screenshot. You can give the condition as **Lower than...** 3:

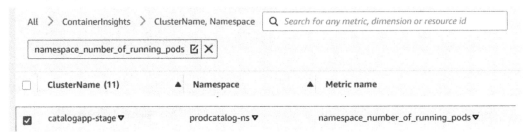

Figure 8.41 – Selecting metrics in CloudWatch

> **Note**
>
> You may not see this metric because we haven't deployed any pods yet, but you can configure this after the first deployment.

9. Once you have created an alarm, install the App Mesh controller in the `catalogapp-stage` EKS cluster. Go to the Cloud9 terminal and run the following commands:

```
# check that helm is installed. If not run curl https://
raw.githubusercontent.com/helm/helm/main/scripts/
get-helm-3 | bash
$ helm list
$ helm repo add eks https://aws.github.io/eks-charts
$ kubectl create ns appmesh-system
$ curl -o controller-iam-policy.json https://raw.
githubusercontent.com/aws/aws-app-mesh-controller-for-
k8s/master/config/iam/controller-iam-policy.json
$ aws iam create-policy \
    --policy-name AWSAppMeshK8sControllerIAMPolicy \
    --policy-document file://controller-iam-policy.json
$ eksctl create iamserviceaccount --cluster catalogapp-
stage \
```

```
      --namespace appmesh-system \

      --name appmesh-controller \

      --attach-policy-arn arn:aws:iam::$ACCOUNT_ID:policy/
AWSAppMeshK8sControllerIAMPolicy  \

      --override-existing-serviceaccounts \

      --approve

$ helm upgrade -i appmesh-controller eks/appmesh-
controller \

      --namespace appmesh-system \

      --set region=$AWS_REGION \

      --set serviceAccount.create=false \

      --set serviceAccount.name=appmesh-controller \

      --set tracing.enabled=true \

      --set tracing.provider=x-ray

$ kubectl create -f mesh.yaml

$ kubectl create -f vgw.yaml
```

Once you have configured App Mesh on the `catalogapp-stage` EKS cluster, raise a PR from the `develop` branch and merge it to the `staging` branch. The following things will take place in sequence the moment code gets merged to the `staging` branch:

1. The `CatalogApp-stageBuild` CodePipeline project will start executing.

2. In this pipeline, all three builds will execute parallelly, but they are not checking for changed files—they are comparing the image versions, and based on that, they update or deploy the new image. Since the pipeline is running for the first time, it will check the deployment. If a deployment doesn't exist, it will deploy the service with the latest image version present in Parameter Store. The process is illustrated in the following screenshot:

```
85
86  Added new context arn:aws:eks:us-east-1:            :cluster/catalogapp-stage to /root/.kube/config
87  Deployment Doesn't exists
88  Deploying the Current Image version ...
89  ***
90  virtualnode.appmesh.k8s.aws/proddetail-v1 created
91  virtualservice.appmesh.k8s.aws/proddetail created
92  virtualrouter.appmesh.k8s.aws/proddetail-router created
93  deployment.apps/proddetail created
94  service/proddetail created
95  Waiting for deployment "proddetail" rollout to finish: 0 of 1 updated replicas are available...
96  deployment "proddetail" successfully rolled out
```

Figure 8.42 – CodeBuild log showing the deployment of the proddetail service

If this executes a second time, then it will check the image version and compare, and based on that, it will make a decision, as illustrated in the following screenshot:

```
Added new context arn:aws:eks:us-east-1:                    cluster/catalogapp-stage to /root/.kube/config
the current image is ***
There is no Change in the Deployment
```

Figure 8.43 – CodeBuild log showing no deployment in case the image version is the same

3. After the deploy stage, you can add an endpoint testing stage, just like the one we added in the develop CodePipeline project. That portion has been skipped in this CodePipeline project, but feel free to add that stage.

4. Once the deployment completes, the next stage is the chaos testing stage, which creates a FIS experiment and starts the experiment, as illustrated in the following screenshot:

```
###############Starting FIS Test###############
===============EKS Node Termination=============
Creating Experiment Template
The Experiment Template id is EXTgEQ6vp4LSCYx
Starting the experiment
EXPE8po1yWxA6KsWAN
experiment is still in progress
experiment is still in progress
experiment is still in progress
experiment is still in progress
Experiment has been completed but pls wait for the test report build to complete
```

Figure 8.44 – CodeBuild log showing creation, execution, and completion of FIS experiment

When this experiment executes, parallelly there is another action that is monitoring a few parameters, such as endpoint health check, number of pods, and number of nodes. In the following screenshot, you can see the moment the experiment started, the endpoint status became 503 and only one worker node is available. The whole point of doing this chaos test is to check the performance of the application. We can see from the timestamp that the application is not available from 17:26:

```
79  ----Endpoint status----
80  Feb 23 17:26:51 HTTP/1.1 503 Service Unavailable
81  ----Pod Status----
82  Feb 23 17:26:51 frontend-node-6cfd4b8cdc-4wsk4   3/3   Terminating      0    8m14s
83  Feb 23 17:26:51 frontend-node-6cfd4b8cdc-9sjkg   0/3   Pending          0    16s
84  Feb 23 17:26:51 prodcatalog-64d8bd9ff7-294mb     3/3   Terminating      0    22m
85  Feb 23 17:26:51 prodcatalog-64d8bd9ff7-4db52     0/3   PodInitializing  0    16s
86  Feb 23 17:26:51 proddetail-56f845d447-zthw5      3/3   Running          0    8m14s
87  ----Node Count Status----
88  Feb 23 17:26:51 ip-192-168-34-202.ec2.internal   Ready   <none>   7m20s   v1.21.5-eks-9017834
```

Figure 8.45 – CodeBuild log showing the status of endpoint, pods, and worker node

Now, in the following screenshot, you can see that the application starts responding from 17:29. That means there was a downtime of 3 minutes:

```
Feb 23 17:29:12 HTTP/1.1 200 OK
----Pod Status----
Feb 23 17:29:13 frontend-node-6cfd4b8cdc-9sjkg      3/3      Running    0      2m38s
Feb 23 17:29:13 prodcatalog-64d8bd9ff7-4db52        3/3      Running    0      2m38s
Feb 23 17:29:13 proddetail-56f845d447-zthw5         3/3      Running    0      10m
----Node Count Status----
Feb 23 17:29:13 ip-192-168-18-14.ec2.internal       Ready    <none>     110s   v1.21.5-eks-9017834
Feb 23 17:29:13 ip-192-168-34-202.ec2.internal      Ready    <none>     9m42s  v1.21.5-eks-9017834
----Endpoint status----
Feb 23 17:29:18 HTTP/1.1 200 OK
----Pod Status----
Feb 23 17:29:19 frontend-node-6cfd4b8cdc-9sjkg      3/3      Running    0      2m44s
Feb 23 17:29:19 prodcatalog-64d8bd9ff7-4db52        3/3      Running    0      2m44s
Feb 23 17:29:19 proddetail-56f845d447-zthw5         3/3      Running    0      10m
----Node Count Status----
Feb 23 17:29:19 ip-192-168-18-14.ec2.internal       Ready    <none>     116s   v1.21.5-eks-9017834
Feb 23 17:29:19 ip-192-168-34-202.ec2.internal      Ready    <none>     9m48s  v1.21.5-eks-9017834
```

Figure 8.46 – CodeBuild log showing the status of endpoint, pods, and worker node

We can see that we are running only one replica of the pod instead of multiple, and only two worker nodes instead of three nodes. By seeing this report, we can decide and increase the replica as well as the number of worker nodes. In this scenario, the CodePipeline project has ended successfully, but you can make it fail and change the worker node and deployment configuration so that the application endpoint remains available even during chaos testing, and if so, then the CodePipeline project will end successfully. You can also integrate it with some third-party tool to generate a graphical or tabular view of the report.

Once the staging CodePipeline project runs successfully, we can merge the code into the `master` branch and deploy the services to the production environment using a canary deployment strategy. We will be using an open source tool, **Flagger**, for canary deployment.

Creating a production CodePipeline project with canary deployment and its analysis using Grafana

The production environment is a critical environment where we do everything carefully. Any mistake could lead to application downtime and affect **business continuity (BC)**. That's why we have all the processes and testing environments set up beforehand. We implemented and tested the application in two environments before we came to deploy the application in the production environment. In this section, we will create a production CodePipeline project along with an EKS production cluster where we will deploy the application with a **canary** deployment strategy and monitor the canary analysis using **Prometheus** and **Grafana**. To know how canary deployment works, you can have a look at the *Introduction to CI and CD Along with a Branching Strategy* section of *Chapter 1, CI/ CD Using AWS CodeStar*, where a canary deployment strategy has been explained in brief.

The production CodePipeline project will have a `CatalogApp` CodeCommit repository `master` branch as the source, followed by a deploy stage, where we have three CodeBuild projects that run in parallel. These CodeBuild projects will perform the same operation as the CodeBuild project of staging CodePipeline performs, meaning it will compare the current image version with the latest image version present in Parameter Store. The only difference is that in the staging CodePipeline project, the deployment strategy was Kubernetes' default deployment strategy, which is **rolling update**. In the production CodePipeline project, we will be deploying one service using a canary deployment strategy. We will do the canary analysis via Grafana. After the canary deployment, we will do a health check of the application. We will also integrate the application stack with an AIOps service, AWS DevOps Guru, that looks for anomalies and create `OpsItem` instances in OpsCenter.

In most scenarios, enterprises—or even start-ups—don't do automated deployment of applications in production. There is a manual intervention during deploying application services in a production environment. As we saw earlier while creating a CodePipeline project, we provide a source, and then **Change detection options** are requested, as shown in the following screenshot:

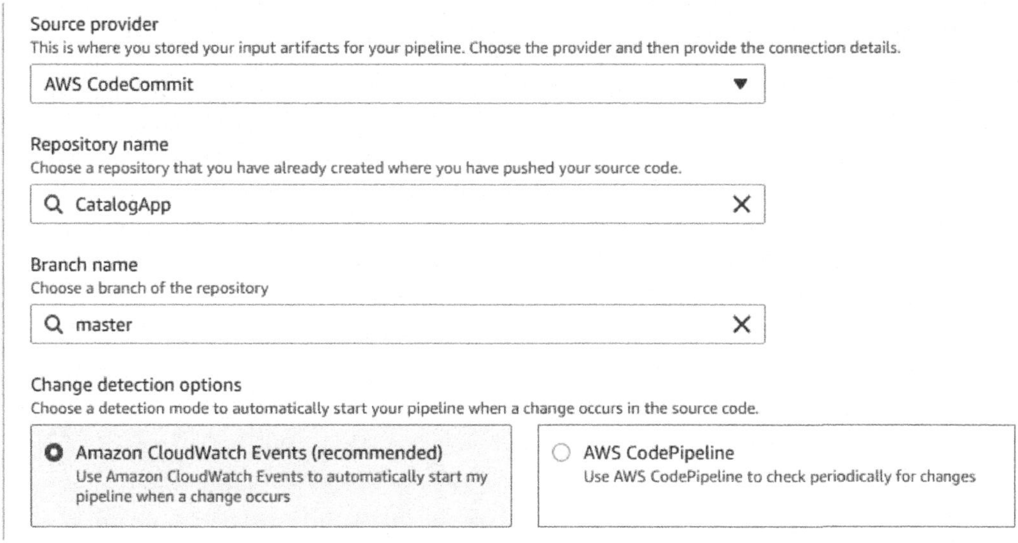

Source provider

This is where you stored your input artifacts for your pipeline. Choose the provider and then provide the connection details.

AWS CodeCommit ▼

Repository name

Choose a repository that you have already created where you have pushed your source code.

🔍 CatalogApp ✕

Branch name

Choose a branch of the repository

🔍 master ✕

Change detection options

Choose a detection mode to automatically start your pipeline when a change occurs in the source code.

⦿ **Amazon CloudWatch Events (recommended)**
Use Amazon CloudWatch Events to automatically start my pipeline when a change occurs

○ **AWS CodePipeline**
Use AWS CodePipeline to check periodically for changes

Figure 8.47 – CodePipeline change detection options via CloudWatch Events

You must need to choose one option, and both options are for starting the CodePipeline automatically. So, in case you are creating your CodePipeline project with the master branch as the source, and somehow if you merge the code into the master branch, then the pipeline will start running, which you probably don't want. You may want to deploy the services after some change request or whichever process your company follows. There is a way where you can stop auto-triggering the CodePipeline project. When we create a CodePipeline project with Amazon CloudWatch Events as the change detection option, it creates a **CloudWatch Events/EventBridge** rule, as follows:

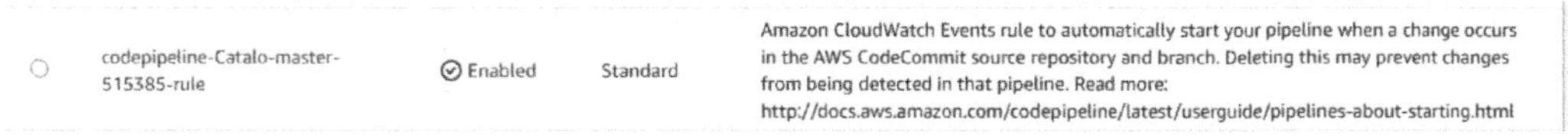

○ codepipeline-Catalo-master-515385-rule   ⊘ Enabled   Standard   Amazon CloudWatch Events rule to automatically start your pipeline when a change occurs in the AWS CodeCommit source repository and branch. Deleting this may prevent changes from being detected in that pipeline. Read more: http://docs.aws.amazon.com/codepipeline/latest/userguide/pipelines-about-starting.html

Figure 8.48 – EventBridge rule responsible for triggering the CodePipeline project

The target of this EventBridge rule is the CodePipeline project. If you remove this EventBridge rule, then the auto-triggering of the CodePipeline project will stop. In this chapter, we are not going for manual deployment and will stick with the auto-triggering way. To create a production CodePipeline project, perform the following steps:

1. You need to create a CodePipeline project and name it `CatalogApp-prodDeploy`. You also need to create stages and a CodeBuild project inside, as in the following screenshot. Refer to the preceding section about creating a CodePipeline project and a CodeBuild project:

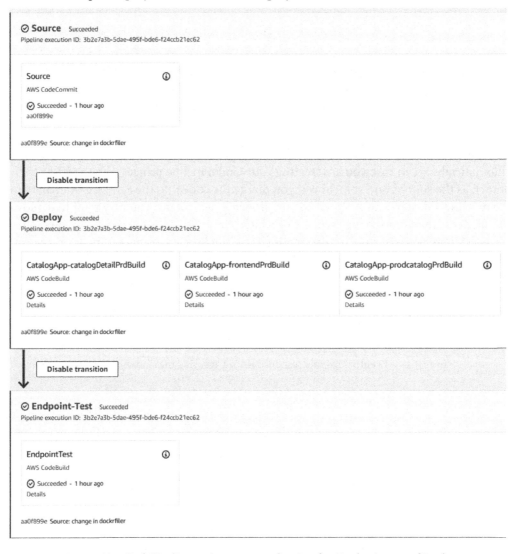

Figure 8.49 – CodePipeline project stages and action for CatalogApp-prodDeploy

> **Note**
>
> While creating a CodeBuild project, if you are getting a `Cannot exceed quota for PoliciesPerRole: 10` error, you just create another IAM role as `CodeBuildServiceRole3` with a similar policy that `CodeBuildServiceRole2` has and add that into the CodeBuild project. Also, make sure to add the IAM role in EKS `aws-auth configmap`, as mentioned in *Step 2* of this section.

2. Once you have created stages and a CodeBuild project, you need to edit the `buildspec` content of the CodeBuild project by pasting the content present inside the files available in the `chapter-08/CICD` folder in the following manner:

- `CatalogApp-catalogDetailPrdBuild` project—`CatalogApp-catalogDetailprdBuild.yaml`

- `CatalogApp-frontendPrdBuild` project—`CatalogApp-frontendprdBuild.yaml`

- `CatalogApp-prodcatalogPrdBuild` project—`CatalogApp-prodcatalogprdBuild.yaml`

- `EndpointTest` project—`EndpointTest.yaml`

Once you are done creating a `CatalogApp-prodDeploy` CodePipeline project, you need to create a `catalogapp-prd` EKS cluster for the production environment, where we will deploy the services via the `CatalogApp-prodDeploy` CodePipeline project. Perform the following steps in the Cloud9 terminal to create a two-node EKS cluster. In the last section, we saw that the application was down for a couple of minutes. In this section, you can spin a three-node cluster and increase the replica of the pod by tweaking the Kubernetes manifest file present in the repository under the `CatalogApp/<servicename>kubespec/canary` folder. But the aim of this section is to demonstrate canary deployment and its analysis, so we are going for two worker nodes. Proceed as follows:

3. Run the following command to create a two-worker-node EKS cluster:

```
$ cd Accelerating-DevSecOps-on-AWS/chapter-08
$ eksctl create cluster --name catalogapp-prd –nodes=2
--node-type=t3.small --zones=us-east-1a,us-east-1b
--with-oidc
$ kubectl create namespace prodcatalog-ns
### You don't need to run the below command if you have
already created this IAM policy in your AWS Account.
```

```
$ aws iam create-policy \
    --policy-name ProdEnvoyNamespaceIAMPolicy \
    --policy-document file://CICD/envoy-iam-policy.json
$ eksctl create iamserviceaccount --cluster catalogapp-
prd \
    --namespace prodcatalog-ns \
    --name prodcatalog-envoy-proxies \
    --attach-policy-arn arn:aws:iam::$ACCOUNT_ID:policy/
ProdEnvoyNamespaceIAMPolicy \
    --override-existing-serviceaccounts \
    --approve
$ kubectl describe sa prodcatalog-envoy-proxies -n
prodcatalog-ns
```

4. Edit the aws-auth EKS cluster config map to grant permission to
    CodeBuildServiceRole2/CodeBuildServiceRole3 (based on whichever
    IAM role you are using in the CodeBuild project, or you can add both if you are
    using both) that is attached to the CodeBuild projects of the CatalogApp-
    prodDeploy CodePipeline project to execute commands on the EKS cluster. The
    code is illustrated in the following snippet:

```
$ kubectl edit cm aws-auth -n kube-system -o yaml
Add the following content and save the file
- rolearn: arn:aws:iam::<YourAccNo>:role/
CodeBuildServiceRole2
  username: CodeBuildServiceRole3
  groups:
  - system:masters
```

5. Now, you need to install **AWS App Mesh** on the EKS cluster by running the following command:

```
$ kubectl create ns appmesh-system
$ kubectl apply -k "github.com/aws/eks-charts/stable/
appmesh-controller//crds?ref=master"
### You don't need to run the below command if you have
already created this IAM policy in your AWS Account.
$ aws iam create-policy \
    --policy-name AWSAppMeshK8sControllerIAMPolicy \
    --policy-document file://CICD/controller-iam-policy.
json
$ eksctl create iamserviceaccount --cluster catalogapp-
prd \
    --namespace appmesh-system \
    --name appmesh-controller \
    --attach-policy-arn arn:aws:iam::$ACCOUNT_ID:policy/
AWSAppMeshK8sControllerIAMPolicy  \
    --override-existing-serviceaccounts \
    --approve
$ helm upgrade -i appmesh-controller eks/appmesh-
controller \
  --namespace appmesh-system \
  --set region=$AWS_REGION \
  --set serviceAccount.create=false \
  --set serviceAccount.name=appmesh-controller
$ kubectl -n appmesh-system get all
```

So far, we have configured the EKS cluster by installing an App Mesh controller. Now, we need to install Flagger and its necessary components. But before that, let's dive into Flagger and understand how it helps in canary deployment.

Canary deployment using Flagger

Flagger is a progressive-delivery Kubernetes operator that automates the release process for services running on Kubernetes clusters. It helps in reducing risk while introducing a new service version in production by gradually shifting the traffic to a newer version of the service while measuring metrics and running conformance tests. If the metrics and tests are not in favor of the newer version, then it also rolls back to the previous stable version. Flagger is a part of the **Cloud Native Computing Foundation** (**CNCF**) project. You can see an overview of a basic Flagger workflow here:

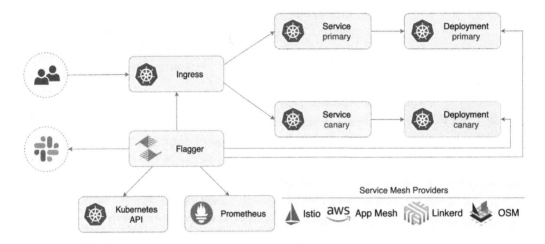

Figure 8.50 – Basic workflow of Flagger

At the moment, Flagger supports the following deployment strategies using a service mesh such as App Mesh, Istio, Linkerd, and **Open Service Mesh** (**OSM**), or an Ingress controller such as nginx, Traefik, and Contour:

- Canary release
- A/B testing
- Blue/green deployment

Flagger uses a custom resource named a canary for the automation of the release process for Kubernetes workloads. We need to register the service with the canary manifest before deploying that service in Kubernetes. In our case, we will be using the `catalogdetail` (we will be using the terms `catalogdetail` and `proddetail` interchangeably, but they are the same) service for canary deployment. So, before we deploy the service, we need to create a canary manifest for the `catalogdetail` service and define all the necessary configurations such as the metrics, interval, and weight of switching the traffic (you can see the canary manifest file in the `chapter-08/catalogdetail-canary.yaml` file). After that, when you apply the canary manifest and then deploy the service, Flagger generates the following items automatically:

- `deployment/<deployment-target-name>-primary`, which in our case would be `deployment/proddetail-primary`. The primary deployment is considered as the stable release of `proddetail`, and by default, all the traffic will be routed to this primary deployment. When you deploy a newer version, Flagger then generates another deployment as `deployment/<deployment-target-name>-canary`, and slowly routes the traffic and promotes it as a new primary deployment.

- Service mesh-related configurations such as `virtualnode`, `virtualservice`, and `virtualrouter`.

- Kubernetes service objects:

  - `<servicename>.namespace.svc.cluster.local` means, in our case, `proddetail.prodcatalog-ns.svc.cluster.local`.

  - `<servicename>-primary.namespace.svc.cluster.local` means, in our case, `proddetail-primary.prodcatalog-ns.svc.cluster.local`.

  - `<servicename>-canary.namespace.svc.cluster.local` means, in our case, `proddetail-canary.prodcatalog-ns.svc.cluster.local`.

  This ensures that traffic to `proddetail.prodcatalog-ns:3000` will be routed to the latest stable release of the `proddetail` service. `proddetail-canary.prodcatalog-ns:3000` is available only during the canary analysis and can be used for conformance and load testing.

You can read more about Flagger here: `https://flagger.app/`.

Since we have a brief understanding of Flagger, let's install it in our EKS cluster, as follows:

1. Install an AppMesh **Prometheus** Helm chart. Prometheus will be used for the metrics collection, and Flagger will also rely on the Prometheus metrics to make decisions in canary deployment. The code is illustrated in the following snippet:

```
$ helm upgrade -i appmesh-prometheus eks/appmesh-
prometheus \
    --namespace appmesh-system \
    --set serviceAccount.create=false \
    --set serviceAccount.name=appmesh-controller
```

2. Install Flagger and the necessary components using a Helm chart, like this:

```
$ helm repo add flagger https://flagger.app
$ kubectl apply -f https://raw.githubusercontent.com/
weaveworks/flagger/master/artifacts/flagger/crd.yaml
$ helm upgrade -i flagger flagger/flagger \
    --namespace=appmesh-system \
    --set crd.create=false \
    --set meshProvider=appmesh:v1beta2 \
    --set metricsServer=http://appmesh-prometheus:9090 \
    --set serviceAccount.create=false \
    --set serviceAccount.name=appmesh-controller
######## Horizontal Pod Autoscaler#########
$ kubectl apply -f https://github.com/kubernetes-sigs/
metrics-server/releases/download/v0.4.1/components.yaml
$ kubectl top nodes
##### Grafana Installation ########
$ helm upgrade -i appmesh-grafana eks/appmesh-grafana
--namespace appmesh-system
```

3. Create a mesh, virtual gateway, a **HorizontalPodAutoscaler** (HPA), and canary configuration for the `proddetail` service, like this:

```
$ kubectl apply -f mesh.yaml
$ kubectl apply -f vgw.yaml
$ kubectl apply -f hpa.yaml
$ kubectl apply -f catalogdetail-canary.yaml
```

4. The moment you apply the canary configuration of the `proddetail` service in the EKS cluster, you can see the logs in Flagger pods, as illustrated in the following code snippet:

```
$ kubectl -n appmesh-system logs deploy/flagger --tail 15
-f | jq .msg
"Waiting for canary informer cache to sync"
"Waiting for caches to sync for flagger\n"
"Caches are synced for flagger \n"
"Waiting for metric template informer cache to sync"
"Waiting for caches to sync for flagger\n"
"Caches are synced for flagger \n"
"Waiting for alert provider informer cache to sync"
"Waiting for caches to sync for flagger\n"
"Caches are synced for flagger \n"
"Connected to metrics server http://appmesh-
prometheus:9090"
"Starting HTTP server on port 8080"
"Starting operator"
"Started operator workers"
"Synced prodcatalog-ns/proddetail"
"deployment proddetail.prodcatalog-ns get query error:
deployments.apps \"proddetail\" not found"
```

You can see that it's searching for the `proddetail` deployment, but it's not available. We will deploy the service using the CodePipeline project since we have done all the initial configurations. You need to raise a PR from the `staging` to the `master` branch and merge the code to the `master` branch. The moment you merge the latest changes to `master`, the `CatalogApp-ProdDeploy` CodePipeline project will get triggered and do the following:

- All three services will get deployed since it's the first deployment to the production environment.

- The `prodcatalog` service will be deployed using the standard **rolling update** strategy. You can see an overview of this in the following screenshot:

```
83  Added new context arn:aws:eks:us-east-1:            :cluster/catalogapp-prd to /root/.kube/config
84  Deployment Doesn't exists
85  Deploying the Current Image version ...
86  virtualnode.appmesh.k8s.aws/prodcatalog created
87  virtualservice.appmesh.k8s.aws/prodcatalog created
88  virtualrouter.appmesh.k8s.aws/prodcatalog-router created
89  deployment.apps/prodcatalog created
90  service/prodcatalog created
91  Waiting for deployment "prodcatalog" rollout to finish: 0 of 1 updated replicas are available...
92  deployment "prodcatalog" successfully rolled out
93
94  [Container] 2022/02/26 13:31:18 Phase complete: BUILD State: SUCCEEDED
95  [Container] 2022/02/26 13:31:18 Phase context status code:  Message:
96  [Container] 2022/02/26 13:31:18 Entering phase POST_BUILD
97  [Container] 2022/02/26 13:31:18 Phase complete: POST_BUILD State: SUCCEEDED
98  [Container] 2022/02/26 13:31:18 Phase context status code:  Message:
```

Figure 8.51 – CodeBuild log showing the deployment of the prodcatalog service

- The `frontend-node` service will also be deployed the same way as the `prodcatalog` service, as illustrated in the following screenshot:

```
Added new context arn:aws:eks:us-east-1:            :cluster/catalogapp-prd to /root/.kube/config
Deployment Doesn't exists
Deploying the Current Image version ...
virtualnode.appmesh.k8s.aws/frontend-node created
virtualservice.appmesh.k8s.aws/frontend-node created
deployment.apps/frontend-node created
service/frontend-node created
Waiting for deployment "frontend-node" rollout to finish: 0 of 1 updated replicas are available...
deployment "frontend-node" successfully rolled out
```

Figure 8.52 – CodeBuild log showing the deployment of frontend-node service

- But the `proddetail` service will be deployed in a different manner since its deployment is handled by Flagger, as illustrated in the following screenshot:

```
 94  Deployment Doesn't exists
 95  Deploying the Current Image version ...
 96  ***
 97  horizontalpodautoscaler.autoscaling/proddetail configured
 98  deployment.apps/proddetail created
 99  Checking Canary status
100  Initialization in Progress
101  Initialization in Progress
102  Initialization in Progress
103  Initialization in Progress
104  Initialization in Progress
105  Initialization in Progress
106  Initialization in Progress
107  Initialization in Progress
108  Initialization in Progress
109  Initialization in Progress
110  Initialization in Progress
111  Initialization in Progress
112  Initialization in Progress
```

Figure 8.53 – CodeBuild log showing the initialization of the proddetail canary

- Once all the service is deployed successfully, then the endpoint test stage will execute and give us the health check status of the endpoint. You can also check the application in your browser by entering the endpoint of the ingress-gw service, as illustrated in the following screenshot:

```
echo "Health Check Passed"
Added new context arn:aws:eks:us-east-1            :cluster/catalogapp-prd to /root/.kube/config
Waiting for end point...
End point ready:
a6926a74eba054282b774956aaf700ea-2e674a00a142dac6.elb.us-east-1.amazonaws.com
Health Check Passed
```

Figure 8.54 – CodeBuild log showing the endpoint health check status

- You can also monitor the health of the service using Grafana. To access Grafana, follow the next steps:

  - Run the following command in a Cloud9 separate terminal (and please don't close the session):

```
$ kubectl -n appmesh-system port-forward svc/appmesh-
grafana 8080:3000
```

- Then, go to **Tools | Preview | Preview Running Application** in the Cloud9 editor, as illustrated in the following screenshot:

Figure 8.55 – Cloud9 IDE Tools tab

- You may see something like this, in which case you need to click the button next to **Browser**:

Figure 8.56 – Cloud9 built-in browser

- Once you do that, you will see the Grafana dashboard. Click on **Home** and then select **AWS App Mesh: Canary Releases**. You will see the activity took place while deploying the `proddetail` service. You can see in the following screenshot that the **Primary** workload is taking all incoming requests:

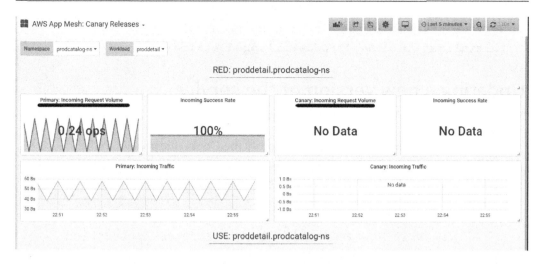

Figure 8.57 – Grafana dashboard monitoring canary status

You can also verify the ongoing status with Flagger pod logs by running the following command:

```
$ kubectl -n appmesh-system logs deploy/flagger --tail 50 -f |
jq .msg
"all the metrics providers are available!"
"VirtualNode proddetail-primary.prodcatalog-ns created"
"VirtualNode proddetail-canary.prodcatalog-ns created"
"VirtualRouter proddetail created"
"VirtualService proddetail created"
"VirtualRouter proddetail-canary created"
"VirtualService proddetail-canary created"
"Deployment proddetail-primary.prodcatalog-ns created"
"proddetail-primary.prodcatalog-ns not ready: waiting for
rollout to finish: observed deployment generation less than
desired generation"
"all the metrics providers are available!"
"proddetail-primary.prodcatalog-ns not ready: waiting for
rollout to finish: 0 of 1 (readyThreshold 100%) updated
replicas are available"
"all the metrics providers are available!"
"Scaling down Deployment proddetail.prodcatalog-ns"
"HorizontalPodAutoscaler proddetail-primary.prodcatalog-ns
created"
```

```
"Service proddetail.prodcatalog-ns created"
```
```
"Initialization done! proddetail.prodcatalog-ns"
```

Updating a new version of the service

Now, you need to verify the complete CI/CD cycle by following the next steps:

1. Create a new `feature` branch and modify the Dockerfile present in the `catalog_detail` folder. You need to enter `app2.js` in place of `app.js` in the last line, as illustrated in the following screenshot:

```
13  # RUN npm install
14  # If you are building your code for production
15  RUN npm ci --only=production
16
17  # Bundle app source
18  COPY . .
19
20  EXPOSE 3000
21  CMD [ "node", "app2.js" ]
```

Figure 8.58 – Editing the Dockerfile in the CodeCommit console

2. Raise a PR to the `develop` branch. The `CatalogApp-Feature-PR` CodeBuild project should get executed successfully.

3. Then, merge the changed code to the `develop` branch. The `CatalogApp-DevBuild` CodePipeline project should get executed successfully. You should be able to see the latest change in the application endpoint by hitting it in the browser. Initially, there was only an ABC.COM catalog, but in the new version, there are two catalogs, which are ABC.COM and XYZ.COM, as illustrated in the following screenshot:

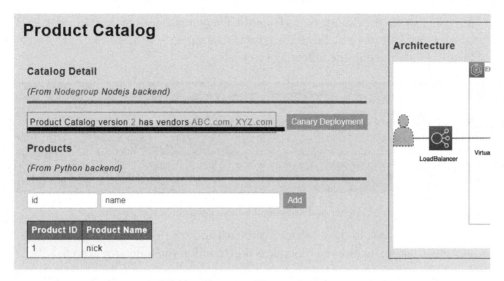

Figure 8.59 – Product Catalog application version 2 UI with two vendors

4. There should not be any effect on the other two services, which are frontend-node and prodcatalog. You can verify this from the build logs as well.

5. Raise a PR and merge the code staging branch, which should trigger the CatalogApp-StageBuild CodePipeline project. The application should be able to pass those FIS experiments present in the CodePipeline stage.

6. Once the staging pipeline has been completed, you can raise a PR and merge the latest change to master, which should trigger the CatalogApp-ProdDeploy CodePipeline project.

7. When the CatalogApp-ProdDeploy CodePipeline project starts, all three builds will run, but only one will get updated—the proddetail service. The moment you go to build logs, you will see that the new version change is in progress, as illustrated in the following screenshot. The canary deployment takes almost 8-9 minutes:

```
Added new context arn:aws:eks:us-east-1            :cluster/catalogapp-prd to /root/.kube/config
the current image is            .dkr.ecr.us-east-1.amazonaws.com/catalogapp/catalog_detail:202202230906-4
There is change in the deployment Image version
Rolling out new version ...
deployment.apps/proddetail image updated
proddetail   Progressing   0       2022-02-26T14:09:12Z
canary.flagger.app/proddetail condition met
Canary deployment has been completed with success
```

Figure 8.60 – CodeBuild log showing the deployment status of proddetail in progress

8. You can also see the canary status from the Flagger pod logs by running `kubectl -n appmesh-system logs deploy/flagger --tail 15 -f | jq .msg`, as illustrated in the following screenshot:

"New revision detected! Scaling up proddetail.prodcatalog-ns"
"Starting canary analysis for proddetail.prodcatalog-ns"
"Advance proddetail.prodcatalog-ns canary weight 5"
"Advance proddetail.prodcatalog-ns canary weight 10"
"Advance proddetail.prodcatalog-ns canary weight 15"
"Copying proddetail.prodcatalog-ns template spec to proddetail-primary.prodcatalog-ns"
"Routing all traffic to primary"
"Promotion completed! Scaling down proddetail.prodcatalog-ns"

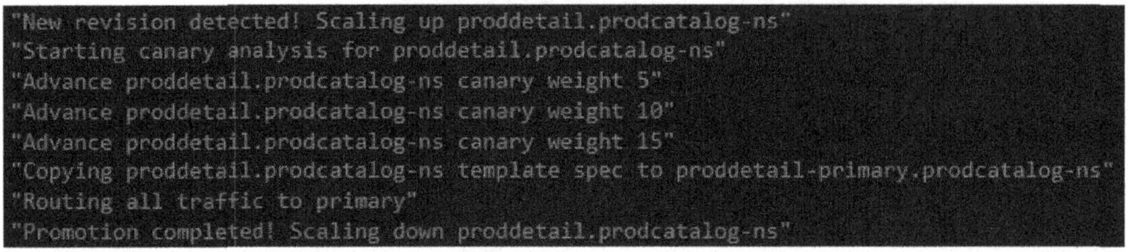

Figure 8.61 – Logs of Flagger pod showing the canary-weighted route to the new version

9. You can also switch to the Grafana dashboard and see that the `canary` object also starts taking incoming requests, as illustrated in the following screenshot:

AWS App Mesh: Canary Releases - Grafana
AWS App Mesh: Canary Releases
Namespace
prodcatalog-ns
Workload
proddetail
RED: proddetail.prodcatalog-ns
Primary: Incoming Request Volume
0.40 ops
Incoming Success Rate
100%
Canary: Incoming Request Volume
0.24 ops
Incoming Success Rate
100%
Primary: Incoming Traffic
Canary: Incoming Traffic
USE: proddetail.prodcatalog-ns

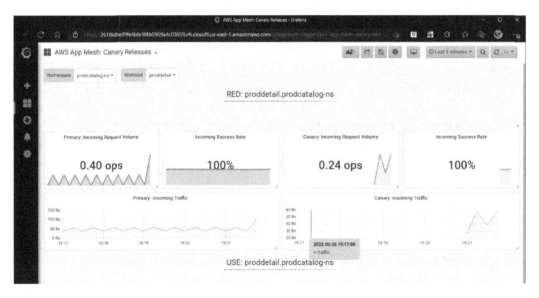

Figure 8.62 – Grafana dashboard showing the canary incoming request in progress

10. When the canary deployment is about to complete, you will be able to see that the requests from the canary side are decreasing and at some point, it will not take any requests. This is illustrated in the following screenshot:

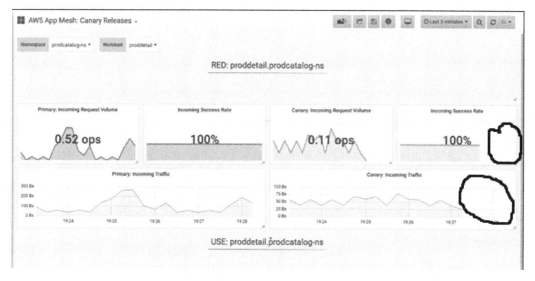

Figure 8.63 – Grafana dashboard showing the canary incoming requests ending

11. You can also try accessing the endpoint of production; sometimes, it will show the result with only one catalog, and sometimes, it will show both. At the point the deployment completes, it will show both catalogs, as illustrated in the following screenshot:

```
deployment.apps/proddetail image updated
proddetail    Progressing    0         2022-02-26T14:09:12Z
canary.flagger.app/proddetail condition met
Canary deployment has been completed with success
```

Figure 8.64 – CodeBuild log showing the successful deployment of the proddetail service

The following screenshot shows the UI of Product Catalog application with both catalog versions:

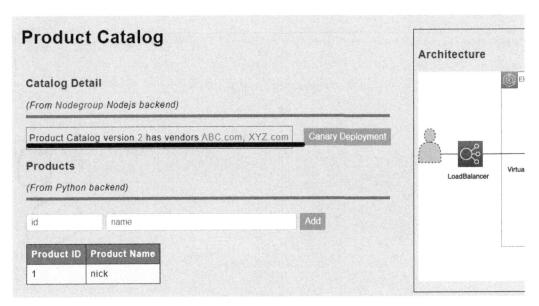

Figure 8.65 – Product Catalog application version 2 UI with two vendors

> **Note**
>
> You can use the Prometheus and Grafana Amazon managed services for canary analysis as well. Read more on this here: `https://aws.amazon.com/blogs/opensource/performing-canary-deployments-and-metrics-driven-rollback-with-amazon-managed-service-for-prometheus-and-flagger/`.

You can improve application availability and detect anomalies by integrating your application with the AWS DevOps Guru service, which detects anomalies in your application. You can read about integrating an application running on an EKS cluster in *Chapter 10, AIOps with Amazon DevOps Guru and Systems Manager OpsCenter*, in the *Enabling DevOps Guru on EKS cluster resources* section.

Summary

In this chapter, we created a CI/CD pipeline for a microservice-based application. We did the planning and defined a strategy before we went ahead and created a pipeline for all three branches. We learned a few loopholes and workarounds in CodeBuild and CodePipeline projects. We saw how to take advantage of CodeGuru Reviewer to scan the source code and place it in CodeBuild steps. We also saw how to scan an image via ECR on demand and fail the build based on the count of vulnerability. We also saw how to automate chaos experiments and get a report of the experiment to improve the performance of the application as well infrastructure. We also deployed the service with a canary deployment strategy via Flagger and did its analysis using Grafana. In the next chapter, we will create a standard **development-security-operations (DevSecOps)** pipeline, which will include some of the industry-wide popular security tools.

DevSecOps Pipeline with AWS Services and Tools Popular Industry-Wide

In the previous chapter, we created a CI/CD pipeline along with the standard branches using AWS native services, as well as integrating CodeGuru Reviewer and ECR image scanning as security tools to detect any vulnerabilities before we deploy services in an environment. In this chapter, we will learn more about security tools and create a pipeline with security in place at every stage that scans the application for vulnerabilities and notifies us of any. We will start with the concepts related to the **Talisman** pre-commit hook, the **Snyk** advisory plugin, **Software Composition Analysis (SCA)**, **Static Application Security Testing (SAST)** (Anchore), **Dynamic Application Security Testing (DAST)** (OWASP ZAP), and **Runtime Application Self-Protection** (**RASP**) (Falco). After this, we will start planning for the pipeline, then we will learn more about the tools and their installation. Finally, we will integrate all the tools in a pipeline and deploy a microservice in an EKS cluster via the secure CI/CD pipeline.

This chapter contains the following main sections:

- DevSecOps in CI/CD and some terminology
- Introduction to and concepts of some security tools
- Planning for a DevSecOps pipeline
- Using a security advisory plugin and a pre-commit hook
- Prerequisites for a DevSecOps pipeline
- Installation of DAST and RASP tools
- Integration with DevOps Guru
- Creating a CI/CD pipeline using CloudFormation
- Testing and validating SAST, DAST, Chaos simulation, Deployments, and RASP

Technical requirements

To perform the tasks mentioned in this chapter, you will need the code and configuration given in the `chapter-09` folder of the following repository:

```
https://github.com/PacktPublishing/Accelerating-DevSecOps-on-AWS.git
```

DevSecOps in CI/CD and some terminology

DevSecOps is the philosophy of adopting security practices along with the DevOps process. A security-focused, continuous-delivery **Software Development Life Cycle (SDLC)** is referred to as DevSecOps. DevSecOps draws on the lessons learned and best practices of DevOps in general. When DevOps ideals are applied to software security, security testing becomes an active, integrated element of the development process. Security has always been considered as a secondary plan, which is bad. Toward the completion of the SDLC, the **information security (InfoSec)** team frequently interacts with development teams. As noble as their objectives may be, discovering security flaws at the end of the SDLC may be annoying.

Why DevSecOps?

In a nutshell, we can state that without security, our technology-driven lifestyles would be jeopardized, hence it is critical to include it early in the SDLC. Cyberattacks have become one of the most serious concerns facing businesses and governments today. Several big corporations have recently had data breaches, leading consumers to lose faith and resulting in massive financial losses each year. So, the question isn't so much *"Why DevSecOps?"* as it is *"How do we perform effectively in the DevSecOps era?"* DevSecOps is a welcome change for individuals encumbered by standard security procedures. This is not a "one-size-fits-all" directive from a centralized organization; solutions may vary depending on your technology stack and architecture.

DevSecOps ensures security checks at every step of software delivery. These days, we use an automated CI/CD process for the fast delivery of software. The DevSecOps culture enables us to take the Shift Left approach and implement security checks at each stage of CI/CD. The curated list of security checks that takes place in software delivery is as follows:

- **Security advisory for source code vulnerabilities in real time**: This security check helps developers to identify source code vulnerabilities as they write the code. The security tools for this sort of check are embedded in the **Integrated Development Environment (IDE)** as some sort of plugin or extension.

  For example, say a developer is importing a library to use in their code. That library has **Common Vulnerabilities and Exposures (CVE)**, but the developer doesn't know. The advisory plugin, which is running in the background, will notify the developer that they shouldn't use this library, or to use the latest version, which doesn't have CVE.

- **Pre-commit secrets check**: This security check helps developers to identify any secrets before they commit the code in a **Version Control System (VCS)**. These security tools are generally installed on the developer's laptop as well as the CI system.

  For example, say a developer finishes writing their code without any vulnerabilities, but somehow, they forgot to remove the secrets of any sensitive data that they were using for their local testing and tried to commit the code to a remote repository. During the commit, this tool will kick in and stop the commit if the scan finds some secret leakage.

- **SCA**: This security check helps to identify vulnerabilities in open source components. This tool doesn't really need to scan the source code, but it scans the libraries and their digital signatures. This tool can be installed as part of the IDE, such as a security advisory plugin. A lot of plugins these days provide source code security checks as well as SCA checks.

For example, say a developer writes their code following the recommendations of a security advisory plugin and uses all the appropriate libraries, which are free from vulnerabilities. But, when they build their code (for example, `npm install`), the library used in the code could look for another dependency and download it. Then, SCA will scan that dependency too, and give the developer the vulnerability report and fixes. SCA generally doesn't have false positives, and most of the time, it has recommendations and fixes.

- **SAST**: This security check is primarily done before code compilation in the build system. The security tool for SAST detects vulnerabilities in proprietary code or code written in-house. This tool also helps to set the standard for code style practices and enforce them to be used companywide. This tool generally scans the entire code and gives recommendations, but it also has a higher number of false positives. Some tools try to suppress those false positives. You should choose the tool that supports the programming language that you use in your application development.

- **DAST**: This security check takes place when your application is deployed in an environment in a running state. This tool simulates all the activities that an attacker would perform in a live application. Common examples are SQL injection, a DDoS attack, and cross-site scripting. DAST does not have any dependencies on language because it interacts with the application from outside means via the application endpoint.

- **RASP**: This security check detects attacks on an application in real time. The security tools are deployed in the application server as agents and kick in when the application runs. This security tool intercepts all the calls from the application to a system, makes sure that they are secure, and validates data requests inside the application.

    For example, say a service Pod is running in **Kubernetes**, and when it gets compromised, the attacker will try to connect to the Pod. During this time, the RASP software can either kick the attacker out or alert the respective application owner.

These are the main security checks implemented in CI/CD, but you are not restricted to only these. DevSecOps is not only responsible for CI/CD but also for the environment. There are plenty of security checks when it comes to the environment, which we covered in *Chapter 2, Enforcing Policy as Code on CloudFormation and Terraform*. In the next section, we will discover and unpack the tools used for these security checks.

Introduction to and concepts of some security tools

In this section, we will discover more about the security tools that cover the preceding security checks. These security tools are picked up based on the features and provide free trials, as well as being open source. So, these tools are great for beginners or for learning purposes. We will be unpacking different types of tools from different vendors so that you get to know more about them.

Snyk – Security advisory for source code vulnerabilities in real time

Snyk Code is a tool developed by Snyk Limited that offers a free plan. Snyk Code comes as a plugin for an IDE. It scans the static code as well as performing SAST at the IDE level. This plugin connects with an online database and gives results in real time. Snyk Code provides three types of checks:

- Open source security
- Code scan security
- Code quality checks

We will be covering the installation and implementation of this plugin in a later section.

Talisman – Pre-commit secrets check

Talisman is an open source tool that basically checks for any secrets present in the code whenever the developer commits to a Version Control System. This tool is installed on the developer's workstation. It works on the basis of pattern matching of large files, content, and entropy that could contain any sensitive data. It also scans for information such as credit card numbers. We will explore its installation and usage in a later section.

Anchore inline scanning and ECR scanning – SCA and SAST

The Anchore inline-scan is a docker image provided by the Anchore company, and it's open source. This docker image scans the application docker image and generates a vulnerability report. The Anchore inline-scan docker image includes a **PostgreSQL** database pre-loaded with Anchore vulnerability data, which gets updated daily. It also contains a docker registry that is used for passing images to Anchore engineers for vulnerability scanning. We will be using the Anchore inline-scan as SCA and SAST in the CodePipeline stage.

ECR scanning is a feature provided by the AWS ECR service. This feature scans the Docker image that is pushed in the registry and finds vulnerabilities. We will be using this feature in our CodePipeline stage after the Anchore inline scan.

Open Web Application Security Project-Zed Attack Proxy (OWASP ZAP) – DAST

The **OWASP** is a worldwide non-profit organization that focuses on improving application security. OWASP ZAP is a popular tool and is totally free. It is a cross-platform tool and can be installed and used in three different ways. You can run it as a desktop application, you can run it in browser mode with a web UI, and you can also install it in such a way that you can perform any task by interacting with the API.

OWASP ZAP's widely used scans are passive and active scans:

- **Passive scan**: A passive scan is a risk-free test that just searches for results and compares them to exploitable vulnerabilities. The data on a website is not changed by a passive scan. As a result, the scan on the websites for which we do not have permission are extremely safe. As you may be aware, the number one vulnerability in 2018, according to OWASP, is still injection. Also, keep in mind that a passive scan will not identify a SQL injection.

- **Active scan**: Active scanning is a technique for finding vulnerabilities on a website that uses well-known techniques. Active scanning can alter data and inject malicious programs into a website. So, when you're ready to thoroughly test your website for security flaws, move it to a different environment and perform an active scan. Only use the active scan on sites for which you have authorization!

We will be installing OWASP ZAP on the server and exposing the API to be consumed and used in the CodePipeline stage. We will be performing an active scan on the application deployed by us.

Falco – RASP

Falco is an open source tool for detecting ongoing risks and threats in Kubernetes, containers, and the cloud. Falco acts as a security camera, detecting unusual behavior, configuration changes, invasions, and data theft in real time.

Sysdig developed it and submitted it to the Cloud Native Computing Foundation. Falco secures and monitors a system via system calls by the following methods:

- At runtime, parsing Linux system calls from the kernel
- Using a sophisticated rules engine to assert the stream

- Sending out an alert when a rule is broken

Falco ships out with a default rule that checks the kernel for unusual behaviors, but you can also create your own rule and feed it into the Falco engine. Falco relies on log stream tools, such as fluent bit, and runs as an agent in the system. We will be looking at its installation and implementation in a later section.

In the next section, we will learn about the planning and strategy of the DevSecOps pipeline that we will create and run.

Planning for a DevSecOps pipeline

In the last chapter, we created a CI/CD pipeline along with a branching strategy with AWS native security services in place, but in this chapter, we will focus more on the security aspect rather than the branching aspect. We will create a single pipeline that will trigger the security tools to scan, provide the result and deploy the application, and then scan the running application. So, this chapter will not cover all the branches, but you can break the stages and place it into multiple pipelines that we are going to create in a single pipeline. The following diagram shows the sequential steps of the DevSecOps CI/CD pipeline:

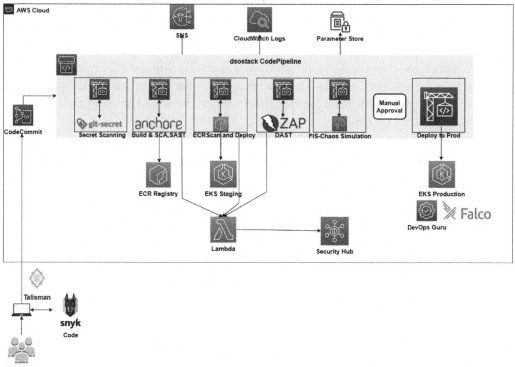

Figure 9.1 – DevSecOps pipeline flow

We are going to perform the following tasks to achieve the DevSecOps pipeline:

1. We will start by installing the Snyk security advisory plugin in the **Visual Studio Code** (**VS Code**) IDE and check for vulnerabilities in the `Catalog_Detail` service code.

2. After that, we will install Talisman on the local workstation and try to put some secrets in the code to check whether it stops us from committing the code.

3. The preceding two steps will be performed in the local machine. After that, we need to prepare the initial setup for the DevSecOps pipeline, as follows:

   - The first step is to create a `CodeCommit` repository, which will store the `CatalogDetail` service code and the `buildspec` files.

   - We will create two ECR repositories and enable **Scan on push**.

   - After that, we will create two EKS clusters for the staging and production environments.

   - Then, we will create an OWASP ZAP instance using CloudFormation.

   - After that, we will install Falco in the EKS environment.

   - Finally, we will integrate the EKS production with AWS DevOps Guru.

4. After the initial setup is done, we will create the DevSecOps CodePipeline project using the CloudFormation template. CloudFormation will not only create the CodePipeline project, but also the related services that will be used in the pipeline, such as **Simple Notification Service** (**SNS**) topics, the AWS Lambda function, and parameter store secrets.

5. Once the CodePipeline creation completes, it automatically starts running, with the latest commit present in the `CodeCommit` repository. Once the pipeline starts running, it does the following in sequence:

   I. The first stage is the `Build-GitSecret` stage. This stage clones the source code from the CatalogDetail `CodeCommit` repository and runs a scan to find any sensitive data or secrets. If the scan doesn't find any secrets, the build succeeds and then executes the next stage.

II. After the successful execution of the previous stage, the next stage is `Build-SCA&SAST`. This stage includes two actions. The first action is SAST analysis. This action builds the application and runs the scan using the Anchore inline scanner, which also generates the report after scanning. If the report includes a critical or high CVE, then it will trigger a Lambda function that will parse the report generated by the Anchore scanner to the **AWS Security Finding Format** (**ASFF**) format and upload it to AWS Security Hub. The second action is `ECR-Scan-and-STG-Deploy`. This action will fetch the ECR scan report and if the report contains a critical or high CVE, then it will trigger the Lambda function and upload the result to AWS Security Hub, or it will deploy the service to the `eks-staging` cluster.

III. The next stage is the **Build-DAST** stage. This stage runs an OWASP ZAP active scan using an API call. During the API call, it fetches the API key from the parameter store. If there are high or critical vulnerabilities, then the Lambda function will be triggered to pass the result to AWS Security Hub, or it will continue to the next stage, which is the Chaos Simulation stage.

IV. The **Build-ChaosSimulation** stage creates the experiment template and runs the experiment. The experiment involves deleting the worker node of the cluster, and parallelly monitoring the health of the application and the counts of Pods and worker nodes. This stage executes for at least 5 minutes.

V. After this, an approval email is sent to approve the production deployment. There will be a manual approval stage as well, where you need to approve it manually with a comment.

VI. After manual approval, the **Deploy-PRD** stage will deploy the service in the `eks-prod` cluster.

7. After the creation of the pipeline, we will run the pipeline. It will fail in all the scanning stages, because the source code, Docker image, and running application will have vulnerabilities. We will try to bypass the vulnerabilities at every stage. We will not fix the vulnerabilities but instead, edit the `buildspec` file to let the `CodeBuild` succeed and move to the next stage.

The application that we are deploying in the EKS cluster will not change the frontend UI. It will remain the same. We are changing the CatalogDetail service deployment image from a public repository image to an ECR repository image. From the next section onward, we will start installing the tools and preparing the environment for the CI/CD pipeline.

Using a security advisory plugin and a pre-commit hook

In this section, we will explore security advisory plugins and how they help in detecting vulnerabilities during the development phase itself rather than the build phase. This makes it easier for the developer to see the vulnerabilities and fix them using the recommendations. There are lots of security advisory plugins available on the market that help you detect vulnerabilities while writing your code in IDE. Lots of industries have their own preferences when selecting a vendor. I have found the Nexus IQ plugin quite powerful and it supports major IDEs such as IntelliJ, VS Code, and Eclipse. In this chapter, we will explore the Snyk vulnerability scanner, which scans your code as well as open source dependencies. Perform the following task on your local machine in which you have your IDE installed. The following test has been performed on VS Code, but the Snyk vulnerability scanner is also available in other major IDEs:

1. Clone the repository and go to the `chapter-09/catalog_detail` folder:

    ```
    $ git clone https://github.com/PacktPublishing/
    Accelerating-DevSecOps-on-AWS.git
    ```

    ```
    $ cd chapter-09/catalog_detail
    ```

2. Open this folder in VS Code. Either type `code` . in your terminal, or open via the GUI and navigate to this folder:

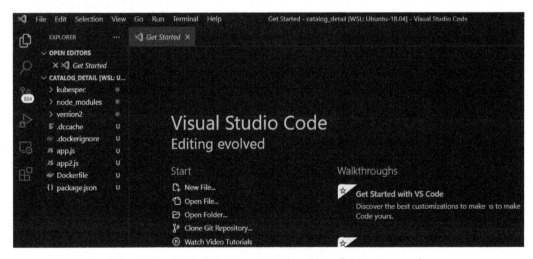

Figure 9.2 – VS Code home page with catalog_detail source code

3. Click on **Extensions** and search for `publisher:"Snyk"` in the search box. You will find **Snyk Vulnerability Scanner**. Click on **Install**:

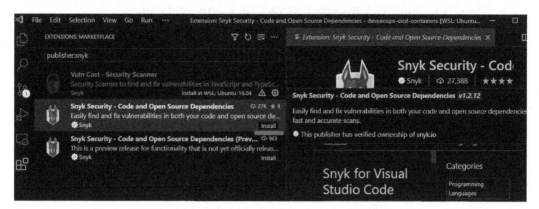

Figure 9.3 – Marketplace showing Snyk Vulnerability Scanner

4. After installation, you will be able to see the Snyk icon in the left navigation bar. Click on that; you will then see a welcome message from Snyk. You will see a **Connect VS Code with Snyk** button. Click on it:

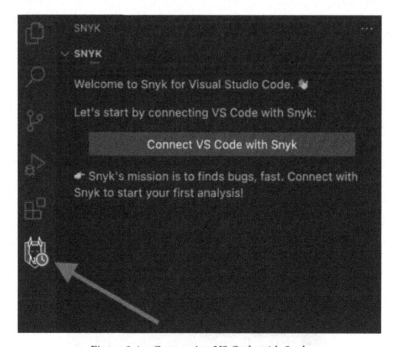

Figure 9.4 – Connecting VS Code with Snyk

5. You will be redirected to the Snyk website, where you will be asked to authenticate. You can create an account for free. Snyk provides a free license for individual users for certain products. Once you sign up, click on **Authenticate**.

Authenticate for CLI

You've reached this page because you ran the `snyk auth` command from our CLI.

Click below to authenticate your machine, so we can confirm that Snyk CLI can be associated with your account. Once completed, you can continue working from the terminal.

Authenticate

Figure 9.5 – Authenticate extension on the Synk server

6. Enable Snyk Code on the Snyk web page and restart VS Code. After that, go to VS Code, where you will be able to see that Snyk took a couple of seconds to analyze a few code-security-related vulnerabilities:

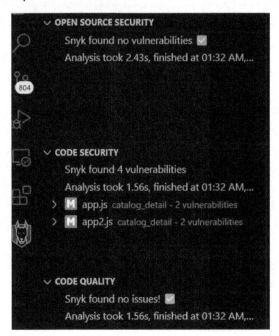

Figure 9.6 – Code scan performed by Snyk

7. If you click on one of the vulnerabilities, in this case, `app.js`, you will be able to see the details with recommendations:

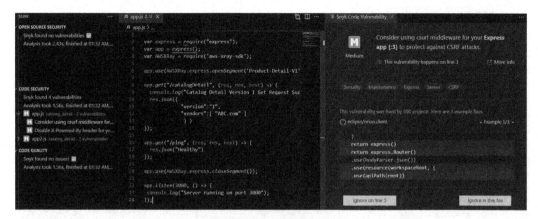

Figure 9.7 – Snyk showing vulnerabilities and recommendations

8. This was about code-related security. Now, let's run `npm install`, which will download the open source libraries, and then see how the Snyk scanner acts. You can open the terminal and run the `npm install` command from there.

9. The moment the command finishes, the Synk **Open Source Security** scanner will start scanning (if it doesn't start the first time, then click on **rescan**). In this case, it didn't find any vulnerabilities in our libraries:

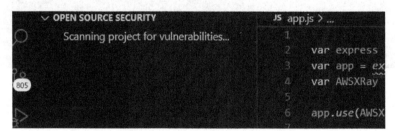

Figure 9.8 – Scanning in progress

When the scan finishes, you can see there are no vulnerabilities:

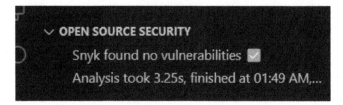

Figure 9.9 – Snyk scan showing no vulnerabilities

10. The following screenshot is the scanning result of another application. You can see the **Open Source Security** vulnerabilities. The right-hand side shows the vulnerabilities in the code:

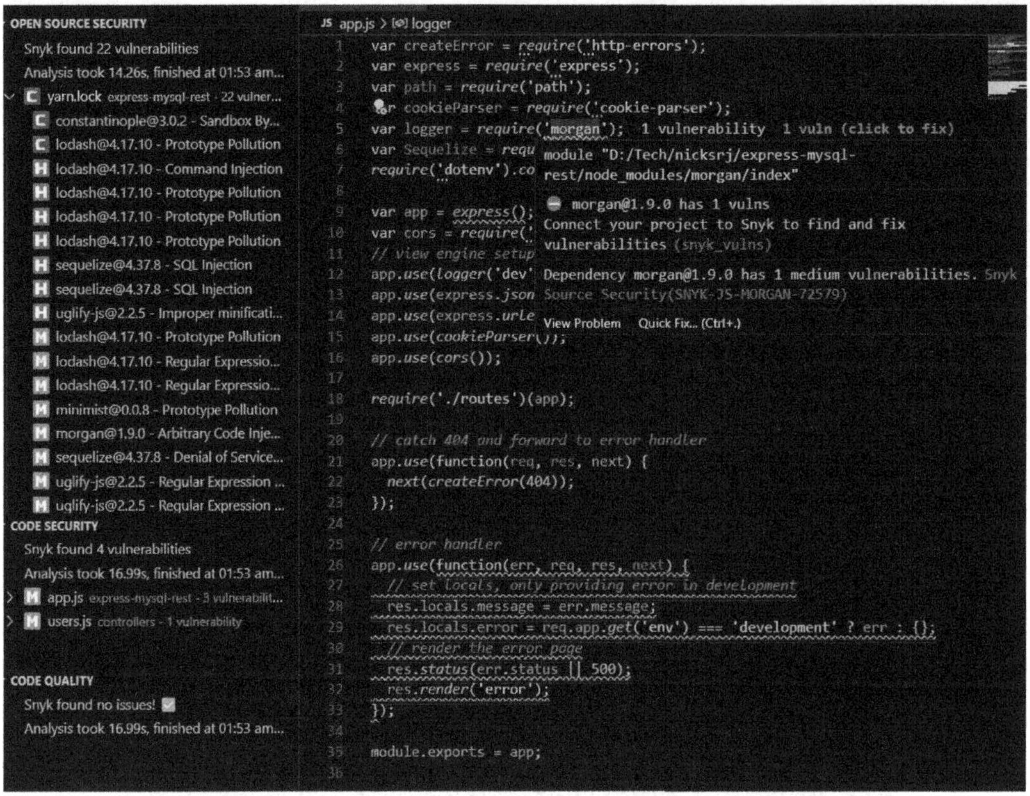

Figure 9.10 – Snyk showing open source vulnerabilities

> **Note**
>
> You can also use the **Nexus IQ** or **Synopsys Code Sight** plugins. The Nexus IQ plugin works with its public online database as well as its private server (you need to pay for the private server, which is Nexus IQ Pro). Code Sight has a 30-day free trial, which you can use for **Proof of Concept** (**POC**) or learning purposes.

So, we just saw how we can leverage the Snyk vulnerability scanner plugin to identify security vulnerabilities before we commit and push the code into a VCS. Now, suppose after fixing all the security vulnerabilities you forgot to remove the API key or any secrets that you were using for development activities, and tried to push into a VCS. If the secrets get uploaded to the repository, it could cause a security breach. So, to have some sort of check before you commit the code or push into a VCS, you can use a pre-commit hook tool called Talisman. Perform the following steps to see how it works:

1. First, we need to inject any sensitive (not really sensitive, but random) data into your code. Go to the `app.js` file of the `chapter-09/catalog_detail` folder in VS Code and add the following line to the beginning of the code:

```
const api_key = 'Xkjhai23JGJIWekUGOOKPPWg38'
```

2. Open the VS Code terminal and delete the unnecessary files if present; these files came because we ran `npm install` before:

```
$ rm -rf node_modules package-lock.json .dccache
```

3. Install Talisman in your home folder where all the Git repositories exist, because it will configure the pre-hook in all the existing repositories as well as the new one that you will clone. Ideally, you should install in `/home/$USER` and follow the interactive instructions. You can customize the installation using configuration parameters that can be found in the documentation of the tool (`https://thoughtworks.github.io/talisman/docs/installation`):

```
$ cd /home/$USER
$ curl -silent https://raw.githubusercontent.com/
thoughtworks/talisman/master/global_install_scripts/
install.bash > /tmp/install_talisman.bash && /bin/bash /
tmp/install_talisman.bash
```

4. Now, run the `git add` and `git commit` commands. You will be able to see that before committing, Talisman scans the files quickly and gives you the report with a **SEVERITY** level:

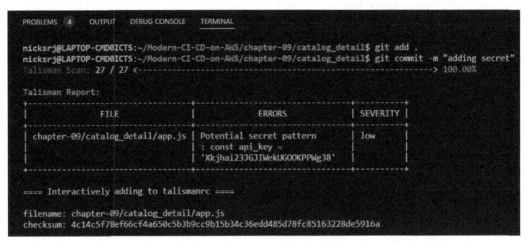

Figure 9.11 – Talisman scanned the code before committing and reported the secret

It is always good to detect these kinds of events, but since this is a local development machine, developers can bypass this as well because they will have full control over Talisman. So, in that case, you must integrate Talisman as a build stage in your CI tool. To learn more about Talisman in the CI stage, you can refer to this blog: `https://praveen-alex-mathew.medium.com/running-talisman-cli-in-the-gitlab-ci-servers-29f15af7b1c7`. In this chapter, we will be using a different tool for secret scanning that has been open sourced by AWS, known as `git-secrets`. This will be part of the CodePipeline stage and scan for any secrets inside the code. In the next section, we will create all the prerequisites for the CI/CD pipeline.

Prerequisites for a DevSecOps pipeline

In this section, we will create all the necessary resources for the DevSecOps pipeline. Perform the following tasks to create the prerequisites:

1. Create a `CodeCommit` repository with the name `CatalogDetail`. Push the source code files available inside `chapter-09/catalog_detail/` and `chapter-09/buildspecfiles/`. The folder structure inside the `CatalogDetail` repository should look like the following:

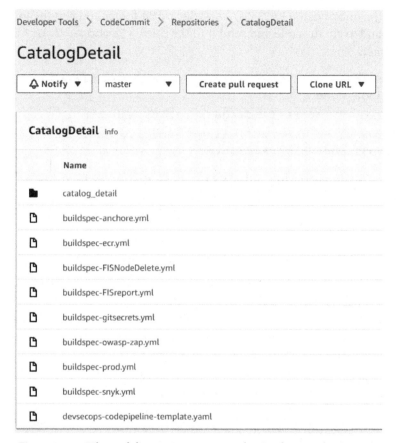

Figure 9.12 – Files and directories present in the CatalogDetail repository

2. Create two ECR repositories and name them `miscimages` and `catalogdetail`. Make sure to enable the **Scan on push** option. Upload the following two images to the `miscimages` ECR repository:

    - `node:14`

    - `anchore/inline-scan:v0.6.0`

3. Edit the `catalog_detail/Dockerfile` file and replace your AWS account number. Similarly, in the `buildspec-anchore.yml` file, replace the `ANCHORE_CI_IMAGE` value with the ECR URL value for `miscimages` that contains the Anchore inline-scan image.

4. Create two S3 buckets and give the names of the S3 buckets as `dsos3lambda-<YourAccountNo>` and `pipeline-artifact-bucket-<YourAccountNo>`.

5. Go to the `chapter-09/CICD/lambda_code` folder and run the following command to zip the code and send it to the `dsos3lambda-<YourAccountNo>` S3 bucket:

```
$ cd Accelerating-DevSecOps-on-AWS/chapter-09/CICD/
lambda_code
$ zip -r import_findings_security_hub.zip .
$ aws s3 cp import_findings_security_hub.zip s3://
dsos3lambda-<YourAccountNo>
```

6. Enable AWS Security Hub and AWS Configuration Recorder in your AWS account. Refer to the third section (*Import AWS Config rules evaluations as findings in Security Hub*) of *Chapter 7, Infrastructure Security Automation Using Security Hub and System Manager*.

7. Spin up two EKS clusters with two worker nodes, one for staging as `eks-staging` and another for production as `eks-prod`:

```
### Command to create first cluster
$ eksctl create cluster --name eks-staging --nodes=2
--node-type=t3.small --zones=us-east-1a,us-east-1b
### Command to create second cluster
$ eksctl create cluster --name eks-prod --nodes=2 --node-
type=t3.small --zones=us-east-1a,us-east-1b
```

Do the context switching to access the staging cluster and then again switch to access the prod cluster:

```
nicksrj@LAPTOP-CMD0ICTS:~$ kubectl config get-contexts
CURRENT   NAME                                          CLUSTER
          nikit@eks-staging.us-east-1.eksctl.io         eks-staging.us-east-1.eksctl.io
*         nikit@eks-prod.us-east-1.eksctl.io            eks-prod.us-east-1.eksctl.io
```

Figure 9.13 – Kubernetes cluster contexts

Currently, you are in the `eks-prod` cluster context, but you can switch to staging by running the following command:

```
$ kubectl config use-context <Context-NAME(in my case
nikit@eks-staging.us-east-1.eksctl.io)>
```

8. Once your cluster is up and running, add the following service role in `aws-auth` `configmap` to both the `eks-staging` and `eks-prod` clusters. This service role is not present right now, but it will be available after the creation of the CodePipeline instance. The format of the service role is `arn:aws:iam::<your account no>:role/dsostack-SecurityCodeAnalysisRole`, as shown here:

```
$ kubectl edit cm aws-auth -n kube-system
```

```
### Add the following content in mapRoles section
    - rolearn: arn:aws:iam::<YourAccountNo>:role/
dsostack-SecurityCodeAnalysisRole
      username: dsostack-SecurityCodeAnalysisRole
      groups:
        - system:masters
```

9. Create an IAM role with the name `FISROLE`, and attach `AmazonEC2FullAccess` and `AmazonSSMFullACCESS`. Edit the trust relationship with the following snippet:

```
{
    "Version": "2012-10-17",
    "Statement": [
        {
            "Effect": "Allow",
            "Principal": {
                "Service": "fis.amazonaws.com"
            },
            "Action": "sts:AssumeRole"
        }
    ]
}
```

10. Go to the CatalogDetail `CodeCommit` repository and edit the `buildspec-FISNodeDelete.yml` file, then replace `roleArn` with the one you just created. Also, replace `Nodegroups-Target-1 resourceArns` with `eks-staging workernode ARN`.

11. Now, deploy the Product Catalog application in both the clusters:

```
$ cd Accelerating-DevSecOps-on-AWS/chapter-09/
$ helm install prodcatalogapp productcatalog_application-
1.0.0.tgz
```

12. You should be able to access the application with the exposed `Loadbalancer` endpoint with port `9000`:

```
$ export LB_NAME=$(kubectl get svc --namespace dsoapp
frontend -o jsonpath="{.status.loadBalancer.ingress[*].
hostname}")
$ echo http://$LB_NAME:9000
```

Enter the output in the browser after a minute to see the application:

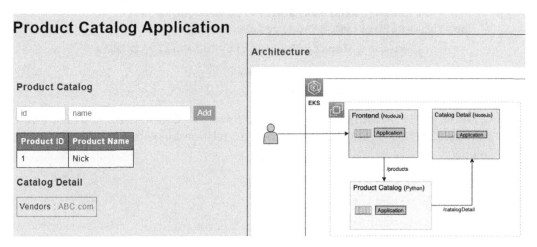

Figure 9.14 – Product Catalog Application UI

13. You can also see the Deployment status in the `dsoapp` namespace:

```
$ kubectl get deployment -n dsoapp
NAME          READY   UP-TO-DATE   AVAILABLE   AGE
frontend      1/1     1            1           7m22s
prodcatalog   1/1     1            1           7m22s
proddetail    1/1     1            1           7m22s
```

So far, we have created the AWS resources for the DevSecOps pipeline. In the next section, we will install some security tools that CodePipeline will leverage to scan the application.

Installation of DAST and RASP tools

In this section, we will install OWASP ZAP in an EC2 instance, which will be used by the DevSecOps pipeline to scan the application once the new service is deployed in an `eks-staging` cluster. After the OWASP ZAP installation, we will install Falco in the EKS cluster.

Installing OWASP ZAP

We will be installing OWASP ZAP using the CloudFormation template. Perform the following tasks to configure OWASP ZAP to be used by CodePipeline:

1. Make sure you have the chapter-09/owasp-zap.yaml file in your local machine.

2. Go to the CloudFormation home page, click on **Create stack**, then select **With new resource**. In the **Specify template** section, select **Upload a template file**. Click on **Choose file** and select the owasp-zap.yaml file, and then click on **Next**.

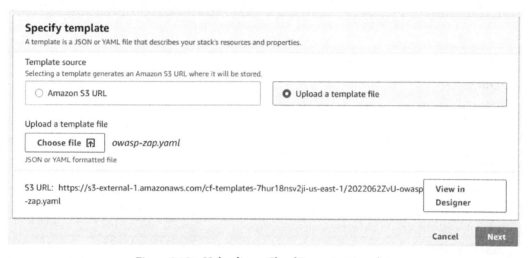

Figure 9.15 – Uploading a CloudFormation template

3.   Enter the stack name as `owasp-zap`. Modify the instance type. It is recommended
     to choose `t2.medium` or above because, during the scan, the CPU utilization of
     this server will spike up. Modify the SSH location to your home/office IP (make sure
     to provide the **Classless Inter-Domain Routing (CIDR)** range) and click on **Next**.

Figure 9.16 – Updating default parameters

4.   Provide the **Tags** key and value and then click on **Next**. Then on the **Review** page,
     click on **Create stack**. It will take 4 to 5 minutes to spin up an EC2 instance, and
     then run a user-data script to install `owasp-zap` and `apache`. You must have
     a default **Virtual Private Cloud (VPC)** in your account, otherwise, the stack will fail.

5.   When you see that the status of the stack is `CREATE_COMPLETE`, go to the **Outputs**
     tab, where you will see the `OWASPZapURL` value. Click on that and you will be
     redirected to the API reference UI page of OWASP ZAP:

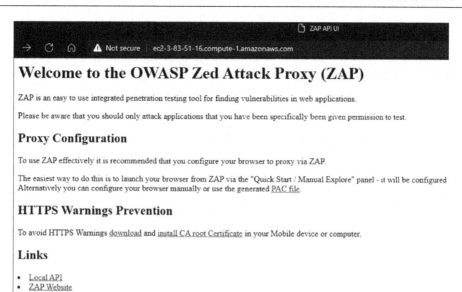

Figure 9.17 – OWASP ZAP API home page

6. Now, we need to register the application endpoint where CodePipeline will run the DAST automation. Select **LocalAPI | spider (not ajazSpider) | scan (url maxChildren recurse contextName subtreeOnly)** in the **Action** section. In **apikey**, enter devsecopsapikey. In **url**, enter the CatalogApp load balancer endpoint with the port number of eks-staging. Enter true in **recurse**. Then, click on **scan**.

ZAP API UI

Component: spider

Action: scan

Runs the spider against the given URL (or context). Option: the spider from seeding recursively, the parameter 'context' subtree (using the specified 'url').

Output Format	JSON ∨
apikey*	devsecopsapikey
Form Method	GET ∨
url	http://a2d3be3f7cf6e4232a4
maxChildren	
recurse	true
contextName	
subtreeOnly	
	scan

Figure 9.18 – ZAP spider scan on application endpoint

7. Once you click on **scan**, it will return the scan ID with 0, as in { "scan" : "0" }.

8. Go back to the ZAP API UI welcome page, then select **LocalAPI | ascan | scan (url recurse inScopeOnly scanPolicyName method postData contextId)** under **Actions**. Enter the same details as before and click on **scan**.

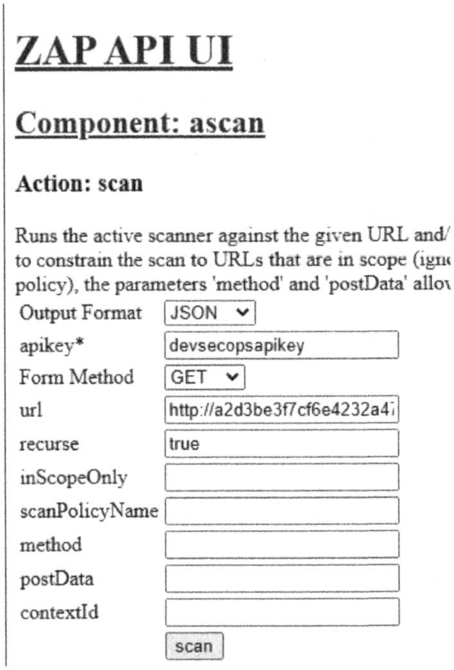

ZAP API UI

Component: ascan

Action: scan

Runs the active scanner against the given URL and/
to constrain the scan to URLs that are in scope (igno
policy), the parameters 'method' and 'postData' allo\

Output Format	JSON ▾
apikey*	devsecopsapikey
Form Method	GET ▾
url	http://a2d3be3f7cf6e4232a4i
recurse	true
inScopeOnly	
scanPolicyName	
method	
postData	
contextId	
	scan

Figure 9.19 – ZAP active scan on application endpoint

9. When you click on **scan**, it will return the scan ID with 0, as in { "scan" : "0" }.

At this stage, OWASP ZAP is ready to scan the application using an API call that will be triggered by one of the CodeBuild projects residing in the DAST scan stage of the DevSecOps pipeline.

Installing Falco

We will be installing Falco using a Helm chart and demonstrating how it sends suspicious activity alerts to CloudWatch. Perform the following tasks to install Falco on eks-staging as well as eks-prod:

1. Go to the chapter-09/falco folder and run the following command to create an IAM policy:

```
$ cd Accelerating-DevSecOps-on-AWS/chapter-09/falco
```

```
$ aws iam create-policy --policy-name EKS-CloudWatchLogs
--policy-document file://iam_role_policy.json
```

2. Attach this policy to the worker node IAM role. You can find the worker node IAM role by running the following command:

```
$ eksctl get nodegroup --cluster eks-staging  -o yaml |
grep NodeInstanceRoleARN
### You will get output something like, Copy the strings
after role/
NodeInstanceRoleARN: arn:aws:iam::<YourAccountNo>:role/
eksctl-eks-staging-nodegroup-ng-9-NodeInstanceRole-
GD3WG0XJX7WO
### Attach the policy created in Step 1 in this Node IAM
Role
$ aws iam attach-role-policy --role-name <THE ROLE THAT
YOU COPIED NOW> --policy-arn 'aws iam list-policies | jq
-r '.[][] | select(.PolicyName == "EKS-CloudWatchLogs") |
.Arn''
```

3. We just attached a policy to an IAM role that allows us to send the logs to CloudWatch. Now, let's install the **FireLens** service, which works in conjunction with Falco. FireLens at the backend works with fluent bit, so the manifest file that we are about to apply contains a fluent beat DaemonSet:

```
$ kubectl create -f configmap.yaml,daemonset.
yaml,service-account.yaml
```

4. Now, we can install the Falco Helm chart on the EKS cluster:

```
$ helm install falco falco-1.17.2.tgz
```

5. You can verify the Pods running in the EKS cluster. At this stage, we will have the following Pods running in the EKS cluster:

```
$kubectl get pods -A
NAMESPACE        NAME                            READY
STATUS     RESTARTS      AGE
default          falco-9w8q9                     1/1
Running    0             2m45s
default          fluentbit-pt22w                 1/1
Running    0             7m28s
dsoapp           frontend-7c856967fd-x8qjm       1/1
```

	Running	0	11m
dsoapp	prodcatalog-664486654d-kvc5d		1/1
Running	0	11m	
dsoapp	proddetail-6744fdccf9-vh6hr		1/1
Running	0	11m	
kube-system	aws-node-6n4dp		1/1
Running	0	48m	
kube-system	coredns-66cb55d4f4-6h8cr		1/1
Running	0	57m	
kube-system	coredns-66cb55d4f4-svgzw		1/1
Running	0	57m	
kube-system	kube-proxy-vpctb		1/1
Running	0	48m	

6. Now, you need to go to the CloudWatch home page and click on **Log groups** in the **Logs** section. You will be able to see the Falco log group. Click on **Falco log group**, and then select **Log stream** present under alerts. You will find that Falco has started sending those logs that violate the rules or checks present in the Falco configuration:

```
▶   2022-03-05T03:21:34.261+08:00        {"log":"Fri Mar 4 19:21:34 2022: Starting internal webserver, listening on port 8765\n","stre…
▼   2022-03-05T03:21:35.192+08:00        {"log":{"output":"19:21:34.212749000: Notice Privileged container started (user=\u003cNA\u003…
    {
        "log": {
            "output": "19:21:34.212749000: Notice Privileged container started (user=<NA> user_loginuid=0 command=container:465cc6bf6a05 k
    node-6n4dp container=465cc6bf6a05 image▓▓▓▓▓▓▓▓▓.dkr.ecr.us-east-1.amazonaws.com/eks/pause:3.1-eksbuild.1) k8s.ns=kube-system k8s.
    container=465cc6bf6a05",
            "output_fields": {
                "container.id": "465cc6bf6a05",
                "container.image.repository": ▓▓▓▓▓▓▓▓.dkr.ecr.us-east-1.amazonaws.com/eks/pause",
                "container.image.tag": "3.1-eksbuild.1",
                "evt.time": 1646421694212749000,
                "k8s.ns.name": "kube-system",
                "k8s.pod.name": "aws-node-6n4dp",
                "proc.cmdline": "container:465cc6bf6a05",
                "user.loginuid": 0,
                "user.name": null
            },
            "priority": "Notice",
            "rule": "Launch Privileged Container",
            "source": "syscall",
            "tags": [
                "cis",
                "container",
                "mitre_lateral_movement",
                "mitre_privilege_escalation"
            ],
            "time": "2022-03-04T19:21:34.212749000Z"
        },
        "stream": "stdout"
    }
▶   2022-03-05T03:21:35.192+08:00        {"log":{"output":"19:21:34.216272000: Notice Privileged container started (user=\u003cNA\u003…
▶   2022-03-05T03:21:35.193+08:00        {"log":{"output":"19:21:34.243430000: Notice Privileged container started (user=\u003cNA\u003…
```

Figure 9.20 – CloudWatch log exported by Falco showing Pods noncompliant with rules

7. You can ignore the preceding log because the `aws-node` Pod needs privilege permission as it's an EKS worker node system Pod.

8. Generally, you won't want someone to make the remote connection to the shell of the Pod. Let's connect to one of the Pods and see what we get in the CloudWatch logs. We can connect to the `prodcatalog` Pod:

```
$ kubectl exec -it <prodcatalogpodwithID> -n dsoapp /bin/
bash
```

9. The moment you run the preceding command, you will see a new thread in the log events like the following. Falco alerted it because a new shell was spawned:

```
2022-03-05T03:36:10.085+08:00              {"log":{"output":"19:36:10.077468228: Notice A shell was spawned in
{
    "log": {
        "output": "19:36:10.077468228: Notice A shell was spawned in a container with an attached
terminal (user=root user_loginuid=-1 k8s.ns=dsoapp k8s.pod=prodcatalog-664486654d-kvc5d
container=ca10fa317262 shell=bash parent=runc cmdline=bash terminal=34816 container_id=ca10fa317262
image=public.ecr.aws/u2g6w7p2/eks-workshop-demo/product_catalog) k8s.ns=dsoapp k8s.pod=prodcatalog-
664486654d-kvc5d container=ca10fa317262",
        "output_fields": {
            "container.id": "ca10fa317262",
            "container.image.repository": "public.ecr.aws/u2g6w7p2/eks-workshop-demo/product_catalog",
            "evt.time": 1646422570077468228,
            "k8s.ns.name": "dsoapp",
            "k8s.pod.name": "prodcatalog-664486654d-kvc5d",
            "proc.cmdline": "bash",
            "proc.name": "bash",
            "proc.pname": "runc",
            "proc.tty": 34816,
            "user.loginuid": -1,
            "user.name": "root"
        },
        "priority": "Notice",
        "rule": "Terminal shell in container",
        "source": "syscall",
        "tags": [
            "container",
            "mitre_execution",
            "shell"
        ],
        "time": "2022-03-04T19:36:10.077468228Z"
    },
    "stream": "stdout"
}
```

Figure 9.21 – CloudWatch log showing the start of a shell session in the prodcatlog Pod

10. You can create a custom CloudWatch insight and an alarm using those metrics. Click on **Logs Insights** in the **Logs** section. Select **falco** in the **Select log group(s)** dropdown. In the text field, provide the snippet shown in the following figure, and then click on **Run query**:

Figure 9.22 – Creating log insights to create an alarm

11. You will be able to see the count of alerts. Now, click on **Add to dashboard**. Click on **Create new** and enter the dashboard name as `dso-falco-alerts`. Click on **Create**, and then click on **Add to dashboard**.

12. Now, you can go to the **Alarms** section. Click on **In alarm**, and then click on **Create alarm**. Click on **Select metric**. In the **AWS namespace** section, click on **Logs**, then **Log Group Metrics**, and then select **falco** with the **IncomingLogEvents** metric name. Click on **Select metric**. In the **Metric** section, select **1 minute** as the period. In the **Condition** section, select **Greater/Equal than 1**, and then click on **Next**. On the **Notification** page, make sure the alarm state trigger is **In alarm**. Select the SNS topic where you want to receive the email of the alert, then click on **Next**. Enter the alarm name as `falco-Terminal-Shell-alarm`, click on **Next**, and then click on **Create alarm**.

13. If you do *Step 8* again, you will receive an alert to the email address provided in the SNS topic:

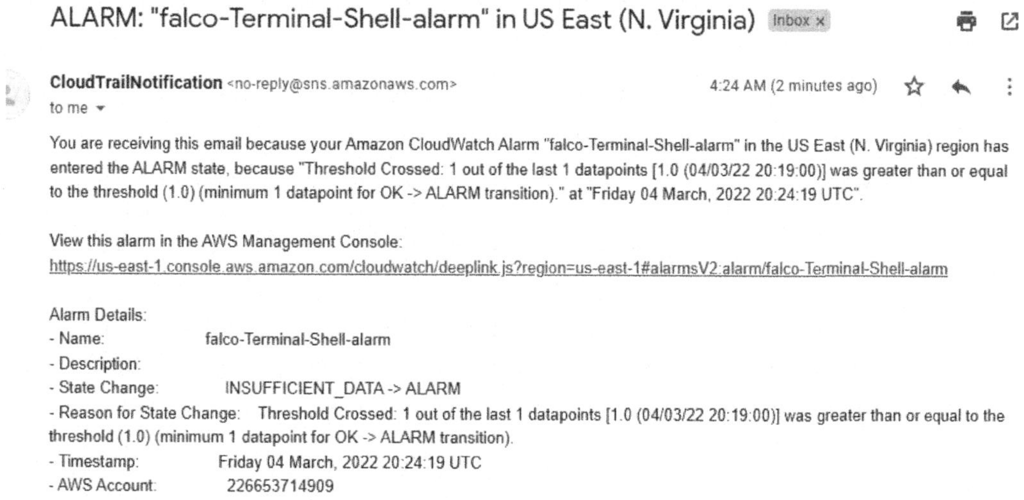

ALARM: "falco-Terminal-Shell-alarm" in US East (N. Virginia) Inbox ×   🖶   ↗

CloudTrailNotification <no-reply@sns.amazonaws.com>   4:24 AM (2 minutes ago)   ☆   ↩   ⋮
to me ▾

You are receiving this email because your Amazon CloudWatch Alarm "falco-Terminal-Shell-alarm" in the US East (N. Virginia) region has entered the ALARM state, because "Threshold Crossed: 1 out of the last 1 datapoints [1.0 (04/03/22 20:19:00)] was greater than or equal to the threshold (1.0) (minimum 1 datapoint for OK -> ALARM transition)." at "Friday 04 March, 2022 20:24:19 UTC".

View this alarm in the AWS Management Console:
https://us-east-1.console.aws.amazon.com/cloudwatch/deeplink.js?region=us-east-1#alarmsV2:alarm/falco-Terminal-Shell-alarm

Alarm Details:
- Name: falco-Terminal-Shell-alarm
- Description:
- State Change: INSUFFICIENT_DATA -> ALARM
- Reason for State Change: Threshold Crossed: 1 out of the last 1 datapoints [1.0 (04/03/22 20:19:00)] was greater than or equal to the threshold (1.0) (minimum 1 datapoint for OK -> ALARM transition).
- Timestamp: Friday 04 March, 2022 20:24:19 UTC
- AWS Account: 226653714909

Figure 9.23 – Email notification in case of Falco rule violation

This way, you can get an alert if any suspicious activity takes place during runtime in your application Pod. Falco alerts on the basis of rules present in the configuration . If you want an intelligent system where the system automatically detects the present working metrics of the application and any anomalies that take place and sends an alert as well as providing recommendations, then you can integrate the application with DevOps Guru, which is an AIOps service provided by AWS. We will integrate the DevOps Guru service with the application running in both staging and prod environments in the next section.

Integration with DevOps Guru

It is strongly recommended that you read *Chapter 10, AIOps with Amazon DevOps Guru and System Manager OpsCenter,* and complete the third section (*Enable DevOps Guru on EKS cluster resources*) with respect to the CloudFormation stack that we created in this chapter, which is eks-staging and eks-prod.

Creating a CI/CD pipeline using CloudFormation

In this section, we will create a CodePipeline project that gets triggered the moment any code change gets pushed to the `CatalogDetail` repository. This CodePipeline project executes the following stages and actions in sequence:

1. The CodePipeline project will first read the changes from the source and then go to the `Build-Secrets` stage.

2. At this stage, the CodeBuild project will start scanning repository code with the `git-secrets` utility and look for any secret leakages. After the completion of this stage, the `Build-SAST` stage will start executing.

3. The `Build-SAST` stage consists of two actions. The first action is SAST analysis, which invokes Anchore to scan the Docker build and then generates the report. Based on the vulnerability status, if there is a high or critical CVE, then the build will fail; otherwise, it will continue to build and push the image to the ECR repository. The next action is `ECR-SAST-and-STG-Deploy`. This action performs the ECR image scanning on the Docker image and, depending on the vulnerability status, it will fail or deploy the image in the staging EKS cluster. Both actions will trigger the Lambda function at the end of the build. This Lambda function uploads the generated report to AWS Security Hub.

4. Once the `Build-SAST` stage succeeds, then `Build-DAST` starts executing. The `Build-DAST` stage includes the `DASTAnalysis CodeBuild` project, which will invoke OWASP ZAP to perform a scan on the catalog app deployed in the `eks-staging` cluster. Depending on the alert status, this build will either fail or succeed. This build also triggers the Lambda function to upload the generated report to AWS Security Hub.

5. Once the `Build-DAST` stage succeeds, the transition goes to the `Build-ChaosSimulation` stage. This stage includes two actions. The first action, `FIS-EKSNodeDelete`, runs the chaos simulation of deleting the worker node using the **Fault Injection Simulator** (**FIS**) experiment template. The second action, `FIS-ReportGenerate`, monitors the worker node, application endpoint, and Pod status.

6. After that, the `Manual Approval` stage will ask for your approval to deploy the application in the production environment.

7. With positive approval, the `Deploy-PRD` stage will deploy the latest service in the `eks-prod` cluster.

This is the entire sequence flow for the CodePipeline. Now let's create the CodePipeline using the `dsopipelineCFT.yaml` CloudFormation template present in the `chapter-09/CICD` folder:

1. Go to the CloudFormation home page, click on **Create stack**, select **With new resources**, and click on **Upload a template file**. Upload the `dsopipelineCFT.yaml` file and click on **Next**.

2. You will see the **Specify stack details** page. Provide the information in the following manner:

   A. **Stack name**: `dsostack`

   B. **BranchName**: `master`

   C. **RepositoryName**: `CatalogDetail`

   D. **EcrRepositoryName**: `catalogdetail`

   E. **EksClusterName**: `eks-staging`

   F. **EksProdClusterName**: `eks-prod`

   G. **SASTTool**: `Anchore`

   H. **DASTTool**: `OWASP-Zap`

   I. **OwaspZapURLName**: **<OWASP-ZAP Endpoint>** (you can get that from the output of the owasp-zap CloudFormation stack)

   J. **OwaspZapApiKey**: `devsecopsapikey`

   K. **ApplicationURLForDASTScan**: **<ELB endpoint of frontend-node kubernetes svc>**

   L. **LambdaPackageLoc**: `dsos3lambda-<YOURACCOUNTNO>`

   M. **LambdaPackageS3Key**: `import_findings_security_hub.zip`

   N. **LambdaHandlerName**: `import_findings_security_hub.lambda_handler`

   O. **PipelineNotificationsEmail**: `YOUREMAILADDRESS`

   P. **PipelineApproverEmail**: `YOUREMAILADDRESS`

   Q. Skip other parameters.

3. Click on **Next** once you are done filling in all the details. Click **Next** to review. Click on the checkbox for IAM resource creation. Then click on **Create**. It will take a few minutes to create all the resources. Once the stack creation completes, you need to go to the **CodePipeline** page and click on **dsostack-pipeline**. You will see the pipeline stages as follows:

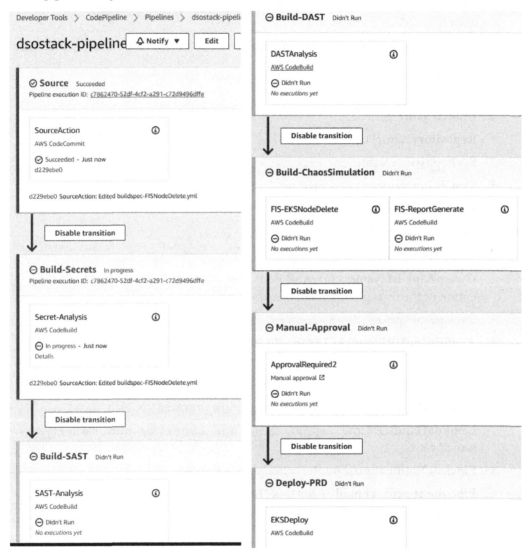

Figure 9.24 – CodePipeline stages for the DevSecOps pipeline

The pipeline will automatically start running. So, we have just created a CodePipeline instance. In the next section, we will validate all the stages.

> **Note**
>
> The `buildspec` files used for the activity have been created with respect to the `us-east-1` region. You may need to modify the `buildspec` files if you are using them in a different region.

Testing and validating SAST, DAST, Chaos Simulation, Deployment, and RASP

In this section, we will be analyzing all the build stages and looking at how the security tools scan, generate the report, and fail the build. We will also try to bypass the vulnerabilities by tweaking the `buildspec` file to go to the next stages because the aim of this chapter is to integrate the security tool, scan, and fail rather than fixing the vulnerability. We will start analyzing with the following sequence:

1. The first stage after the source is `Build-Secrets`. If you navigate to the logs of this CodeBuild project, you will see that this stage first clones the repository and then runs a `git secrets` scan on the source code. Since there are no secret leakages, this stage succeeds and moves to the next stage, which is `Build-SAST`:

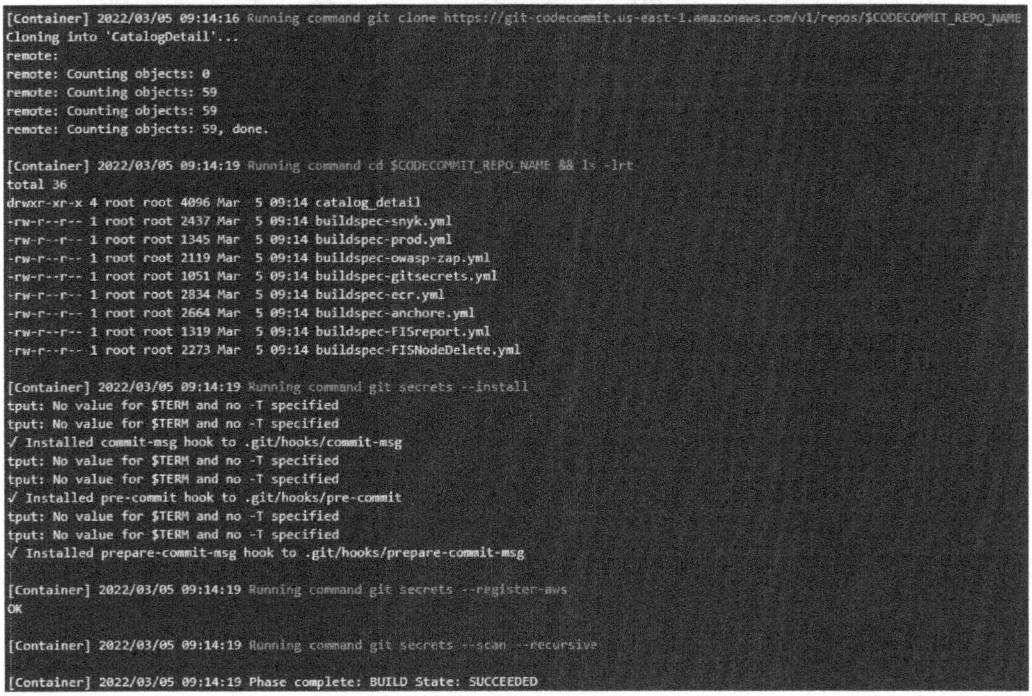

Figure 9.25 – CodeBuild logs showing the git secrets scan on source code

2. In the `Build-SAST` stage, if you go to the build logs of the `SAST-Analysis` action, you will see that the Anchore scanner has identified lots of vulnerabilities with `High`, `Critical`, and `Medium` severities. Depending on the logic given in `buildspec-anchore.yml`, the build should fail if it finds `High` or `Critical` vulnerabilities. So, the `SAST-Analysis` action failed, by pushing the generated report to AWS Security Hub via the Lambda function:

```
1117            "severity": "High",
1118            "severity": "High",
1119            "severity": "High",
1120            "severity": "High",
1121            "severity": "High",
1122            "severity": "High",
1123            "severity": "High",
1124            "severity": "High",
1125            "severity": "High",
1126            "severity": "High",
1127            "severity": "Critical",
1128            "severity": "High",
1129            "severity": "High",
1130            "severity": "Critical",
1131            "severity": "High",
1132            "severity": "High",
1133            "severity": "High",
1134            "severity": "High",
1135            "severity": "High",
1136 {
1137        "StatusCode": 200,
1138        "FunctionError": "Unhandled",
1139        "ExecutedVersion": "$LATEST"
1140 }
1141 LAMBDA_SUCCEDED
1142 There are critical or high vulnerabilities.. failing the build
```

Figure 9.26 – CodeBuild project build failed due to the presence of Critical and High vulnerabilities

You can also go to the **AWS SecurityHub** console to see the findings as follows:

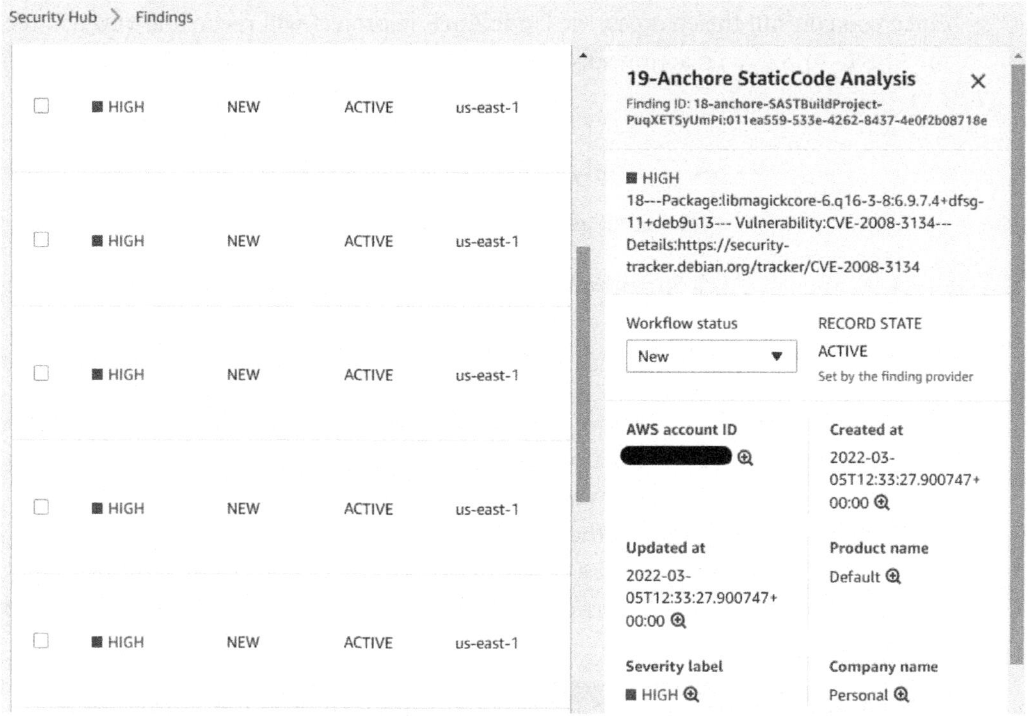

Figure 9.27 – The Security Hub console showing the Anchore vulnerability report

Now, based on the findings, we can see that there are lots of OS- and language-related vulnerabilities that we need to fix. The main lesson here is to build our own (internal) base Docker image, continuously scan and fix it, and provide that Docker image to developers where they will build their application code. It's a similar concept to using the custom patched and secured AMI. Now, to bypass this, we need to tweak the `buildspec-anchore.yml` file and commit it. Go to the **CodeCommit** console and edit the `buildspec-anchore.yml` file. In the `post_build` command's `if` condition, remove `High|Critical` and enter `Random` instead. In the `elif` condition, enter `High|Critical|Medium`, and commit the changes. It should look like the following:

```
if (grep -E 'Random' payload.json); then
    aws lambda invoke --function-name ImpToSecurityHubEKS --payload file://payload.json anchore
    echo "There are critical or high vulnerabilities.. failing the build"
    docker push $REPOSITORY_URI:latest
    exit 1;
elif (grep -E 'High|Critical|Medium' payload.json); then
    aws lambda invoke --function-name ImpToSecurityHubEKS --payload file://payload.json anchore
    docker push $REPOSITORY_URI:latest
else
    docker push $REPOSITORY_URI:latest
fi
```

Figure 9.28 – Editing the buildspec-anchore.yaml file

Once you commit the changes, the CodePipeline project will rerun and you will see the SAST-Analysis action succeed:

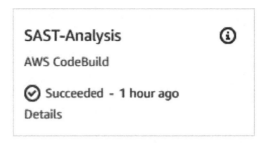

Figure 9.29 – SAST-Analysis CodeBuild project succeeded

After the SAST-Analysis action, the ECR-SAST-and-STG-Deploy action will run. This action will retrieve the ECR image scan result and compare the vulnerability severity status. If the severity matches with **HIGH** and **CRITICAL**, then the build will fail; otherwise, it will deploy the service to the eks-staging cluster. In this case, we got the result of 35 high and 2 critical severities, and that led to the build failing:

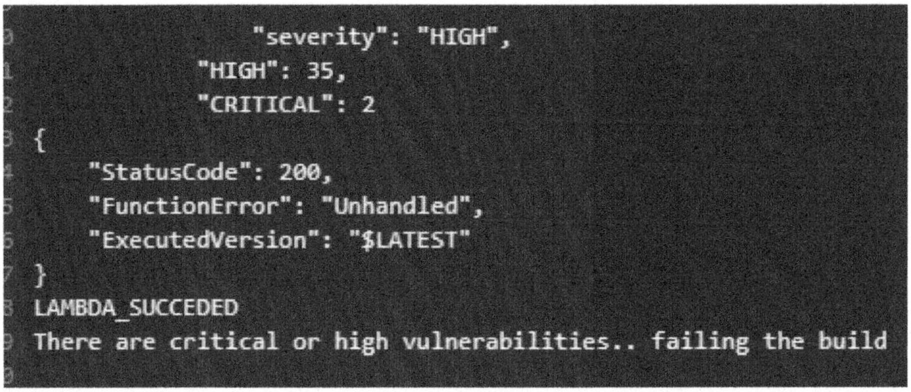

```
              "severity": "HIGH",
          "HIGH": 35,
          "CRITICAL": 2
{
    "StatusCode": 200,
    "FunctionError": "Unhandled",
    "ExecutedVersion": "$LATEST"
}
LAMBDA_SUCCEDED
There are critical or high vulnerabilities.. failing the build
```

Figure 9.30 – CodeBuild project build failed due to the presence of critical and high vulnerabilities

So, this is another layer on which we can scan for vulnerabilities. You can find the generated report as a finding in Security Hub:

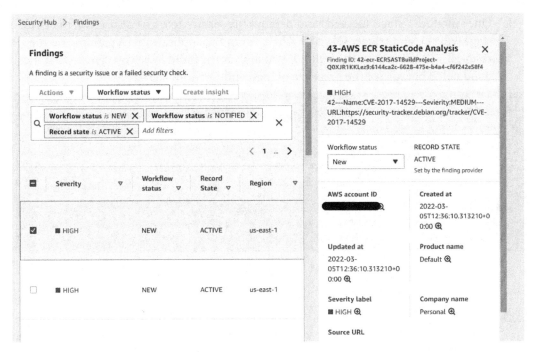

Figure 9.31 – Security Hub console showing the ECR vulnerability report

We will bypass this stage also by modifying the `buildspec-ecr.yml` file. We will tweak `if-else-logic` in the `post_build` commands to allow the `HIGH` and `CRITICAL` string and commit the changes (use a word such as `bridions` instead of `random` in this case):

```
if (grep -E 'BRIDIONS' ecr_scan_result.json); then
    aws lambda invoke --function-name ImpToSecurityHubEKS --payload file://p
    echo "There are critical or high vulnerabilities.. failing the build"
    exit 1;
elif (grep -E 'HIGH|CRITICAL|MEDIUM' ecr_scan_result.json); then
    aws lambda invoke --function-name ImpToSecurityHubEKS --payload file://p
fi
```

Figure 9.32 – Editing the buildspec-ecr.yaml file

Once you commit the changes, CodePipeline will re-run and this time, the build will succeed and the latest image will be pulled in the **proddetail** deployment in EKS cluster. The latest image will replace the existing one, which was a public Docker image. You will be able to see the application running with the latest image. You can describe the `proddetail` deployment in the EKS cluster to verify the image version:

3.   Once the SAST stage succeeds and deploys the service to `eks-staging`, the DAST stage will run and trigger OWASP ZAP to scan the application. Depending on the result, it will fail or pass the build. If you look at the build logs, you can see that the build failed because of the presence of high and medium alerts:

```
[Container] 2022/03/05 13:27:42 Running command if [ $high_alerts != 0 ] || [ $medium_a
failing the build" && exit 1; else exit 0; fi
there are high or medium alerts.. failing the build

[Container] 2022/03/05 13:27:42 Command did not exit successfully if [ $high_alerts !=
medium alerts.. failing the build" && exit 1; else exit 0; fi exit status 1
[Container] 2022/03/05 13:27:42 Phase complete: POST_BUILD State: FAILED
[Container] 2022/03/05 13:27:42 Phase context status code: COMMAND_EXECUTION_ERROR Messa
|| [ $medium_alerts != 0 ]; then echo "there are high or medium alerts.. failing the bu
[Container] 2022/03/05 13:27:42 Phase complete: UPLOAD_ARTIFACTS State: SUCCEEDED
[Container] 2022/03/05 13:27:42 Phase context status code:  Message:
```

Figure 9.33 – CodeBuild project build failed due to the presence of high and medium alerts

You can verify this and analyze the DAST result in Security Hub:

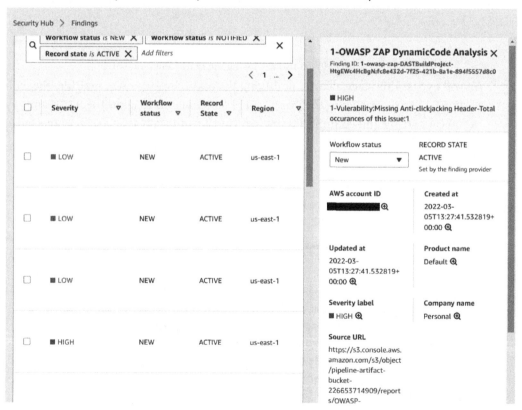

Figure 9.34 – CodeBuild project build failed due to the presence of high and medium vulnerabilities

You need to comment out the last line of the `post_build` commands in the `buildspec-owas-zap.yml` file and commit the changes:

```
aws lambda invoke --function-name ImpToSecurityHubEKS --payload file://payload.json o
#  | if [ $high_alerts != 0 ] || [ $medium_alerts != 0 ]; then echo "there are high or m
tifacts:
type: zip
```

Once you commit the changes, the CodePipeline will rerun and, this time, the DAST stage will succeed and trigger the next stage, which is Chaos Simulation:

4. In the `Build-ChoasSimulation` stage, there are two parallel actions. The first action will delete 50% of worker nodes in a `nodegroup` and the second action will monitor it for 5 minutes:

```
###############Starting FIS Test################
==============EKS Node Termination============
Creating Experiment Template
The Experiment Template id is EXTDAkE8PiSfBcWwS
Starting the experiment
EXP7jFupvWcv4FDKPY
experiment is still in progress
experiment is still in progress
experiment is still in progress
Experiment has been completed but pls wait for the test report build to complete

[Container] 2022/03/05 15:25:48 Phase complete: BUILD State: SUCCEEDED
```

Figure 9.35 – CodeBuild log showing FIS experiment completion

The following figure shows the report of the FIS experiment that shows the unavailability of Pods and nodes:

```
----Pod Status----
Mar 05 15:30:20 frontend-7c856967fd-rfg5k        0/1    Running              0        3m4s
Mar 05 15:30:20 prodcatalog-664486654d-wz94n     0/1    ContainerCreating    0        3m4s
Mar 05 15:30:20 proddetail-5464c77fd-qjs2w       0/1    Running              0        3m4s
----Node Count Status----
Mar 05 15:30:20 ip-192-168-40-231.ec2.internal   NotReady    <none>    5s     v1.21.5-eks-9017834
Mar 05 15:30:20 ip-192-168-8-19.ec2.internal     Ready       <none>    2m5s   v1.21.5-eks-9017834
----Endpoint status----
----Pod Status----
Mar 05 15:30:26 frontend-7c856967fd-rfg5k        1/1    Running    0    3m10s
Mar 05 15:30:26 prodcatalog-664486654d-wz94n     0/1    Running    0    3m10s
Mar 05 15:30:26 proddetail-5464c77fd-qjs2w       0/1    Running    0    3m10s
----Node Count Status----
Mar 05 15:30:26 ip-192-168-40-231.ec2.internal   NotReady    <none>    11s    v1.21.5-eks-9017834
Mar 05 15:30:26 ip-192-168-8-19.ec2.internal     Ready       <none>    2m11s  v1.21.5-eks-9017834
----Endpoint status----
```

Figure 9.36 – CodeBuild logs showing the worker node and Pod are in the restarting and not ready state

The following figure shows the report that the endpoint, Pod, and nodes are available at their full capacity:

```
----Endpoint status----
Mar 05 15:32:39 HTTP/1.1 200 OK
----Pod Status----
Mar 05 15:32:40 frontend-7c856967fd-rfg5k        1/1      Running   0              5m24s
Mar 05 15:32:40 prodcatalog-664486654d-wz94n     1/1      Running   0              5m24s
Mar 05 15:32:40 proddetail-5464c77fd-qjs2w       1/1      Running   0              5m24s
----Node Count Status----
Mar 05 15:32:40 ip-192-168-40-231.ec2.internal   Ready    <none>    2m25s   v1.21.5-eks-9017834
Mar 05 15:32:40 ip-192-168-8-19.ec2.internal     Ready    <none>    4m25s   v1.21.5-eks-9017834
```

Figure 9.37 – CodeBuild logs showing the endpoint, Pod, and node status

5. Once the Build-ChaosSimulation stage succeeds, there will be an email sent to the email address that you provided during the creation of the dsostack CodePipline for approval, and then there will be a manual approval required too. You need to allow that to deploy the latest image in the production EKS cluster:

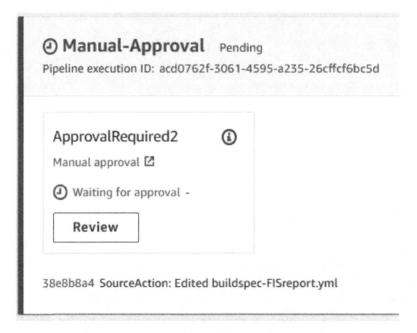

Figure 9.38 – CodePipeline manual approval stage waiting for approval

The following figure shows what happens when you click on **Review** and it asks you to leave comments:

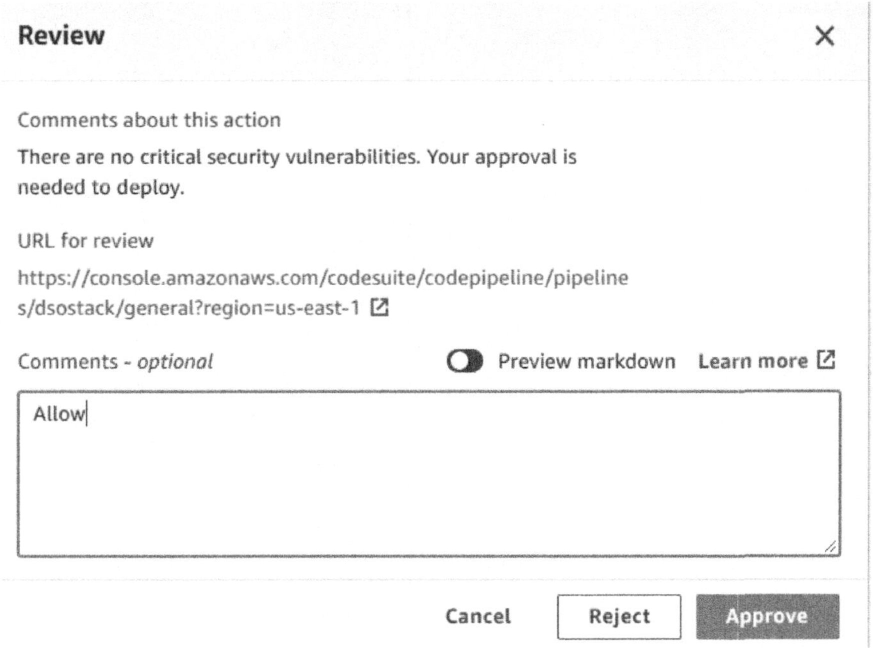

Figure 9.39 – CodePipeline approval page

6. Once you provide the approval, the `Deploy-PRD` stage will deploy the latest image in the `eks-prod` cluster:

Figure 9.40 – CodeBuild log showing the deployment of a service

7. In the end, your entire pipeline will look like this:

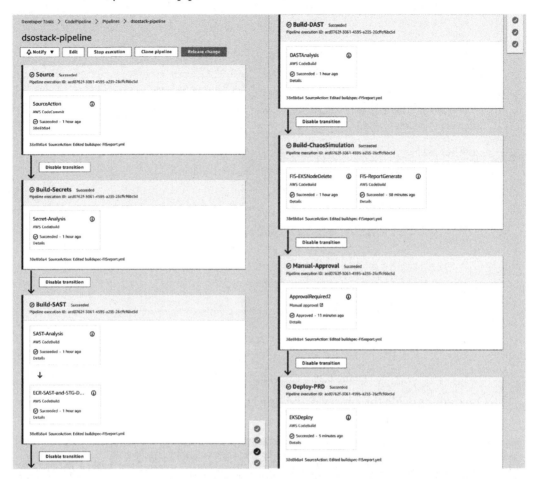

Figure 9.41 – Overall CodePipeline stage succeded

These are the steps that CodePipeline project executed using native services as well as the open source security tools. You can verify the Falco functionality by connecting to any Pod; you will receive an email alert with the subject `falco-terminal-shell-alarm`.

You can replace the `catalog_detail` service code by entering your own service code, and tweak the `buildspec` files to have a smooth run for CodePipeline. So, we have just validated the functionality of security tools and their integration with AWS services. We haven't covered the validation of DevOps Guru yet, because we are covering it in the next chapter. Before we dive into DevOps Guru, there are certain machine learning concepts that you must be aware of. We wanted to isolate the security concepts so that they don't overlap, but since we have finished our final DevSecOps pipeline, in the next chapter, we will learn more about the AWS AIOps service, DevOps Guru.

Summary

In this chapter, we learned about the importance of implementing security at the early stages of software delivery. We discussed the various techniques for security checks that can be implemented in a CI/CD pipeline. We covered the important concepts of security advisory tools, pre-commit secret checks, SCA, SAST, DAST, and RASP. We learned more about the tools by installing and validating them. We created an end-to-end pipeline with a microservice and deployed it to an EKS cluster. We validated all the security checks at every stage of the pipeline. Now, you can easily create a robust pipeline within your environment with your use cases. Remember that security is everyone's responsibility. With great power and freedom also comes greater responsibility to use that freedom in a secure manner.

10

AIOps with Amazon DevOps Guru and Systems Manager OpsCenter

This chapter will introduce you to the concepts of **artificial intelligence (AI)** and **machine learning (ML)**. We will also learn about **AIOps**, why we need it, and how it is applied to IT operations. We will cover some of the areas where AIOps can be helpful. We will learn about the AWS **DevOps Guru** AIOps tool and implement two use cases. We will deploy a serverless application and inject some failure, and then analyze the insights and remediation provided by Amazon DevOps Guru. Then, another use case will be covered about identifying anomalies in CPU, memory, and networking within an **Elastic Container Service for Kubernetes (EKS)** cluster.

This chapter contains the following main sections:

- AIOps and how it helps in IT operations
- AIOps using Amazon DevOps Guru
- Enabling DevOps Guru on EKS cluster resources

- Injecting failure and then reviewing the insights

- Deploying a serverless application and enabling DevOps Guru

- Integrating DevOps Guru with Systems Manager OpsCenter

- Injecting failure and then reviewing the insights

Technical requirements

To implement the solutions mentioned in this chapter, you will need an AWS account with DevOps Guru enabled.

The github repo for this chapter can be found here:

```
https://github.com/PacktPublishing/Accelerating-DevSecOps-on-
AWS/tree/main/chapter-10
```

AIOps and how it helps in IT operations

AI is a hot topic everywhere and, unlike previously, lots of people now really understand the meaning of AI and how it is applied in real-life scenarios or use cases. Before jumping right to AIOps, we first need to set the context by understanding AI and ML.

AI is the broadest term and has been around for decades as a research topic. AI allows a computer to perform any task that normally requires human intelligence. ML is a subset of AI that solves specific tasks by learning from patterns and data and making predictions without explicitly being programmed. This phrase of *explicitly being programmed* is the key factor that translates some huge opportunities to transform how we do IT operations today. ML is one approach to AI, recently popular due to big data and cheap compute through cloud computing. Broadly, there are two types of ML algorithms:

- **Supervised learning algorithms** take the raw data that you are inputting, and they also have a set of training labels or examples that provide the algorithm with an illustration of how you correctly interpret that data and create correct outputs.

- **Unsupervised learning algorithms** take only the raw data and analyze and cluster the unlabeled datasets. These algorithms find hidden patterns or data grouping without human intervention. Most of the time in IT operations, we generally have data that is not labeled.

	Inputs	Applications
Supervised	Raw Data + Training Labels	**Classification**: Is this image a cat or dog? **Prediction**: What will the temp be tomorrow?
Unsupervised	Raw Data Only	**Clustering**: Group these news articles by topic **Anomaly Detection**: Is this an unusual credit card charge?

Figure 10.1 – Examples of supervised and unsupervised learning

Different types of input data are usually a better fit for one approach or the other and result in different end user experiences, but ultimately, supervised and unsupervised are just implementation details. Two things impact the IT operations team every day, which are the **open box** and **black box** approaches to ML.

A black box approach means an algorithm where you give it an input and you get an output, but you don't know anything about exactly how that output was arrived at. In some cases, this could have serious implications; for example, a credit card company might use ML to provide credit, and they might be compliant with foreign regulations that require them to be able to go back and explain to someone who applies for a credit card why an algorithm may have reached a certain decision.

An open box approach to ML is easy to explain and for the IT operations team, the openness is really an important property to improve adoption and outcomes. In brief, open box ML is explainable, editable, and insightful, as follows:

- **Explainable**: The logic produced by ML is expressed in a format that humans can see and understand.

- **Editable**: The logic produced by ML can be edited, so you can tweak it based on human knowledge and experience.

- **Insightful**: You can preview the results of the ML logic against a historical dataset (for example, monitoring alerts collected during a critical outage window).

So, basically, there are three factors that are important while adopting ML-based tools for IT operations, and those are **transparency**, **control**, and **trust**.

AIOps is a term coined by Gartner and it originally meant **algorithmic IT operations**, but later changed to **artificial intelligence for IT operations**. It's a new label for the category of tools that take ML capabilities and applies to the IT operations space. There are three main categories in IT operations where we can apply ML:

- Monitoring and dealing with alert and metrics data

- IT service desk or **IT Service Management** (**ITSM**)

- Automation in general

The following diagram shows the workflow of AIOps:

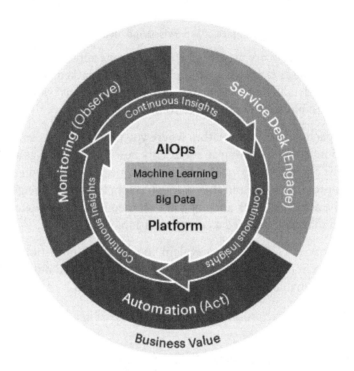

Figure 10.2 – Core workflow of AIOps

But why do we need AIOps? Everything is working fine right now. What are the challenges that lead us to use AIOps-powered tools?

In the past, IT teams have been very internally oriented, meaning that they mostly think about what they can accomplish with the technology, how can they reduce and control the cost structures, and how to organize all the processes within IT to be the most efficient organization.

But in the age of digital transformation, IT teams are more focused on where the business is going. Instead of thinking about cost reduction, they are focusing on revenue generation. There are lots of changes happening throughout the business. In any software development organization, they are incorporating lots of automated processes, such as **Infrastructure as Code (IaC)** to spin up the application infrastructure and **CI/CD (Continuous Integration/Continuous Delivery or Deployment)** to deliver the new features quickly. We are also seeing lots of changes in the infrastructure models of the public cloud and hybrid cloud. All these changes are creating a seismic shift. Ten years ago, we had fewer tools, and application delivery was a bit slow, but nowadays we have so many tools and every now and then new features are released. These things create lots of noise, issues, and maintenance, and we can't simply employ more and more people to resolve and maintain this. Now the question remains: what is happening to IT and IT operations and how is it impacting IT operations? What sort of changes are required in IT operations to support this large infrastructure, smooth application delivery, and the maintenance of it?

IT operations teams must keep up with a more dynamic IT landscape, including containers, serverless functions, microservices, cloud-native architectures, and public and hybrid cloud deployments. IT operations teams also must support innovation and digital transformation but at the same time they still need to maintain the legacy and traditional infrastructure because IT operations is additive so they still have to maintain previous responsibilities. Now, at this point, IT operations teams leverage automation and ML-based tools and capabilities to ensure that they can handle the scale and complexity.

IT operations teams are already using some tools such as rule-based engine automation, which works for now, but it just doesn't handle all scenarios. The rule-based tools work in the following manner:

1. Select a specific subset of your data to focus on.
2. Experts help determine how to process that data.
3. Translate expert process to rules.
4. The machine follows the rules.
5. Observe and refine rules to deal with exceptions.

But the problem is, when you scale, you have tens and thousands of those rules. Another problem is how to manage those thousands of rules, and how those rules are aligned with the subset of target data. Now, at this juncture, ML can help.

As the data comes to your system, ML can learn about your environment. It can leverage all the institutional knowledge to handle the *known knowns*, but also leverage the intelligence in the system to be able to handle the *unknown unknowns* at a large scale. It can autonomously respond 24 hours a day, 365 days a year. Most importantly, if you are using open-box ML, you can control and modify the logic as well.

Now that we understand how ML-based tools or AIOps tools help IT operations teams, let's discover how AIOps works.

AIOps tools comprise three fundamental technology components, and those are big data, ML, and automation. It uses a big data platform to aggregate siloed IT operations data in one place. This data can include historical performance, event data that streams real-time operation events, system logs and metrics, and network data. Then, AIOps applies focus analytics and ML capabilities to separate significant event alerts from the noise. It uses analytics such as application rules and pattern matching to comb through the operational data and separate signals from the noise and significant abnormal event alerts. It then helps in identifying and proposing solutions. It uses industry-specific or environment-specific algorithms to correlate abnormal events with other event data across environments to identify the cause of an outage or performance problem, and eventually suggests remedies or solutions. AIOps then automates responses as well as a real-time proactive resolution. AIOps also automatically routes alerts and recommended solutions to the appropriate IT teams or even creates response teams based on the nature of the problem and the solution. In lots of scenarios, AIOps processes the results from ML to trigger automatic system responses that address problems in real time, before IT teams are even aware of them. AIOps also learns continuously and independently in order to improve how it handles future problems. It uses the results of the analytics to change the algorithm or create a new one to identify the problem even earlier and recommend more effective solutions.

AIOps encompasses a broad category of tools that IT operations face today, such as the following:

- AIOps for incident and problem management
- AIOps for IT operations analytics
- AIOps for infrastructure management
- AIOps for capacity management

There are some amazing companies that provide effective AIOps tools, such as **Splunk**, **Moogsoft**, and **BigPanda**. AWS has recently announced an AIOps service, DevOps Guru, which is at an early stage but is improving quite rapidly. In the next section, we will learn more about Amazon DevOps Guru and how we can use it to improve IT operations.

AIOps using Amazon DevOps Guru

AWS has been hearing customers' feedback and acting on it by providing amazing managed services. One of the recently launched AWS services is Amazon DevOps Guru, which is powered by ML to improve an application's operational performance and availability. It helps detect behaviors that act differently from normal operating patterns so that you can easily identify operational issues long before they impact your application.

DevOps Guru uses ML models built on information that has been collected by years of Amazon and AWS operation excellence to identify anomalous application behavior (for example, resource constraints, error rates, and increased latency) and raise critical issues beforehand so that they do not cause any potential outages or service disruptions. Once DevOps Guru identifies an issue, it automatically sends an alert and provides information and a summary related to anomalies, root cause, timestamp, and the location where the issue has occurred. It also provides recommendations on how to remediate the issue.

DevOps Guru has the following main features:

- **Aggregate operational data from multiple sources**: DevOps Guru analyzes and composes streams of operations and maintenance data from multiple sources, such as CloudWatch metrics, AWS Config, CloudFormation, and X-Ray, and provides you with a dashboard to browse for and observe anomalies in your operational information, expelling the need for multiple tools. This delegated administrator may then browse, sort, and filter insights from all accounts within your company to create an organization-wide snapshot of the health of all monitored apps without any extra modification.

- **Provide ML-powered insights**: ML-powered advice helps DevOps Guru increase application availability and resolve operational issues faster and with less human work. It continually collects and analyzes metrics, logs, events, and traces in order to define typical application behavior boundaries. DevOps Guru then searches for outliers and combines anomalies to generate operational insights based on component interactions in your application. Using CloudTrail events, the insights show which components are impacted, the identification of associated problems, and advice on how to address them.

- **Automatically configure alarms**: DevOps Guru can be used by developers and operators to customize and set up alerts for their applications. DevOps Guru automatically identifies new resources and ingests associated metrics as your applications change and you accept new services. It then notifies you when a change occurs from regular operating patterns, without needing any manual rule or alarm modifications.

- **Detect critical issues with minimal noise**: DevOps Guru leans on years of expertise running widely accessible applications such as Amazon.com, as well as ML models built on internal AWS operational data, to deliver accurate operational insights for crucial application issues.

- **Integrate with AWS services and third-party tools**: Amazon DevOps Guru directly interacts with CloudWatch, Config, CloudFormation, and X-Ray to discover and track interconnections and dependencies between application components. AWS Systems Manager and EventBridge can also be integrated with DevOps Guru. DevOps Guru produces an OpsItem in OpsCenter for each insight it generates due to the interface with AWS Systems Manager. This allows you to make use of OpsCenter's capability to gain a better understanding of, investigate, and resolve operational issues more quickly. DevOps Guru also provides integration with third-party incident management systems such as PagerDuty and Atlassian, which can ingest SNS notifications from DevOps Guru and manage incidents for you automatically.

DevOps Guru is a managed service so you can enable it's feature with a single click. It doesn't need any additional software to deploy and manage. Before jumping to perform any operation on DevOps Guru, let's get familiar with some terminologies related to DevOps Guru:

- **Anomaly**: An anomaly is one or more connected metrics recognized by DevOps Guru that are strange or unexpected. DevOps Guru produces anomalies by analyzing metrics and operational data linked to your AWS resources using ML. When you set up Amazon DevOps Guru, you define which AWS resources you want to be evaluated.

- **Insight**: An insight is a collection of abnormalities discovered during the investigation of the AWS resources specified when DevOps Guru is configured. Each insight includes observations, recommendations, and analytical data that may be used to improve operational performance. There are two types of insights:

  - **Reactive**: A reactive insight detects unusual behavior as it occurs. It includes anomalies with recommendations, relevant data, and events to assist you in understanding and addressing the issues right now.

  - **Proactive**: A proactive insight alerts you to unusual conduct before it occurs. It provides abnormalities as well as advice to assist you in addressing the issues before they occur.

- **Metrics and operational events**: Analyzing the data given by Amazon CloudWatch and operational events released by your AWS services generates the anomalies that comprise an insight. You may examine the metrics and operational events that generate an insight to assist you in better understanding issues in your application.

- **Recommendations**: Each insight includes tips to help you enhance the performance of your application.

In the next section, we will deploy a container-based application on an EKS cluster and detect the anomalies using DevOps Guru.

Enabling DevOps Guru on EKS cluster resources

Because of the vast number of abstractions and supporting infrastructure, observability in a container-centric system gives new issues for operators. Hundreds of clusters and thousands of services, tasks, and pods can operate concurrently in many companies. This section will demonstrate new features in Amazon DevOps Guru that will assist in simplifying and increasing the operator's capabilities. Anomalies are grouped by metric and container clusters to increase context and facilitate access, and more Amazon CloudWatch Container Insight metrics are supported.

We will first deploy an EKS cluster using `eksctl` and then deploy the **OpenTelemetry Collector** to aggregate all the metrics and provide them to CloudWatch. Then, we will enable DevOps Guru for the EKS cluster resources.

Perform the following steps to enable DevOps Guru on EKS cluster resources:

1. Deploy an EKS cluster using the `eksctl` command:

```
$ eksctl create cluster --name=dgo-cluster --nodes=1
```

2. The previous command will create an EKS cluster using two CloudFormation stacks. One stack creates an EKS cluster and another one creates a node group, which consists of a worker node:

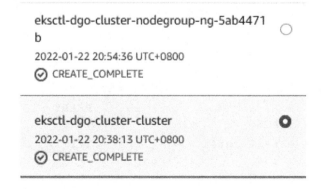

Figure 10.3 – CloudFormation stacks of an EKS cluster

3. We will modify the **Identity and Access Management (IAM)** role of the worker node and attach a policy that allows CloudWatch to gather metrics from the worker node. Go to the EKS cluster console. Click on the **dgo-cluster** cluster. Then, click on **Configuration**, followed by **Compute**, as shown here:

Figure 10.4 – An EKS cluster configuration showing the node group

4. Click on the node group name and click on **Node IAM role ARN value**. You will be redirected to the **IAM role** permission page. Click on **Attach policies** and select **CloudwatchAgentServerPolicy**.

5. Once you have attached the policy, deploy the OpenTelemetry Collector on the EKS cluster:

```
$ curl https://raw.githubusercontent.com/
aws-observability/aws-otel-collector/main/deployment-
template/eks/otel-container-insights-infra.yaml | kubectl
apply -f -
```

6. You can verify the pod by running the following command:

```
$ kubectl get pods -n aws-otel-eks
NAME                              READY     STATUS
RESTARTS     AGE
aws-otel-eks-ci-rgt4l             1/1       Running
0            1h
```

7. Once you have deployed the OpenTelemetry Collector, go to **AWS CloudWatch** and click on **Metrics**, then click on **All metrics**. You will be able to see **ContainerInsights** in **Custom namespaces**:

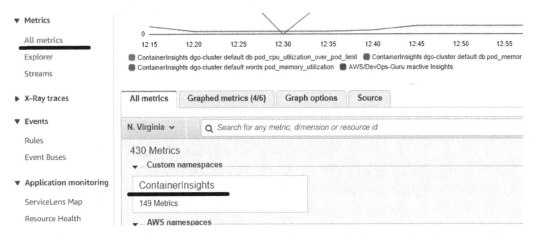

Figure 10.5 – The CloudWatch ContainerInsights metrics

8. Now, go to the Amazon DevOps Guru home page and click on **Get started** to configure the DevOps Guru settings. It comes with a free tier for 3 months:

Figure 10.6 – The Amazon DevOps Guru home page

9. You will see a **Get started** page where, under the Amazon DevOps Guru analysis coverage, you will be asked to select the resources that will be analyzed by DevOps Guru. Click on **Choose later**:

Amazon DevOps Guru analysis coverage

DevOps Guru analyzes the operational data for your AWS resources based on your selection. You pay for the number of AWS resource hours analyzed, for each active resource. A resource is only active if it produces metrics, events, or log entries within an hour. See the pricing page ☑ for complete details.

Choose which AWS resources to analyze by specifying the coverage boundary

○ Analyze all AWS resources in the current AWS account in this Region

● Choose later
     You can specify specific AWS resources to analyze using AWS CloudFormation stacks as your coverage boundary.

Figure 10.7 – Selecting resources for analysis coverage

10. Under **Specify an SNS topic**, click on **Create a new SNS topic**, give it the name dgsns, and click on **Enable**.

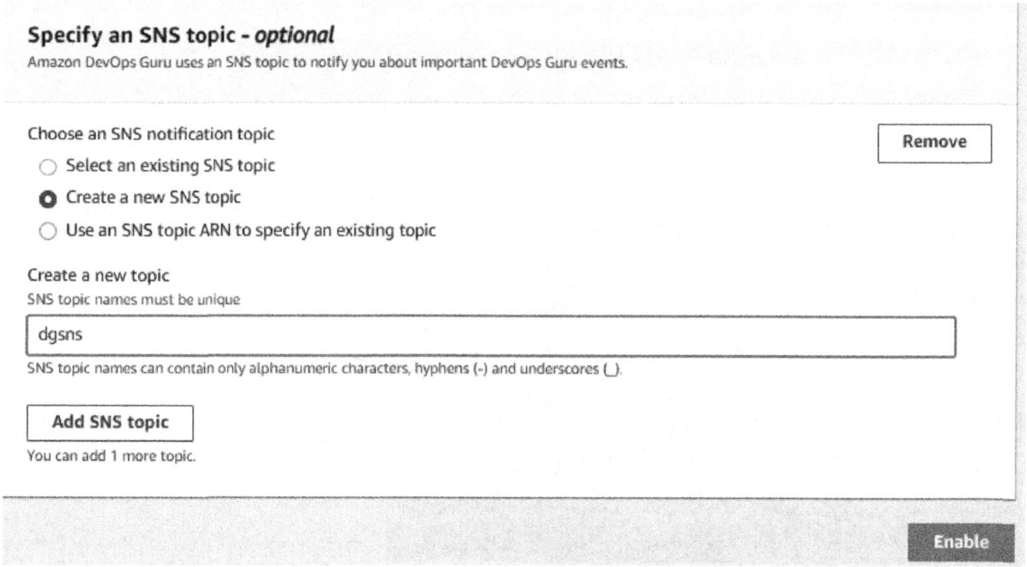

Specify an SNS topic - *optional*

Amazon DevOps Guru uses an SNS topic to notify you about important DevOps Guru events.

Choose an SNS notification topic   Remove

○ Select an existing SNS topic

● Create a new SNS topic

○ Use an SNS topic ARN to specify an existing topic

Create a new topic

SNS topic names must be unique

dgsns

SNS topic names can contain only alphanumeric characters, hyphens (-) and underscores (_).

Add SNS topic

You can add 1 more topic.

Enable

Figure 10.8 – Creating a new SNS topic

11. Then, go to **Settings** and click on **Analyzed resources**. Click on **Edit** and select **CloudFormation stacks**. This basically allows DevOps Guru to choose the resources to analyze. Select the CloudFormation stack name that helped to create the EKS cluster and worker node. Then, click on **Save**:

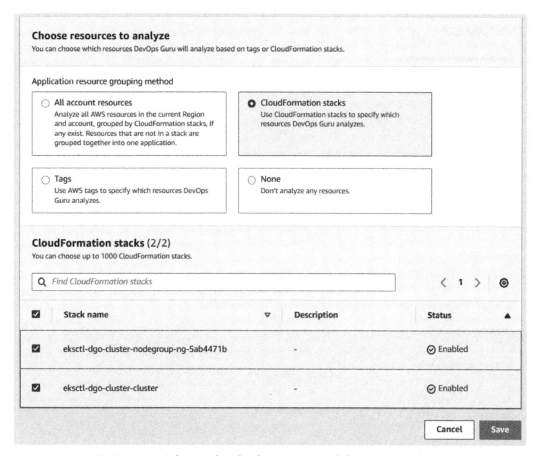

Figure 10.9 – Selecting the CloudFormation stack for analysis coverage

12. Once we have configured that, DevOps Guru will analyze the resources created via the CloudFormation stack and show the health in the main **Dashboard**. As we can see, both of the resources are in a healthy condition:

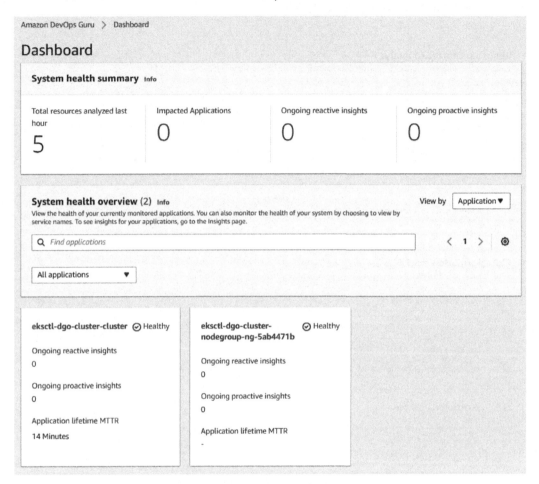

Figure 10.10 – Dashboard showing the health of resources after analysis

This way, we have enabled DevOps Guru on an EKS cluster. DevOps Guru will basically monitor and analyze the following metrics to detect the anomalies:

- `cluster_failed_node_count`
- `cluster_node_count`
- `namespace_number_of_running_pods`
- `node_cpu_limit`
- `node_cpu_reserved_capacity`

- `node_cpu_usage_total`
- `node_cpu_utilization`
- `node_filesystem_utilization`
- `node_memory_limit`
- `node_memory_reserved_capacity`
- `node_memory_utilization`
- `node_memory_working_set`
- `node_network_total_bytes`
- `node_number_of_running_containers`
- `node_number_of_running_pods`
- `pod_cpu_reserved_capacity`
- `pod_cpu_utilization`
- `pod_cpu_utilization_over_pod_limit`
- `pod_memory_reserved_capacity`
- `pod_memory_utilization`
- `pod_memory_utilization_over_pod_limit`
- `pod_number_of_container_restarts`
- `pod_network_rx_bytes`
- `pod_network_tx_bytes`
- `service_number_of_running_pods`

In the next section, we will deploy an application and inject a failure in it and see how DevOps Guru analyzes and provides the recommendation to resolve the anomalies.

Injecting a failure and then reviewing the insights

In this section, we will deploy an application that we deployed in previous chapters, and then we will inject a failure and validate how DevOps Guru analyzes those anomalies and provides the recommendation to resolve the anomalies.

Perform the following steps:

1. Deploy the application on an EKS cluster:

```
$ curl -o starkapp.yaml https://raw.githubusercontent.
com/nikitsrj/kube-app-golang/master/kube-deployment.yml
$ kubectl create -f starkapp.yaml
```

2. Get the **Elastic Load Balancer** (**ELB**) endpoint and paste it in the browser to access the application:

```
$ kubectl get svc web
NAME    TYPE              CLUSTER-IP      EXTERNAL-IP
PORT(S)           AGE
web     LoadBalancer      10.100.1.2
a4ce7bd79683043d5ae122943d00d2c4-1894525087.us-east-1.
elb.amazonaws.com      80:31536/TCP    85m
```

The following screenshot shows the application UI:

Figure 10.11 – The Stark app in the browser

3. Now, we need to inject a failure by modifying the db pod resource limit. You need to add the resource limit in the deployment file and save the file as follows:

```
$ kubectl edit deployment db -o yaml
```

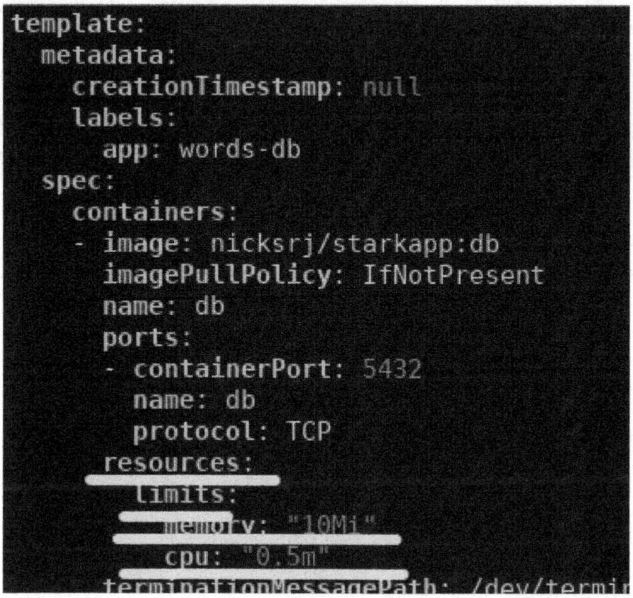

```
template:
  metadata:
    creationTimestamp: null
    labels:
      app: words-db
  spec:
    containers:
    - image: nicksrj/starkapp:db
      imagePullPolicy: IfNotPresent
      name: db
      ports:
      - containerPort: 5432
        name: db
        protocol: TCP
      resources:
        limits:
          memory: "10Mi"
          cpu: "0.5m"
      terminationMessagePath: /dev/termi
```

Figure 10.12 – Adding the resource limit in a db deployment

4. Once you do the previous step, it will delete the db pod and create a new one.

5. Now, you need to simulate minor traffic on the website. Enter the following command in your terminal, which will call the website every second. This will spike the CPU utilization of the pod more than the limit:

```
$ watch -n 1 curl http://<URLOFWEB>
```

6. You will be able to see the db pod keep on restarting:

```
$ watch kubectl get pods -A
```

The following screenshot shows the db pod status:

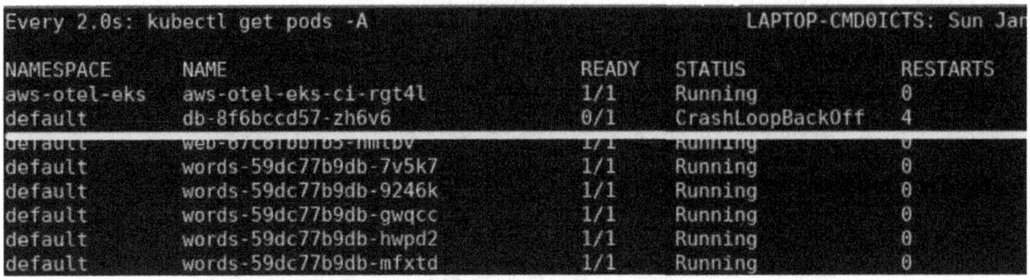

```
Every 2.0s: kubectl get pods -A                                    LAPTOP-CMD0ICTS: Sun Jan

NAMESPACE        NAME                        READY    STATUS              RESTARTS
aws-otel-eks     aws-otel-eks-ci-rgt4l       1/1      Running             0
default          db-8f6bccd57-zh6v6          0/1      CrashLoopBackOff    4
default          web-67c61bb1b5-nmtbv        1/1      Running             0
default          words-59dc77b9db-7v5k7      1/1      Running             0
default          words-59dc77b9db-9246k      1/1      Running             0
default          words-59dc77b9db-gwqcc      1/1      Running             0
default          words-59dc77b9db-hwpd2      1/1      Running             0
default          words-59dc77b9db-mfxtd      1/1      Running             0
```

Figure 10.13 – The db pod keeps on restarting

You can also check the application in the browser. The words in the application box will be missing:

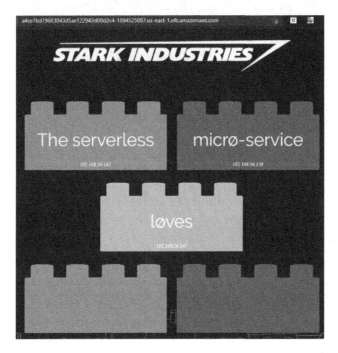

Figure 10.14 – The Stark app UI without words in the box

7. Now, if you go to the DevOps Guru dashboard, you will see one of the application systems is unhealthy:

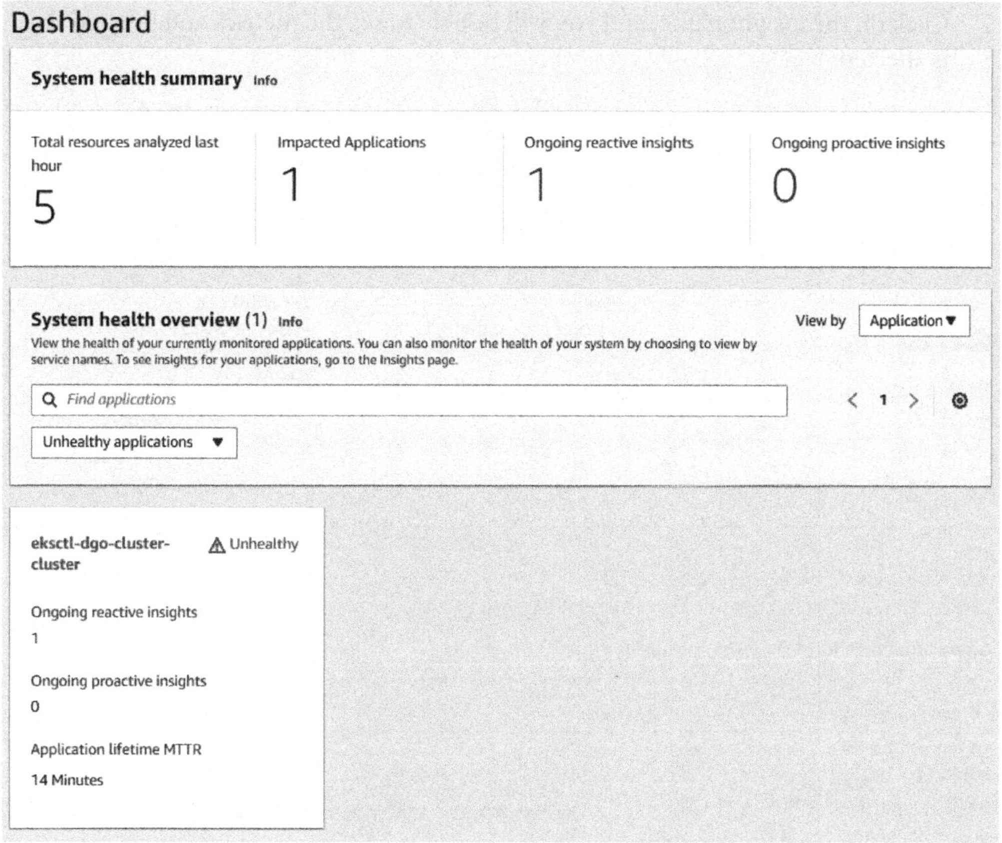

Figure 10.15 – The DevOps Guru dashboard

8.   Go to **Insights**, where you will be able to see an ongoing insight:

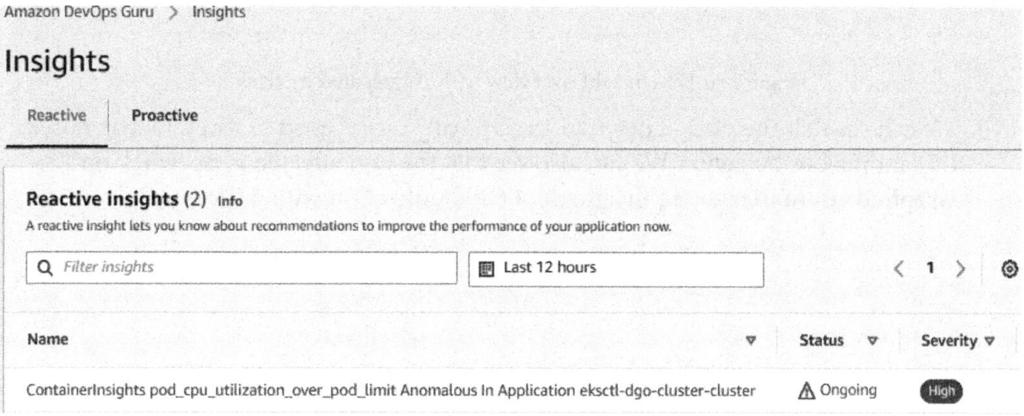

Figure 10.16 – The DevOps Guru Insights page showing reactive insights

9. Click on the insight name, and you will be able to see the metrics and the pod that is affected:

Insight overview   View recommendations

Description
On - anomalous behavior was detected on the pod_cpu_utilization_over_pod_limit ⤤ metric. DevOps Guru has provided you with 1 recommendation to resolve the issue.

Insight severity   Start time   Last update time
High severity   January 23, 2022 15:32 UTC   January 23, 2022 15:30 UTC

Status   End time   OpsItem ID
⚠ Ongoing   -   -

Affected applications
1

Aggregated metrics | **Graphed anomalies**

Aggregated metrics (1) January 23, 15:32–Now Info   Group by   No grouping ▼

Metrics in your AWS account are analyzed to find anomalies in an insight. The timeline shows the start time of the anomaly to current time.

Q Find metric by metric name, application, service name   〈 1 〉   ⊖ ⊕

Metrics ⤤			23:55 12/31	23:56 12/31	23:57 12/31	23:58 12/31	23:59 12/31	00:00 01/01	00:01 01/01	00:02 01/01	00:03 01/01	00:04 01/01
Application	Service name	Resource names ⤤										
▼ pod_cpu_utilization_over_pod_limit (dgo-cluster)												
	ClusterName:dgo-cluster												
db												
	r	ContainerInsights ClusterName:dgo-cluster, Service:db, Namespace:default										

Figure 10.17 – Insight overview with Aggregated metrics

10. We can see that the `pod_cpu_utilization_over_pod_limit` metric raised this anomalous behavior. We can also see that the pod affected is `db`. Click on **Graphed anomalies** to see the graph of CPU utilization with a timestamp:

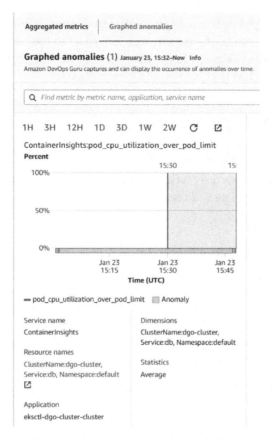

Figure 10.18 – Insight overview with Graphed anomalies

11. Amazon DevOps Guru also provides the recommendation for this anomaly. Since, in this case, the problem occurred because of CPU utilization, it is recommended to scale the deployment. So, DevOps Guru recommended automatic scaling:

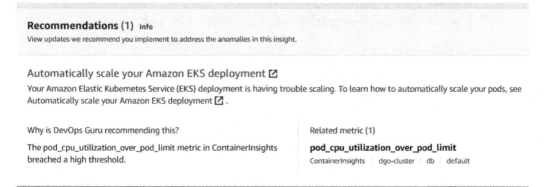

Figure 10.19 – A DevOps Guru recommendation

We just saw how DevOps Guru caught anomalies in the insight and provided a recommendation. We can configure this step in CI/CD to have a strong AIOps solution along with the application delivery. In the next section, we will deploy a serverless application and enable DevOps Guru on the serverless stack.

Deploying a serverless application and enabling DevOps Guru

In this section, we will deploy a serverless application using a CloudFormation template. This CloudFormation template will create a few resources, as follows:

- A DynamoDB table

- Two Lambda functions and some roles

- One API gateway and methods

This CloudFormation template has been cloned and modified from the AWS DevOps Guru sample repository provided by AWS, but we will be using this only to create application-related AWS resources with some modification. After that, we will enable DevOps Guru on the application stack.

Perform the following steps to deploy the stack:

1. Configure the awscli credentials and configure the output as json. Install jq by running the following command:

   ```
   $ sudo yum install jq -y
   ```

2. Install python3.6 and pip 20.2.3:

   ```
   $ sudo yum install python36 -y
   $ sudo python3 -m pip install --upgrade pip
   ```

3. Install Python modules:

   ```
   $ pip3 install requests
   ```

4. Clone the sample code:

```
$ git clone https://github.com/PacktPublishing/
Accelerating-DevSecOps-on-AWS.git
$ cd Modern-CI-CD-on-AWS/chapter-10
```

5. Before we deploy this application, let's take a look into the dynamodb table resource configuration of cfn-cartoon-code.yaml. The readcapacity parameter is set to 1:

```
Resources:
  ShopsTableMonitorOper:
    Type: AWS::DynamoDB::Table
    Properties:
      KeySchema:
        - AttributeName: name
          KeyType: HASH
      AttributeDefinitions:
        - AttributeName: name
          AttributeType: S
      ProvisionedThroughput:
        ReadCapacityUnits: 1
        WriteCapacityUnits: 5
```

6. Deploy the application infrastructure using CloudFormation. It will take few minutes to deploy all the resources:

```
$ aws cloudformation create-stack -stack-name
gdo-serverless-stack -template-body file://cfn-cartoon-
code.yaml -capabilities CAPABILITY_IAM CAPABILITY_NAMED_
IAM
```

7.   You can go to the AWS CloudFormation console and see the status. Once it's completed, then get the DynamoDB table name.

Figure 10.20 – The CloudFormation stack of a serverless application

The following command gives you the DynamoDB table name:

```
$ dynamoDBTableName=$(aws cloudformation list-stack-
resources --stack-name gdo-serverless-stack | jq
'.StackResourceSummaries[]|select(.ResourceType ==
"AWS::DynamoDB::Table").PhysicalResourceId' | tr -d '"')
```

8.   Update the database table name in the json file and populate the table using the json file data:

```
$ sudo sed -i s/"<YOUR-DYNAMODB-TABLE-
NAME>"/$dynamoDBTableName/g cartoon-shops-dynamodb-table.
json
$ aws dynamodb batch-write-item --request-items file://
cartoon-shops-dynamodb-table.json
{
    "UnprocessedItems": {}
}
```

9. Get the API gateway `ListRestApiEndpointMonitorOper` `OutputValue` URL and paste it in the browser to view the data:

```
$ aws cloudformation describe-stacks --stack-name
gdo-serverless-stack --query 'Stacks[0].Outputs'
[
    {
        "OutputKey": "ListRestApiEndpointMonitorOper",
        "OutputValue": "https://unuoirftn0.execute-api.
us-east-1.amazonaws.com/prod/",
        "ExportName": "ListRestApiEndpointMonitorOper"
    },
    {
        "OutputKey": "CreateRestApiEndpointMonitorOper",
        "OutputValue": "https://lq8dlzs36m.execute-api.
us-east-1.amazonaws.com/prod/",
        "ExportName": "CreateRestApiEndpointMonitorOper"
    }
]
```

The following screenshot shows the application output in the browser:

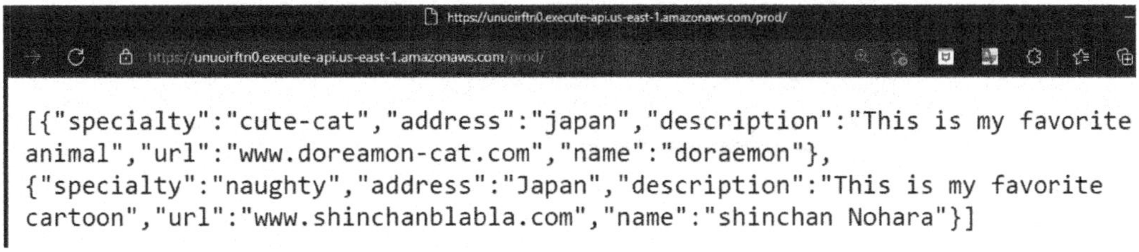
https://unuoirftn0.execute-api.us-east-1.amazonaws.com/prod/
https://unuoirftn0.execute-api.us-east-1.amazonaws.com/prod/
[{"specialty":"cute-cat","address":"japan","description":"This is my favorite animal","url":"www.doreamon-cat.com","name":"doraemon"},
{"specialty":"naughty","address":"Japan","description":"This is my favorite cartoon","url":"www.shinchanblabla.com","name":"shinchan Nohara"}]

Figure 10.21 – Serverless application output

10. At this point, the application is running fine. Now, let's put this application's CloudFormation stack under the analysis coverage of DevOps Guru. Go to the DevOps Guru console, click on **Analyzed resources**, and select **CloudFormation stacks**. Then select the name of the stack and click on **Save**:

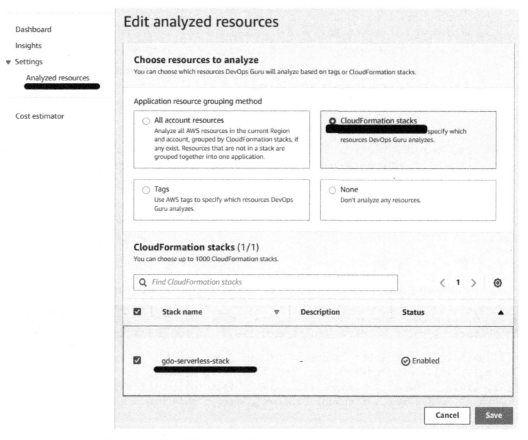

Figure 10.22 – Adding a serverless stack under analysis coverage

11. DevOps Guru takes some time to analyze the stack resources and then show them on the dashboard:

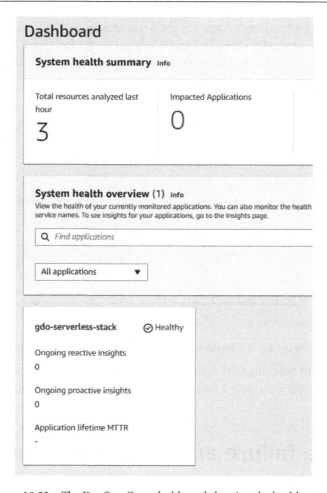

Figure 10.23 – The DevOps Guru dashboard showing the healthy status

Let DevOps Guru analyze the application for at least 2 hours for a baseline before injecting any failure. Sometimes it takes 4-5 hours to analyze. It is very important for DevOps Guru to understand the current working metrics of the application. In the next section, we will be integrating DevOps Guru with Systems Manager OpsCenter.

Integrating DevOps Guru with Systems Manager OpsCenter

Whenever there is any insight taking place within DevOps Guru, it is recommended that some engineer is at least aware of the insight status. With the integration of DevOps Guru and OpsCenter, the response team can easily be notified with an OpsItem whenever there is a new insight taking place in DevOps Guru.

AWS has made it simple when it comes to integration between the services. To enable DevOps Guru to create an OpsItem in OpsCenter, go to the DevOps Guru console, click on **Settings**, and click on the checkbox under **Service: AWS Systems Manager**:

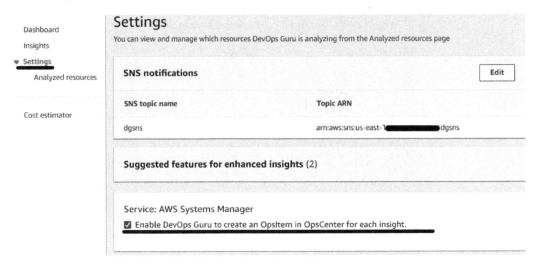

Figure 10.24 – Enabling DevOps Guru to create an OpsItem

Any new insight will automatically lead DevOps Guru to create an OpsItem in OpsCenter. In the next section, we will inject a failure and analyze the recommendation from DevOps Guru.

Injecting a failure and then reviewing the insights

In the previous section, we enabled DevOps Guru on the `gdo-serverless-stack` serverless application. We also enabled the integration between DevOps Guru and Systems Manager OpsCenter. Now, let's inject some failure and see the insight.

Perform the following steps to inject the failure:

1. Edit the Python script and place the `ListRestApiEndpointMonitorOper` URL as the `url variable` value and save the file.

2. Run the following Python script in four different tabs of your terminal to inject the large traffic. You need to keep this script running for at least 10 minutes. You will see there will be lots of failure requests with a `502` error code:

```
$ python3 sendAPIRequest.py
```

3. After some time, you will be able to see the anomaly insight in the DevOps Guru console. The total analyzed resources may vary in your scenario:

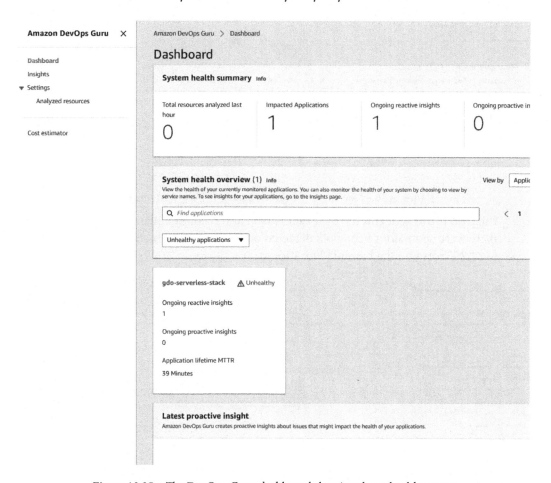

Figure 10.25 – The DevOps Guru dashboard showing the unhealthy status

4.   Once you click on **Insights**, you will be able to see an insight. The insight status is **Closed** in the following screenshot because I kept it for a longer period and stopped the traffic injection, so it automatically turned into a **Closed** state. But, if you keep monitoring it, you may see it with an **Ongoing** status:

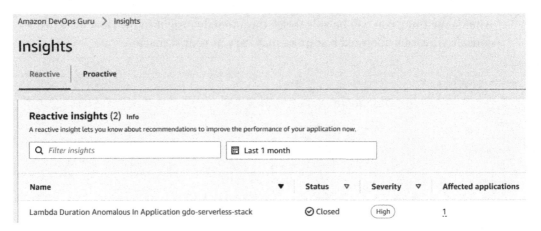

Figure 10.26 – DevOps Guru showing reactive insight anomalies

5.   Click on the insight and see the exact reason and recommendations. We can see that there were anomalous behaviors detected on five metrics, which were mostly related to 5XX errors and the Lambda Duration sum:

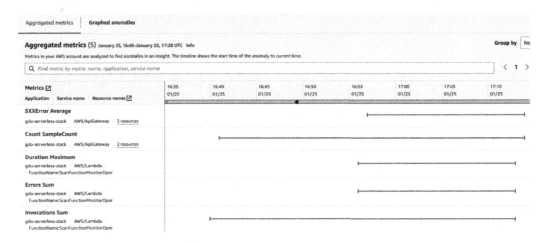

Figure 10.27 – An insight overview with Aggregated metrics

6.   We can also have a look at graphed anomalies by clicking on **Graphed anomalies** next to **Aggregated metrics**, which shows a snippet of API gateway 5XX errors and Lambda errors:

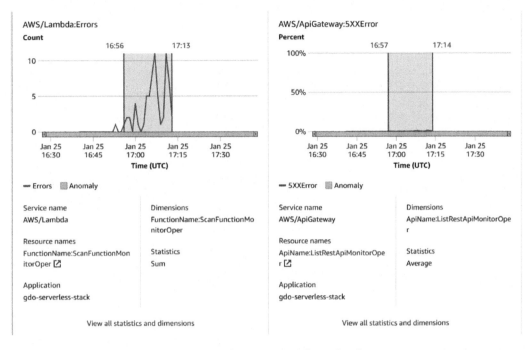

Figure 10.28 – Insight overview with graphical statistics

7. When you scroll down, you will see the **Recommendations** section, where you will find a few recommendations provided by DevOps Guru:

Recommendations (3) Info

View updates we recommend you implement to address the anomalies in this insight.

Troubleshoot errors and set up automatic retries in AWS Lambda [Z]

Your Lambda function is throwing a high number of errors. To learn about common Lambda errors, their causes, and mitigation strategies, see Troubleshoot errors and set up automatic retries in AWS Lambda [Z] .

Why is DevOps Guru recommending this?	Related metric (1)
The Errors metric in Lambda breached a high threshold.	**Errors**
	Lambda ScanFunctionMonitorOper

Troubleshoot errors in Amazon API Gateway [Z]

Your API Gateway is throwing a high number of errors. To learn about common API Gateway errors and how to handle them, see Troubleshoot errors in Amazon API Gateway [Z] .

Why is DevOps Guru recommending this?	Related metric (1)
The 5XXError metric in ApiGateway breached a high threshold.	**5XXError**
	ApiGateway ListRestApiMonitorOper

Configure provisioned concurrency for AWS Lambda [Z]

Your Lambda function is having trouble scaling. To learn how to enable provisioned concurrency, which allows your function to scale without fluctuations in latency, see Configure provisioned concurrency for AWS Lambda [Z] .

Why is DevOps Guru recommending this?	Related metric (1)
The Duration metric in Lambda breached a high threshold.	**Duration**
	Lambda ScanFunctionMonitorOper

Figure 10.29 – Recommendations provided by DevOps Guru to address anomalies

8. Now, let's have a look at the top section of the page, **Insight overview**, where you will see **OpsItem ID**:

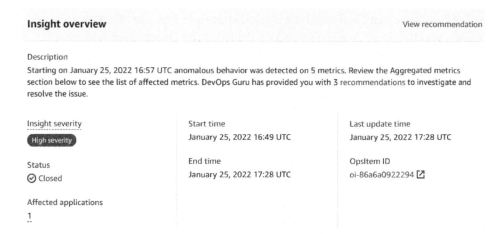

Figure 10.30 – Insight overview showing OpsItem ID

9. Once you click on **OpsItem ID**, you will be redirected to the Systems Manager OpsCenter console, where you can see details of the anomaly. If OpsCenter is integrated with **Incident Manager**, then the incident team will get a notification or SMS based on the incident configuration, after which the incident team can investigate this issue immediately:

Figure 10.31 – The OpsItem console

So far, we have seen that DevOps Guru created an insight because of a 5XX error. The reason was the ReadCapacityUnits value for the DynamoDB table was 1. Let's change it to 5 and let DevOps Guru baseline for a while. Then, we will change ReadCapacityUnits back to 1 and inject the traffic again and see what sort of insight and recommendation DevOps Guru produces. Perform the following steps to change ReadCapacity to 5 and inject traffic:

1. Edit the cfn-cartoon-code.yaml template file and change ReadCapacityUnits to 5:

```yaml
Resources:
  ShopsTableMonitorOper:
    Type: AWS::DynamoDB::Table
    Properties:
      KeySchema:
        - AttributeName: name
          KeyType: HASH
      AttributeDefinitions:
        - AttributeName: name
          AttributeType: S
      ProvisionedThroughput:
        ReadCapacityUnits: 5
        WriteCapacityUnits: 5
```

2. Update the dgo-serverless-stack CloudFormation stack:

```
$ aws cloudformation update-stack --stack-name
gdo-serverless-stack --template-body file:///$PWD/
cfn-cartoon-code.yaml --capabilities CAPABILITY_IAM
CAPABILITY_NAMED_IAM
```

3. Once the stack is updated, inject a minor amount of traffic for a while and stop the traffic, so that DevOps Guru baselines the condition of the application.

4. Repeat *Step 1*, but with a `ReadCapacityUnits` value of `1`, and update the stack again by running the command from *Step 2*.

5. Now, inject the traffic again by running the following command in four different tabs of the terminal for at least 10 minutes:

```
$ python3 sendAPIRequest.py
```

6. You will see a new insight in DevOps Guru caused by the `ReadThrottleEvents` sum:

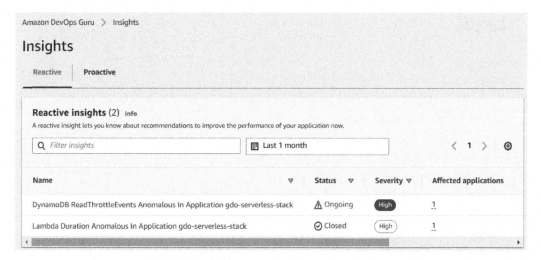

Figure 10.32 – Different reactive insight generated for a serverless application stack

7. Click on the insight to get more details:

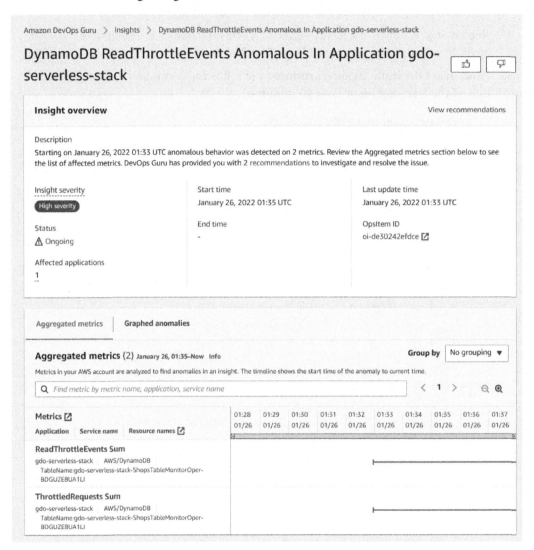

Figure 10.33 – Insight overview page showing the metrics for anomalies

8. You can also see the recommendation of rolling back the DynamoDB table configuration, which caused this anomaly:

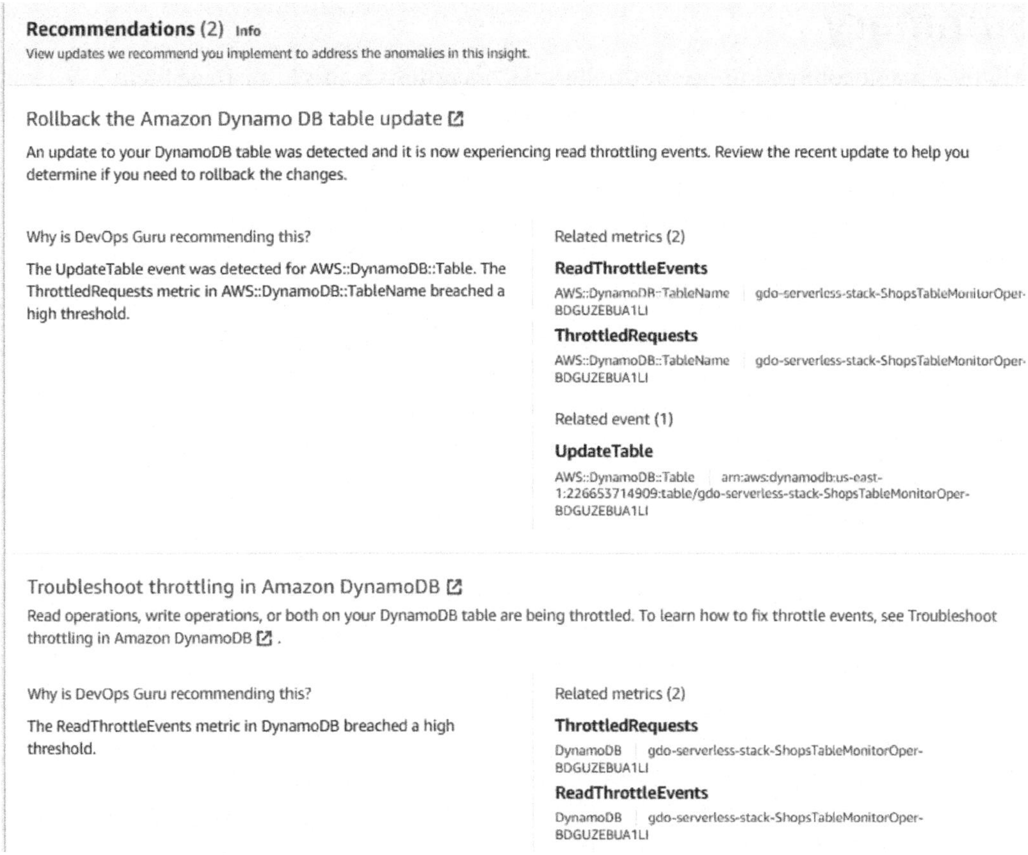

Recommendations (2) Info

View updates we recommend you implement to address the anomalies in this insight.

Rollback the Amazon Dynamo DB table update

An update to your DynamoDB table was detected and it is now experiencing read throttling events. Review the recent update to help you determine if you need to rollback the changes.

Why is DevOps Guru recommending this?

The UpdateTable event was detected for AWS::DynamoDB::Table. The ThrottledRequests metric in AWS::DynamoDB::TableName breached a high threshold.

Related metrics (2)

ReadThrottleEvents

AWS::DynamoDB-TableName   gdo-serverless-stack-ShopsTableMonitorOper-
BDGUZEBUA1LI

ThrottledRequests

AWS::DynamoDB::TableName   gdo-serverless-stack-ShopsTableMonitorOper-
BDGUZEBUA1LI

Related event (1)

UpdateTable

AWS::DynamoDB::Table   arn:aws:dynamodb:us-east-
1:226653714909:table/gdo-serverless-stack-ShopsTableMonitorOper-
BDGUZEBUA1LI

Troubleshoot throttling in Amazon DynamoDB

Read operations, write operations, or both on your DynamoDB table are being throttled. To learn how to fix throttle events, see Troubleshoot throttling in Amazon DynamoDB .

Why is DevOps Guru recommending this?

The ReadThrottleEvents metric in DynamoDB breached a high threshold.

Related metrics (2)

ThrottledRequests

DynamoDB   gdo-serverless-stack-ShopsTableMonitorOper-
BDGUZEBUA1LI

ReadThrottleEvents

DynamoDB   gdo-serverless-stack-ShopsTableMonitorOper-
BDGUZEBUA1LI

Figure 10.34 – Recommendation from DevOps Guru to address anomalies

So, you can see that DevOps Guru also analyzes the changes before and after the insight and gives the recommendation.

DevOps Guru is still at an early phase, but AWS is continuously adding new features to this service. Recently, they also added metrics such as database load and wait time to analyze the RDS anomalies. DevOps Guru is a black box AIOps tool, but there are lots of other features such as seamless integration, which is a good reason to opt for this service.

Summary

AIOps is the upcoming important thing for IT operations teams to manage their activity. In this chapter, we looked at the need for AIOps tools and how they help in revolutionizing IT operations. We learned some important concepts of ML, which also helps you analyze which AIOps tool to use, based on the open box and black box approaches. We learned about the new and managed AIOps service DevOps Guru and enabled it on containerized applications. We also enabled DevOps Guru on a serverless application and integrated it with OpsCenter to create an OpsItem for a generated insight. After reading all the chapters of this book, you should be able to create successful, secure, and intelligent CI/CD pipelines for applications as well as infrastructure.

Index

`Packt.com`

Subscribe to our online digital library for full access to over 7,000 books and videos, as well as industry leading tools to help you plan your personal development and advance your career. For more information, please visit our website.

Why subscribe?

- Spend less time learning and more time coding with practical eBooks and Videos from over 4,000 industry professionals
- Improve your learning with Skill Plans built especially for you
- Get a free eBook or video every month
- Fully searchable for easy access to vital information
- Copy and paste, print, and bookmark content

Did you know that Packt offers eBook versions of every book published, with PDF and ePub files available? You can upgrade to the eBook version at `packt.com` and as a print book customer, you are entitled to a discount on the eBook copy. Get in touch with us at `customercare@packtpub.com` for more details.

At `www.packt.com`, you can also read a collection of free technical articles, sign up for a range of free newsletters, and receive exclusive discounts and offers on Packt books and eBooks.

Other Books You May Enjoy

If you enjoyed this book, you may be interested in these other books by Packt:

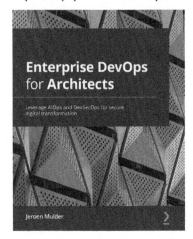

Enterprise DevOps for Architects

Jeroen Mulder

ISBN: 9781801812153

- Create DevOps architecture and integrate it with the enterprise architecture
- Discover how DevOps can add value to the quality of IT delivery
- Explore strategies to scale DevOps for an enterprise
- Architect SRE for an enterprise as next-level DevOps
- Understand AIOps and what value it can bring to an enterprise
- Create your AIOps architecture and integrate it into DevOps
- Create your DevSecOps architecture and integrate it with the existing DevOps setup
- Apply zero-trust principles and industry security frameworks to DevOps

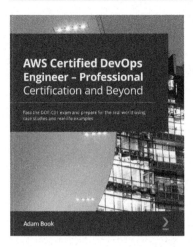

AWS Certified DevOps Engineer - Professional Certification and Beyond

Adam Book

ISBN: 9781801074452

- Automate your pipelines, build phases, and deployments with AWS-native tooling
- Discover how to implement logging and monitoring using AWS-native tooling
- Gain a solid understanding of the services included in the AWS DevOps Professional exam
- Reinforce security practices on the AWS platform from an exam point of view
- Find out how to automatically enforce standards and policies in AWS environments
- Explore AWS best practices and anti-patterns
- Enhance your core AWS skills with the help of exercises and practice tests

Packt is searching for authors like you

If you're interested in becoming an author for Packt, please visit `authors.packtpub.com` and apply today. We have worked with thousands of developers and tech professionals, just like you, to help them share their insight with the global tech community. You can make a general application, apply for a specific hot topic that we are recruiting an author for, or submit your own idea.

Share Your Thoughts

Now you've finished *Accelerating DevSecOps on AWS*, we'd love to hear your thoughts! Scan the QR code below to go straight to the Amazon review page for this book and share your feedback or leave a review on the site that you purchased it from.

https://packt.link/r/1-803-24860-2

Your review is important to us and the tech community and will help us make sure we're delivering excellent quality content.

Made in the USA
Columbia, SC
20 August 2023

21904148R00285